GW00374819

The contributors to this collection of essays in honour of the distinguished medieval historian Edward Miller pay tribute by writing on the society and economy of England between the eleventh and the sixteenth centuries. They address many of the most important themes in an era which experienced profound change in rural, commercial, urban and industrial life, and they focus in particular on the progress which was achieved and the problems which were encountered.

Each of the essays is original and contains the fruits of new research. The subjects covered include the growth of London, the commercial and urban development of the north, Italian merchants and banking, overseas trade, taxation, farm servants, hunting and poaching, changing relations between landlords and tenants, the expansion of the economy in the twelfth century and the great slump of the fifteenth. The book has been written by leading experts, and is a major contribution to English medieval economic and social history.

Progress and problems in medieval England

Progress and problems in medieval England

ESSAYS IN HONOUR OF EDWARD MILLER

EDITED BY

RICHARD BRITNELL
University of Durham

AND

JOHN HATCHER
University of Cambridge

CAMBRIDGE
UNIVERSITY PRESS

Published by the Press Syndicate of the University of Cambridge
The Pitt Building, Trumpington Street, Cambridge CB2 1RP
40 West 20th Street, New York, NY 10011–4211, USA
10 Stamford Road, Oakleigh, Melbourne 3166, Australia

© Cambridge University Press 1996

First published 1996

Printed in Great Britain at the University Press, Cambridge

A catalogue record for this book is available from the British Library

Library of Congress cataloguing in publication data
Progress and problems in medieval England: essays in honour of Edward Miller/edited by
Richard Britnell and John Hatcher.
p.   cm.
ISBN 0–521–55036–X (hardcover)
1. Great Britain – History – Medieval period, 1066–1485.
2. England – Economic conditions – 1066–1485. I. Miller, Edward, 1915–
II. Britnell, R. H. III. Hatcher, John.
DA175.P74 1966
942–dc20   96–3488 CIP

ISBN 0521 55036 X hardback

Contents

Figures

Maps

Tables

Contributors

JEAN BIRRELL, *Honorary Fellow, Institute for Advanced Studies in the Humanities, University of Birmingham*

IAN BLANCHARD, *Professor of Medieval Economic History, University of Edinburgh*

RICHARD BRITNELL, *Reader in History, University of Durham*

WENDY CHILDS, *Senior Lecturer in Medieval History, University of Leeds*

CHRISTOPHER DYER, *Professor of Medieval Social History, University of Birmingham*

DAVID FARMER, *Late Professor and Head of the History Department, St Thomas More College, University of Saskatchewan*

EDMUND FRYDE, *Emeritus Professor of History, University College of Wales, Aberystwyth*

JOHN HATCHER, *Professor of Economic and Social History, University of Cambridge, and Fellow of Corpus Christi College, Cambridge*

GEORGE HOLMES, *Emeritus Chichele Professor of Medieval History, University of Oxford, and Fellow of All Souls College, Oxford*

JENNY KERMODE, *Senior Lecturer in Local History, University of Liverpool*

EDMUND KING, *Professor of Medieval History, University of Sheffield*

PAMELA NIGHTINGALE, *Leverhulme Research Fellow, Ashmolean Museum, Oxford*

AMBROSE RAFTIS, *Emeritus Professor of History, University of Toronto*

ANTHONY TUCK, *Emeritus Professor of Medieval History, University of Bristol*

Edward Miller: an appreciation

E DWARD MILLER came from a background in the north of England
which inclined him to an interest in the land and agriculture. It was not
surprising therefore that his first book, *The Abbey and Bishopric of Ely* (1951),
was a substantial study of a great medieval landowner, which investigated
the economic and social history of the English countryside. That was published after he had been for some years a Fellow of St John's College,
Cambridge (that position interrupted by five years of war service), and Dir-
ector of Studies in History, a role which allowed him to begin to encourage
the careers of younger historians. The work on Ely also sprang, of course,
partly from the strong Cambridge tradition of medieval economic and social
history recently enlivened by M.M. Postan, to which Ted was to contribute
so much.

Those who were his pupils in those days (the present writer first saw him
crossing second court in uniform; would that have been in 1946?) remember
him as the liveliest and most invigorating of teachers, who fired their enthusiasm for the study of medieval economy and society. They remember his
wife Fanny's kindness to them, and those who have become professional
historians will remember also their young son, John, now also a professor
of history. Much of the research for Ely must have been done before 1939,
but Ted's enthusiasm both for research and for stimulating the young has
remained undiminished in the 1990s as his bibliography shows.

In 1961, when he had just published a history of the college, *Portrait of
a College: A History of the College of St John the Evangelist, Cambridge*, he left
St John's to become Warden of Madingley Hall, just outside Cambridge,
and then, from 1965 to 1971, Professor of Medieval History at the University
of Sheffield. Willingness to undertake demanding administrative positions
has been a feature of his life. But historical research was not interrupted,
though its geographical centre, which had begun to move earlier, was re-

directed to some extent by his move to Yorkshire. The *Victoria County History of the City of York* (1961) contains an important chapter on 'Medieval York', his second major piece of research and a change from country to city. In 1963 came the third volume of the *Cambridge Economic History of Europe*, dealing with *Economic Policies and Organization in the Middle Ages*, part of a series of volumes with which Postan had been much concerned. In this case Ted was joint editor and also author of a section on the economic policies of the governments of England and France, marking a new interest in government as well as in society.

From 1971 to 1981 he was Master of Fitzwilliam College, Cambridge, the summit of his career in academic administration. But in 1978 he published, jointly with John Hatcher, the book which has probably made him most widely known to students – Ely and York being more appropriate to the specialist – *Medieval England: Rural Society and Economic Change, 1086–1348*, added by all of us to reading lists and recommended to the young.

Ted has been the author of many important articles, well known to the *cognoscenti* of medieval economic, social and political history. Medieval economic history is a field of study in which an article can be revolutionary and no account of Ted's work should underestimate the influence of 'The English Economy in the Thirteenth Century' (1964), 'The Fortunes of the English Textile Industry during the Thirteenth Century' (1965) and 'England in the Twelfth and Thirteenth Centuries: an Economic Contrast?' (1971). He has also been a generous contributor of time and energy to the organisation of the Victoria County Histories and the History of Parliament, and his editorial skills secured the publication of a substantially revised second edition of volume II of the *Cambridge Economic History of Europe* in 1987. If anything the flow of Ted's scholarship has swelled in recent years. In 1991 the third volume of the *Agrarian History of England and Wales* appeared under his editorship, containing wide-ranging and perceptive contributions by him on agriculture and rural society in the later Middle Ages, particularly relating to Lancashire and Yorkshire and to the southern counties of England; just a few months ago we welcomed the publication of *Medieval England: Towns, Commerce and Crafts, 1086–1348*; and in the near future the Cambridgeshire Record Society will publish his calendar of the Ely Coucher Book of 1251. It is difficult to think of anyone whose career has involved more fruitful and enduring work in the history of medieval English society. His friends and colleagues, who have contributed to this volume, salute him as one who has been for so long in the creative forefront of their field of study and look forward to the further illuminations he will give them.

GEORGE HOLMES

Abbreviations

AHEW, II	H.E. Hallam (ed.), *Agrarian History of England and Wales, II: 1042–1350* (Cambridge, 1988)
AHEW, III	E. Miller (ed.), *Agrarian History of England and Wales, III: 1348–1500* (Cambridge, 1991)
AHEW, IV	J. Thirsk (ed.), *Agrarian History of England and Wales, IV: 1500–1640* (Cambridge, 1987)
Cal. Chart. Rolls	*Calendar of Charter Rolls*, 6 vols. (HMSO, London, 1903–27)
Cal. Close Rolls	*Calendar of Close Rolls*, 46 vols. (HMSO, London, 1892–1963)
Cal. Fine Rolls	*Calendar of Fine Rolls*, 20 vols. (HMSO, London, 1911–49)
Cal. Inq. Post Mortem	*Calendar of Inquisitions Post Mortem*, 16 vols. (HMSO, London, 1904–75)
Cal. Pat. Rolls	*Calendar of Patent Rolls*, 54 vols. (HMSO, London, 1891–1916)
Pipe Roll	*The Great Roll of the Pipe*, 5 Henry II to 5 Henry III, Pipe Roll Society, 58 vols. (London, 1884–1990)
VCH	*The Victoria History of the Counties of England* (London, 1900 – in progress)

1

Economic development in the early twelfth century

EDMUND KING

THE SOURCES for an economic history of England between the death of the first Norman king in 1087, and the accession of his great-grandson, the first Angevin king, in 1154, are not considerable. They are the by-products of government, royal, lay and ecclesiastical. They have provided the material for some distinguished studies of various aspects of government, of politics and of law. They are not at first sight promising for those of economic interests. Yet there are in the *acta* of kings and magnates, in the narrative passages that connect the charters in such sources as the Abingdon cartulary and the *Liber Eliensis*, and in the records of the royal exchequer and of local estate management, indications of the assumptions which governed men's attitudes to land and wealth. It might seem a little ambitious to broaden the discussion to consider economic policy at this time, but we have in Edward Miller's work clear evidence of the benefits to be gained from this approach, and important clues as to how best to proceed. We may start with some necessary caveats. 'The study of government policies can be based on no straightforward progression through time; and it is also difficult to lay down hard and fast criteria defining what was and what was not a "state".'[1] The Anglo-Norman territorial state may seem advanced in ambition and achievement by the standards of the eleventh century, but still this is a period in which 'government' can be difficult to distinguish from 'estate management'.[2] Neither central administrators nor local estate managers could function effectively without the protection of a *pax*;[3] and at the end of the

---

[1] Edward Miller, 'Government Economic Policies and Public Finance 1000–1500', in Carlo M. Cipolla (ed.), *The Fontana Economic History of Europe, I: The Middle Ages* (London, 1972), pp. 339–73, quotation p. 339.

[2] Edward Miller, 'The Economic Policies of Governments', in M.M. Postan *et al.* (eds.), *Cambridge Economic History of Europe, III: Economic Organization and Policies in the Middle Ages* (Cambridge, 1963), pp. 281–340, quotation p. 285.

[3] *Ibid.*, p. 282.

period under discussion there was a protracted civil war, the 'nineteen long winters in which Christ and his saints were asleep'.

In England the records of central government might seem particularly impressive. Domesday Book is incomparable. So also is the one surviving pipe roll from Henry I's day, that of 1129–30. There are from the same reign a group of estate surveys, with information more detailed than in the text of Domesday. It was the suggestion of the late Lewis Warren that the written records of Henry I's time showed an administrative machine facing a crisis, due in large part to the loss of the Anglo-Saxon memory: 'a crisis in the management of the Anglo-Saxon inheritance developed as the old hands passed away'.[4] In this interpretation, it is no coincidence that the surveys appeared 'at that moment in time when the Normans were having to learn to cope for themselves'.[5] It is good to have noted the importance of local estate managers, and more will be said about these, but the general thesis cannot be sustained. Marjorie Chibnall sees the surveys rather as part of the normal process of efficient estate management.[6] The *Leges Henrici Primi* envisage a close questioning of staff when the manor is returned to the lord: 'they must be questioned about increases in the number of men and cattle, about whether the manor has decreased in value in respect of demesne land or tenants, pastures or woods, about whether any occupant has increased his due payments or whether anyone has unjustly withheld them, about what is held in the granaries and what has been sown'.[7] The Peterborough survey specifies the villein services, renders to the monastery in cash and in kind, and the livestock on the demesne. It gives no indication as to whether the manors were farmed, but it does have sufficient information for a farm contract to be drawn up.[8] Now this survey was made at a time of vacancy, in 1125–8: 'This is the survey (*descriptio*) of the manors of the abbey of Peterborough as Walter the archdeacon received them, and seized them into the king's hands.'[9] At exactly the same time, a survey which has not survived was made at Battle, by William of Ely and John Belet, 'who made a brief survey of the entire abbey and its appurtenances'.[10] The coincidence is sufficient to suggest that in the late 1120s it was the standard practice of the exchequer to require a written survey to be made at a time of vacancy.

[4] W.L. Warren, 'The Myth of Norman Administrative Efficiency', *Trans. Royal Hist. Soc.*, 5th ser., 34 (1984), pp. 113–32, quotation p. 118.

[5] *Ibid.*, p. 118 and n. 13, quotation p. 119.

[6] *Charters and Custumals of the Abbey of Holy Trinity Caen*, ed. Marjorie Chibnall (Records of Social and Economic History, n.s., V, London, 1982), p. xxix.

[7] *Leges Henrici Primi* c. 56, 3, ed. L.J. Downer (Oxford, 1972), pp. 174–5.

[8] *Chronicon Petroburgense*, ed. T. Stapleton (Camden ser. XLVII, London, 1849), pp. 157–68.

[9] *Ibid.*, p. 157.

[10] *The Chronicle of Battle Abbey*, ed. Eleanor Searle (Oxford, 1980), pp. 132–3.

It is tempting to go on to suggest that what we see here is what in the jargon of modern quality control is termed the dissemination of good practice.

If a survey were not made during the vacancy, it would be made by a prudent new incumbent. This was done by Nigel the second bishop of Ely, immediately on his appointment in 1133,[11] after up to a decade of service as the first court treasurer.[12] He was the nephew of Roger of Salisbury, and father of the author of the *Dialogus*. He 'had no match in his day for knowledge of the exchequer'.[13] His knowledge of good practice was second to none. A prudent landlord would also ride out and survey his demesnes in person. Thus Walter de Lucy 'shortly after his institution' as abbot of Battle in 1139 'planned to make a visitation to the manors and possessions in distant parts, as is the custom of those who undertake new administrations'.[14] Walter was the brother of Richard de Lucy, who came to exercise much of the influence of Roger of Salisbury, and was justiciar under Henry II. Henry of Blois made a similar visitation on his appointment as abbot of Glastonbury in 1126, which office he would hold for forty-five years, in plurality with the bishopric of Winchester from 1129. He has left an account of his actions as abbot, the first English landlord to do so, his confidence and his care for detail thrusting out from the page.[15] The following passage describes his discovery that fertile land had been passed off as worthless:

> A certain Ralph of Sainte-Barbe asked my predecessor, Abbot Herluin [1100–18], for some land adjacent to the river Axe in the Brent marshes, which he disingenuously argued had been of no use to the church, was not of use now and never would be. As it was spoken of in these terms, and so described in a charter, the land was given to him as a gift. Then one day when I had gone to the manor I speak of and was wandering about via some causeways in disrepair to tour the bounds of my territory, I came across this piece of land, surrounded on one side by a circular bank and on the other by a deep watercourse. I saw there waving corn, golden in colour, making a soft murmur

---

[11] *English Lawsuits from William I to Richard I*, ed. R.C. Van Caenegem, 2 vols. (Selden Soc., CVI-CVII, London, 1990–1), I, no. 287. (No other reference will normally be cited for texts that appear in this invaluable collection of documents.) Edward Miller, *The Abbey and Bishopric of Ely: The Social History of an Ecclesiastical Estate from the Tenth Century to the Early Fourteenth Century* (Cambridge, 1951), pp. 167–74.

[12] C. Warren Hollister, 'The Origins of the English Treasury', *Eng. Hist. Rev.*, 93 (1978), pp. 262–75, at pp. 269–75; repr. in his *Monarchy, Magnates and Institutions* (London, 1986), pp. 209–22, at pp. 216–22.

[13] *Dialogus de Scaccario*, ed. Charles Johnson (London, 1950), p. 50.

[14] *Chronicle of Battle*, pp. 238–9.

[15] First printed in *Adami de Domerham Historia de Rebus Gestis Glastoniensibus*, ed. T. Hearne, 2 vols. (Oxford, 1727), II, pp. 305–15; more recently, with useful commentary, in *English Episcopal Acta, VIII: Winchester 1070–1204*, ed. M.J. Franklin (London, 1993), pp. 202–13; and there are some sections in translation in *English Lawsuits*, I, pp. 221–3, 246.

in the breeze, so level and so even that no foreign shoot poked up above it, while below no weed sprouted to push apart the dense cornstalks, close-ranked enough to present the reaper with bunches rather than single ears. When I asked the name of this field, I was told that the knight previously mentioned had called it 'useless' (*nullius proficui*). Thereafter on the appointed day, in the presence of many people, this great deception was exposed, and by their judgement I rightfully received this piece of land, whose name was suitably changed.[16]

The *Libellus* is a remarkable text, which would repay a close exegesis. It need not be questioned that we have here the authentic voice of Henry of Blois; and it will be heard again in what follows.

So much of the wealth of England in the early twelfth century was in land that references to land as a commodity, to its value and to its capacity for improvement are worth attention. In 1147 at the consecration of the new church at Lewes William III de Warenne said that tithes should increase if his demesnes increased: it would seem that he is thinking of an increase in wealth – primarily at least – as following an increase in territory.[17] But in a grant by the abbot of St Mary's York to Ralph the sheriff in the very early years of Henry II's reign, an increase in value was clearly seen to be tied to an increase in effort (*industria*).[18] The *Leges Henrici Primi* had envisaged disputes arising between the lord and the farmer, 'in regard to the tallies or to a subsequent increase in value'.[19] The charters give evidence of many such disputes, often prompted by the need to specify to whom the profits of improvement should go.[20] If land was not to be improved this might need

---

[16] *Ibid.*, I, p. 222.

[17] 'et si dominium meum aut redditus mei creuerint eotenus crescat et decima monachorum': *Early Yorkshire Charters*, I–III, ed. W. Farrer (Edinburgh, 1914–16), IV–XII, ed. C.T. Clay (Yorkshire Arch. Soc., Leeds, 1935–65), VIII, no. 32. The concession nonetheless was worth having. To see one religious corporation being distinctly less magnanimous with another, note Fountains Abbey compounding the tithes of Aldburgh to the local church for 6d. a year: 'precium quidem paruum est, quia non fuit ibi multum terre arabilis quando primum data est eis, sed fere totum monachi postea sartauerunt': *Charters of the Honour of Mowbray 1107–1191*, ed. D.E. Greenway (Records of Social and Economic History, n.s., I, London, 1972), no. 97.

[18] 'Concedimus eciam ad jus suum pertinere quicquid sua uel nostra industria in eadem tenura poterit adcrescere': *Early Yorkshire Charters*, IV, no. 106.

[19] *Leges Henrici Primi*, c. 56, 1, ed. Downer, pp. 174–5.

[20] At the conclusion of a life-tenure conceded by the abbot of Ramsey to Reinald de Argentine, the abbot was to hold 'cum omni augmentatione et emendatione quam Reinaldus faciet super terram illam': *Regesta Regum Anglo-Normannorum 1066–1154*, ed. H.W.C. Davis, C. Johnson, H.A. Cronne and R.H.C. Davis, 4 vols. (Oxford, 1913–69), II, no. 580. Here also the churchmen might wish to have it both ways. When the canons of Guisborough received a carucate of land in 1160 for the term of twenty years, they specified that the grantor or his heirs should pay the value of their buildings, 'justa estimacio pretii', at the end of the term, otherwise they would be razed to the ground: *Early Yorkshire Charters*, II, no. 754.

to be specified.[21] Baldwin de Redvers, earl of Exeter, in granting St James, Exeter, as a Cluniac priory, conceded to the monks that 'they and all their men should have in all their lands any measure and every freedom to buy and sell to allow their goods to multiply in every way that is proper'.[22] This was a daughter-house of St Martin des Champs in Paris, then seeing its own goods multiplying wonderfully, through the profits of trade, particularly along the Seine. They might have wished to be assured that the west country was not an economic backwater.

London certainly was not. The following charter of Stephen's queen Matilda mentions the *profituum* as a part of the calculation involved in the repayment of a mortgage taken out with Gervase of Cornhill.

> Know that I give Gervase the justice of London ten marks-worth of land in the township of Gamlingay for his service. The remainder of the township, besides this ten marks-worth of land, I give to him free and quit, until I shall have repaid the debt which I owe him, so that within this term he shall have the profits which arise from this township. When I shall have repaid the debt to him or his heirs, then they shall keep the stock which they will have put on my land.[23]

Gervase was one of the great men of the city of London, and he had a reputation as a usurer; but this charter contains nothing exceptional. The same standards applied in the fens. We find living in Chatteris in the middle of Henry I's reign one Bricstan. He was a model citizen: 'he was neither very rich nor very poor, but managed his affairs and those of his family after the fashion of a layman with a modest competence'. He was, however, accused by a royal official with concealment of treasure trove and usury; and it took St Etheldreda, in one of her finest cameo roles, to secure his release.[24] There had been debt ever since Eve took the apple from the tree. It was a part of the human condition. In the preamble to a charter Archbishop Thurstan wrote simply: 'it happens frequently that clerics just as other men, from necessity or human frailty, pass from this world burdened with various debts'.[25] Thurstan had been another man close to Henry I, and had served

[21] This happens in an early charter, of *c.* 1108, from the Norwich collection: 'land which was then [pre-1087] cultivated shall be arable, and land then uncultivated shall remain waste': *English Episcopal Acta, VI: Norwich 1070–1214*, ed. C. Harper-Bill (London, 1990), no. 5.

[22] *Charters of the Redvers Family and the Earldom of Devon, 1090–1217*, ed. Robert Bearman (Devon and Cornwall Rec. Soc., n.s., 37, Exeter, 1994), no. 27.

[23] *Regesta*, III, no. 243.

[24] Parallel accounts, though with a different view of Bricstan's guilt, are found in the *Liber Eliensis* and the *Ecclesiastical History* of Orderic Vitalis, and translated in *English Lawsuits*, I, no. 204, pp. 167–76.

[25] *Early Yorkshire Charters*, I, no. 149, dated to the last months of Thurstan's life in *English Episcopal Acta, V: York 1070–1154*, ed. Janet Burton (London, 1988), no. 80.

as his almoner, 'possibly in charge of the privy purse'.[26] He had seen it all.

It may be too early to speak of a market for land at this date,[27] but in charters and in chronicles it is assumed that land could be bought and sold in Anglo-Norman England. Purchase was one of a range of options, the choice to be determined by the status of the parties and the relationship between them, the nature of the tenure, and by the economic environment. It was a sign of confidence that at Battle under Henry I's firm peace, 'the abbot and the brothers started to look for lands to buy and to recover lands that had been lost'.[28] At another monastery William of Malmesbury wrote in a matter of fact way, and from first-hand experience, of the authority of Roger bishop of Salisbury: 'anything bordering his property that suited his requirements he extracted at once by prayer or price, otherwise by force'.[29] In the 1140s Robert of Bethune bishop of Hereford acquired land 'et precibus et pecunia et amore' from Roger earl of Hereford and his sub-tenant.[30] The prayer of a powerful man might be indistinguishable from force. In his *Libellus* Henry of Winchester described himself as 'defeated' by a request from Henry I.[31]

A very clear statement about sale of urban property and title to it is found in the Ramsey cartulary.

> Be it known to all the sons of Holy Church that Wulnoth of Walbrooke from London has sold to abbot Reginald of Ramsey some land of his, which he had on the Walbrooke . . . and also a house of stone and a cellar which he had built on that land with iron doors and windows upstairs and downstairs, and also some wooden houses which he had build with his own money on some other adjacent land, which he held in fee and inheritance from the church and the abbot of Ramsey.[32]

The consideration was ten pounds *in denariis*, which the abbot gave him in the presence of the whole husting. It was still worth specifying the nature of the title to the property. A confirmation for Gloucester Abbey in 1114 confirmed in detail individual grants of rural property, concluding with a broad sweep of the hand, 'and all their lands and houses in Gloucester by

[26] Frank Barlow, *The English Church 1066–1154* (London, 1979), p. 83.
[27] Paul R. Hyams, 'The Origins of a Peasant Land Market in England', *Econ. Hist. Rev.*, 2nd ser., 23 (1970), pp. 18–31, has points of more general significance.
[28] *Chronicle of Battle*, pp. 118–19.
[29] *Historia Novella*, ed. K.R. Potter (London, 1955), p. 38. 'uel prece uel precio' was a borrowing from the classics, but this does not weaken the point: it was seen to be appropriate to the circumstances of the early twelfth century.
[30] *English Episcopal Acta, VII: Hereford 1079–1234*, ed. Julia Barrow (London, 1993), no. 28.
[31] 'victus tandem prece regis': *English Lawsuits*, I, p. 222.
[32] *Ibid.*, I, no. 270

gift or purchase'.[33] One feature in the market for property in London was the need for major landowners to have appropriate lodging in the capital. Henry of Winchester, here as elsewhere, provides an exemplary study. Royal charters show his purchase of land in Southwark;[34] but his authentic voice provides the better record. He and his predecessors, he said, had been gravely inconvenienced coming to London on urgent royal and other business, 'for the lack of a house of our own in that city'.[35] He had needed to spend a very large sum of money indeed to remedy the lack (*altiori precio comparaui*); and this from a man whose wealth was legendary.

References to the sale of rural property are proportionately more scarce than references to the sale of urban property in charters of the early twelfth century. In royal charters they are scarce indeed. The subject index in the volume for Stephen's reign shows three only in over a thousand entries. It cannot be a coincidence that all three concern Henry of Winchester. One relates to the purchase of land in Southwark just noted.[36] The second concerns land bought from Berner de Ferrers in West Hatch, Somerset.[37] These two are charters for Winchester: the third concerns Glastonbury. This was the purchase of the manor of Siston in Gloucestershire, 'for the agreed purchase of which Racindis received forty marks of silver from the monies of that church by the hand of my brother Henry bishop of Winchester'.[38] There is further information in the *Libellus*. This reveals negotiations going back a decade, and vigorous competition for the property from other religious houses.[39] The list of purchases referred to in royal charters might be extended,[40] but even so would not be long. As the Siston example shows, a royal charter was at several removes from the transaction which it recorded. It was not necessary for the diplomatic of the charter for cash to be mentioned, and it may have been reckoned bad form to do so. In some cases there may have been reservations about the propriety of a sale. A charter early in the reign of Henry II spells this out. Roger le Bret of Markingfield granted Fountains Abbey thirty-six acres of land, receiving in his need twenty marks and 20s., a plough-team and a horse, 'so that he might retain the rest

[33] *Regesta*, II, no. 1041.
[34] *Ibid.*, III, nos. 956–8.
[35] *Winchester Acta*, ed. Franklin, no. 24.
[36] *Regesta*, III, nos. 956–8.
[37] *Ibid.*, III, no. 954.
[38] *Ibid.*, III, no. 342.
[39] *Winchester Acta*, ed. Franklin, pp. 208–9. The bishop later lost control of Siston to the earl of Gloucester: see R.H.C. Davis, *King Stephen*, 3rd edn (London, 1990), p. 168, no. 342a.
[40] *Regesta*, III, nos. 104 (Duke Henry for monks of Biddlesden), 861 (Stephen for the Templars).

of his inheritance'.[41] The mention of necessity becomes a routine phrase in charters recording sales in the late twelfth century and beyond.

Roger of Howden described Richard I immediately after his coronation in 1189 gathering resources for his crusade: 'he put up for sale everything he had – offices, lordships, earldoms, castles, towns, lands, the lot'.[42] Even with the reticence of the sources, enough survives to suggest that at the beginning of the twelfth century, just as at its end, England was a land in which everything had its price. Norwich in the 1140s, illuminated by the searchlights trained on the murdered William of Norwich, absolutely reeks of money. When the Jews were first accused they sought aid from the sheriff, 'who had been wont to be their refuge'. 'Look you,' they said to him, 'we are placed in a position of great anxiety, and if you can help us out of it, we promise you a hundred marks.' The sheriff, 'delighted at the number of marks', promised to keep their secrets, and swore to secrecy also the chief witness, Aelward Ded.[43] Elsewhere a smaller consideration might suffice. We find one man asking simply for 'a dog that he wanted';[44] another for 'ten marks and a monk's raincoat';[45] while 3d. for cherries purchased the attention of the schoolboys of London for sufficient time for them to note the purchase of an acre of land by the canons of St Paul's.[46] Service as well as land had its value. In the mid-1140s, dark days for the see of York, the provost of Beverley often rode over to York at the archbishop's request, and was given twenty bovates of land in augmentation of his prebend in consideration of his expenses.[47] At a less elevated level we find Torfin holding twelve bovates of land in a hamlet of Harkness, and additionally a toft worth 8d. a year to enable him to represent the interests of the monks of Whitby in the village. It was specified that for this latter the monks would get precisely 8d. worth of advice (*secundum valenciam ipsorum denariorum*).[48] Torfin was a true Yorkshireman.

Aelward Ded of Norwich was not a Yorkshireman, but he also, in the case just quoted, was careful to specify that the promise to keep quiet would only last until he lay on his death-bed. There different considerations applied. The *locus classicus* here, made so by another distinguished historian from north-east England, is Nigel d'Aubigny's restitution to the monks of

[41] 'ut per ipsam pecuniam retinerem me et heredes meos in residuum hereditatis nostre ne plus aut eciam totum amitteremus'; *Early Yorkshire Charters*, XI, no. 158.
[42] John Gillingham, *Richard the Lionheart*, 2nd edn (London, 1978), p. 133.
[43] *English Lawsuits*, I, no. 321.
[44] *Chronicle of Battle*, pp. 120–1.
[45] *Early Yorkshire Charters*, III, no. 1528.
[46] *English Lawsuits*, I, no. 329.
[47] 'negotiis ecclesie nostre exigentibus prefatum T. Ebor' venire sepius sollicatamus': *York Acta*, ed. Burton, no. 83, correcting the date given in *Early Yorkshire Charters*, I, no. 155.
[48] *Early Yorkshire Charters*, XI, no. 223.

Durham early in the reign of Henry I.[49] It has been quoted because of the loyalty it shows between king and magnate.[50] It is worth quoting also because of the constraints upon his freedom of action which Nigel d'Aubigny perceived. He seems in fact confident that he can restore his disseisins, but he felt obliged to offer land in exchange: thus he envisaged, 'the restoration of lands which I make to my men whom I have disinherited; and the exchanges which I have given for those lands to my men to whom I have given them'. The restoration was as peremptory as the disseisin. In many cases, however, land granted away could not be restored since its recipients were seen as enjoying secure title. This consideration clearly influenced Archbishop Theobald when in 1146 he accepted from Henry of Rye an exchange for land that had been alienated from Canterbury, 'in such a way that he could in no way revoke it in favour of the church'.[51]

Eleanor Searle is right to point out that material of this kind is of great significance for the questions of economic development in the twelfth century. A lord could even dispossess an improving tenant, and keep land and chattels without compensation.[52] Both this, and the need to leave a profit for the farmer, were a check on investment. Good husbandry provides its own satisfaction, as the case of Henry of Winchester surveying the growing corn makes clear, but the real money was not here. Rather it lay in jurisdiction. 'Holders of large manors with extensive assets of grazing, woodland, moorland and, best of all, jurisdiction of a hundred attached, successfully exploited numerous possibilities of exacting a wide range of rents and dues from a large number of people.'[53] Recent work has served to highlight the importance of the lordship exercised from hundredal centres.[54] The Abingdon chronicle prints two charters of Henry I in favour of the abbey, one granting the hundred of Hormer, the other the market of Abingdon. Behind these there was a story. The abbey's rights to these had been called in question, and they were only vindicated when the abbot produced a charter of Edward the Confessor, and offered 300 marks for the royal confirmation. To raise the sum he 'thoroughly polished up the reliquary of St Ethelwold,

[49] *Mowbray Charters*, no. 3, the centre-piece of a 'remarkable series of charters', *ibid.*, nos. 2–10, ed. Greenway, p. xxv n. 3.
[50] R.W. Southern, 'King Henry I', in his *Medieval Humanism and Other Studies* (Oxford, 1970), pp. 220–1.
[51] *English Lawsuits*, I, no. 311.
[52] Searle, in *Chronicle of Battle*, pp. 12–13.
[53] Sally P. J. Harvey, 'The Extent and Profitability of Demesne Agriculture in England in the Later Eleventh Century', in T.H. Aston *et al.* (eds.), *Social Relations and Ideas: Essays in Honour of R.H. Hilton* (Cambridge, 1983), pp. 45–72, quotation p. 70.
[54] Edmund King, 'The Anarchy of King Stephen's Reign', *Trans. Royal Hist. Soc.*, 5th ser., 34 (1984), pp. 133–53, at pp. 138–41; Paul Dalton, *Conquest, Anarchy and Lordship: Yorkshire 1066–1154* (Cambridge, 1994).

which was made of gold and silver, and obtained the price of more than 300 marks for it'.[55] It should not be assumed that the hundred was valued at this sum, which might rather be seen as a relief,'hidden from the more scrupulous as a confirmation of liberty. In this entry the hundred centre and the market went together, and might be seen to be coterminous.[56] It is thus appropriate to turn to sources reflecting the regulation and the profits of trade.

The surviving charters suggest that one of the first acts of Henry of Blois when he became abbot of Glastonbury was to secure a charter in protection of the fair of Glastonbury.[57] This was one of many fairs competing for custom in a market which nonetheless could not support more than a few fairs of international significance. When Henry was promoted to Winchester he succeeded to one of these. The story of the build up of this fair may be traced in outline from the royal confirmations, all doubtless after the event: first in 1096 the grant of a three-day fair by William Rufus; then in 1110 the period was extended to eight days by Henry I; then in 1136 Stephen added a further six days, making fourteen days in all; while in March 1155, ignoring the grant by Stephen, Henry II increased the fair yet further, to sixteen days.[58] For the whole of the period thus systematically extended, the bishop enjoyed the rights of the crown throughout the city. Later, to symbolise the transfer of power, the official measures were solemnly taken up St Giles Hill;[59] and such theatre was in every way characteristic of Bishop Henry. This background is necessary to explain the famous correspondence between Brian fitz Count and Henry of Winchester. It called forth, and is best remembered for, Brian fitz Count's recollection of the good days of Henry I, 'who gave me land and an honour'.[60] But it was precipitated by the baron seizing goods that were on their way to the bishop's fair at Winchester. The standard writ of protection stated that all bound for a fair should have the king's firm peace.[61] Brian fitz Count's reply suggested not that no firm peace could be looked for in the circumstances of the early 1140s, but, more insidiously, that what was needed was a private arrangement. The men of Wallingford

[55] *English Lawsuits*, I, no. 246.
[56] On markets in hundredal centres, see R.H. Britnell, *The Commercialisation of English Society 1000–1500* (Cambridge, 1993), pp. 20–1.
[57] *Regesta*, II, no. 1590.
[58] Martin Biddle (ed.), *Winchester in the Early Middle Ages* (Winchester Studies, 1, Oxford, 1976), pp. 286–9.
[59] Martin Biddle (ed.), *Survey of Winchester*, 2 vols. (Winchester Studies, 2, Oxford, 1985), II, pp. 1091–123, at p. 1115.
[60] H.W.C. Davis, 'Henry of Blois and Brian fitz Count', *Eng. Hist. Rev.*, 25 (1910), pp. 297–303.
[61] The bishop would have relied on *Regesta*, III, no. 952: 'omnes homines illuc venientes et ibi morantes et inde redeuntes in eundo et redeundo habeant meam firmam pacem'.

would later have privileged rights in the fair of Winchester; and the confirmation of its privileges, as they had been under Henry I, was Henry of Winchester's first request of Henry II.[62]

Roger of Salisbury and his nephews the bishops of Lincoln and Ely were no less active. In September 1131, when oaths were once again sworn in support of the empress's succession, Roger of Salisbury was granted by the crown the abbey of Malmesbury *ut dominium suum et sedem propriam*.[63] And very soon after he had helped Stephen to come to power in December 1135 he obtained from him the borough of Malmesbury and the hundreds and customs pertaining to it.[64] He took a similar proprietary interest in the other boroughs and towns of his diocese and beyond. The boundaries of his diocese came up to the town walls of Oxford, and by the end of Henry I's reign he had acquired rights in the fair that had been granted to the canons of St Frideswide's.[65] As he lay on his death-bed, his examination of conscience, in contrast to that of Nigel d'Aubigny, turned on a range of economic issues, and he specifically restored the fair of Oxford to the canons.[66] The work of his nephew Alexander of Lincoln at Newark may similarly be taken as exemplary.[67] This is well known as one of the castles confiscated after 'the arrest of the bishops' at Oxford in 1139.[68] But the town and its castle were buttressed by privileges largely economic in nature. It was very carefully done. First the bishop was given permission to divert the Fosse Way, 'as he might chose'; then a bridge was built over the Trent to serve the castle; a part of the knight-service of the bishopric was transferred there; and a fair of five days confirmed. Those issuing the charter in regard to the bridge, in Hampshire, among them Roger of Salisbury, showed sufficient awareness of the topography and trade of the north midlands to specify that the new bridge should not be to the detriment of Lincoln or Nottingham, the royal boroughs which it served to link.[69]

---

[62] Biddle (ed.), *Winchester in the Early Middle Ages*, p. 287 n. 3.

[63] *Regesta*, II, no. 1715. Henry I's grants of the fair are *ibid.*, II, nos. 494, 971.

[64] *Ibid.*, III, no. 784.

[65] *Ibid.*, II, no. 1957; and cf. an earlier grant, *ibid.*, II, no. 1345. Roger's interest is explained by Edward J. Kealey, *Roger of Salisbury: Viceroy of England* (Berkeley, 1972), pp. 121–2, but in terms of religious patronage not the pursuit of economic advantage. It needs to be noted that the city of Oxford was not in the Salisbury diocese.

[66] Kealey, *Roger of Salisbury*, pp. 265–9.

[67] The group of charters need to be taken together: *Regesta*, II, nos. 1660–1, 1770, 1772–3, 1791. There is a useful discussion in *Documents relating to the Manor and Soke of Newark-on-Trent*, ed. M.W. Barley (Thoroton Soc., Rec. Ser., 12, Nottingham, 1956), pp. xvi–xxiv, though no special emphasis is given to this phase of development.

[68] Henry of Huntingdon, *Historia Anglorum*, ed. T. Arnold (Rolls Ser., 74, London, 1879), 266; *Historia Novella*, pp. 25, 27.

[69] *Regesta*, II, no. 1770.

A little to the south, in the fenland, the abbots of the great monasteries were no less single-minded in their pursuit of economic advantage. At St Ives the abbot of Ramsey had a winner. The grant of fair of eight days in 1110 was notified by the king not just to the bishop of Lincoln and the sheriff of Huntingdon, but to 'his lieges and merchants' of England.[70] The abbot's neighbours could not compete in the same league, but they tried very hard to do so. The ambition of the abbot of Thorney was closely focussed on the river bank at Yaxley. Early in Stephen's reign, he obtained from Henry the son of the king of Scots confirmation of the market and quay at Yaxley, with toll and other customs, 'so that those coming and going thence may have my firm peace in perpetuity'.[71] But that peace was of no long duration, and in the 1140s a matching pair of charters were issued by earl Simon of Senlis.[72] Additionally, he exempted the lands of the monks from *tenseria* and all works.[73] The compiler of the 'Red Book of Thorney' showed a good sense of the realities of power in Stephen's reign in copying these magnate charters, uniquely, in the section devoted to royal *acta*.

The amount of economic business coming before the chancery in the early twelfth century is striking, particularly since the survival rate for documents of this kind is likely to have been poor. Thus the Abingdon cartulary contains at least fifteen writs relating to economic privileges from Henry I's reign alone.[74] Among these the largest group relates to tolls. These writs can be useful in providing specific information about the commodities and the direction of trade, and the impediments that might be placed in its path. The abbot of Abingdon complained more than once concerning Warin the reeve of Southampton and his servants, who had taken toll and customs from the monastery's goods.[75] Several abbots of eastern England complained of the abbot of Peterborough and his agents, for they controlled the access of Barnack stone to the Welland and the Nene, and were levying toll from

[70] *Ibid.*, II, no. 953; cf. *ibid.*, II, no. 1916. Already by this date the court of the barony was held here: *English Lawsuits*, I, no. 182 (from 1109). See also M.W. Beresford and J.K.S. St Joseph, *Medieval England: An Aerial Survey*, 2nd edn (Cambridge, 1979), pp. 182–3, figs. 73A, 73B.

[71] *Regesta Regum Scottorum, I: Acts of Malcolm IV, 1153–65*, ed. G.W.S. Barrow (Edinburgh, 1960), nos. 15–16, pp. 141–2.

[72] Cambridge Univ. Library, Add. MS 3020, fol. 21r-v.

[73] This reference to *tenseria* gains an added interest from its geographical proximity to Peterborough, where the term appears in the famous passage in Anglo-Saxon Chronicle: *The Peterborough Chronicle*, ed. Cecily Clark, 2nd edn (Oxford, 1970), s.a. 1137, pp. 55–7; quoted with discussion in King, 'Anarchy of Stephen's Reign', pp. 135–7.

[74] *Regesta*, II, nos. 520 (carriage service), 550, 565 (building materials), 566 (salt), 576, 615 (improvement), 814–15, 854–5, 937–8, 1258 (aspects of trade on the Thames), 1510, 1612 (trade *via* Southampton).

[75] *Regesta*, II, no. 1510. Reading Abbey had similar problems in the reign of Stephen: *ibid.*, III, no. 676. It should be noted that the lord of the men of Southampton might at this stage have been Henry of Winchester: *Historia Novella*, p. 75.

and distraining upon the boats of their brother monks.[76] A number of the earliest writs seem specifically in support of a particular building project. A writ for Ely specified an exemption for timber and lead and iron and stone, and anything else that the monks had need of for building their church.[77] If there was some reluctance, on the part of the chancery, to grant a more general protection, it had clearly been overcome by the middle years of Henry I's reign. The majority of charters, as always, are for religious corporations, but they were also issued to favoured laymen.[78] The first privileges for the Cistercians were issued to the order as a whole. A writ surviving in the Fountains cartulary offered protection to all Cistercian houses, on proof of status or production of the writ.[79] Another, from that of Rievaulx, stated that the horses, the goods and the men of Citeaux be quit of taxes on trade. The writ was addressed generally, but specifically, to the reeves of Southampton, Hastings, Dover, Barfleur, Caen, Ouistreham and Dieppe, which conveniently gives us a list of the most popular cross-Channel ferries of the day.[80]

The monks of Citeaux thought it worthwhile, in advance of their journey to England, to send for a writ of protection whose general address was a simple statement of authority. This would not be the case under Stephen. As his reign progressed, the area of his effective authority shrank, and those engaged in trade could find themselves with written instruments that were worthless. The problem, which may often have called for some diplomacy, may be introduced by citing a couple of Stephen's writs. Early in his reign, the king wrote to his justices and ministers of Boulogne and Wissant granting the monks of Canterbury freedom from toll and other dues.[81] His writ ran in the honour of Boulogne, and continued to do so. In a writ of 1138, at Hereford, witnessed by Brian fitz Count, Stephen granted freedom from toll to the local bishop, the writ here addressed to his ministers of the whole of

---

[76] *Regesta*, II, nos. 585 (Thorney), 694 (Bury St Edmunds), 1410 (Ramsey), 1733 (Bury St Edmunds).

[77] *Ibid.*, II, no. 771. The surviving texts here might suggest that duplicates were issued, as certainly happened later in the century. There are two originals of *ibid.*, III, no. 495, issued by Duke Henry for Lire Abbey at Rouen in 1154; and a charter of Richard I for the burgesses of Exeter in 1190 survives in three originals, one of them illustrated in Edmund King, *Medieval England* (Oxford, 1988), p. 90.

[78] Writs for Michael of Hanslope and for William Mauduit II are found side by side in the *Beauchamp Cartulary*, ed. Emma Mason (Pipe Roll Soc., n.s., 43, London, 1980), nos. 169–70 (= *Regesta*, II, nos. 1674, 1846).

[79] *Regesta*, II, no. 1820.

[80] *Ibid.*, II, no. 1720. The identical list, with the exception of Ouistreham, is found in a charter of Henry II in favour of the Cistercian house of Meaux: *Early Yorkshire Charters*, III no. 1389.

[81] *Regesta*, III, no. 141; but note 'sicut precepi per alia brevia mea': this was not the first time he had had occasion to write on this topic.

England and Wales.[82] Within a few months this writ will have had at best
an archival interest. The hard-headed archivist of Kirkham priory – by
profession, at least, a Yorkshireman – noted they had a charter of Stephen
granting freedom of toll, *sed carta Henrici melior est et perpetualior*.[83] There
was if anything a greater discrepancy, between the promise and the actuality,
in the writs and charters of Stephen's opponents. In the summer of 1141 the
empress wrote to 'my ministers of the whole of England and the sea-ports',
offering protection and her firm peace to 'my burgesses of Devizes'.[84] It
cannot have lasted long; and the subsequent settlement there of the most
pale of remnants of an imperial court must have been a mixed blessing for
the townsmen. We may know that in 1150 and 1151 Duke Henry of Normandy
was the coming man, but his promises to the citizens of Rouen of their
portus at Dowgate, and quittance of customs in London, and freedom to go
with their goods to all the fairs of England, were more than he could deliver
at that date.[85] He alone of the protagonists, however, offered the prospect
of a union of England and Normandy; and his father's death in 1151 and his
marriage in 1152 increased still further the scope of the free-trade area that
he could offer. This was a powerful attraction to the merchants not just of
Rouen and the major towns in Normandy but in Flanders also. They were
to provide the financial muscle behind the future Henry II. As Edward Miller
noted, the first fruits of the new free trade were offered to the burgesses of
Wallingford.[86]

New ports grew up in eastern and southern England, and there was
vigorous competition for the profits of the trade which ran through them.
Let us start on the seashore, at Yarmouth, and with a commodity that was
almost an international currency,[87] 'those fish that in common parlance are
called herrings'.[88] 'There was at that time on the beach at Yarmouth a certain
tiny chapel in which divine services were only celebrated in the season of
the herring fishery, for there were no more than four or five little houses
here provided for the reception of the fishermen.'[89] The bishop sought from
the king licence to build a church with parochial rights, and appointed a

---

[82] *Ibid.*, III, no. 383; and note, about the same time, a similar writ in favour of the monks
of Worcester, *ibid.*, no. 968.

[83] *Ibid.*, III, no. 426.

[84] *Ibid.*, III, no. 253.

[85] *Ibid.*, III, no. 729.

[86] Miller, 'Economic Policies of Governments', p. 309; the best version of the charter is in
Charles Gross, *The Gild Merchant*, 2 vols. (Oxford, 1890), II, pp. 244–5.

[87] *Regesta*, III, no. 288, for Eye Priory: 'concedo eis quod decima eorum de Donewico
[Dunwich] crescat quoque anno in denariis et harengis et in omnibus aliis rebus
secundum hoc quod redditus mei ibidem crescent'.

[88] *Ibid.*, III, no. 329.

[89] *English Lawsuits*, I, no. 173.

full-time chaplain. This mission to seamen was rudely interrupted when 'the men of the adjacent ports' showed up, and 'evicted the said chaplain by force of arms'. We can be confident that behind the struggle for the chapel lay a conflict over the control of trade. We find a similar conflict at Sandwich, between Christ Church, Canterbury and St Augustine's.[90] Again we find 'little houses', here built on the other side of the harbour 'because of the ships coming there'; there were toll and customs taken illicitly 'from the foreigners who put in there'; and a new ferry-boat started to ply back and forth. 'Whence many disputes and quarrels without number broke out.' It hardly matters which side was which. Tolls on goods taken by water were particularly difficult to enforce. The abbot of Abingdon claimed custom 'for every ship of the city of Oxford that travels southwards on the Thames', namely 'a hundred herring or the equivalent in money'. The boatmen were supposed to pay without being asked, but many did not. The abbot went to law, and his custom was confirmed.[91] If the Thames boatmen were recalcitrant, the more so were the fishermen of the East Riding. The abbot of Whitby and the prior of Bridlington came to an agreement in the 1120s: the fishermen of Whitby putting in at Filey, and those of Filey putting in at Whitby, should pay tithes where they landed.[92]

Henry I's charter for the bishop of Norwich in Lynn granted him 'his customs and exchange and market and port'.[93] The mention of exchange (*bursa*) might seem surprising, for of all the royal monopolies the control of the coinage was the most tenaciously defended, by the use of the most severe penalties. It need not be so. Henry I's system, at least until his latter years, left a good deal of scope for seigneurial involvement. The charter in which he set the standard, issued Christmas Day 1100, was designed to protect the quality of the coinage.[94] It contained the interesting provision that no moneyer was to engage in exchange outside his shire, and if he operated outside his home town he had to coin in the presence of two witnesses of the shire. Some clues as to what enterprise might be lawful are found in the Peterborough survey of the late 1120s, where under Stamford the abbey's revenues included 20s. 'from the moneyers for the exchange of the markets of Oundle and Peterborough'.[95] The crown might also license the presence of seigneurial moneyers in the mint towns. After Roger's exem-

---

[90] *Ibid.*, I, no. 254.

[91] *Ibid.*, I, no. 191.

[92] *Early Yorkshire Charters*, II, no. 874.

[93] *Regesta*, II, no. 1853; and on the growth of Lynn, see *The Making of King's Lynn: A Documentary Survey*, ed. Dorothy M. Owen (Records of Social and Economic History, n.s., IX, 1984), pp. 5–12.

[94] *Regesta*, II, no. 501.

[95] 'reddunt monetarii de cambitione mercati Undele et Burch in Pascha 20s et de torno monete 20s': *Chronicon Petroburgense*, p. 166.

plary treatment of 'the moneyers of the whole of England' in 1125, the abbot
of Bury sought to have his minting rights confirmed 'after justice has been
done upon his moneyer'.[96] The researches of Mark Blackburn into the coinages of Henry I and Stephen have shown a significant reduction in Henry
I's last type in the number of mints, and the restoration of many of those
closed down in the first type of Stephen.[97] The coinage remained centrally
controlled. As the reign progressed, this control was lost, and this provides
very clear evidence of anarchy. In Wales, in the west country and in Yorkshire, if not elsewhere, there were baronial coinages. The Box hoard of
1994 has added to the list the greatest magnate of them all, Robert earl of
Gloucester,[98] a most apposite demonstration of the regional authority of
which the chroniclers spoke.[99] In this context, the question of what exactly
was a 'baronial' coinage is worth attention. A new mint was opened at Hedon
in Stephen type 7. If the 'distinctive York coins in the name of Stephen can
properly be regarded as the baronial issues' of William of Aumale, earl of
York,[100] the same point could be made even more strongly of Hedon. And
it might be extended to other regions. A mint was opened at Castle Rising
during Stephen type 2, bearing the king's name, but a sign of the enterprise
of William d'Aubigny earl of Sussex.[101] We might finally look to consider
what the coinage of the anarchy tells us of economic development. The
answer here may be looked for in the evidence of hoards. They might suggest
an increased localisation of trade,[102] with particular difficulties experienced
by tradesmen on the shifting internal frontiers of England.[103] Henry II moved
quickly to restore the customs of his grandfather.

   A vacancy was a time of weakness. Political circumstances might create
the equivalent of a vacancy in the lord's lifetime. This was particularly true

[96] *Anglo-Saxon Chronicle*, s.a. 1125, ed. Dorothy Whitelock (London, 1961), p. 191; *Regesta*,
     II, no. 1430.
[97] M. Blackburn, 'Coinage and Currency under Henry I: A Review', *Anglo-Norman Studies*,
     13 (1991), pp. 49–81, esp. pp. 64–71; M. Blackburn, 'Coinage and Currency', in E. King
     (ed.), *The Anarchy of King Stephen's Reign* (Oxford, 1994), pp. 145–205, esp. pp. 153–61.
[98] There were coins struck, by several moneyers at Bristol, also at Trowbridge and at
     Cirencester: information from Marion Archibald.
[99] The earl and his supporters 'put almost half of England, from sea to sea, under their
     own laws and ordinances', *Gesta Stephani*, ed. K.R. Potter and R.H.C. Davis, 2nd edn
     (Oxford, 1976), pp. 148–51.
[100] Blackburn, in King (ed.), *Anarchy of Stephen's Reign*, p. 185.
[101] *Ibid.*, pp. 153, 159–61.
[102] Note the contrast in the range of places of issue of coins between Prestwich, Lancs.
     (1972) and Coed-y-Wenallt, Glam. (1980), in summary in King, 'Anarchy of Stephen's
     Reign', p. 149; Coed-y-Wenallt is published in full in G.C. Boon, *Welsh Hoards 1979–
     1981* (Cardiff, 1986), pp. 37–82. The evidence of the hoard from Box, Wilts. (1994)
     makes the point no less strongly.
[103] The finding of the Box hoard gives an added resonance to the remarks of William of
     Malmesbury on the quality of the coinage: *Historia Novella*, p. 42.

of Stephen's reign, but not exclusive to it, for this was symptomatic of the competitive lordship of the Anglo-Norman kings. In 1100 Henry I succeeded, and Ranulf Flambard fell from power, and went overseas to Normandy. In 1101 he was restored, but one year's loss of lordship took several years to undo. Writ after writ winged their way north, instructing his men and his cattle to return at once to his lordship. Even his cathedral chapter needed a writ from the king before they would receive him back. Men such as this, we are told, owed everything to the king. When the king's favour was withdrawn, they had a lot to lose.[104] The arrest of Roger of Salisbury and his nephews in 1139 had a similar impact in a variety of locations. The canons of St Frideswide's, Oxford, asked for the protection of the papal legate.[105] A writ from King Stephen at Oxford instructed Hugh de Escalers and Stephen his nephew to restore to the monks of Ely their farm, as they best held 'before I captured the Isle of Ely'; and then a writ from Bury St Edmunds to Geoffrey de Mandeville asked him to ensure that this was done.[106] Their lord had taken refuge in Gloucester,[107] and in his absence those who relied on his protection suffered – not just the monks. Edward Miller has the vivid image of the knights of the bishopric of Ely being driven into Ely with their legs tied beneath their horses.[108] Word of the arrest had quickly reached London also: a few lads went out on the town, and through the vigilance of the canons of St Martin le Grand, who have preserved one of the best archives for the study of Stephen's reign, they can be named as the sons of Hubert Juvenis.[109] Stephen protected his brother Henry whilst he was away in Rome, noting that he was absent 'with my permission and by the apostolic command'.[110] William of Malmesbury's epitaph for Roger of Salisbury provides for his day the definitive treatment of a man whose lordship has been destroyed.[111] Cash and precious vessels were stripped from the altar of his cathedral church. He left nothing behind.

Roger of Salisbury had issued charters in the king's name, often as presiding officer at the exchequer, and could expect them to be obeyed. After his death, it could no longer be presumed that royal charters were good against

[104] Southern, 'Ranulf Flambard', in *Medieval Humanism*, pp. 183–205, at pp. 196–8; H.H.E. Craster, 'A Contemporary Record of the Pontificate of Ranulf Flambard', *Archaeologia Aeliana*, 4th ser., 8 (Newcastle, 1930), pp. 33–56.

[105] *Winchester Acta*, ed. Franklin, no. 90.

[106] *Regesta*, III, nos. 264–5; and note two further charters from the mid-1140s, nos. 266–7.

[107] *Gesta Stephani*, pp. 100–1.

[108] Miller, *Ely*, p. 172; *Liber Eliensis*, ed. E.O. Blake (Camden, 3rd ser., XCII, London, 1962), p. 319.

[109] The king orders the restitution to Roger of Salisbury and the canons of all land of which they had been dissesised 'postquam discordia incepit inter nos': *Regesta*, III, no. 525.

[110] *Ibid.*, III, no. 535.

[111] *Historia Novella*, pp. 37–9.

all men, and for all time. The year 1141 was one of particular uncertainty. The 'second charter' of Stephen to Geoffrey de Mandeville, issued at Christmas, confirmed 'all the tenements which he held, from whomsoever they were held, on the day on which I was detained at Lincoln and captured'.[112] Earlier in the same year the empress had offered Stephen's brother, Henry of Winchester, confirmation of the estates of Glastonbury as they had been on the day of Henry I's death and as they had been held latterly on the third Sunday in Lent, 'when he came and spoke to me at Wherwell, this being the day before the Monday on which this prelate and the citizens of Winchester received me honourably' within the city.[113] The insistence of the Angevins that nothing that Stephen did was legitimate is one of the reasons that the text of the 1153 peace agreement is so long. 'In the whole kingdom of England,' it concluded, 'both in that part which pertains to the duke and in that part which pertains directly to me, I shall exercise royal justice.'[114] England would remain a divided realm until Stephen died. And problems lasted into the next reign. Henry II sent a letter offering his protection to the dean of York: though he had never sworn homage either to his mother or to himself, nonetheless he enjoyed the king's confidence and his lordship should be protected.[115] This forms part of a large archive of documents relating to the see of York, in some way comparable to that relating to Flambard in Durham, showing how the prolonged vacancy impacted on the whole region.

Among these, a particular interest attaches to the charters relating to St Peter's (later known as St Leonard's) hospital in York. The lordship of such a house lay exclusively in charity and co-operation, and its very existence was challenged when these virtues came under threat. Its charters show how this came about, the particular problems that were identified, and the solutions proposed.[116] The first charter is that of William Rufus in the 1090s confirming the 'ancient endowment' of the hospital, namely 'one thrave of corn from each plough at work in the province of York'.[117] This was a lot of ploughs. Regular reminders were needed, and protection offered to their servants (*ministri*), but particular problems arose after the death of Thurstan in 1140. John of Hexham saw this as the beginning of a decade of anarchy in the north of England, defined as a period of 'unrestrained disputes, shameless contempt of the clergy, irreverence of the laity towards ecclesiastical laws and persons: the unity of the kingdom was destroyed, because each

[112] 'die qua impeditus fui apud Lincolniam et captus': *Regesta*, III, no. 276.
[113] *Ibid.*, III, no. 343.
[114] *Ibid.*, III, no. 272.
[115] *Early Yorkshire Charters*, I, no. 140.
[116] *Ibid.*, I, nos. 166–99, pp. 141–67.
[117] *Ibid.*, I, no. 166.

man's will was his law'.[118] Here we have a good case study. At some time in the 1140s Stephen ordered a general protection of the house, and specifically freedom from pleas concerning any land they had held 'in the time of king Henry and archbishop Thurstan'. The king wanted them to have peace, 'so that they may more freely and securely pray for me to God and do good works'.[119] A decade later their requests were being addressed not to the king but to the Archbishop Theobald, the papal legate, from whom the hospital procured no less than four charters.[120] In one of them he wrote, clearly echoing the case put to him, that the hospital could no longer perform its work, 'by reason of the destruction of their house, the plunder of their livestock, the depopulation of their townships and the devastation of the countryside'.[121] The word used here for the region affected was *provincia*, a word that had a particular resonance in the context of the relationship between the archbishops of Canterbury and York; but if Theobald was tempted to contrast his lordship with the situation in the north of England, it was a temptation he resisted. Possibly around the same time, the dean of York wrote slightly forlornly to the parishioners of the diocese to order the payment of Peter-corn, asking their priests additionally to ensure that death-bed bequests were carried out.[122] Anarchy here is manifest as simple inertia. The lines between the extraction of the peasant surplus and the work of the hospital were long, and the *ministri* of both powers, king and archbishop, were called to account.

It is not in question that the lordship that was most attenuated in the reign of Stephen was that of the king himself. It may be that it is from this angle that we should approach the well-known and extensively discussed figures that would seem to quantify 'the devastation of the countryside' to which archbishop Theobald referred. These are the figures for 'waste' which are provided in the pipe roll of 1155–6, when Henry II restored one of the 'customs' of his grandfather Henry I, and levied a geld. These figures require attention in any study of the English economy in the first half of the twelfth century, since they provide figures that have been interpreted as statistics relating to the English economy in the 1150s. An article by H.W.C. Davis

---

[118] John of Hexham, in *Symeonis Monachi Opera Omnia*, ed. T. Arnold, 2 vols. (Rolls Ser., 75, London, 1882–5), II, p. 305. On the significance of Thurstan's death see Dalton, *Conquest, Anarchy and Lordship*, pp. 151–2.

[119] *Early Yorkshire Charters*, I, no. 172, dated to 1140s; and in *Regesta*, III, no. 991, with date 1140. The date of 1140 is provided by reading 'Bernardi episcopo Sancti Davidi' for 'A. episcopo Sancti Laudi' in the manuscript. As Algar was bishop of Countances 1132 × 1150, the emendation seems both extremely bold and completely unnecessary; and the text reads better with a longer interval of time between its issue and Thurstan's death.

[120] *Early Yorkshire Charters*, I, nos. 180, 183–5.

[121] *Ibid.*, I, no. 183.

[122] *Ibid.*, I, no. 182.

drew attention to the importance of the information, and thereafter it has been extensively discussed, most recently and most fully by Emilie Amt.[123] When the figures for each county are tabulated, the median is about 25 per cent, and the closest to the median is Wiltshire at 26 per cent. Wiltshire was also the wealthiest county in terms of its geld assessment. What does it mean to say that a quarter of Wiltshire was waste? The debate has been extensive, and it will not be reviewed again here. The suggestion which we now have, which is helpful, is that 'the condition of the country, at least in some regions, would not bear the weight of all the taxes being demanded'.[124] It is useful then to turn attention, as Amt does, to 'the enormous expenditure' on restocking in the first few years of the reign. 'In 1156, such expenditure occurs in 21 county farms and eleven separately farmed estates, and the total spent, £1178, is a substantial sum, equal to a tenth of the potential revenue from county and manor farms this year, and representing thirty percent of all expenditure recorded on the roll.'[125] In some cases, and particularly on separately farmed estates, there is clear evidence linking this restocking with increased productivity. The entry for Taunton in Devon is quoted: 'And the same sheriff renders account for 20s 2d from Taunton. Into the treasury 20s 2d. And he is quit. And in restocking of the same manor £6 2s 4d, which is credited to the sheriff as *superplusagium*. And from now on he should render to the treasury £13.'[126] It might be noted here that Taunton was one of the major estates of the bishopric of Winchester, and that it was in hand because Bishop Henry was in exile.[127] In looking at these figures for restocking, anyone who has studied a medieval estate will feel themselves on familiar ground. According to the Ramsey Abbey chronicle, after the depredations of Geoffrey de Mandeville, the incoming abbot found 'on all the demesne lands of the abbey only one and a half plough teams, and no provisions'.[128]

The condition of the royal estate, in a majority of counties, was better than this. It had nonetheless been a close shave. This at least was the official view of the exchequer. The author of the *Dialogus*, the son of Nigel of Ely,

---

[123] H.W.C. Davis, 'The anarchy of Stephen's Reign', *Eng. Hist. Rev.*, 18 (1903), pp. 630–41. The figures are from the pipe roll of 1155–6, *Pipe Rolls 2–4 Henry II* (London, 1844), pp. 3–68; the entries are tabulated in Emilie Amt, *The Accession of Henry II in England: Royal Government Restored 1149–1159* (Woodbridge, 1993), p. 139.

[124] Amt, *Accession of Henry II*, p. 141.

[125] *Ibid.*, p. 142.

[126] *Ibid.*, p. 146; *Pipe Roll 2–4 Henry II*, p. 48.

[127] He was in exile 1155–7: Franklin, in *Winchester Acta*, pp. xlvii–xlviii. Soon after his return, on 11 October 1158, he issued a charter there in which he referred repeatedly to 'my vill of Taunton': *ibid.*, no. 113; cf. *Regesta*, III, no. 953.

[128] *Chronicon Abbatiae Ramesiensis*, ed. W.D. Macray (Rolls Ser., 83, London, 1886), pp. 333–4; cited with similar texts in David Knowles, *The Monastic Order in England*, 2nd edn (Cambridge, 1963), pp. 268–72.

in a famous passage stressed his father's contribution to continuity. 'Frequently asked by the great king Henry, he restored the knowledge of the exchequer, which had almost perished during the long years of war, and like another Ezra, the diligent restorer of the Bible, renewed its form in all its details.'[129] A part of this *scientia*, the historic memory of the exchequer,[130] was – it may be suggested – concerned with estate management. It is tempting to suggest further, *pace* Warren, that the exchequer was in some respects more ambitious in Henry I's reign than it was later in the twelfth century. It is very likely that the confidence of estate administrators was high. At the very beginning of the reign Geoffrey of Saint-Calais was appointed administrator at Battle. He found the abbey's principal manor fragmented (*distractum*) and demanded from its reeve an account of his management. Geoffrey was described as 'supremely shrewd, prudent and worldly wise'.[131] Here was the very model of a medieval abbot or a modern head of house. There can be no mistaking the voice of the manager in Henry of Blois' *Libellus* from Glastonbury; and that voice is seldom absent throughout his long career. The group that brought Stephen to power comprised churchmen of great capacity and exceptional confidence. Stephen's 'charter of liberties' for the church was at the same time a blueprint for its more effective management. But it is not just churchmen who show this managerial confidence. The material relating to Lewes Priory in the Warenne volume in *Early Yorkshire Charters*, among the jewels in the crown of that great enterprise, shows this particularly well. One writ from the 1130s gains a particular immediacy from its *viva voce* instruction to the earl's steward to make sure his instructions are carried out.[132] A licence to fish, in any age a solitary pursuit, was granted only on condition that an officer of the earl was present.[133] Even Geoffrey de Mandeville, 'the most perfect and typical presentment of the feudal and anarchic spirit that stamps the reign of Stephen', according to J.H. Round, was remembered at Waltham as an excellent manager.[134] In the anarchy lines of communication broke down, and confidence was lost. With the Restoration in 1154 there came a more favourable environment for the routine pursuit of economic advantage. It was nicely

---

[129] *Dialogus de Scaccario*, p. 50.
[130] See John Hudson, 'Administration, Family and Perceptions of the Past in Late Twelfth-Century England: Richard FitzNigel and the *Dialogue of the Exchequer*', in Paul Magdalino (ed.), *The Perception of the Past in Twelfth-Century Europe* (London, 1992), pp. 75–98.
[131] *Chronicle of Battle*, pp. 108–13; and also in *English Lawsuits*, I, no. 174.
[132] *Early Yorkshire Charters*, VIII, no. 24.
[133] *Ibid.*, VIII, no. 38.
[134] J.H. Round, *Geoffrey de Mandeville: A Study of the Anarchy* (London, 1892), p. v; *The Waltham Chronicle*, ed. Leslie Watkiss and Marjorie Chibnall (Oxford, 1994), pp. 78–9. Note his concern over the transfer of his market from Newport to Walden, in *Regesta*, III, no. 274, and his seizure of land in Smithfield to make a vineyard, *ibid.*, III, no. 507.

symbolised 'at the first Pentecost after the concord made between the king and the duke of Normandy', when the bishop of Lincoln established a new fair at Banbury; and for its better publicity he secured the agreement of the monks of Eynsham that the Pentecostal processions from the neighbouring rural deaneries be diverted there.[135] It was business as usual.

---

[135] *English Episcopal Acta*, I: *Lincoln 1067–1185*, ed. D.M. Smith (London, 1980), no. 116; and see discussion in P.D.A. Harvey, 'Banbury', in M.D. Lobel (ed.), *Historic Towns*, I (London, 1969), p. 5.

2

Lothian and beyond: the economy of the 'English empire' of David I

IAN BLANCHARD

THE REIGNS of Stephen and Matilda (1135–54) witnessed momentous changes on England's northern borders.[1] Within a month of Henry I's death in December 1135 David I, ostensibly supporting his niece the Empress Matilda's claim to the English throne, invaded the realm, initiating a two-phase programme of territorial aggrandisement. Initially, from 1136–8, this resulted in the annexation of Cumberland. Then, after the setbacks following his defeat at the battle of the Standard, it led, during the years 1140/2–51 to the further acquisition of Northumberland and Westmorland proper, to the creation of 'client states' in Durham and southern Westmorland or Kentdale and to the extension of Scottish influence deep into Yorkshire. By the mid-twelfth century David had created a vast 'English empire', to the south of Lothian, which he and his successor Malcolm IV continued to hold until 1157. He managed, moreover, to settle these territories with a host of knights, drawn largely from the western and southern lands of the English realm. Yet the reasons for either the Scots king's interest in these territories or the attraction they held for would-be immigrants remain obscure, and, accordingly, will be investigated in this essay.

Certainly, in the closing years of Henry I's reign, few would have considered these lands as worthy of much attention. They comprised a remote wilderness whose inhabitants were not noted for their wealth (Map 2.1). At that time the city of Carlisle, for so it was called (*civitas*) contemporaneously, was essentially a place of refuge under the protection of the castle built in

---

[1] An earlier version of this chapter was presented at the Third Anglo-American Seminar on Medieval Economy and Society, Chester, 14–17 July 1989. I should like to thank all present, and particularly Edmund King and Paul Harvey, for their helpful comments on that occasion. I should also like to thank Marion Archibald of the Department of Coins and Medals at the British Museum for making available to me a complete list of the coins in the Prestwich hoard, and for a most illuminating discussion on the Scots issues contained therein.

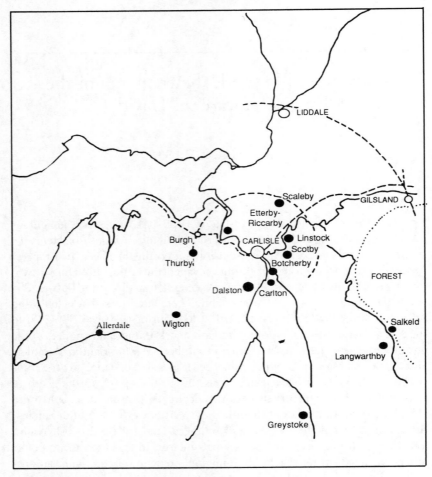

Map 2.1　Cumberland in the twelfth century.

1092,[2] existing within the administrative framework established by Henry I after about 1120/1 when Ranulf le Meschin, on becoming earl of Chester after the death of his cousin in the White Ship, surrendered his own earldom of Carlisle into the crown's hands.[3] The bulwarks of this structure on its exposed northern frontier were the great baronies of Gilsland and Liddale

[2] *The Anglo-Saxon Chronicle*, ed. and trans. G.N. Garmonsway, 2nd edn (London, 1954), p. 227.

[3] *The Royal Charters of the City of Carlisle*, ed. R.S. Ferguson (Carlisle, 1894), p. xiii. The subsequent account of the situation in Cumberland in 1130 is largely based on *Magnum Rotulum Scaccarii vel Rotulum Pipae de Anno Tricesimo-Primo Regni Henrici Primi*, ed. J. Hunter (Rec. Comm., London, 1833) (hereafter *Pipe Roll 31 Henry I*), p. 142.

guarding the passes to Scotland by land and Burgh protecting the seaward approaches. To the south, were the equally strategically significant lordships, like Scaleby, Etterby, Harraby and Botcherby, which with the royal manors, such as Scotby and Dalston, encircled Carlisle, reserved by the crown to itself together with the forest of Cumberland to the east. It was this inter-acting system of lordships which shaped the structure of the emergent town-ship, whose grandiose title belied its contemporary form. Administratively of primary immediate importance within the system of lordships were the lands of Étard (Etterby), acquired by the knight Richard in 1130, on the old 'Roman' road to the sea north-west of the city beyond the Eden, and, the lands of Bochard, on the same road to the south-east beyond the river Petteril, whose incumbents seem to have enjoyed a special responsibility for administering those areas within the walls of the city which subsequently echoed these earlier arrangements in assigning to the wards the names Rick-ergate and Botchergate. Within this area, still being enclosed with a wall in 1130, each of the lords of the region maintained a house, a refuge in times of trouble, which was probably looked after in their absence by the royal janitors under the general supervision of the two guardians referred to above. This then was the city of Carlisle in the years prior to 1133, in one respect at least a part of the military structure created by Henry I in Cumberland.

It was also, however, part of the royal demesne, subject to the sheriff's authority, and by no means economically the most important part. The city's ground rents, even when compounded with the returns from the royal manors, could only be farmed to the sheriff for about £71, a figure far less than that yielded by the crown's forest lands. Even setting to one side the revenues of Salkeld and Langwathby straddling the Eden on the south-western edge of the forest, which were included in the farm of the city and royal manors, receipts from activities in the forest were considerable. Of primary importance was the *geldum animalium* or noutgeld, a crown rent paid in cattle, the staple agrarian product of the region. During the years 1125/6–1127/8 these beasts, who were the responsibility of the ubiquitous knight Richard, had been partly deployed to stock the royal manors, but in the following two years 1128/9 and 1129/30 they had been sold, the receipts of £85 8s. 8d. suggesting that the animals involved in the levy should be numbered in the thousands.[4] Nor did this exhaust the potential of these lands as a source of revenue. Mines, probably discovered in *c.* 1125, yielded the crown a not inconsiderable revenue and provided a major raison d'être for the settlement at Carlisle. In 1130 the crown enjoyed, as later, rights

[4] Calculated on the basis of the price of cattle recorded in the pipe roll of 1130 which may be set in context by reference to A.L. Poole, 'Livestock Prices in the Twelfth Century', *Eng. Hist. Rev.*, 55 (1940), pp. 284–95.

associated with, and appendant to, the workings which were encompassed in the word *minaria* (variously spelt and misspelt in the genitive form *mineir-iae* and *manariae*) but at this time restricted to those rights embodied in the silver mine (*argentaria*) itself. Anciently rented out, the *firma minariae argentariae* or 'old farm' had yielded the diminutive sum of £5, but in 1130 as production expanded with the opening of new veins an enhanced farm of £40 was added to the original sum. A growing quantity of ore, deriving from the crown's levy on the industry which may have comprised about a tenth of production, was coming on to the market to be smelted and refined into lead and silver and the group who were prepared to take up the farm and acquire the minerals is described in the pipe roll of 1130 as the burgesses of Carlisle (*burgenses de Caerliolio*) who may possibly be identified with the commonalty of the silver mines at Carlisle (*comunitas minerarum de argen-teria Caerleolio*) of the subsequent 1133 lease. If this is correct then the nature of the mining 'camp' in the 1130s is revealed. In the wild frontier society of these years the community of miners, who worked in the Silverbeck mine, sought the security of Carlisle's as yet unfinished walls in establishing their residences. In the process they became the community (or burgesses) of the city. Mining 'camp' and 'city' were one and each individual, in his own person, enjoyed the customary privileges of miner and townsman. He also, in both capacities, was subject to the fiscal and legal authority of the sheriff. Initially, during the years to 1133, therefore, the mining 'camp' and 'city' of Carlisle formed a unitary structure, providing the base for a mining com-munity exploiting the neighbouring silver mine within the bounds of the royal forest and constituting an important element in the economy of the royal demesne.

Yet even considering the extensive pastoral and mining activity encom-passed within the royal demesne, the overall impression suggested by the accounts submitted by the sheriff to the exchequer, is one of poverty and endemic cash shortages. The payments to the knights and serving men in the castle absorbed half of the revenues from the noutgeld in 1128/9 and after payments had been made to the exchequer there was little left over for anything else. Thus in 1130 the walls of the diminutive township were still uncompleted.[5] Similarly St Mary's, begun after Henry I's visit to the city in 1122, was still in the process of construction eight years later.[6] The priory, initially endowed by Walter the chaplain, had been heavily dependent on royal patronage from the beginning and had been the recipient of a steady stream of gifts: Linstock and Carleton for an annual rent in cattle valued at

[5] *Pipe Roll 31 Henry I*, p. 142.
[6] *Symeonis Monachi Opera Omnia*, ed. T. Arnold, 2 vols. (Rolls Ser., no. 75, London, 1882–5), II, p. 267.

37s. 4d. which anyway was subsequently pardoned them; pasturage rights in the forest and, by a charter perhaps drawn up at Rouen in 1123, the churches of Newcastle upon Tyne and Newburn, together with the reversion of the churches of Warkworth, Corbridge, Whittingham and Rothbury in Northumberland.[7] The absence of any considerable temporalities in the royal gifts, however, is noteworthy and, in the context of a major construction programme serious cash flow problems remained, only slightly alleviated by modest royal cash gifts like the £10 paid to the canons in 1130 'for the building of their church'.[8] Overall the royal demesne was too poor to support major construction programmes designed for the furtherance of Henry's political, ecclesiastical and military ambitions.

Within a quinquennium, however, the whole situation was transformed as news began to circulate in 1133 that veins of silver had been discovered at Carlisle and the miners who dug for it in the bowels of the earth had paid £500 a year to the king, as rent for the mine. For a brief moment a nation's interest suddenly centred on this lonely fell land in a remote border county as news percolated throughout the realm of the fabulous silver find.[9] Nor were the expectant rumours unfounded, for a small band of miners, working on the slopes of a mountain from which welled the waters of Tyne, Wear and Derwent, had struck a lode which was to sustain a production unrivalled in contemporary Europe. The whole area, upon the slopes of the silver mountain where three counties met, was soon littered with prospectors and production was opened up over wide tracts of land (Map 2.2). How extensive the workings were, however, only becomes apparent from subsequent grants from the patrimonies of the English and Scots royal houses which originally during the years 1125–54 encompassed all mining activity on the hill. At the centre of the field were the mines of Silverbeck-Minerdale in Cumberland, on the limestone moors east of the Crossfell escarpment, where production had begun to expand even before 1133 and where output was sustained at high levels during the subsequent years of the first mining bonanza from c. 1133–58.[10] Further east below Burnhope Head the workings continued in an arc through the episcopal hunting forest to the area beyond the Wear below Middlehope Moor, where a complex of veins provided the

[7] *Liber Feodorum*, 2 vols. in 3 (HMSO, London, 1920–31), I, p. 199; W. Farrer, 'An Outline Itinerary of King Henry the First', *Eng. Hist. Rev.*, 34 (1919), nos. 458, 525, pp. 523, 538; W. Dugdale, *Monasticon Anglicanum*, ed. J. Caley, H. Ellis and B. Bandinel, 6 vols. in 8 (London, 1817–30), VI, p. 144.

[8] *Pipe Roll 31 Henry I*, p. 142.

[9] Robert of Torigni, in *Chronicles of the Reigns of Stephen, Henry II and Richard I*, ed. R. Howlett, 4 vols. (Rolls Ser., no 82, London, 1884–9), IV, p. 123; *Eulogium Historiarum*, ed. F.S. Hayden, 3 vols. (Rolls Ser., no. 9, London, 1858–63), III, p. 64.

[10] The situation prevailing immediately before and in 1130 is revealed in *Pipe Roll 31 Henry I*, p. 142.

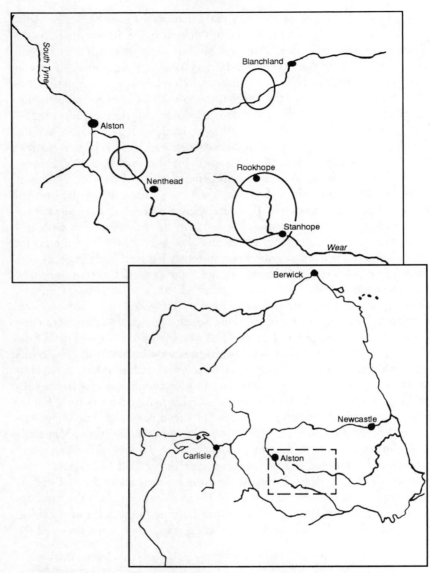

Map 2.2   The 'Carlisle minery'.

focus for an important production centre which dominated mining activity in the region during both the first (*c.* 1150–80) and the second (*c.* 1180–1210) production-cycles of the second bonanza. This centre remained with the crown until 1154 when, in one of his final acts of patronage, Stephen granted it to the princely bishop of Durham.[11] Initially production here was concentrated on the Burtree Pasture vein at Rookhope which sustained intense activity during the years *c.* 1150–80 before the worked-out mine was granted to the refounded hospital of Kepier to provide lead for the roof of the church and infirmary.[12] During the second phase of mining activity this centre was replaced by new workings at Stanhope on the neighbouring Red vein. Finally, continuing beyond the Derwent the arc was completed with the inclusion of the Northumberland workings which lay within the peculiar of the archbishop of York, probably, from the description of John of Hexham, at or near the later mines of Blanchland.[13] The centre of intense mining activity which wrought havoc in the archepiscopal forest during the first phase of the second bonanza, and the focus of lesser workings during the second, these mines were retained in the hands of either Scots or English kings throughout the twelfth century save for a brief interlude between 1189 and 1193 when they passed with the earldom of Northumberland into the de Puiset empire.[14] Thus lay in a semi-circle below Nenthead the mine or 'minery of Carlisle', the most productive area of silver mining to be known in medieval England, for a short time (1125–54) unified under the English or Scottish crowns but thereafter divided.

The discovery of 1133 marked the beginnings of the first great regional mining boom which at its height in *c.* 1136–8 yielded an output of some three or four tonnes of silver a year, or some ten times more than had been produced in the whole of Europe during any year of the past three-quarters of a millennium (Figure 2.1).[15] For slightly more than a decade vast quantities

---

[11] Durham University Library, Dean and Chapter of Durham, Reg. no. 16, printed in *Historiae Dunelmensis Scriptores Tres*, ed. J. Raine (Surtees Soc., no. 9, Durham, 1839), appendix no. xxvii, pp. xxxiii–xxxiv.

[12] Public Record Office (hereafter PRO), Durham Cursitor Roll 43, m.6, no. 31; *Boldon Book*, ed. W. Greenwell (Surtees Soc., no. 8, Durham, 1852), appendix x, p. xlvi.

[13] *Symeonis Monachi Opera Omnia*, ed. Arnold, II, p. 328; *The Priory of Hexham, its Chroniclers, Endowments and Annals*, ed. J. Raine, 2 vols. (Surtees Soc., nos. 44, 46, Durham, 1864–5), I, p. 166.

[14] *Pipe Roll 2 Richard II*, p. 55; Durham University Library, Dean and Chapter of Durham, Pontificalia E.1, printed in *Historiae Dunelmensis Scriptores Tres*, appendix no. xlii, p. lxiii; Roger of Howden, *Chronica*, ed. W. Stubbs (Rolls Ser., 51, London, 1868–71), III, p. 15. William of Newburgh and Richard of Devizes, in *Chronicles of the Reigns of Stephen, Henry II and Richard I*, II, p. 438, III, p. 386.

[15] I. Blanchard, 'Technical Implications of the Transition from Silver to Lead Smelting in Twelfth-Century England', in L. Willies and D. Cranstone (eds.), *Boles and Smeltmills: Report of a Seminar on the History and Archaeology of Lead Smelting Held at Reeth, Yorkshire, 15–17 May 1992* (Historical Metallurgical Soc., Matlock Bath, 1992), pp. 9–11.

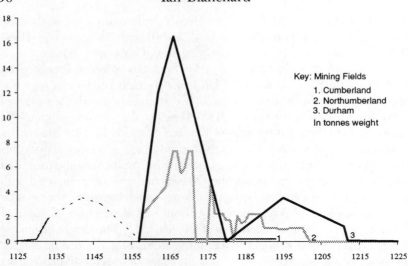

Figure 2.1 The 'Carlisle minery': silver production, 1125–1225.

of silver poured forth from the mines of Silverbeck-Minerdale in Cumberland, on the limestone moors east of the Crossfell escarpment, before decline set in and an industrial diaspora carried production to new centres in Northumberland, Durham and Yorkshire, laying the foundations for the second mining 'bonanza' which after 1157 would carry production to even greater heights.

The impact of this first great mining 'bonanza' on the local economy, whether under English (1133–5 and 1139–41) or Scots (1136–8 and 1142–57) rule, was dramatic. Under Henry I, from 1133 to 1135, the Crown's share of mine output, alone amounting to £500 a year in 1133, was considerable, being more than twice as much as the total receipts of the royal demesne three years earlier. Dreams, unrealised because of a lack of cash in previous years, could now be fulfilled and work unfinished, like the city walls, completed. That grand politico-ecclesiastical design involving St Mary's, first conceived in 1122 when, during his visit to Carlisle, Henry had seen Bishop John of Glasgow dedicating churches and carrying out other ecclesiatical functions in Cumberland even though he paid allegiance to neither the king nor his Archbishop Thurstan of York, could finally be brought to fruition.[16] In 1133 the priory was completed and Aethelwulf, who had seen the chaplain Walter's ideas realised, appointed bishop of the new see contemporaneously created. Whether Aethelwulf combined the offices of prior and bishop, as

[16] *Joannis de Fordun Scotichronicon cum Supplementis et Continuatione Walteri Boweri*, ed. W. Goodall, 2 vols. (Edinburgh, 1775), lib. 5, cap. xxxix, pp. 289–90.

is suggested in a much later document, is uncertain but it is quite clear that for the first time Thurstan's authority, exercised through his new bishop, now reigned supreme in Cumberland, undermining the influence of the Scots Bishop John and gaining a major point in the protracted battle between the prelates which dated back to John's consecration in 1118.[17] Thanks to the abundant resources now available to them, the king and his archbishop had won that great victory which had been so long denied them and Carlisle, as the focal point of the northern see, had, at last, earned the title *civitas* which it had for so long borne.

Nor were the mighty alone in the realisation of their aspirations. The burgess-miners who brought their silver to the newly established Carlisle mint[18] for coining acquired the means to fulfil their own more mundane desires and merchants were not long in arriving to satiate their demands. Throughout the next twenty-five years of the first mining 'bonanza' (*c.* 1133–57) merchants flocked to the northern city, transforming its internal structure and endowing the title *civitas* with an economic as well as an administrative reality (Map 2.3).[19] Traversing the old 'Roman' road from either the sea, by way of the wath which crossed the Eden to the north-west of the city, or, from the landward side, past the towers guarding the Petteril approach on its south-eastern side, the merchants came, ultimately forming a major component within the city's population and altering the structure of urban society. Outside the walls, within the area between the city and the castle known as Caldew through which passed the 'Roman' road, foreign merchants began to settle. The solitary priory and church of St Cuthbert with adjacent housing soon sounded to the hubbub of commercial activity and the discordant noise of foreign tongues. Between the priory and the gate of Bochard, along the south-eastern section of the 'Roman' road, was the Fleming quarter (or *vicus Flandrensis*) joining at the bridge of the Caldew, below the castle, the road from that bridge to the Caldew gate which provided access to the market within the walls. This latter highway also housed the other alien communities. It traversed, in the section closest to the bridge, the suburb

---

[17] *Early Scottish Charters prior to 1153*, ed. A.C. Lawrie (Glasgow, 1905), pp. 267–70.

[18] The issues of the Carlisle mint during the first years of the mining boom are represented by only solitary examples of Henry's last two types, but these reveal at work the two moneyers, Erembald and Durant, who were to dominate the northern mining scene until *c.* 1140. Both are recorded in G.C. Brooke, *A Catalogue of English Coins in the British Museum: The Norman Kings*, 2 vols. (London, 1916) (hereafter *BMC Norman*), I, pp. cciv-ccv, Durant's coin being further described and illustrated *ibid.*, nos. 8 and 11, pl. xliv, p. 302. The dating of the types here follows the chronology proposed in M. Dolley, *The Norman Conquest and the English Coinage* (London, 1966).

[19] The description of Carlisle's topography below is based on materials contained in B.C. Jones, 'The Topography of Medieval Carlisle', *Transactions of the Cumberland and Westmorland Antiquarian and Archaeological Society* (hereafter *Trans. CWAAS*), n.s., 45 (1946), pp. 77–96. The interpretation differs somewhat from that of the author.

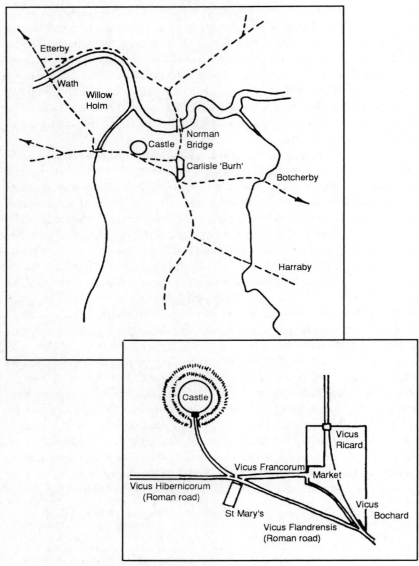

Map 2.3   Twelfth-century Carlisle.

of the Gaelic-speaking traders (*vicus hybernicorum*) whose commerce spanned the western seas,[20] and, in the section below the city wall, the quarter of the Franks (*vicus francorum*). Nor was the intra-mural city immune from these same forces, a large community of English merchants also settling therein. Gradually the older elements in urban society, the lords who maintained temporary residences in the city and the miners who had legally and economically dominated the settlement during the years prior to 1133, were submerged under a welter of commercial activity which gave the merchants a predominant position in urban life. When the merchants formally displaced the miners as the main group within the city is uncertain but this may date to the 1150s when the gradual displacement of mining activity eastward undermined the locational advantages which Carlisle had previously enjoyed as a mining settlement. Almost certainly, however, the English merchants had earlier established an economic superiority vis-à-vis the miners and had acquired the privileges appertaining to a merchant guild which were confirmed to them in *c.* 1157/8 by Henry II.[21] Such rights afforded them total superiority, allowing them to insert themselves between the miners and the foreign merchants and to acquire the miners' silver before minting and to sell to them the foreign merchants' wares to which they otherwise had no access. Henceforth, accordingly, the foreigners were confined to the *portus* of Burgh-Caldew whilst their English counterparts, from Carlisle and elsewhere, travelled about the mining areas selling both imported English and foreign wares and acquiring silver which they then transported to their home towns for minting.

Nor did this situation change when Cumberland and its mines passed under Scots rule in 1136 and for some twenty years until 1157 Carlisle became the administrative focus of an extensive territory encompassing on occasion the lands between the Forth and the Tees of the erstwhile kingdoms of Bernicia and Cumbria–Strathclyde and even extending to English lands beyond their bounds.[22] Silver, now in the form of the newly instituted Scots

[20] I should like to express my thanks to Geoffrey Barrow for drawing to my attention the similarity between this settlement at Carlisle and those western suburbs of Scottish burghs inhabited by Gaelic-speakers usually called 'Argyll', as in Glasgow (whence Argyle street), St Andrews (Argyle just west of the West Port), Dundee and elsewhere.

[21] *Royal Charters of the City of Carlisle*, pp. xx–xxi.

[22] The English occupation of the southern part of this territory during the years 1092–1135/8 followed a long period of its subjection to the Scottish crown. On the situation in Cumbria–Strathclyde to 1092, see D.P. Kirby, 'Strathclyde and Cumbria: A Survey of Historical Development to 1092', *Trans. CWAAS*, n.s., 62 (1962), pp. 77–94, and P.A. Wilson, 'On the Use of the Terms "Strathclyde" and "Cumbria"', *Trans. CWAAS*, n.s., 66 (1966), pp. 57–92. The continuing claims of Scots kings after 1092 for a restoration of their rights throughout all of these lands are discussed in G.W.S. Barrow, 'The Scots and the North of England', in E. King (ed.), *The Anarchy of King Stephen's Reign* (Oxford, 1994), pp. 231–53.

coinage,[23] remained the staple export of the region and either passed overseas or along the 'Roman' road to England, where a tiny fraction of the flow, avoiding reminting, entered general circulation. The re-amalgamation of the southern Cumbrian economy with that of Lothian, however, meant that the Carlisle merchant community no longer enjoyed a monopoly position in these trades and it was not long before they had to face the competition from Scots traders who invaded their preserves. A rapid growth in the size of the mining community coupled with an overpricing of local provisions opened up dazzling prospects for producers and merchants alike. By c. 1136–8, accordingly, the economies of Cumbria and Northumbria, Lothian and even Scotia itself felt the full impact of the mining boom (Map 2.4).[24] As production from Silverbeck-Minerdale mines rapidly increased during these years the tentacles of the provisioning system extended ever outwards beyond

[23] Hoard evidence reveals that during the late tenth and early eleventh centuries English coins were widely utilised in western Scotland and the islands: J.D.A. Thompson, *Inventory of British Coin Hoards*, A.D. 600–1500 (British Numismatic Soc., Special Publications, no. 1, London, 1956), nos. 61, 66, 144, 196, 198, 201, 357. However, as elsewhere, from c. 1050 the quantities of new coins arriving from England gradually diminished (S.E. Rigold, 'The Trail of the Esterlings', *British Numismatic Journal*, 3rd ser., 6 (1949–51), pp. 38ff) causing monetary stocks to dwindle, and creating until c. 1135 that monetary vacuum in these lands which has been described by W.W. Scott, 'The Use of Money in Scotland, 1124–1230', *Scot. Hist. Rev.*, 58 (1979), pp. 106–7. It was to relieve this 'monetary famine' that David not only caused the moneyer, Erembald, to mint at Carlisle the new Scots coinage but also to promote a process of 'liberalisation' in the silver trade.

[24] The coin suggested here to be the earliest of David's issues (Scots. types IVb) bears the name and portrait of the monarch on the obverse and utilises an English type for the reverse. Known only by Erembald's issues at Carlisle, this is a reverse-type XV of Henry I. Dating perhaps from c. 1136, it is represented by a solitary example now preserved in the British Museum: I.H. Stewart, *The Scottish Coinage* (London, 1955), no. 6, pl. 1. The later type IVc was a much more substantial and varied issue, minted at Roxburgh, Edinburgh, Perth, Newcastle and Carlisle. Examples of coins from all these mints have been found in the Prestwich hoard: M. Dolley and I.D. Brown, *Coin Hoards*, I (Royal Numismatic Soc., London, 1975), no. 360. Erembald minted coins of this type at Edinburgh, surviving examples of which were struck from the same obverse die: D.M. Metcalf, *Sylloge of Coins of the British Isles, XXXV: Scottish Coins in the Ashmolean Museum, Oxford, and the Hunterian Museum, Glasgow* (London, 1987), nos. 1a–2a, pl. 1. The moneyer Richard struck a long series of this type in Carlisle which may be divided into two groups. The first was of fine workmanship marred only by rather crude lettering: E. Burns, *The Coinage of Scotland*, 3 vols. (Edinburgh, 1887), I, p. 29, no. 24. The second was of inferior manufacture with a retrograde and partially transposed obverse: an example from the Dartford hoard is recorded in J. Rashleigh, 'An Account of Some Baronial and Other Coins of King Stephen's Reign', *Numismatic Chron.* (hereafter *NC*), 1st ser., 13 (1851), p. 189, and illustrated in Stewart, *Scottish Coinage*, no. 7, pl. 1. The Roxburgh type IVc coin of DEREND, has a similar retrograde obverse: Burns, *Coinage*, I, p. 30, no. 25. As indicated above, an example of Scot. type IVc was found in the Dartford hoard in a context suggesting a date before 1140. The absence of these coins from the Bute hoard, which contains a representative distribution of Scots coins from c. 1138–60, tends to confirm this dating. Moreover, the minting of type IVc at Newcastle, which before 1140 was held by the Scots only briefly in 1136 and 1138, is further suggestive of this chronology. It thus seems probable that these coins were first minted after David's occupation of Carlisle, type IVb being issued in 1136 and type IVc in 1137–8.

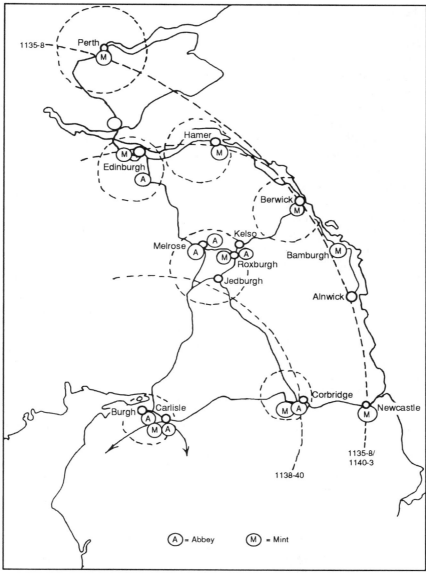

Map 2.4   Northern British commercial networks, *c.* 1135–8 to 1143.

the reaches of southern Cumbria to the provisioning grounds of the Merse, the rich grain lands of the Lothians and the Northumbrian seaboard and even central Scotia. Merchants from towns along the great northern trading routes, which stretched eastward from Carlisle to Newcastle and north through Roxburgh and Edinburgh to Perth, flocked each year to Cumberland to acquire silver, bringing the produce of their region to exchange and carrying the white metal home to be minted. The impact of the silver boom imposed itself, through the effects of a trade boom, on a wider and wider area. At the height of the mining boom in c. 1136–8 the effects wrought on the local economy were truly awesome.

Nor in c. 1141–6 when the Scots once more, after a brief interlude, held the mine was the situation significantly different. Production might now be slightly lower than during the 'boom years' of c. 1136–8 but as the Silverbeck-Minerdale mines still echoed to the noise of a workforce who could perhaps be numbered in the hundreds and a flood of silver poured forth from the caverns dug deep into the hill, the provisioning system of the mine remained extensive (Map 2.4).[25] Through the medium of a major trade boom the inflationary effects of the mining 'bonanza' continued to be diffused throughout the northern economy, the wealth of the indigenes of that region creating a secondary effect as alien merchants flocked to the termini of the 'silver road' bringing exotic wares to tease the appetites of the northerners and to obtain the fine silver coins and ingots they so desired. The estuaries of the Tweed and Lothian Tyne were full each year with ships bringing Flemings in search of 'Scottish' silver and laden with wares for distribution through Hamer (Whitekirk) and Berwick. At the southern terminus of the road the impact was similar. From the anchorage at Burgh by Sands there was a steady traffic along the 'Roman' road to Carlisle as Flemings, Gaels and

---

[25] In Scotland, following the reacquisition in 1141 of the lost conquests (including the 'Carlisle minery') a major monetary reform was undertaken. During subsequent years mints were re-established at Berwick, Roxburgh and an uncertain place known only by the letters HA at the beginning of the mint name, which may be Hamer (Whitekirk) in the Lothians, where a team of moneyers headed by Folpalt began the minting of an new and original design. This is Scot. I, a type whose sterlings are noted for their fine manufacture and good weight, a feature which may owe something to the recapture of the Cumberland mines. The obverse has a reasonable profile portrait and the legend DAVIT REX or in the case of Folpalt's Berwick issues DAVIT REX CSOCIE (presumably for SCOCIE) in well-formed letters: Stewart, *Scottish Coinage*, p. 3. The normal reverse was an original design embodying a cross fleurie with a pellet in each quarter. In Scotland the new coinage established a supremacy in the circulating media never again to be rivalled by any other Scots coin, as is revealed by both the Bute and Bamburgh hoards: 'Miscellanea', *NC*, n.s., 3 (1863), pp. 216–17; J.H. Pollexfen, 'On a Hoard of Gold Ornaments and Silver Coins Found in Bute', *NC*, n.s., 5 (1865), pp. 57–72: Burns, *Coinage*, I, pp. 8ff. Others traversed further afield, passing either by the eastern ports or via Roxburgh to England where, in spite of prohibitions on their circulation and their enforced reminting, a tiny fraction of the flow entered into the currency of the realm to be preserved in hoards like that of Shelden.

Franks transported their wares to their compatriots settled at Caldew, below the walls of the city. Within those walls were the English merchants, organised into their own guild, who received goods from England along the same 'Roman' road to the south-east and who distributed these wares and those of the alien merchants through the hinterland of the city, returning with silver to pay their debts and fill their coffers. Within the lands under Scottish rule the mining boom engendered intense commercial and minting activity.

When the process of slow silver production decline which had characterised the years after c. 1141 gave way to a collapse in output is difficult to assess but by the late 1140s there were already signs that the earlier impetus was spent and that a phase of contraction was under way. Commercial activity diminished and the boundaries of the trading network retreated. Outlying mints in Lothian closed their doors and within Scotland activity became concentrated at Roxburgh.[26] The economy was reverting to a situation similar to that which had prevailed in c. 1133–5 but in a more attenuated form. Yet as Cumberland silver production diminished changes were afoot in the industry as mining activity was displaced towards new centres in the east and south. By 1152 a new mine was already well established in the vicinity of Blanchland in Northumberland whose workmen excited the wrath of Henry Murdac, archbishop of York, for their depradations in his forest lands and it is probably from about the same period that workmen first discovered the rich deposits at Rookhope in the episcopal hunting forest of Weardale and the minor ones at Skipton.[27] Contraction was thus associated with structural change within the industry which wrought fundamental alterations in the fabric of the commercial economy dependent upon it (Map

---

[26] The period spanned by the issue of the fine Scot. I pieces possibly extend no later than to c. 1143. The official dies which produced these coins were apparently not always replaceable, and thus Scot. type I merged gradually into Scot. type II as local engravers at the mints seem to have assumed responsibility for making the dies. The basic coinage had undergone a mutation: Stewart, *Scottish Coinage*, pp. 4–5. Type II sterlings, which retained the types of group I, were now characterised by blundered legends on both sides of the coin, executed in imitation of the officially made dies. The moneyer's name on the reverse is usually very blundered, as is the name of the mint, whilst the rendering of the king's name is sometimes a scrawly imitation of AVIT R, occasionally retrograde but more often as nearly as unintelligible as the reverse. Not only were these coins barbarous in design, however, but amongst those surviving there are many of decidedly light weight. At some time during the minting of types II and III – the latter being even more debased in the form of the legends, which comprised a completely incoherent jumble of letters – the weight standard which had characterised group I was abandoned and coins weighing no more than 16–17 grains may have been entering circulation by c. 1147.

[27] Durham University Library, Dean and Chapter, Reg. no. 16, printed in *Historiae Dunelmensis Scriptores Tres*, appendix no. xxvii, pp. xxxiii–xxxiv.

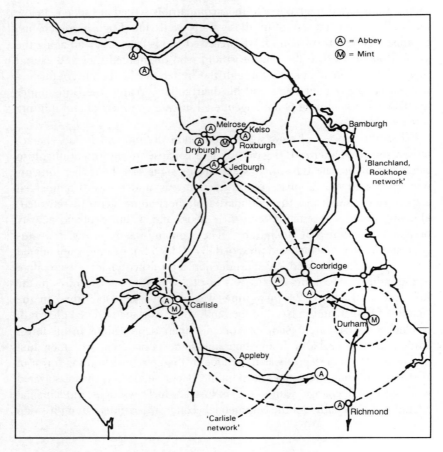

Map 2.5   Northern British commercial networks, *c.* 1155.

2.5). Within the pre-existing western supply network producers on the upper
Tweed and middle Tyne now found that they had other markets in the
new easterly mining camps and, turning aside at least a proportion of their
provisions to these centres, created a provisioning 'crisis' at the Carlisle mine
and its Yorkshire satellite. The denizens of these mining camps, accordingly,
began to cast covetous eyes elsewhere, to the grain lands of the upper Eden.
As the Carlisle supply network was thus rebuilt to incorporate new provisioning centres to the south, changes of equal significance were also taking
place further east. The new mining centres of Blanchland and Rookhope
now began to attract provisions not only from the regions of the middle
Tyne and upper Tweed, but also from production centres along the North-

umbrian and Durham coastal plain, the silver passing back in exchange providing the basis for mint activity at Bamburgh and the city of Durham. As the 'Carlisle minery' thus underwent an internal metamorphosis the focus of economic activity shifted southward. Within the 'new' networks, however, the tempo of commercial activity was diminishing as the new eastern mining centres failed to compensate for the decline in silver production further west. Mint output which previously had supplied not only local needs but also had yielded an abundant volume of coins for export now began to assume a parochial character. The circulation of coins struck in the early 1150s rarely transcended the region in which they were minted.[28] An acute silver crisis was beginning to emerge and whilst David might in 1151, with his accustomed liberality, compensate Yorkshire churches for damages incurred during the campaign of that year with handsome gifts of silver chalices the material basis of his generosity was disintegrating as the mining boom gradually drew to its close.[29]

Within a mere twenty years from 1133 to 1152 the lands of the Scottish king in Lothian, Cumbria and Northumbria had been transformed, fully justifying the statement of Ailred of Rievaulx that the kingdom was now 'no longer a beggar from other countries, but of her abundance relieving the wants of her neighbours – adorned with castles and cities, her ports filled with foreign merchandise and the riches of distant nations.'[30] The material resources available to its king were no less transformed. As the mining 'bonanza' ran its course he was able, on occasion, to make direct grants from mine revenues to would-be followers.[31] Far more important to him, however, were the indirect effects of the boom. As its inflationary effects were diffused through the economy of the Lothians and the lands beyond, property values within the supply network of the mines increased rapidly, making such land an ideal gift for either ecclesiastical supplicants or would-be knightly followers – a gift which David dispensed with both liberality and political judgement, creating a new and powerful feudal state in the north.

At each node of the commercial network, which reached its greatest extent during the years c. 1136–8, a mint was established to fabricate the silver which was obtained by local merchants in exchange for the provisions and manufactures they carried to the Cumberland mines. The large quantities of coin obtained by the merchants were then distributed through a carefully regulated regional trade network to local craftsmen and members of rural

[28] For the coinages of Henry, earl of Northumberland in the later 1140s, see the Appendix.
[29] John of Hexham, in *Priory of Hexham*, I, p. 326.
[30] Ailred of Rievaulx, 'Eulogium Davidis', in J. Pinkerton, *Vitae Antiquae Sanctorum qui Habitaverunt in ex Parte Britanniae Nunc Vocata Scotia* (London, 1789), pp. 439–56.
[31] G.W.S. Barrow, 'The Scots Charter', in H. Mayr-Harting and R.I. Moore (eds.), *Studies in Medieval History Presented to R.H.C. Davis* (London, 1985), p. 154.

society as they acquired new wares for their trade, enhancing cash incomes
and creating amongst the local population a demand for manufactures which
the merchants satisfied, from either local sources or abroad, through the
same carefully regulated trade systems. In the absence of productivity
changes, as inflationary pressures were diffused through the economy of
Scotia, the Lothians, Cumbria and Northumbria, denizens of the regional
economies enjoyed enhanced monetary incomes, obtained in coin which had
a markedly enhanced purchasing power abroad. To protect and stimulate
this trade, whilst maintaining a stable, ordered form of society, David actively
intervened into the economy employing both traditional and contemporary
means to achieve his ends. Foreign merchants, who threatened to swamp
the Scottish economy with their wares, were largely confined to those coastal
settlements which were encompassed within a *portus* system, where local
burgesses had first option of buying wares from the ships which could only
land at these places appointed by the crown.[32] Such produce as escaped
these pre-emptive practices and was carried up-country by the aliens was
further disadvantaged in being subject to the king's internal tolls from which
denizens of the royal burghs engaged in inter-regional trade were exempt.[33]
The prices at which alien wares were sold by foreign and denizen merchants
to Scottish consumers were thus equilibrated, the latter group thereby being
afforded protection from foreign competition. In the acquisition of raw materials (particularly wool and hides or cloth for finishing) craftsmen in the
Scottish burghs enjoyed similar pre-emptive rights which again allowed them
to sell their wares at prices which were competitive with those of their alien
rivals.[34] As the silver boom ran its course and inflationary pressures enhanced
incomes, David thus ensured price equilibration between foreign and
domestic wares. He also, by channelling trade exclusively through burgh
markets where transactions were validated before witnesses, ensured that
bargains (made in accord with prevailing rights of pre-emption and the
payment of taxes) would be honoured and that those disruptive 'free-market'
practices, which threatened his artfully contrived price structure, would be
eliminated. By his interventionary commercial policies David thus ensured
that rising incomes would not be associated with social disorder and that

[32] *Liber S. Thome de Aberbrothoc*, ed. C. Innes and P. Chalmers, 2 vols. (Bannatyne Club,
no. 86, Edinburgh, 1848–56), I, no. 1, p. 3; *Regesta Regum Scottorum*, ed. G.W.S. Barrow
et al., 8 vols. projected (Edinburgh, 1960–), II, nos. 166, 475, pp. 230–1, 437–8; *Leges
Burgorum*, cc. 8, 9, 16 and 25 in *Ancient Laws and Customs of the Burghs of Scotland,
1124–1424*, ed. C. Innes (Scottish Burgh Records Soc., Edinburgh, 1868).
[33] G.W.S. Barrow, *Kingship and Unity. Scotland 1000–1306*, 2nd edn (Edinburgh, 1989),
pp. 99–100.
[34] *Ibid.*

each and every member of society would benefit from the inflationary effects of the mining boom in conditions of peace and tranquility.

That society itself was also changing, however, as the inflationary effects of the mining boom, which were diffused through the economy of Scotia, the Lothians, Cumbria and Northumbria, caused land values within the supply network of the mines to increase rapidly. David thus found, in the royal demesne, assets which he could grant to others without diminishing royal revenues. In such a manner were the royal burghs created. Equally he now possessed the means to create those knights' fees and baronies of the new feudal order. A knight could now be sustained on a fraction of the land which had once been required for a royal thegn and thus at the nodes of the new commercial system such land, encompassed within the royal demesne, became an ideal gift which David liberally dispensed to either ecclesiastical supplicants or would-be knightly followers.

The effects of such liberality on the political landscape have been revealed in the case of Edinburgh with its dependent shire and natural hinterland.[35] Here at the start of David's reign, before the region felt the indirect effects of the mining boom, within the lands below the castle the ancient churches of the area were already endowed with extensive lands, rights and sanctuaries, including Liston belonging to the bishops of St Andrews; Cramond which belonged in part to the bishops of Dunkeld; St Cuthbert under the castle, with a dependent territory embracing Corstorphine, Hailes (Colinton) and Liberton; Lasswade, another property of the see of St Andrews, on which Roslin, Glencorse and Dalkeith were dependent; and Inveresk, which included Musselburgh. The royal patrimony was no less extensive, ranging from the 'king's waste and forest of Pentland' (i.e. the Pentland hills) to the burgh itself, the Dean Mills on the Water of Leith, and the haven at the mouth of that stream.[36] It was also complemented by a primary tier of richer local lords – Cospatric, son of Waltheof, at Dalmeny, Maelbeatha of Liberton, Alfwin MacArchill at Newton north of Dalkeith and Thor, son of Swein, at Tranent – and a secondary tier of substantial freeholders with such extensive estates as Braid, Gilmerton, Craigmillar, Edmonstone, Falside, Smeaton and Restalrig.

Before the end of the reign, in the context of the commercial changes associated with the mining boom, the region had been subjected to dramatic

---

[35] The following two paragraphs are based on the studies of Edinburgh and its shire in G.W.S. Barrow, *David I of Scotland (1124–1153): The Balance of New and Old* (Reading, 1985), pp. 11–12, and G.W.S. Barrow, 'Midlothian – or the Shire of Edinburgh?', *The Book of the Old Edinburgh Club*, 35 (1985), pp. 141–8.

[36] It seems probable that the royal *portus* was Leith at this time, the neighbouring estate of Inveresk enjoying only *villa* status: *Registrum de Dunfermelyn* (Bannatyne Club, no. 74, Edinburgh, 1842), nos. 1, 237, pp. 3–4, 151–3.

changes. The burgh, during the years after about 1135, had become one of
the first recipients of those privileges based on the customs of Newcastle
upon Tyne which were subsequently embodied in the 'Laws of the Four
Burghs'.[37] It was also complemented at this time by a new burgh – the
Canongate – created by the Augustinian canons, who had settled at Holyrood
in 1128, to provide a commercial focus for their new estate which encompassed part of Arthur's Seat, rights in royal mills and other perquisites in
and around the burgh of Edinburgh and the entire *parochia* of St Cuthbert.
The commercial institutions, through which the effects of the trade boom
would be translated into enhanced land values, were in place and local
patterns of property ownership were transformed. The new religious orders
benefited enormously. The Benedictines, introduced to Dunfermline originally by David I's mother, Queen Margaret, in the 1080s and raised by her
son to abbatial status in 1128, came to possess the whole shire of Inveresk,
with the churches of Inveresk, Hailes, Newton and Woolmet. The Tironen-
sians of Kelso were given Duddingston and most of Arthur's Seat thereby
becoming neighbours to the Augustinian canons of Holyrood. In 1140 the
Cistercian monks of Melrose hived off a vigorous colony at a site known as
the 'rough haugh', otherwise Newbattle, on the South Esk by Dalkeith. They
quickly acquired not only a good deal of land but also vast tracts of hill and
upland grazing. Finally the Knights of the Temple of Solomon in Jerusalem
came to possess by the king's gift the large upland estate of Balantroddach,
since known simply as Temple. Nor were David's close secular associates
neglected and many may be found amongst the new landowners of the
Edinburgh region towards the end of his reign. Two were comparative
latecomers to the king's service: Geoffrey de Melville and Alexander of Seton.
Geoffrey obtained, whether by marriage, escheat or simple force, the whole
estate formally of Malbeatha of Liberton. Seton was established in a ring of
estates about Edinburgh, at Winchburgh, Winton and Seton itself. Otherwise, it is chiefly the long-established favourites who came to dominate the
land market. The Avenels of Eskdale held Abercorn and part of Cramond;
Ranulf de Soules of Liddesdale held Gilmorton; the Lisures family, related
to the Engaines of Huntingdon and Northants, held Gorton in Lasswade;
the Ridels of Huntingdon and Rutland held Cranston; the Steward held
land on the south side of the burgh, whilst the Grahams probably held at

---

[37] This follows the conclusions as to the dating of the 'Laws of the Four Burghs' expressed
in Barrow, *Kingship and Unity*, pp. 97–8, a topic that has given rise to much debate. Cf.
W.M. MacKenzie, *The Scottish Burghs* (Edinburgh, 1949), pp. 21–31, and more recently
in H.L. MacQueen and W. J. Windram, 'Laws and Courts in the Burghs', in M. Lynch,
M. Spearman and G. Stell (eds.), *The Scottish Medieval Town* (Edinburgh, 1988), pp.
209–11. The evidence on p. 223 n. 16 of this latter work is particularly important in the
dating of this document to the years *c.* 1135–57.

this time those knights' fees at Gogar, Pentland and Couston which are first discernible in William I's reign.

At this, one of the most important of the five principal nodes of the extended commercial network formed in the years 1136–8, David showed his intent, surrounding his fortified royal residence with mercantile and ecclesiastical satellites and a ring of close friends and supporters, bound to him and his heirs by feudal obligation, and capable of rendering him military and administrative service of the most up-to-date kind. In the process he fully validated that picture of his realm as being adorned with castles and cities, its havens filled with alien ships and merchandise, which was subsequently presented by Ailred of Rievaulx in his eulogy of a king whose reign was to appear as a 'golden age' in the difficult times that followed.

Appendix: coinages of Henry, earl of Northumberland

Organisationally the northern border lands held by David's son, Henry, were divided into two parts. During the five to seven years before his death in 1152, he employed the moneyer William the son of Erembald to produce two distinct coinages, type Hen. II and type Hen. IIIa, distinguished by their very different different reverses but united by a common obverse with the legend N. ENCI. CON, which may be extended to indicate *Henricus Comes*, i.e. Henry, earl (of Northumberland). At Carlisle, in the occupied territories outside the earldom of Northumberland, he minted coins (type Hen. II) which recognised the subordination of these lands to Scotland by incorporating the standard Scottish reverse: the basic cross fleurie (but without the pellets) and the moneyer's and mint name, in this case WILLEN ON CARDI C, the latter letter c perhaps indicating Cumberland.[38] In contrast, at Bamburgh within the earldom of Northumberland, which he held in his own right, he minted coins with his own distinctive and unique design for the reverse (type Hen. IIIa): a cross crosslet with in each angle a cross pattée suspended from a crescent resting on the inner circle.[39] These also bore the moneyer's name WILLELM and the mint nomenclature ON C(ASTR)I B(AEMBURGI). The products of two independent jurisdictions under the authority of the earl, types Hen. II and Hen. IIIa were also distinguished by the standard to which they were struck. Coins from the Cumberland mint, like their contemporary Scottish counterparts, were distinctly light-weight, surviving examples approximating to a norm of only 16–17 grains. At the Northumberland mint they were of both better workmanship and weight, conforming to the Anglo-Scottish mint standard of 22.5 grains, but thereby, in the conditions of the 1140s, inviting that clipping which characterises so many surviving examples. In the erstwhile lands of Bernicia and Cumbria, therefore, from the mid-1140s the coinage, like its Scottish counterpart, began to deteriorate either through the application of mint policies or the operation of market forces which adjusted coin weights towards

---

[38] This type is illustrated by Stewart, *Scottish Coinage*, no. 9, pl. 1, from the time when the coin was in the hands of B.A. Seaby, Ltd, after the Ryan Sale of 1954 and by D.M. Metcalf, in *Sylloge*, XII, no. 292, pl. xi, after it had passed to its present location in the Ashmolean.

[39] G. Askew, 'The Mint at Bamburgh Castle', *NC*, 5th ser., 20 (1940), pp. 51–6; Stewart, *Scottish Coinage*, pl. 1.10; *BMC Norman*, II, no. 1, pl. lix; Metcalf, *Sylloge*, XII, no. 291, pl. xi.

a new norm of 16–17 grains in line with higher silver prices. The circulation of these coins also began to contract. In the Bute hoard, deposited in the mid-1160s, there are no examples at all of Henry's issues or indeed of any other alien coins of the 1140s, this period being represented only by local group II coins. They are similarly absent from English hoards where such coins might be expected to be found – those deposited at Awbridge *c.* 1168, Dartford *c.* 1150, Nottingham *c.* 1158 and Winterslow *c.* 1154.[40] Indeed, almost all of the surviving coins of Henry's late issues come from the hoard deposited at Outchester *c.* 1170, which encompassed the major issues entering local circulation during the years *c.* 1145–50.[41]

---

[40] H.A. Grueber, 'A Find of Coins of Stephen and Henry II at Awbridge, near Romsey', *NC*, 4th ser., 5 (1905), pp. 354–63; *BMC Norman*, II, pp. xxx–xxxi.

[41] *BMC Norman*, I, pp. xcviiiff; D.F. Allen, *A Catalogue of Coins in the British Museum: The Cross-and-Crosslets (Tealby) Type of Henry II* (London, 1951), pp. xlixff.

3

Boroughs, markets and trade in northern England, 1000–1216

RICHARD BRITNELL

FOR LOCAL trade in the north of England, as it is now, the coming of the Normans was a great divide – so great that there is a danger of exaggerating its significance. This territory, whose ultimate control was disputed between the kings of Scotland and England for much of the period under present consideration,[1] is defined here as England to the north of York. It comprises the North Riding of Yorkshire, the Furness district of Lancashire and the four counties of Cumberland, Westmorland, Northumberland and Durham, as they were before county boundaries were altered in 1974. Before the late eleventh century there is little evidence either of urban development or of any formal trading institutions in all this region. The only borough was York on its southern margin. Domesday Book describes it twelve times as a city (*civitas*) and four times as a town (*urbs*), but its population included burgesses (*burgenses*). York had over 636 inhabited messuages in 1086; though the Domesday survey does not permit an exact count, the city's reduced population was perhaps below 5,000.[2] The mint there was the most northerly in England throughout the late Saxon period.[3] Durham was an important monastic centre, but the urban settlement there was as yet a small one. Neither Carlisle nor Newcastle existed. Outside York and perhaps Durham no markets and fairs are recorded. Yet between the time of the Norman conquest of the north and the end of King John's reign the number of boroughs and markets grew right across the region (Map 3.1) – Alnmouth, Berwick, Carlisle, Durham, Newcastle upon Tyne, Norton, Richmond and Whitby are recorded by 1150, Alnwick, Appleby, Bamburgh, Barnard Castle, Brough, Darlington, Gateshead, Hartlepool, Kendal, Kirkby

---

[1] G.W.S. Barrow, 'The Scots and the North of England', in E. King (ed.), *The Anarchy of King Stephen's Reign* (Oxford, 1994), pp. 231–53.

[2] E. Miller, 'Medieval York', in *VCH Yorks.: The City of York*, p. 40; D.M. Palliser, *Domesday York* (Borthwick Papers, no. 78, York, 1990), pp. 8, 14.

[3] D. Hill, *An Atlas of Anglo-Saxon England* (Oxford, 1981), pp. 126–32, 141–2.

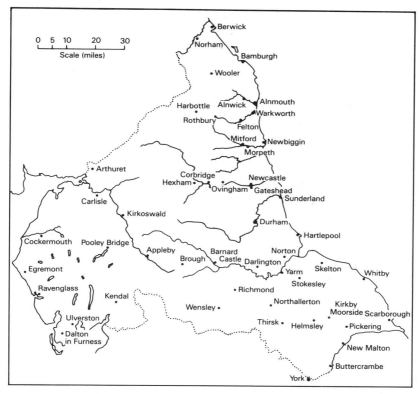

Map 3.1 Early markets and boroughs of northern England.

Moorside, Mitford, New Malton, Norham, Rothbury, Scarborough, Sunderland and Thirsk by the time of John's accession in 1199, Arthuret (perhaps), Buttercrambe, Cockermouth, Corbridge, Egremont, Felton, Helmsley, Kirkoswald, Newbiggin by the Sea, Pickering, Pooley Bridge, Ravenglass, Ulverston, Wensley and Wooler by 1216. This implies a list of forty boroughs and markets that go back to the period before the end of King John's reign. Their names are perhaps more striking than their numbers, since the list includes the major centres of urban development in the north up to the modern period. The numerical estimate would increase to fifty if it were allowed to include market towns with no known royal charter that occur in thirteenth-century sources – that is, Dalton in Furness, Harbottle, Hexham, Morpeth, Northallerton, Ovingham, Skelton, Stokesley, Warkworth and Yarm.[4] Most of these, if not all, are likely to have been

---

[4] References to the earliest occurrence of markets and fairs here and elsewhere in this paper are given in the Appendix.

founded by 1200 since by then a royal claim to license new markets and fairs was recognised throughout the realm, and later royal grants are quite well recorded.

A few other early boroughs and markets may be overlooked in the following discussion for want of a sufficiently early reference. For example, the borough at Stockton on Tees in the Palatinate of Durham may date back to the twelfth century, but it does not occur in the records before 1283[5] and no presumption of greater antiquity can safely be made; new markets in Durham were licensed by the bishop, not the king, and the episcopal records from the thirteenth century are exceedingly poor. At a much later period there was a Saturday market at Lindisfarne whose origins are wholly obscure. Raine surmised that 'it must have been established by an early bishop of Durham', but no date can be assigned to the event; it is unlikely to have been before the later twelfth century when a monastic community is first in evidence there.[6] Penrith may have been one of the earlier commercial centres of the north-west, but it has to be excluded from the following discussion because no institutional development is on record there before a market and fair were formally instituted in the king's name in 1222.[7] Newburn, in Northumberland, has likewise been excluded on the grounds that though there are quite strong indications that it was an ephemeral borough in King John's reign it is not described as such.[8]

By 1215 there was a line of boroughs and market towns along the north-east coast (Berwick, Bamburgh, Alnmouth, Warkworth, Newbiggin by the Sea, Sunderland, Hartlepool, Whitby, Scarborough), but no comparable activity in the north-west, where none of the early boroughs was coastal. Many of the inland boroughs were strategically placed on routes along river valleys, especially at points where rivers were forded or bridged. The largest inland group of new marketing centres was strung along the Tyne valley – Newcastle, Gateshead, Ovingham, Corbridge and Hexham – marking this as a major focus for the formation of boroughs in the north. On the other side of the country, Carlisle, Appleby and Brough suggest the importance of the

[5] Stockton borough occurs in 1283: T. Madox, *The History and Antiquities of the Exchequer*, 2nd edn, 2 vols. (London, 1769), II, p. 720, note u.

[6] J. Raine, *The History and Antiquities of North Durham* (London, 1852), p. 154n, A.J. Piper, 'The First Generation of Durham Monks and the Cult of St Cuthbert', in G. Bonner, D. Rollason and C. Stancliffe (eds.), *St Cuthbert: His Cult and his Community* (Woodbridge, 1989), p. 444.

[7] A.J.L. Winchester, *Landscape and Society in Medieval Cumbria* (Edinburgh, 1987), p. 124; *Rotuli Litterarum Clausarum*, ed. T.D. Hardy, 2 vols. (Rec. Comm., London, 1833–4; hereafter *Rot. Litt. Claus.*), I, p. 513a.

[8] *Pipe Roll 3 John*, p. 249. On this evidence it is included as a borough in M. Beresford and H.P.R. Finberg, *English Medieval Boroughs: A Handlist* (Newton Abbot, 1973), p. 145.

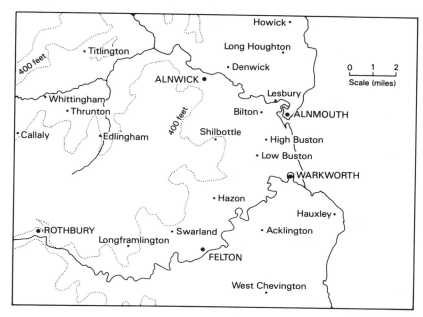

Map 3.2   A region of commercial development in central Northumberland.

Eden valley. Kendal and Alnwick (as their names imply) were on the Ken and the Aln respectively. Cockermouth was on the Derwent, Norham on the Tweed, and Morpeth on the Wansbeck. Wooler was in the Till valley, Yarm, Darlington and Barnard Castle were all in the Tees valley. Durham commanded a loop in the river Wear. Of the early north Yorkshire boroughs, Helmsley was in Ryedale, Richmond in Swaledale, Wensley in Wensleydale, New Malton on the Derwent and Stokesley on the Leven. The hinterland of Alnmouth Bay in mid-Northumberland, where five markets and boroughs had been founded within a few miles of each other by 1216, is an impressive illustration of these various developments, for besides Alnmouth on the coast, there were then centres of trade at Alnwick on the river Aln and at Warkworth, Felton and Rothbury on the Coquet (Map 3.2).

So far boroughs and markets towns have been counted together, but this needs to be justified, since it is not obvious that boroughs and markets were the same thing. There is a chronological divide in the evidence, as Table 3.1 shows. Most of the places that are under consideration on the strength of evidence from before 1199 occur as boroughs in the first instance, without there being direct evidence of a market or fair until a much later date. The only recorded markets in the north before John's accession were at

Table 3.1 *The status of early northern boroughs and markets at the time they are first recorded*

First recorded appearance	First occurring as borough	First occurring as market	First occurring as both borough and market	Total
Before 1150	6	1	1	8
1150–99	15	2	0	17
1199–1215	4	10	1	15
After 1215	4	6	0	10
Total	29	19	2	50

Source: Appendix.

Alnmouth, Durham, Kendal, Newcastle upon Tyne, Norton, Helmsley and probably Mitford. By contrast, most of the places in the list because of evidence from 1199 onwards first occur as markets. This divide coincides both with the earliest systematic recording of royal market charters and with a more determined attempt by the crown to enforce its right to license markets and fairs in the north. The pipe rolls suggest that it was only from John's accession that northern landlords normally concerned themselves with the need to acquire charters for markets and fairs. In order to derive any meaning from this list of places, it will be necessary to establish that there really was some close analogy between earlier-recorded borough founding and later-recorded market founding in the region.

Though early boroughs were often favourably situated for communication by land or water, it is often not obvious that they were centres of trade. In many instances their location betrays a meaning of non-commercial character. Many twelfth-century boroughs were at centres of baronial and ecclesiastical authority. Two (Newcastle upon Tyne and Carlisle) were major royal strongholds and centres of local government, six were at the head manors of baronies,[9] and seven others were hard by the castles of secular lords, probably from the beginning of their existence.[10] The borough of Cockermouth was founded by about 1210, beside the castle of the lords of

---

[9] Alnwick, Appleby, Mitford, Morpeth, Richmond, Thirsk: I. J. Sanders, *English Baronies: A Study of their Origin and Descent, 1086–1327* (Oxford, 1960), pp. 65–6, 103–4, 131–2, 140–1, 146–7.

[10] Bamburgh, Barnard Castle, Berwick, Brough, Harbottle, New Malton, Scarborough. For these castles, see D. J. Cathcart King, *Castellarium Anglicanum*, 2 vols. (New York, 1983), I, pp. 134, II, pp. 326–7, 334, 491, 521, 525; D.F. Renn, *Norman Castles in Britain* (London, 1968), pp. 98, 120, 200, 239, 306–7.

the honour of Cockermouth.[11] Durham and Norham had early episcopal castles, and Durham, like Whitby, was an important monastic centre. Dalton in Furness, too, was a monastic borough. These political connections cast some initial doubt on the wisdom of assigning any commercial significance to early borough foundations. A borough might be a device to attract tenants in a colonial context by granting them a favourable status at law and offering them the protection of nearby seigneurial defences. Burgage tenure was attractive in that properties could be freely bought and sold. In Sunderland, for example, a burgess was free to sell any land acquired by purchase without his heir's consent, and he was free to sell up his property and leave the borough so long as his title was not currently subject to legal investigation.[12] Burgesses also had the distinction of paying their rents mostly in the form of money. There was no reason why such conditions should be extended to privileged rural tenants, and indeed some Anglo-Irish boroughs were purely agrarian communities.[13] Such tenures could be created as a means of increasing rent, or to attract a more dependable local following in a hostile land, or as a recognised mark of status, signifying local power over land and men, and none of these meanings would directly imply that a borough was a centre of marketing. The burgesses of Egremont were obliged by their charter to supply military aid in time of war.[14]

Doubts about the nature of northern boroughs are heightened by some regional oddities. Durham has so far been counted as a single borough, but the real situation was more complicated. By 1200 there were four Durham boroughs, two in the lordship of the priory, one in the lordship of the bishop and one in the lordship of Kepier Hospital. Only the bishop's borough had a market place, and the other three must be counted as unusual instances of boroughs that did not have markets.[15] There are other reasons for doubting whether all northern boroughs were marketing centres. In 1293, when reporting to the king's commissioners on markets in the bishop of Durham's

[11] A.J.L. Winchester, 'Medieval Cockermouth', *Transactions of the Cumberland and Westmorland Antiquarian and Archaeological Society* (hereafter *Trans. CWAAS*), 86 (1986), p. 109. A charter of *c.* 1210 is a grant of liberties to the 'free men of Cockermouth', but there is no reference to a borough. Unlike Newburn, however (above, p. 48), Cockermouth is here treated as a borough (a) because in other respects the document recognisably has the form of a borough charter, and (b) because Cockermouth was later described as a borough in 1260: Beresford and Finberg, *English Medieval Boroughs*, p. 83.

[12] *Boldon Book*, ed. W. Greenwell (Surtees Soc., no. 25, 1852), pp. xli–xlii.

[13] J. Bradley, 'Planned Anglo-Norman Towns in Ireland', in H.B. Clarke and A. Simm (eds.), *The Comparative History of Urban Origins in Non-Roman Europe*, 2 vols. (British Archaeological Reports, International Series, no. 255, Oxford, 1985), pp. 411, 425.

[14] E.H. Knowles, 'The Charters of the Borough of Egremont', *Trans. CWAAS*, 1st ser., 1 (1866–73), p. 282.

[15] M. Bonney, *Lordship and the Urban Community: Durham and its Overlords, 1250–1540* (Cambridge, 1990), pp. 41–9.

liberty, local jurors reported only the bishop's markets and fairs in Durham, Darlington and Norham, the Scottish king's market in Barnard Castle and Robert de Brus' market at Hartlepool.[16] There is no reference to a market at Gateshead or Sunderland, and it has been surmised that no formal markets were there.[17]

The force of any argument from feudal geography concerning the nature of boroughs is reduced, however, by the fact that the connection between baronies, castles and early markets is nearly as strong as that between baronies, castles and early boroughs. Of the twenty places under consideration that first occur as markets, six were at the head manors of baronies[18] and three were beside castles.[19] This does not establish that early boroughs and markets were of any great economic significance, but it implies that the location of early boroughs beside large households should not count strongly against the idea that they were intended to be marketing centres.

To strengthen this conclusion, it can be shown that without exception all the places described as boroughs by 1199 had markets at some date in the thirteenth or fourteenth centuries, usually by prescriptive right. A market at Scarborough is known to have existed in 1256,[20] at Richmond in 1268,[21] at Bamburgh in 1279,[22] at New Malton in 1283,[23] at Whitby in the early fourteenth century[24] and at Yarm in 1368.[25] The *Quo Warranto* inquests of Edward I's reign pick out unchartered markets at Carlisle, Helmsley, Thirsk, Alnwick, Harbottle, Corbridge, Norham, Barnard Castle, Darlington, Durham and Appleby.[26] Some later markets in established boroughs are known from grants of market rights by the crown, as at Hartlepool (1218 or 1229 and again in 1234),[27] Cockermouth (1221),[28] Berwick (1253),[29] Kirkby Moorside (1254)[30] and Ulverston (1280).[31] The fact that these places were given later market charters does not disprove the suggestion that they had

[16] *Placita de Quo Warranto*, ed. W. Illingworth (Rec. Comm., London, 1818; hereafter *Placita*), p. 604.
[17] M.H. Dodds, 'The Bishops' Boroughs', *Archaeologia Aeliana*, 3rd ser., 12 (1915), p. 108.
[18] Kendal, Mitford, Ovingham (Prudhoe), Skelton, Stokeley, Wooler.
[19] Kirkoswald, Pickering, Warkworth.
[20] *Cal. Pat. Rolls, 1247–58*, p. 477.
[21] *VCH, Yorks. North Riding* (hereafter *NR*) I, p. 27.
[22] *Three Early Assize Rolls for the County of Northumberland*, ed. W. Page (Surtees Soc., no. 88, Durham, 1891), p. 352.
[23] *Cal. Pat. Rolls, 1281–92*, p. 76.
[24] G. Young, *A History of Whitby and Streoneshalh Abbey*, 2 vols. (Whitby, 1817), I, p. 322.
[25] *VCH, Yorks. NR*, II, p. 323.
[26] *Placita*, pp. 120, 189, 218, 587, 593, 595, 604, 792.
[27] *Cal. Chart. Rolls*, V, 191.
[28] *Rot. Litt. Claus.*, I, p. 458b.
[29] *Cal. Chart. Rolls*, I, 416.
[30] *Cal. Pat. Rolls, 1247–58*, p. 385.
[31] *Cal. Chart. Rolls*, II, p. 231.

formal marketing institutions by 1216, since new charters were required if a market day was changed. At Rothbury, for example, though the borough is known from as early as 1196, the first mention of a market is from 1223, when the market day was changed by charter from Sunday to Monday.[32] The ten places added to the list from thirteenth-century sources were mostly recorded then as markets, and some had evidently existed as such before the time of their first mention. There was already a market at Hexham in 1222, when the market day was changed from Sunday to Monday, and similarly at Warkworth in 1223, when the day was changed from Sunday to Wednesday.[33]

It is also relevant to this argument that a number of those twenty early boroughs and markets which are first recorded as early markets were described as boroughs in later documentation. This suggests that the establishment of a market had been simply one element in a more extensive operation. This is the case with Keswick, for example, which was founded as a Saturday market in 1189 and which occurs as a borough in the reign of Henry III.[34] Felton and Kirkoswald, where markets were chartered in 1200 and 1201 respectively, both occur as boroughs in later records. Hexham, Newbiggin by the Sea, Pooley Bridge, Skelton and Stokesley are similarly all recorded as boroughs after first occurring as markets.[35] It would be tempting to suppose that the market charter to Norton represents the origin of the later borough of Stockton, which was in the parish of Norton, except that there is no hint of burghal development at Stockton in Boldon Book or in any other source between 1109 and 1283.

In southern England it is a characteristic of the earliest recorded markets, and those that may be presumed to have an early origin, that they stood a better chance of survival as centres of local trade than those founded later. An equivalent pattern of development is to be seen if the northern-eastern boroughs are analysed as if they were marketing centres. Of the fifty places considered above, thirty-two continued to function as market towns in the sixteenth and seventeenth centuries (Table 3.2). This proportion (64 per cent) is appreciably higher than that of markets licensed by the crown between 1216 and 1350, of which only eleven out of seventy-one (15 per cent) survived into the early modern period.[36] A difference of this magnitude

---

[32] *Rot. Litt. Claus.*, I, p. 543.

[33] *Ibid.*, I, pp. 515, 543.

[34] J. Munby, 'Medieval Kendal: The First Borough Charter and its Connections', *Trans. CWAAS*, 85 (1985), p. 97.

[35] For their burghal status, see Beresford and Finberg, *English Medieval Boroughs*, pp. 144, 188; Winchester, *Landscape and Society*, p. 122.

[36] The latter calculation ignores the Palatinate of Durham, in which the very few new markets of the period after 1216 were licensed by the bishop.

Table 3.2 *The longevity of the early boroughs and markets of northern England as market towns*

First recorded appearance	Number recorded	Number surviving as market towns after 1500	Percentage surviving
Before 1150	8	6	75
1150–99	17	12	71
1199–1215	15	8	53
After 1215	10	6	60
Total	50	32	64

Source: Appendix, Table 3.1 and A. Everitt, 'The Marketing of Agricultural Produce', in J. Thirsk (ed), *Agrarian History of England and Wales*, IV: *1500–1640* (Cambridge, 1987), pp. 468–75.

would be difficult to explain unless the early northern boroughs were well established as local markets at an early date.

It must be granted that boroughs in the north often retained some rural features. Hugh de Puiset, bishop of Durham, granted the free burgess of Norham pasture and marshland that had been part of their endowment in the time of his predecessor Ranulph Flambard. Probably Flambard had established the borough here between the time he built the castle in 1121 and his death in 1128.[37] Similar grants of pasture rights are common in northern borough charters.[38] Yet such interests in agriculture were general amongst English boroughs, even the larger ones, and have no particular significance for the characteristics of the north.[39] The bishop of Durham's boroughs, Norham, Durham, Gateshead and Sunderland, can all be shown to have been centres of regular commerce. Boldon Book records that about 1183 the bishop received toll and stallage in the borough of Norham.[40] Durham had not only a market but a mint by 1100, and a distinctly commercial sort of society was already growing up; by about 1107 the priory had been authorised to hold Elvet, across the river, so that the monks could have

[37] Raine, *History and Antiquities of North Durham*, p. 257 and note.
[38] A. Ballard, *British Borough Charters, 1042–1216* (Cambridge, 1913), pp. 58–63 (Alnwick, Barnard Castle, Corbridge, Egremont, Gateshead, Norham, Sunderland); A. Ballard and J. Tait, *British Borough Charters, 1216–1307* (Cambridge, 1923), pp. 70–84 (Alnwick, Barnard Castle, Helmsley, Morpeth); Munby, 'Medieval Kendal' (Ulverston, Kendal).
[39] F.W. Maitland, *Township and Borough* (Cambridge, 1964), pp. 44–67.
[40] *Boldon Book*, p. 41.

forty houses for tradesmen there.[41] Hugh de Puiset's charter to Gateshead prohibited foresters from impeding trade between the forest and the borough.[42] His more extensive charter of the 1180s to 'the burgesses of Wearmouth' (later known as the borough of Sunderland) regulated trade between burgesses and ships applying to the shore there, and envisaged the existence of a grain trade between the burgesses and the surrounding countryside.[43]

Similar references to regular trade occur in the liberties granted to burgesses elsewhere. Sometime in the period 1190–1210 Robert de Ros II granted to Byland Abbey freedom of tolls on all sales and purchases made in the town and market of Helmsley.[44] In 1200 the burgesses of Appleby were granted freedom of tolls throughout England on the same terms as the burgesses of York.[45] The burgesses of Egremont were allowed freedom of trade within the borough and freedom from tolls on their own goods on Richard de Luci's lands.[46] About 1210 Alice de Rumeli gave the free men of Cockermouth, among other customs, the assize of bread, wine and ale as enforced at Carlisle.[47] The regulation of textile operations is provided for in the early borough charters of Ulverston, Egremont and Kendal.[48] A charter of Henry II's privileged the cloth industries of the royal boroughs of Kirkby Moorside, New Malton, Thirsk and Scarborough as well as those of Beverley and York; the growth of clothmaking in these new centres may indeed have been damaging York's interests by John's reign.[49] It is not surprising that there should be evidence of extensive trade from the principal new urban centres at Newcastle and Carlisle. Already before 1135, Henry I granted the burgesses of Newcastle liberties that implied sea-going ventures, a regular trade in salt, herrings, wool and hides, and a cloth-finishing industry,[50] and

[41] *Durham Episcopal Charters, 1071–1152*, ed. H.S. Offler (Surtees Soc., no. 179, Durham, 1968), p. 8; M. Allen, 'The Durham Mint before Boldon Book', in D. Rollason, M. Harvey and M. Prestwich (eds.), *Anglo-Norman Durham, 1093–1193* (Woodbridge, 1994), pp. 384, 396. See too below, pp. 59–60.

[42] *Boldon Book*, p. xl.

[43] *Ibid.*, pp. 6, xli–xlii; R. Surtees, *The History and Antiquities of the County Palatine of Durham*, 4 vols. (London, 1816–40), I, pp. 297–8.

[44] *Early Yorkshire Charters*, I–III, ed. W. Farrer (Edinburgh, 1914–16), IV–XII, ed. C.T. Clay (Yorkshire Arch. Soc., Leeds, 1935–65; hereafter *Early Yorks. Chart.*), X, no. 95, pp. 147–8.

[45] *Rotuli Chartarum*, ed. T.D. Hardy (Rec. Comm., London, 1837; hereafter *Rot. Chart.*), p. 41.

[46] Ballard, *British Borough Charters*, pp. 193, 216.

[47] R. Hall, 'An Early Cockermouth Charter', *Trans. CWAAS*, 77 (1977), p. 77.

[48] Munby, 'Medieval Kendal', pp. 100, 103; Knowles, 'Charters of the Borough of Egremont', p. 284.

[49] *Cal. Pat. Rolls, 1345–8*, pp. 199–200; *Early Yorks. Chart.* I, no. 349, p. 263; Miller, 'Medieval York', p. 44.

[50] W. Stubbs, *Select Charters and Other Illustrations of English Constitutional History*, 9th edn, ed. H.W.C. Davis (Oxford, 1913), pp. 133–4.

in 1158 Henry II granted the merchants of Carlisle the right to have a guild merchant.[51] In this latter year Carlisle and Newcastle both had mints, supplied from the silver mines at Alston, whose proximity is believed to have contributed greatly to Carlisle's trade up to the 1160s.[52]

Further evidence for the real economic significance of northern boroughs is that the financial returns to those who had lordship over them were often high. Newcastle, perhaps not surprisingly, was the most valuable town in the north. In 1156 the burgesses were recorded to owe the king the fixed sum of £50 a year.[53] In 1201 Newcastle was farmed for £50 still, Corbridge for £30 and Rothbury for £20.[54] The borough of Norham, with its various sources of income, was valued in the 1180s at £16 13s. 4d.[55] In 1183 the bishop of Durham leased his part of the city for either £16 or £40, depending on which version of the text of Boldon Book one chooses to believe. Gateshead was perhaps already a valuable borough in 1183, though the sum of £40 at which it is valued in Boldon Book contains arable land of considerable dimensions as well as the borough with its associated mills, fisheries and ovens.[56] Scammell observes that the farms of Durham and Gateshead in the late twelfth century 'were equal to those of Bury St Edmunds, Colchester, Hereford, Oxford and Yarmouth'.[57] Darlington was smaller, worth £5 or so.[58] In Yorkshire the borough of Richmond was paying a fee farm of £29 to its earl within thirty years of its foundation.[59] The annual sum owed by the burgesses of Scarborough to the crown increased by several stages from £20 in 1163 to £76 in 1201, which seems to be evidence not only of economic significance but of impressive development as well.[60]

The high proportion of boroughs, and the small number of recorded markets, that characterises the twelfth-century evidence for commercial development in the north can be related, in part, to the region's distance from the core region of either English or Scottish royal authority and the correspondingly slower development of legal practice and terminology relat-

---

[51] Ballard, British Borough Charters, p. 205. For discussion of this charter, see K. Smith, 'The Dating of Carlisle's First Charter', Trans. CWAAS, new ser., 54 (1954), pp. 272–3, and H.R.T. Summerson, Medieval Carlisle: The City and the Borders from the Late Eleventh to the Mid-Sixteenth Century, 2 vols. (Kendal, 1993), I, pp. 59–61.

[52] Summerson, Medieval Carlisle, I, p. 68.

[53] H. Bourne, The History of Newcastle upon Tyne (Newcastle upon Tyne, 1736), p. 184.

[54] Pipe Roll 3 John, p. 249. In this same context Newburn was farmed for £30, but for want of any clear description of it as a borough it has been excluded from consideration in this survey.

[55] Boldon Book, p. 41.

[56] Ibid., p.2.

[57] G.V. Scammell, Hugh de Puiset, Bishop of Durham (Cambridge, 1956), p. 216n.

[58] Boldon Book, p. 17.

[59] M.W. Beresford, New Towns of the Middle Ages: Town Plantation in England, Wales and Gascony (London, 1967), p. 518.

[60] Early Yorks. Chart., I, p. 285.

ing to regalian rights over the licensing of markets. The earliest known royal charter relevant to the north licensed a market at Norton in 1109. The licensee, Ranulph Flambard, bishop of Durham and former chief minister to William II of England, had presumably been associated with the implementation of the legal requirement that all new markets required authorisation by the crown. The only other northern grants of market or fair recorded in the twelfth century either by a surviving English royal charter or in the pipe rolls were somewhere in Northumberland (probably Mitford) about 1158, at Kendal in 1189 and at Wooler in 1199.[61] The loss of authority by the English crown under King Stephen is well illustrated by an unusual charter of the years 1152–c. 1155 by which a market at Alnmouth was licensed by the earl of Northumberland, to be held as freely as any market in Northumberland.[62] By implication, the earl claimed the regalian privilege of licensing markets and fairs in his earldom. As a result of the weak impact of royal claims in this respect, northern estates probably retained rather longer than elsewhere a certain indifference to definitions which were becoming standardised both in Scotland and in England further south. For example, as late as 1290, when the prior of Tynemouth was alleged to have a Sunday market at Tynemouth he denied that this was true. He had no market, he said, but there was a tumbrel, fishermen and brewers, an oven that he leased, and stalls for setting out goods such as bread, meat and fish for sale 'as is the practice in other villages of those parts'. This doubtless appeared naive to the king's justices, who told him that if he did not claim a market or port at Tynemouth he ought to suppress any signs of one.[63]

Borough-founding can safely be interpreted as a feature of commercial organisation in the region. Whether or not the new northern boroughs should be regarded as culturally specific signs of feudal lordship – and the frequency of their association with Norman castles and baronies suggests that they should – the fact that they symbolised power over land and men was clearly not incompatible with their also being investments of real commercial significance. None of the northern boroughs of the twelfth century seems likely to have been a purely agrarian development. The Durham example, though it shows that not all formally distinct boroughs had markets, can only be understood on the understanding that the four boroughs were urban, and indeed together constituted the centre of the modern city of Durham. The numerous links between boroughs, markets, baronies, castles and abbeys match a distinctly Anglo-Norman pattern that can be observed in

---

[61] References to all three are cited in the Appendix.
[62] *Regesta Regum Scottorum*, ed. G.W.S. Barrow *et al.*, 8 vols. projected (Edinburgh, 1960–), II, no. 3, pp. 124–5. Earl William later became king of Scots in 1165.
[63] *Rotuli Parliamentorum*, 6 vols. (Rec. Comm., London, 1783), I, pp. 28–9.

south-western England, in Wales and the Welsh marches, in Anglo-Norman Ireland, or in Scotland after the creation of feudal institutions there by King David I.[64] Boroughs were, indeed, a well-tried component in the twelfth-century practice of estate management in areas of colonisation, but this was not a code to be applied routinely without regard to local commercial conditions. Some territorial lords, like the bishops of Durham, planned new boroughs on a grand scale, but many others did not. There were northern baronies, like Ellingham, Embleton, Greystoke, Kirklinton, Topcliffe, Wark or Whalton, that had no boroughs at their head estate by 1216, even if they received market charters later.[65] There were also twelfth-century castles with no boroughs at their gate, as at Brougham and Pendragon (both in Westmorland), or at Kilton and Middleham (both in North Riding).[66] This implies that boroughs were founded in such contexts only when it was appropriate to do so, and that when landlords did decide to invest in this way they had first reasoned about the potential economic benefits.

Even if the commercial aspect of twelfth-century borough-founding is conceded, however, this does not establish that it accompanied any significant restructuring of northern economic activity. Did a new institutional marketing structure really represent commercial development, or was an older system simply being brought into line with Norman lordship? It is conceivable that the fettering of existing patterns of trade by predatory lords could actually have reduced the incentives to trade, and so brought about commercial contraction. In order to establish that new boroughs and markets encouraged trade, it is necessary to show positive evidence of associated commercial expansion, or at the very least to establish that their creation was achieved without the forcible imposition of controls detrimental to the interests of traders.

There were already informal centres of trade in the north before the twelfth century. Some of these were ancient, centring perhaps on major local churches or the administrative headquarters of large estates, though the disruption of both ecclesiastical and political organisation during the ninth century is likely to have created discontinuity in the location and organisation of marketing. It may be that some of the places occurring as boroughs in the twelfth century, or as prescriptive markets in the thirteenth century or later, were at focal points of eleventh-century commerce. Hexham was a

---

[64] R.H. Britnell, 'Les marchés hebdomadaires aux Iles Britanniques avant 1200', in *Foires et marchés dans les campagnes de l'Europe médiévale et moderne, VIIe–XVIIIe siècles* (Actes des 14ᵉˢ Journées Internationales d'Histoire, Editions Flaran) (forthcoming); A. Preston-Jones and P. Rose, 'Week St Mary: Town and Castle', *Cornish Arch.*, 31 (1992), pp. 143–53.

[65] Sanders, *English Baronies*, pp. 41–2, 50, 58–9, 148–50.

[66] King, *Castellarium Anglicanum*, II, 491, 493, 519, 521.

major ecclesiastical centre and, as already observed, had a prescriptive market in 1222. Amongst the centres of secular power with some importance as local meeting places for trade and other business, Bamburgh should perhaps be included, as the centre of Northumbrian royal power up to 954 and the seat of the earls of Northumbria thereafter, though its importance had probably declined since the ninth century. There was a borough there in 1170. Corbridge and Darlington were well-established settlements on important roads by major river crossings.[67] On the east coast, Wearmouth was a port in the eighth century, and may have retained some local importance even before the restoration of monasticism there in about 1076–8.[68] At Whitby, too, despite the destruction of the monastery in the years 867–70, the port seems to have been used in the period before the restoration of the monastery in about 1078.[69] On the west side of the Pennines there was less commercial activity before the twelfth century. Carlisle was of some importance in the eleventh century for its churches and as a centre of secular lordship, and it was probably a focus for north-western trade.[70] Penrith's case to be considered as an early commercial centre is based both on its location and its important early church.[71] In all these places there may have been continuity between late Saxon and Norman trade networks, though undoubtably new developments were needed to create the institutional framework for trade on record from the period after 1100.

North of York, Durham is the only place for which there is any evidence of formal provision for local trade in the eleventh century. The town became a centre of local importance after the body of St Cuthbert was brought there in about 995; there is no earlier archaeological record.[72] Symeon of Durham's account of a Scottish raid on the city in 1040 states that there was a market place at that date.[73] In the early Norman period the feast of St Cuthbert was the occasion for a big meeting of the bishop's barons, thegns, drengs and others, who were given the saint's special protection on their way to Durham.[74] A miracle story relating to the late eleventh century confirms that, as in later days, this festival was already the occasion for buying and selling; the anonymous author reports that some people went to Durham for pious

[67] A.E. Smailes, *North England* (London, 1960), pp. 110–11.

[68] Dodds, 'Bishops' Boroughs', pp. 83–4; D. Knowles, *The Monastic Order in England* (Cambridge, 1950), p. 168.

[69] *VCH Yorks. NR*, II, p. 506; Knowles, *Monastic Order in England*, p. 168.

[70] Summerson, *Medieval Carlisle*, I, pp. 11–13.

[71] Winchester, *Landscape and Society*, p. 124.

[72] P. Lowther *et al.*, 'The City of Durham: An Archaeological Survey', *Durham Arch. Jl*, 9 (1993), p. 108.

[73] Bonney, *Lordship*, p. 26.

[74] *Historiae Dunelmensis Scriptores Tres*, ed. J. Raine (Surtees Soc., no. 9, Durham 1839), appendix, no. cccxxxii, pp. ccccxxx–ccccxxxi.

reasons, and others for the sake of trade.[75] The September feast of St Cuthbert was later famous for its fair.[76]

Smaller centres of inland trade were probably quite numerous. At the most local level, trade was often associated with attendance at church. A later northern example of informal Sunday trading is that reported in Crosthwaite churchyard in 1291, whose informal nature was demonstrable from absence of seigneurial tolls on transactions.[77] In the north, as elsewhere in the country, landlords of the twelfth and thirteenth centuries sometimes formalised such a congruence of the sacred and the profane by setting up regular Sunday markets. Other local centres of trade probably developed along regularly used routes through the countryside, perhaps at places where there was accommodation for travellers. Perhaps Chopwell in Durham acquired its name in this way.[78] The possibilities for trade were not circumscribed by the existence of deliberately created marketing institutions, and, indeed, the relationship between the volume of trade and the extent of an institutionalised structure of markets is problematic. The abundant evidence for 'hidden trade' in the later Middle Ages cannot be paralleled from the eleventh century for want of sources, but there can surely be no doubt that by that time, even without regular markets, there were established patterns of marketing in northern England.

The significance of an additional fifty or so marketing institutions in the region under discussion, many of them of very doubtful value, could arguably have been swamped by commercial changes outside that structure of which there is no surviving record. On the other hand the parallel evidence of urban development constitutes good evidence that the institutional developments of the twelfth century were signs of commercial expansion. The new centres of trade were not simply market places with a set of rules, replacing the old informality of bargaining in roadside houses or country churchyards. The fact that so many markets were developed as boroughs suggests that they mostly served concentrations of families who did not primarily depend on agriculture. The creation of boroughs characteristically implied the setting out of smallish plots around a market place and in adjacent streets, often without any attached farmland. A number of the northern boroughs were newly created communities of just this sort, with markedly urban features, and are listed amongst Professor Beresford's new towns of the Middle Ages. Alnmouth was earlier known as Newbiggin in the

[75] 'De Miraculis et Translationibus Sancti Cuthberti', in *Symeonis Monachi Opera Omnia*, ed. T. Arnold, 2 vols. (Rolls Ser., 75, London, 1882–5), II, p. 336.

[76] Dodds, 'Bishops' Boroughs', p. 106.

[77] *Placita*, p. 115b.

[78] J.R. Ellis, 'Chopwell: A Problematical Durham Place-Name', *Nomina*, 12 (1988–9), pp. 65–76.

1150s, implying that the development of the site represents a new enterprise on the part of the Vesci family. Morpeth is described as a new town in a charter of Roger III de Merlay.[79] In the North Riding, New Malton, Richmond and Thirsk all qualify as new towns of the twelfth century, and so similarly do Barnard Castle and Hartlepool in Durham, Appleby and Brough in Westmorland.[80] The most successful examples of urban growth are convincing on this point. Newcastle clearly took its name from a castle that was first built in 1080, and there is no evidence to suggest any earlier community resident upon the site.[81] Archaeological evidence suggests that, whatever its local importance as an administrative centre may have been, Carlisle had no urban features before the twelfth century.[82] During the 150 years under discussion, towns developed in the north to an extent unprecedented in any earlier period.

This could not have come about without commercial growth. A direct analogy may be made with the Scottish lowlands in the same period, where the founding of boroughs is strongly associated with agrarian development and the monetisation of the economy from a very low earlier level. There was no Scottish currency until about 1136, in the reign of King David I (1124–53).[83] The eleventh-century kings of Scotland had received the returns from their estates in the form of payments in kind, and it was only in the twelfth century that they began to depend upon an income in cash. The use of money for the payment of rents seems to date only from about 1140, and it was initially most marked in the south-eastern part of the kingdom nearest to Northumbria.[84] The chronology of monetisation in Cumbria was probably very similar.[85] The association of markets with these new boroughs is just what should be expected from an increase in the proportion of the population employed outside agriculture.

Is it possible to suggest which economic signals encouraged landlords to establish new boroughs? The successful founding of a borough in the twelfth century – unlike some of the more desultory later schemes – hinged upon the ability of the project to attract tenants. A new borough was, first and foremost, a scheme for settling tradesmen and artisans on an estate in order for the landlord to benefit from an increase in money rents, tolls and other

[79] *Chartularium Abbathiae de Novo Monasterio*, ed. J.T. Fowler (Surtees Soc., no. 66, Durham, 1878), p. 6.

[80] Beresford, *New Towns*, pp. 516–19.

[81] *Ibid.*, pp. 473–4.

[82] Summerson, *Medieval Carlisle*, I, p. 13.

[83] *Regesta Regum Scottorum*, I, pp. 53–4, and II, pp. 52–3; A.A.M. Duncan, *Scotland: The Making of the Kingdom* (Edinburgh, 1975), p. 463; above, chapter 2, pp. 33–4.

[84] Duncan, *Scotland*, pp. 394–5; W.W. Scott, 'The Use of Money in Scotland, 1124–1230', *Scot. Hist. Rev.*, 58 (1979), pp. 112–19, 123.

[85] Summerson, *Medieval Carlisle*, I, pp. 7, 42.

dues. Secondly, and much more indirectly, a new borough was a way of improving marketing opportunities for tenants by creating a new focus of market demand. If tenants could sell their produce with greater ease, this would facilitate levying money rents and payments from them. Marketing institutions as such (the new market places with their weighing apparatus and so on) were much less important, both as sources of seigneurial income and as commercial facilities for tenants, than concentrations of new burgesses lucratively employed. So the signals that would induce a landlord to found a borough were, on the one hand, indications of good opportunities for local employment in industry and trade, and, on the other, evidence that some particular site – especially if associated with the residence of a big-spending household – was likely to attract artisans and tradesmen if provided with an appropriate institutional infrastructure. Successful borough-founding depended upon accurate perception of these two points, not on the mechanical implementation of some Norman ideal of regional planning, nor on bullying unwilling tenants to force an old trading system into a new shape.

It remains only to describe more generally the circumstances in which opportunities for borough-founding occurred as they did in northern England during the twelfth century. One answer, though it can account only for a minority of the boroughs, is growth in the demand for northern products and transport services across the North Sea and in other regions of England. The development of the north-eastern ports in this period, and especially of Newcastle, suggests that the region benefited from a higher level of long-distance trade. What this trade consisted of is more a matter for guesswork than informed comment. In the later Middle Ages minerals (coal, lead, iron, salt) were an important resource of the north-east, and it is certain that silver and lead, at least, already featured as regional exports in the twelfth century.[86] Probably, too, agricultural products (grain, wool and hides) were sent abroad to Scandinavia or the Low Countries, or to more densely populated regions further south. More importantly, however, urban development in the north was stimulated by rising demand within the region itself. This encouraged urban development on the coast, both for the handling of imported goods, such as wine,[87] and for the expansion of sea-fishing, which is referred to in charters both for Newcastle and Sun-

---

[86] Above, chapter 2, pp. 33–6; R.A. Lomas, *North-East England in the Middle Ages* (Edinburgh, 1992), pp. 198–206; Scammell, *Hugh de Puiset*, pp. 215, 217.

[87] E.g. E. Miller, 'Rulers of Thirteenth-Century Towns: The Cases of York and Newcastle upon Tyne', in P.R. Coss and S.D. Lloyd (eds.), *Thirteenth Century England*, I (Woodbridge, 1986), p. 134; Scammell, *Hugh de Puiset*, p. 207; G. Tate, *The History of the Borough, Castle and Barony of Alnwick*, 2 vols. (Alnwick, 1866–9), I, p. 86.

derland.[88] Rising demand for manufactures and services also accounts for the proliferation of inland urban centres. Excavations in Durham have identified shoemaking and pottery as two of the urban crafts of this period.[89] Some of this increased expenditure was by greater landlords and their dependants, and some by the monasteries whose number increased in the course of the century. This is part of the reason why boroughs were founded by castles and monasteries. But more important still was the more diffuse demand for goods and services from the lesser landlords and villagers of the north. Average holdings were probably larger in the north than in southern England, and rents were moderate, which encouraged the consumption of purchased commodities in village societies.[90] Such increasing demand, in this predominantly agrarian economy, depended upon an increase in the amount of marketable produce that could only have arisen through agricultural development.

Edward Miller's studies of northern agriculture and rural settlement have demonstrated just the sort of expanding rural economy in which pronounced commercial growth was likely. Opportunities for expanding the arable area were particularly great in twelfth-century Yorkshire and farther north, partly because earlier economic development had been less extensive than in the south, and partly because of the recent ravages of war.[91] During the twelfth century both population and agricultural production increased much more in the north than they could do in the south, simply because there was more land to be taken up.[92] Forest land was cleared for farming, as village settlements, abbeys and granges multiplied.[93] The development of wool production attested by thirteenth-century records was already under way before the end of the twelfth century.[94] Between 1165 and 1174, for example, the monks of Holmcultram were licensed by William I of Scotland to trade freely in wool and other produce in the Scottish boroughs.[95] These conclusions powerfully reinforce the view that the twelfth century was an age of marked economic

---

[88] Stubbs, *Select Charters*, p. 133; *Boldon Book*, p. xli. For the fishermen of Whitby, see above, chapter 1, p. 15.
[89] Bonney, *Lordship*, p. 32.
[90] E. Miller, 'Social Structure: Northern England', in *AHEW*, II, pp. 688–90, 695.
[91] Miller, 'Farming in Northern England during the Twelfth and Thirteenth Centuries', *Northern Hist.*, 11 (1975), pp. 4–6.
[92] E. Miller and J. Hatcher, *Medieval England: Rural Society and Economic Change, 1086–1348* (London, 1978), p. 32.
[93] Miller, 'Farming in Northern England', pp. 6–7; E. Miller, 'New Settlement: Northern England', in *AHEW*, II, pp. 247–55.
[94] Miller, 'Farming in Northern England', pp. 11–12, Scammell, *Hugh de Puiset*, pp. 212–13.
[95] *Regesta Regum Scottorum*, II, no. 87, p. 184.

development.[96] New institutions, agricultural expansion and commercial growth together created a powerful regional dynamism in the north, so that in this hitherto unurbanised region of England the marketing network of the thirteenth century was already substantially in place by 1216.

---

[96] E. Miller, 'England in the Twelfth and Thirteenth Centuries: An Economic Contrast?', *Econ. Hist. Rev.*, 2nd ser., 24 (1971), pp. 5–7.

Appendix: the first references to the early markets and boroughs of northern England

CUMBERLAND

Arthuret (perhaps), market and two fairs chartered *c.* 1200: *Pipe Roll 2 John*, p. 244.[97]

Carlisle, borough occurs 1130: *Pipe Roll 31 Henry I*, p. 142.

Cockermouth, borough chartered *c.* 1210: Hall, 'Early Cockermouth Charter', pp. 75–81, Winchester, 'Medieval Cockermouth', pp. 109–32.

Egremont, borough chartered *c.* 1202: Knowles, 'Charters of the Borough of Egremont', pp. 282–5.

Kirkoswald, Thursday market and a fair chartered by John, 1 March 1201: *Rot. Chart.*, p. 89a.

Ravenglass, Saturday market and a fair chartered by John, 20 August 1208, *Rot. Chart.*, p. 182a.

WESTMORLAND

Appleby, borough occurs *c.* 1179: J. Nicolson and R. Burn, *The History and Antiquities of Westmorland and Cumberland*, 2 vols. (London, 1777), I, pp. 310–11 note. The new town was founded in the early twelfth century: Beresford, *New Towns*, p. 502; Winchester, *Landscape and Society*, p. 126.

Brough, borough occurs 1196: *Pipe Roll 8 Richard I*, p. 98.

Kendal, Saturday market chartered by Richard I, 1189: Nicolson and Burn, *Hist. and Antiq. of Westmld. and Cumb.*, I, p. 67 note.

Pooley Bridge ('Barton'), Thursday market and a fair chartered by John, 22 September 1214: *Rot. Chart.*, p. 201a; *Pipe Roll 16 John*, p. 94.

---

[97] Summerson suggests that this grant to William de Stutevill (at an unnamed place in Cumberland) was for a market at Kirkoswald, but the market at Kirkoswald chartered in 1201 was a grant to Hugh de Morevill: *Rot. Chart.*, p. 89a; Summerson, *Medieval Carlisle*, I, p. 66. The grant in question was presumably for a parcel of the barony of Liddell Strength, and somewhere in Arthuret is the likeliest place. There was a later market charter for Arthuret of 1307: *Cal. Chart. Rolls*, III, p. 81. There may be some connection between these early grants and the origins of Longtown.

FURNESS

Dalton in Furness, market occurs 1292: *Placita*, pp. 370–1. There are earlier charters for fairs: *Cal. Chart. Rolls*, I, pp. 243, 295.

Ulverston, borough chartered *c.* 1200: Munby, 'Medieval Kendal', pp. 97–9.

NORTHUMBERLAND

Alnmouth, borough occurs 1147: Tate, *Hist. of Alnwick*, II, appendix, p. viii.

Alnwick, borough occurs 1157×85: Tate, *Hist. of Alnwick*, II, appendix, p. i.

Bamburgh, borough occurs 1170: *Pipe Roll 16 Henry II*, p. 52.

Berwick, borough occurs 1119×24: G.S. Pryde, *The Burghs of Scotland: A Critical List* (London, 1965), p. 3.

Corbridge, borough occurs 1201: *Rot. Chart.*, p. 87b; *Pipe Roll 3 John*, p. 249.

Felton, Monday market and a fair chartered by John, 27 April 1200: *Rot. Chart.*, p. 50b.

Harbottle, borough occurs 1245: *Cal. Inq. Post Mortem*, I, no. 49, p. 12.

Hexham, Sunday market occurs 1222: *Rot. Litt. Claus.*, I, p. 515.

Mitford (probably), market granted 1157–8; a market occurs there in 1250: *Pipe Roll 2–4 Henry II*, p. 178; J. Hodgson, *A History of Northumberland*, 3 parts in 6 vols. (Newcastle, 1820–58), II(2), p. 65.

Morpeth, borough occurs 1188×1239: Hodgson, *Hist. of Northumberland*, II(2), p. 480.

Newbiggin by the Sea, Friday market and a fair chartered by John, 25 February 1204: *Rot. Chart.*, p. 119b.

Newcastle upon Tyne, borough charter referring to market chartered by Henry I, 1100×1135: Stubbs, *Select Charters*, pp. 133–4.

Norham, borough occurs 1153×1195: Raine, *Hist. and Antiq. of N. Durham*, p. 257 note h.

Ovingham, Sunday market and a fair occur 1292: *Placita*, p. 593.

Rothbury, borough occurs 1196: *Pipe Roll 8 Richard I*, p. 96.

Warkworth, Sunday market occurs 1223, *Rot. Litt. Claus.*, I, p. 543.

Wooler, Thursday market chartered by John, 21 August 1199: *Rot. Chart.*, p. 11a.

DURHAM

Barnard Castle, borough occurs *c.* 1175: Surtees, *Hist. and Antiq. of the County Palatine of Durham*, IV, p. 71.

Darlington, borough occurs *c.* 1183: *Boldon Buke*, p. 17.

Durham, borough occurs 1130: *Pipe Roll 31 Henry I*, pp. 130, 132.

Gateshead, borough chartered 1153×95: *Boldon Book*, p. xl.

Hartlepool, borough occurs 1162×85: *Cal. Pat. Rolls, 1396–9*, p. 172.

Norton, market chartered by Henry I, 1109: *Regesta Regum Anglo-Normannorum*, ed. H.W.C. Davis, C. Johnson, H.A. Cronne and R.H.C. Davis, 4 vols. (Oxford, 1913–69), II, no. 925, p. 89.

Sunderland ('Wermouth', 'Weremue'), borough occurs *c.* 1183: *Boldon Book*, pp. 6, xli–xlii; Surtees, *Hist. and Antiq. of the County Palatine of Durham*, I, pp. 297–8.

NORTH RIDING

Buttercrambe, Saturday market and a fair chartered by John, 23 April 1200: *Rot. Chart.*, p. 54b.

Helmsley, market and borough occur 1190×1210: *Early Yorks. Chart.*, X, nos. 95, 100, pp. 147–8, 155.

Kirkby Moorside, borough occurs 1154×1179: *Cal. Pat. Rolls, 1345–8*, p. 200; *Early Yorks. Chart.*, I, no. 349, pp. 199–200.

New Malton, borough occurs 1154×1179: *Cal. Pat. Rolls, 1345–8*, p. 200; *Early Yorks. Chart.*, I, no. 349, pp. 199–200.

Northallerton, borough occurs 1267–8: *VCH Yorks. NR*, I, p. 422. There is an earlier charter for a fair: *Rot. Chart.*, p. 37.

Pickering, market occurs 1201: *Rot. Chart.*, p. 85b.

Richmond, borough occurs 1136×1145: *Early Yorks. Chart.*, IV, nos. 20, 21, pp. 22–3.

Scarborough, borough occurs 1155×1163: *Early Yorks. Chart.*, I, no. 364, pp. 283–4.

Skelton, market occurs 1227: *Cal. Close Rolls*, 1227–31, p. 9.

Stokesley, market occurs 1279×1281: *Placita*, p. 194.

Thirsk, borough occurs 1163: *Cal. Pat. Rolls, 1345–8*, p. 200; *Early Yorks. Chart.*, I, no. 349, pp. 199–200.

Wensley, Thursday market granted *c.* 1202: *Pipe Roll 4 John*, p. 65.

Whitby, borough occurs 1122: *Regesta Regum Anglo-Normannorum*, II, no. 1335, p. 174.

Yarm, borough occurs 1273: *Cal. Close Rolls, 1272–9*, p. 46.

4

Peasant deer poachers in the medieval forest

JEAN BIRRELL

T HE RECORDS of the forest courts of the thirteenth and fourteenth centuries together contain many hundreds of brief accounts of hunting expeditions; they constitute a unique source for an activity which is perhaps better known from the idealised descriptions in hunting treatises or imaginative literature.[1] The hunters whose real-life exploits are described in forest eyres, or in the general inquisitions which replaced them during the fourteenth century, came from all ranks of society, and the interest of their stories is by no means confined to what they tell us about hunting techniques, precious though this is. In their descriptions not only of how, but of where and when and in whose company, men – and, very occasionally, women – hunted, the forest records provide scores of vignettes of English medieval rural social life. We see barons and bishops, knights and squires, the rough soldiery of castle garrisons, parish clergy, monks, servants of every type, craftsmen from the towns, local villagers and a host of others at work and at play, travelling and brawling, in the company of family and friends. We are given a unique perspective on rural life and relationships.

It is on the peasant hunters, and the light their activities throw on peasant life and experience, that I propose to concentrate here. For despite the prohibitions of forest law, the danger contained in encounters with forest officers and the severity of the penalties which might follow detection, the peasantry of forest villages continued to take deer in the royal forests. There were regular poachers who used a range of methods, many of them exclusive

---

[1] For some recent examples, see F. Barlow, 'Hunting in the Middle Ages', *Report and Transactions of the Devonshire Association*, 113 (1981), pp. 1–11; J. Cummins, *The Hound and the Hawk. The Art of Medieval Hunting* (London, 1988); N. Orme, 'Medieval Hunting; Fact and Fancy', in B. Hanawalt (ed.) *Chaucer's England* (Minneapolis, 1992), pp. 133–53. J.M. Gilbert, *Hunting and Hunting Reserves in Medieval Scotland* (Edinburgh, 1979), and G.K. Whitehead, *Hunting and Stalking Deer in Britain through the Ages* (London, 1980), are based on a wider documentation.

to their class, which suited both the circumstances in which they hunted and their needs. These were methods which often demanded a knowledge of the habits and movements of the different types of deer and a degree of self-discipline and manual dexterity on the part of the hunter which might be thought to fit ill with the disdain for them which pervades the hunting treatises, and even to compare favourably with the aristocratic methods which the same treatises extol. But whilst much peasant poaching was carefully planned and performed, much was opportunistic, even parasitical on the hunting of others. Either way, the circumstances throw light on peasant life, attitudes and experience. In the way they created and seized opportunities, reacted to the ever-present threat of forest officers and dealt with and ultimately disposed of their booty, peasant deer poachers were in some ways like and in others unlike their social superiors; both similarities and differences can be equally instructive.

Before looking in more detail at these themes, it is necessary to say something about sources and method. As with all court records, we need first to ask how accurate is the information they contain. In the eyre rolls, the entry usually takes the form of a presentation by the forest officers which is 'proved', that is recorded as the truth.[2] Clearly, these entries cannot all be taken at face value. Evidence of lying, false accusation and intimidation often surfaces, and was no doubt more common than at first appears. Further, when we are in a position to compare the information recorded at the preliminary special inquisitions with the information that eventually found its way into the eyre roll, we see a number of discrepancies.[3] Some, but not all, are simply the result of the greater compression of the later account. That the final record in the eyre roll is far from comprehensive is, in any case, often obvious. It would be foolish to conclude, for example, that a particular baron went into a forest alone to poach because no companions are mentioned, though we may well believe that the single peasant alleged to have laid snares at night really was operating alone.

However, our prime interest here is not so much in the offences committed by particular persons as in the nature of peasant deer stealing, and, with this aim in mind, there are many positive indications which inspire confidence in the eyre record. First, the entries describing venison offences are largely free of formulaic language. One aspect of this is that the degree of

[2] The best discussion of forest law remains that of G.J. Turner in his introduction to *Select Pleas of the Forest* (Selden Society, 13, London, 1901). For the frequency of the forest eyre and other aspects, see C.R. Young, 'The Forest Eyre in England during the Thirteenth Century', *American Journal of Legal History*, 18 (1974), pp. 321–31, and, more generally, C.R. Young, *The Royal Forests of Medieval England* (Leicester, 1979).

[3] Many of the limited number of surviving special inquisitions and the eyre rolls based on them are printed in *Select Pleas*, ed. Turner.

detail varies considerably from one eyre to another, and even within eyre rolls; though some entries are, from the historian's point of view, unhelpfully terse, others are very full. Further, when details are recorded, they frequently have a ring of truth. Descriptions of the behaviour of the different types of deer or dogs, for example, are recognisably true to life: poachers set their greyhounds at herds of fallow does and hinds; stags lead running dogs and men on long chases; fawns are discovered in the bracken in June; deer are tempted into traps by deer-browse in the winter, and so on.[4] Also, however varied the incidents described, we find consistent and coherent patterns of behaviour on the part of different categories of poacher, which again inspires confidence. It seems reasonable to assume that the problems are not serious enough or of a type to cast serious doubt on the accuracy of what survives as evidence of the circumstances and nature of peasant hunting.

Another problem is the identification of the peasant poachers whose activities I propose to discuss. Every eyre roll contains the names of many poachers whose status it is probably impossible ever to establish. But there are many poachers whose status can be identified by one of a number of means. Before surnames were normally inherited, they could be informative; Ralph, son of Richard le Potter of Hamstall Ridware, who poached in Cannock Forest in 1275, was almost certainly the son of a village potter. Or occupation or status is noted – as, for example, with many parish clergy. Or the company kept or some other detail is recorded in connection with the offence – the man at work in the forest with an axe, for example, was probably a woodcutter. The penalty imposed may supply relevant evidence, since penalties related, very roughly, to the wealth and status of the offender, and might be waived because of the offender's poverty. Even the nature of the offence may offer some clue, though there is clearly a danger of circular argument here. All in all, we can safely identify a substantial minority of peasant poachers, even though we may shrink from estimating what proportion of the total they constituted.[5] As far as possible, I will confine myself

[4] See, for example, Public Record Office (henceforward PRO), E.32/132, mm. 6, 5d; *The Sherwood Forest Book*, ed. Helen E. Boulton (Thoroton Society Record Series, 23, Nottingham, 1964), p. 118; F.H.M. Parker, 'Some Stories of Deer-Stealers', *Transactions of the Cumberland and Westmorland Archaeological and Antiquarian Society*, n.s., 7 (1907), pp. 7, 10; for fawns and deer-browse, see below.

[5] But see the estimates of the number of poachers hunting 'from need', as opposed to for 'social' reasons, in J. West, 'The Administration and Economy of the Forest of Feckenham during the Early Middle Ages', unpublished Birmingham University PhD thesis (1964), pp. 172–4; West thinks about half the poachers at the 1270 eyre fell into the former category, about two-thirds at the 1280 eyre. For a recent discussion of peasant hunting, not only of deer, based largely on literary evidence, see Richard Almond, 'Medieval Hunting: Ruling Classes and Commonalty', *Medieval History*, 3 (1993), pp. 150–5.

here to those poachers whose peasant status is made clear by one or more of the means indicated above.

Given that my prime interest is in the specifically peasant dimension of deer poaching in the royal forest, I have also largely excluded those men who, though peasants or of peasant origin, were hunting either in the company of men of higher social status or alone but in their capacity as servants. This is both a quantitively and a qualitatively important aspect of peasant life and experience, but it is one which would take us beyond the scope of this study, since the peasants concerned were participating in or adopting the hunting methods of a different social class. The average villager was not in a position to hunt with leashes of greyhounds, for example, though many a servant did so, using his master's hounds, with or without his knowledge or connivance. For similar reasons, I have excluded the many townsmen – also, no doubt, often of peasant origin – who made poaching expeditions into a nearby forest.

In what follows, I will look first at the various ways, both planned and opportunistic, in which peasants poached deer, and then at how they dealt with the problem of getting their booty safely away. Many poachers, of course, failed to manage this, and I will look next at how peasants acted when discovered. Lastly, I will discuss how they disposed of their booty, and make a few observations about the peasant deer stealers themselves.

I

The most characteristic peasant method of hunting deer, as, indeed, of hunting lesser beasts, was the trap or snare. Three words are used in these records for the devices employed by lower-class poachers: *laqueus, trappa* and *ingenium*. The former, the snare, was perhaps the most common. At more or less every forest eyre, local men were accused of taking deer *cum laqueis*, or of being in possession of incriminating snares. In use, snares are described either as 'set' – as when two habitual poachers, Henry Willock and his son, John, took a hind with *laqueis suis positis* in the wood of Mansfield, in Sherwood Forest, in the early fourteenth century – or, less often, as 'stretched' or 'extended' – as when five men repairing the fencing of Guildford Park (Surrey) in 1259 *tetenderunt laqueos* to catch deer coming to browse on the branches felled for new pales.[6] Such snares were probably home-made, of materials which came readily to hand. Five snares 'for taking fawns or hares' in Brigstock Park in 1246 were of horsehair.[7] For larger animals, stronger materials were required: one New Forest poacher used a

---

[6] PRO, E.32/132, m. 8; *Select Pleas*, pp. 55–6 (these snares were later described as *extensos*).
[7] *Select Pleas*, ed. Turner, p. 83

snare of withies in 1249.[8] But the most common material was probably cord or rope. Even the largest deer found in the medieval forest could be taken this way, like the 'great hart' caught in a snare of rope at Langley, in the New Forest, in 1277.[9] The offence was often simply recorded as placing 'cords to catch deer': thus Robert and Thomas Hale, common poachers, 'stretched and fixed' cords in Rockingham Forest in 1346; in Whittlewood Forest, in 1364, Henry at Church of Norton, having taken two does one winter night in Hanley Hay 'with cords', returned to the same spot a fortnight later to place a further seven cords.[10]

Snares of horsehair or withies or cord were relatively inconspicuous when in position in the forest, though there was always the risk that they would be discovered by a zealous forester who knew where to look, not to speak of the risk of the poacher being observed busy at the spot or nearby: this was the fate of Robert Bulewrot, found in the New Forest in 1249 alongside his snare, where blood on the ground bore witness to his recent success.[11] Snares were generally small and light enough to be easily carried and concealed when not in use, an enormous advantage for the poacher. They were, nevertheless, often discovered when foresters searched houses or even sacks which aroused their suspicions: officers of Rockingham Forest struck doubly lucky in 1246 when three suspected poachers, realising they were being following, panicked and fled, abandoning a sack which turned out to contain a snare, a flayed doe and its hide.[12]

In these records, the word 'trap' seems to be reserved for devices which, though they might incorporate a snare, involved some sort of wooden frame. A trap found in a house search by foresters and verderers in Sudborough in Rockingham Forest in 1250, for example, had wooden parts and a cord; it had recently been used, as the cord, which was broken, still bore traces of deer hair.[13] The word engine (*ingenium*) had a less precise meaning. Indeed, it was frequently used as a sort of catch-all term, as when poachers were accused of using 'snares and other engines' or 'traps and other engines' or even 'bows and arrows and other engines'.[14] Occasionally, the nature of the 'engine' is spelled out. A poacher in the Forest of Chute (Hants and Wilts.) in the 1270s, for example, used 'engines called cuppes'.[15] Another trick was

---

[8] *A Calendar of New Forest Documents AD 1244– AD 1334*, ed. D. J. Stagg (Hampshire Record Series, 3, Winchester, 1979), no. 68.

[9] *Ibid.*, no. 234.

[10] PRO, E.32/99, inquisition held June 1346; E.32/305A, inquisition held 1364.

[11] *New Forest Documents*, no. 68.

[12] *Select Pleas*, ed. Turner, pp. 84–5.

[13] *Ibid.*, p. 94.

[14] PRO, E.32/161, m. 13; E.32/72, m. 4; E.32/30, m. 8d.

[15] PRO, E.32/161, m. 10d.

to lay caltrops on the ground, so as to lame any deer that trod on them.[16] The 'engine' which crops up most frequently, over a wide geographical area, consisted of sharpened stakes on which the deer were impaled; Adam Calf of Brigstock was found in a wood in Rockingham Forest around 1270 in possession of 'a certain engine, that is a certain sharpened stake (*pelo acuto*) for catching deer'; William, son of Ralph of la Woodhouse, took a deer in a croft in the Forest of Chute with a stake (*pilum*) one August night in 1272; at the 1334 eyre for Pickering Forest, it was alleged that William of Settrington was 'wont to place sharp spears' (*acutas cathias*) in the forest to catch deer.[17]

Some of these snares and traps were designed to entangle the antlers and head of the animal; cords were hung 'above a ditch' by two men in the New Forest in the 1320s, whilst two brothers – habitual poachers, it was alleged at the 1334 eyre – took a hind in Clipston wood in Sherwood Forest with snares 'placed in such a way as to strangle' the animal.[18] Other snares were intended to trap the feet, such as the 'noose attached to a stake' which caught a young buck in Rockingham Forest in 1253.[19] Two ingenious labourers attacked on both fronts in Duffield Frith (Derb.) in 1321 by placing cart-ropes in an opening in the paling fence of Shottle Park, with halters suspended in the trees overhead.[20] Though he disapproved of their use, Gaston Phoebus of Foix described many of these devices in the greatest of all medieval hunting treatises, written in the late 1380s, and they were carefully drawn by his illustrators;[21] they would feature in accounts of deer poaching for many centuries to come.[22]

A successful poacher had to know not only how to devise traps, snares 'and other engines' but when and where and in what conditions to employ them. The poachers mentioned above who set snares while working in Guildford Park in November knew that deer would be attracted by the leaves of the felled oak branches; similarly, poachers in Rockingham Forest in 1255 'stretched . . . four cords' round a container of water which they knew would

[16] *Pipe Roll 9 John*, pp. 149–50. For the use of caltrops in the seventeenth century, see R.B. Manning, *Hunters and Poachers. A Cultural History of Unlawful Hunting in England 1485–1640* (Oxford, 1993), p. 25.

[17] PRO, E.32/72, m. 7; E.32/161, m. 10; *Honor and Forest of Pickering*, ed. R.B. Turton, 4 vols. (North Riding Rec. Soc., n.s., I–IV, London, 1894–7), II, p. 93. See also *Cal. Pat. Rolls, 1272–81*, p. 270.

[18] *New Forest Documents*, no. 453; PRO, E.32/132, m. 4.

[19] *Select Pleas*, ed. Turner, p. 112.

[20] Quoted in J.C. Cox, *The Royal Forests of England* (London, 1905), p. 58; see also p. 271.

[21] See, in particular, P. Ménard, 'Littérature et iconographie. Les pièges dans les traités de chasse d'Henri de Ferrières et de Gaston Phébus', in Colloque de Nice, *La Chasse au Moyen Age: Actes du Colloque, 1979* (Nice, 1980), pp. 159–88.

[22] See, for example, C. Chevenix Trench, *The Poacher and the Squire. A History of Poaching and Game Preserves in England* (London, 1967), p. 119.

be likely to attract deer.[23] Animals which left the shelter of the forest in search of food in village fields were a frequent target. They were still protected by forest law, but local villagers, hardly surprisingly, set snares and traps to catch them. At Langley, in the New Forest, 'all the men of the vill' were in the habit of setting snares to take beasts 'in their grain and hay', according to the foresters; some twenty men were named as offenders at the 1280 eyre, and the village as a whole amerced the considerable sum of twenty marks.[24] Similarly, one September night in Sherwood Forest in 1319, a notorious poacher, with the aid of some friends and his dog, drove a stag out of a Woodborough village field into nets he had laid to ensnare it.[25] But traps and snares were probably more often set deep in the forest, where peasant poachers used their knowledge of deer movements and habits to capture them. This was the case with the poacher who, sometime around Michaelmas 1275, set snares in Bromley Hay in Cannock Forest to catch a certain buck 'which frequented the spot' (*qui ibidem frequentabatur*).[26]

Snares, traps and engines of the sort described probably did not usually kill deer outright, but rather brought them within the peasant poacher's reach, where they could more easily be finished off. It was by no means uncommon for deer to contrive to break free of traps and snares, but even if a beast managed to get away, it was likely to be wounded or at the least encumbered and so less able to escape pursuing men or dogs. This was what happened to the young buck which got its feet caught in a noose attached to a stake in Rockingham Forest in 1255; it got away, but dragged the stake with it, so that it eventually got entangled between two trees, when it was caught.[27]

The ultimate silent and inconspicuous weapon was the sling, and it was a weapon some peasants were able to use with devastating effect. Even stags, that is the adult male red deer, could be killed with stones from a sling: this was the fate of a stag in Sherwood Forest in September 1280, killed by a poacher with a well-aimed shot.[28] On this occasion, the poacher got away with the venison, but another Sherwood villager, John Gate, the Ollerton village hayward, was less successful: he broke the leg of a hind with a stone from his sling, one day in 1325, but the deer escaped him, though only to die later of its wound.[29]

---

[23] *Select Pleas*, ed. Turner, p. 113.
[24] *New Forest Documents*, no. 234.
[25] PRO, E.32/132, m. 4d.
[26] PRO, E.32/188, m. 5d.
[27] *Select Pleas*, ed Turner, p. 112.
[28] PRO, E.32/127, m. 4.
[29] PRO, E.32/132, m. 5; see also *Honor and Forest of Pickering*, ed. Turton, II pp. 27–8.

Peasants also used nets to trap deer, as we have seen, but this was a method by no means exclusive to them. A hunting treatise like Edward duke of York's *Master of Game* might condemn the use of nets, but in practice they were commonly employed by deer hunters at all social levels, whether hunting professionally or for sport, legally or illegally; in the thirteenth and fourteenth centuries, royal huntsmen, knights and barons all took deer by driving them into nets, just as the huntsman in Aelfric's Colloquy had done in the eleventh century.[30] For peasant poachers, on the other hand, it was a method which had its problems. On the one hand, nets designed to catch deer were relatively bulky and conspicuous to transport or lay; on the other, they were tedious and difficult to make, or, alternatively, relatively expensive to buy.[31] This was a particular disadvantage given the risk that they might be lost to forest officers; the nets confiscated from one notorious peasant poacher in Sherwood Forest in 1319, for example, were valued at 3s., a large enough sum to represent a serious blow to a poor man.[32]

Peasant poachers also used bows and arrows to shoot deer: one group active in the Forest of Dean in the 1260s were described as 'common malefactors with bows and arrows, snares and other engines'; another band in the same forest in the 1270s used 'bows and arrows and other engines'.[33] Part of a bloody and broken arrow was found in a house in Rockingham in 1246; there were five arrows as well as some venison in a chest searched in Inglewood Forest in the 1270s.[34] But bows and arrows seem not to have been particularly favoured by peasant poachers, and were, in any case, also commonly used by hunters from higher up the social scale. For peasants, a bow and arrows may have been too conspicuous to carry in the forest. Also, even with a well-aimed arrow from a longbow, it was much easier to wound a deer than kill it outright, and there was a strong likelihood of a shot deer managing to escape, even if it was doomed later to die as a direct or indirect consequence of its wound. It took Thomas Ketel of Lyndby, who had shot a buck in Sherwood Forest one Thursday in September 1324, three days to find it, so that it was not until the following Sunday, that, with the aid of

[30] See the discussion in Cummins, *The Hound and the Hawk*, pp. 234–6. For the widespread use of nets, see *Cal. Close Rolls, 1251–3*, pp. 27, 453; *Cal. Pat. Rolls, 1272–81*, p. 296; *VCH Yorks.*, I, pp. 510–11; PRO, E.32/30, mm. 10, 14d; Jean R. Birrell, 'Who Poached the King's Deer? A Study in Thirteenth-Century Crime', *Midland History*, 7 (1982), p. 18; *Honor and Forest of Pickering*, ed. Turton, IV, pp. 13–20; *Aelfric's Colloquy*, ed. G.N. Garmonsway (London, 1939), pp. 23–4. For the practice in the early modern period, see Manning, *Hunters and Poachers*, p. 25.

[31] See, for example, D. Hay, 'Poaching and the Game Laws on Cannock Chase', in D. Hay, P. Linebaugh, J.G. Rule, E.P. Thompson and C. Winslow (eds.), *Albion's Fatal Tree. Crime and Society in Eighteenth-Century England* (London, 1975), p. 194.

[32] PRO, E.32/132, m. 4d.

[33] PRO, E.32/27, m. 4d; E.32/30, m. 8d.

[34] *Select Pleas*, ed. Turner, p. 85; Parker, 'Some Stories of Deer-Stealers', pp. 28–9.

Adam Tynker, a fellow-villager, he was at last able to carry it back home.[35] Not all poachers were so persistent or so lucky, and many a deer shot by poachers, peasant or other, was never found, at least by whoever had shot it. This is a point to which I will return.

With all these methods, a good dog was an invaluable aid. The solitary poacher 'with a snare and a dog' was a familar figure in every forest.[36] Knightly and baronial poachers hunted mostly with greyhounds (*leporarii*) – dogs which coursed the deer, hunting by sight – or with 'running dogs' (*canes currentes*) – which hunted by scent[37] – but the typical peasant poacher relied on a single dog. For him, if a chase was necessary, the shorter and more silent the better; the last thing he wanted was for dogs to bark and large numbers of deer to be stampeded, attracting undesirable attention. The word used for the peasant poacher's dog was usually the unspecific *canis*, though dogs were often identified by colour or even by size. Peasant dogs came in all colours: a peasant who shot a doe in Sherwood Forest in 1317 took it 'with a brown dog'; two poachers in the same forest in March 1333 used a white dog; whilst two brothers from Blakeney were caught in the Forest of Dean in 1278 'with a black dog'.[38] Three peasant poachers from Brockenhurst and Battramsley caught in the New Forest in 1278 had simply 'a small dog'.[39] But peasant poachers also sometimes favoured the fierce and sturdy mastiff, unworried by its unrefined appearance; this was the dog used, for example, by a gang of peasant poachers to take a doe in Rockingham in the 1280s.[40] Peasants also, though perhaps less often, used the bercelet, a hound which could track down a wounded deer: it was with a bercelet that two Bloxwich brothers took a buck they had shot in Cannock Forest in the 1270s, whilst a group of poachers in Sherwood Forest in 1329 had with them a fawn bercelet.[41] Much rarer was the beagle used to take a buck by a group of what sound very like peasant poachers in Pickering Forest in 1311.[42]

Interestingly, though lower-class methods of hunting deer might be scorned, implicit recognition of peasant skills and knowledge was made when they were employed as guides (*ductores*) by hunting parties from higher up the social scale who were less familiar with the terrain and the local deer population. This was one of many ways in which enterprising peasants could cash in on the poaching activities of others within the royal forest. A typical

---

[35] PRO, E.32/132, m. 5.
[36] PRO, E.32/127, m. 2.
[37] For hounds, see Cummins, *The Hound and the Hawk, passim*.
[38] PRO, E.32/132, mm. 4, 7; E.32/30, m. 8.
[39] *New Forest Documents*, no. 242.
[40] PRO, E.32/76, m. 13. For the 'visually unsuitable' mastiff, see Cummins, *The Hound and the Hawk*, p. 15.
[41] PRO, E.32/188, m. 7d; E.32/132, m. 6.
[42] *Honor and Forest of Pickering*, ed. Turton, II, pp. 101–2.

guide was Hugh of Worhale of Woodborough, a regular poacher, who operated both during the day and under cover of night in the years preceding the 1334 Sherwood Forest eyre. He used a variety of methods, including nets, and was often accompanied by his dog. He sometimes poached alone, but often also joined larger, heterogeneous gangs. His skills never made him rich – he was too poor to pay an amercement at the eyre – but they were enough to make him frequently in demand as a guide to other poaching parties.[43] Such services might be well-rewarded; another Sherwood Forest *ductor* early in the fourteenth century, Richard of Pillays, received two strikes of oats and 18d. on one occasion, a mantle of frieze and a cartload of hay on another, from parties to whom he sold his services.[44]

II

Alongside the regular peasant poachers, there existed a rather different category, the opportunists, themselves a disparate group. There were many peasants who worked in or near forests where deer were regularly to be seen. They must often have eyed them longingly, as well as gaining a degree of familiarity with their movements; they were equally familiar with the movements of the many hunters at large within the forest, legitimate or illegitimate. Those archetypal forest workers, woodcutters and charcoal burners, are prominent amongst the men who exploited their legitimate presence in the forest to seize any opportunity that offered to lay their hands on some venison: William the charcoal burner of Geddington appropriated a buck he found dead in Rockingham Forest in 1250; the sound of woodcutting by night was alone enough to arouse the suspicions of foresters in Brigstock Park at about the same date.[45] Men working in or traversing the forest were often already wielding potentially lethal tools, which they were quick to use on deer if and when the opportunity arose: Walter Musard of Lyndhurst killed a buck in the New Forest in the 1270s 'with an axe he was carrying'; a shepherd in Pamber Forest in 1294 finished a deer off with his staff; a man carting in Sherwood Forest in 1329, coming upon a young stag on the ground, promptly struck and killed it with his iron fork.[46]

Dead or dying deer were frequently to be found in the forest. Deer died of natural causes or of hunger or disease or the assaults of predators, and their flesh was not scorned by meat-hungry peasants who discovered them.

[43] PRO, E.32/132, mm. 4d, 5.
[44] PRO, E.32/132, m. 4d.
[45] *Select Pleas*, ed. Turner, pp. 33, 94–5.
[46] *New Forest Documents*, no. 245; PRO, E.32/161, m. 8d; E.32/132, m. 6. See also *Honor and Forest of Pickering*, ed. Turton, II p. 77; *Select Pleas*, ed. Turner, p. 11.

Two men who came upon a doe in the process of being 'partly eaten at the front and the back' by hounds in Sherwood Forest in 1325 rescued what they could for their own consumption.[47] In a few forésts at this period, deer were still at risk from wolves, who might abandon their prey half-eaten or, more likely, retreat in the face of a determined approach by a man: Geoffrey, son of Bernard, who found a beast killed (*jugulatam*) by wolves in the Forest of Dean in the 1250s, managed to get away with two shoulders;[48] some thirty years later, poor Dean villagers were still stealing whatever they could rescue of carcasses of deer killed by wolves.[49]

Even better from the point of view of local villagers, aristocratic hunters and poachers, who could afford to be profligate in their behaviour, frequently shot deer with their arrows, but failed to track them down if they ran off. The deer often later died of their wounds. How many carcasses simply rotted undiscovered or were consumed by pigs or vermin, we can never know, but many were discovered and filched by peasants who came upon them by chance.[50] In fact, so frequent are such incidents that one begins to suspect that forest peasants actively sought them out. The sound of hounds barking alerted two men in the Forest of Dean to the presence of a hunting expedition in 1265; they followed the noise and found a dead doe, which they promptly appropriated.[51] A beast left dead by a hunting party which included the young John of Brabant in Rockingham Forest in 1285, for example, was picked up by a Cottingham man, Hugh of Paty, who concealed it under a cartload of hawthorn to get it safely home.[52] Sometimes, peasants were able to snatch deer from in front of their pursuers, even royal huntsmen, during the course of a hunt: two brothers got away with a stag in this way in 1279 in the Forest of Bagshot.[53] In Alice Holt and Woolmer, in 1276, a man was sharp enough to take advantage of the fact that a party of hunters who had started a stag outside the royal forest dared not pursue it inside; he managed to take the stag where it was being held at bay by six greyhounds the original hunting party had failed to call off.[54] A deer which had once been wounded by hunters made a relatively easy target: a hind shot by poachers in Kinver

---

[47] PRO, E.32/132, m. 5. For prohibitions in Penitentials on eating the 'impure' flesh of animals half-eaten by domesticated or wild beasts, see P. Bonnassie, 'Consommation d'aliments immondes et cannibalisme de survie dans l'occident du Haut Moyen Age', *Annales ESC*, 5 (Sept.–Oct., 1989), pp. 1035–56, especially pp. 1038, 1042. I am grateful to Maria Moisa for drawing my attention to this discussion.

[48] PRO, E.32/28, m. 3d.

[49] PRO, E.32/30, mm. 10d, 7, 13.

[50] PRO, E.32/184, m. 6; *New Forest Documents*, nos. 452, 250. See also *Select Pleas*, ed. Turner, pp. 6–7, 62; E. 32/76, m. 9.

[51] PRO, E. 32/29, m. 4d.

[52] PRO, E. 32/76, m. 11d. See also E. 32/184, m. 2d.

[53] PRO, E. 32/161, m. 12d.

[54] *Ibid.*, m. 9. See also E. 32/132, m. 7.

Forest in 1285 escaped them only to fall into the hands of a gang of eight men from two neighbouring villages, who set to and killed it, before sharing the venison between them.[55]

Deer that strayed out of the forest covert, as we have seen, were another tempting and relatively easy target. The protection still afforded by forest law must have been particularly resented when deer fed on village fields, orchards or gardens. In these circumstances, men and women alike were ready to seize and kill an animal which came within their reach, like the husband and wife from Sowerby who finished off a hart in their garden within Inglewood Forest in 1280.[56] It was corn fields in August which tempted the deer at Langley, in the New Forest, in the incident described above, but it was probably more often in winter, when fodder in the forest was in short supply, that deer strayed out into danger. It was in February 1287 that a group of five men and women took a young deer that had found its way into the village of Carlton from Rockingham Forest, and it was in March 1245 that a buck was taken in the field of Wennington (Hunts.).[57] Such hunting might be seen as, strictly speaking, primarily defensive, but one suspects that incidents of this type might have been much enjoyed, both during and after the event, by all who participated, attracting considerable local attention. One Sunday in June 1276, for example, in the Forest of Buckholt, four men started a buck which had strayed into a village field; they chased it to another village, where they managed to kill it in a garden; by this time, some dozen others had arrived on the scene; they helped to drag the carcass into a bakehouse belonging to the owner of the garden, where it was shared out between them.[58]

In a quite different type of opportunistic 'hunting', peasants searched out the newly born fawns left lying concealed in the bracken when their mothers went elsewhere to graze during the fence month. These young animals could be picked up fairly easily by someone who knew where to look, and if there was not much meat on the carcass, at least the skins could be used or sold. This practice, the very antithesis of the aristocratic hunt as a display of skills and bravery, in which the prey was required to show some resistance, was common. In one such wholly typical incident, a poor man from Aure killed a fawn in the Forest of Dean at the beginning of July 1278 and carried it off to sell in Newnham concealed under a load of firewood; a Sherwood Forest villager who, one June in the 1270s, had taken two fawns and put them temporarily in an enclosure (*caula*), had a nasty shock on his return: the

---

[55] PRO, E. 32/188, m. 4.
[56] Parker, 'Some Stories of Deer-Stealers', p. 14.
[57] PRO, E. 32/76, m. 13; *Select Pleas*, ed. Turner, p. 18.
[58] PRO, E. 32/161, m. 11d.

fawns had been stolen. Yet another Sherwood villager, the young son of a shepherd of Skegby, who was discovered in June 1314 carrying a fawn 'in the bracken', presumably, that is, very close to where he had found it, was made to put it back; whether, the eyre roll laconically adds, he later went back to get it was not known.[59]

III

Peasant slings, snares, traps and other engines were effective in taking deer one at a time or in very small numbers, which was all most peasant poachers wanted or could cope with. For a poor man, one deer was riches enough, whether the carcass was destined to be sold off or eaten locally, a point to which we will return; the range of joints specified in the eyre rolls – shoulder, haunch, neck, rib, collar, side, etc. – is a reminder of just how much meat a carcass represented for a poor man.[60] In any case, as for any poacher, getting the carcass safely away was a difficult and dangerous job, where the risks of discovery were great. The task was all the harder for a solitary poacher or tiny group. A poacher in Cannock Forest, who killed a deer, but not before it had taken refuge in the river Tame, had to pay a passer-by 1d. to help him to drag it out.[61] At a pinch, a strong man could carry a deer on his shoulders, and many a poacher was caught attempting to get his booty out of the forest unaided in this way: this was the fate of Roger Prigge of Lyndhurst, who had found a deer dead in the New Forest in the 1270s, and was discovered carrying it away in a sack.[62] A horse or a horse and cart, as we have seen, made things easier: one man who, with some associates, had shot and killed a stag in the Forest of Woolmer in 1273, hastily stowed the whole carcass into a covered cart, alongside a certain Amya, already in occupation, and drove off into Sussex and what he hoped was safety; a shepherd and a carter from Hucknall Torkard (Notts.) who came on a deer being attacked by greyhounds in Sherwood Forest one December day in 1333 put the hounds to flight, loaded the venison on to the cart and returned home with their booty.[63] One poacher in the Forest of Dean had to borrow a horse from another to carry a load of venison away.[64] Bracken and firewood were useful camouflage, and we may guess that many a deer was successfully

---

[59] PRO, E. 32/30, m. 10; E. 32/132, mm. 4, 7d. See also *Sherwood Forest Book*, pp. 114, 132.
[60] PRO, E. 32/30, m. 15 (a collar and two shoulders); *New Forest Documents*, nos. 226 (a shoulder and a haunch), 459 (a side); *Select Pleas*, ed. Turner, pp. 8, 37–8 (a rib, a shoulder and two necks).
[61] E. 32/187, m. 6.
[62] *New Forest Documents*, no. 250. See also PRO, E. 32/72, m. 4d.
[63] PRO, E. 32/161, m. 9; E. 32/132, m. 7.
[64] PRO, E. 32/30, m. 8.

smuggled out of the forest under such a load for every one that was discovered.

One or two limbs were clearly easier and less conspicuous to carry than a whole deer, and, especially when there was more than one poacher, carcasses were often skinned and divided up on the spot. Men were frequently found attempting to smuggle parts of a carcass out of the forest, like the poor wretch found in Dean in the 1270s 'with one limb'.[65] But skinning a carcass was a time-consuming and messy job which left marks which were difficult wholly to conceal; it must have been bad for the nerves of the participants, as it was so often the moment when poachers were discovered.[66] Once the carcass was broken up, unwanted parts could be disposed of on the spot or nearby. But, however carefully they had been hidden or buried, there was still a danger that they would be found, like the head and entrails inadequately buried in Weybridge Park in 1248, or the four deer feet discovered by a forester in some charcoal workings in the Forest of Dean in the 1260s.[67]

Even when the poacher got all or the best parts of the carcass safely away, his problems were far from over. Foresters could search the houses of suspects in the presence of verderers, and this was common practice. Venison, as well as traps and snares or other incriminating material, was frequently discovered: meat was found in a chest in the house of one suspect in Inglewood Forest in the 1270s; the head, neck, two shoulders and skin of a doe were found in a house in Minstead, in the New Forest, in 1314.[68] Sometimes, it was the offal alone that remained, as in a house at Boldre in the New Forest, the venison itself having already been disposed off.[69] A frequent find was the skin. It was clearly dangerous to hang on to the hide of a poached beast, but, on the other hand, it was too valuable to throw away: the skin of a 'putrid' hind found in Sherwood Forest in 1334 was valued at 2s.[70] The hides of poached deer were often sold: one Pickering man who sold the skin of a stag he had snared in York in 1311 used the proceeds to buy some fur to trim his overcoat.[71] But a sale took time to arrange and was in itself a risky business, another frequent occasion for discovery.

One way of reducing the risks of being caught was to operate under cover of night. This was when many peasant poachers set or visited their traps

[65] PRO, E. 32/30, m. 13d; see also m. 5.
[66] PRO, E. 32/29, m. 4d; Parker, 'Some Stories of Deer-Stealers', pp. 3–4.
[67] *Select Pleas*, ed. Turner, pp. 23, 74 (see also pp. 4, 30–1, 86); PRO, E. 32/29, m. 4d.
[68] Parker, 'Some Stories of Deer-Stealers', pp. 28–9 (see also *ibid.*, p. 8; PRO, E. 32/72, m. 7); *New Forest Documents*, no. 448 (see also no. 447). For other searches, see PRO, E. 32/72, m. 6; *Select Pleas* ed. Turner, pp. 304, 9.
[69] *New Forest Documents*, no. 232. See also PRO, E. 32/72, m. 6d.
[70] PRO, E. 32/132, m. 5.
[71] *Honor and Forest of Pickering*, ed. Turton, II, p. 107. See also PRO, E. 32/29, m. 4d.

and snares; it was 'at night', for example, that Simon Drake of Brigstock and his son were taken with a trap in Brigstock Park in January 1274.[72] Even when deer were taken during the day, the poachers often waited until nightfall to carry their booty out of the forest; two men who had taken a buck in the Forest of Alice Holt and Woolmer one August day in 1276, for example, hid the venison till nightfall, when they carried it back home.[73] In their appreciation of the possibilities of a moonlit night, however, peasants were not alone. Some upper-class hunters, too, took advantage of a dark night to poach, or deigned to smuggle their booty out of the forest at night. And, unfortunately for the poachers, these possibilities were appreciated equally by foresters; over and over again, it was at night, either in the forest or attempting to leave it, that poachers were discovered.[74]

IV

Peasant poachers were at all stages heavily influenced by the need to escape detection. For them, this could have serious, even disastrous, consequences. The fate of offenders was very variable, and this is not the place to discuss it at length. Suffice it to say that lower-class poachers, when arrested, were frequently taken off to some local prison, from which they had first to negotiate their release. At the eyre, which admittedly might be many years later, they, their pledges and even fellow-villagers, risked what, for them, were heavy amercements. It is true that many offenders were pardoned because of their poverty; it is equally true that many fled and suffered outlawry rather than submit to the processes of forest law.[75] It is also very clear that they went to considerable lengths to avoid detection or capture.

At all times, day or night, peasant poachers were on the lookout for forest officers, either patrolling the forest or lying in wait for their return home.[76] If discovered and accosted, their most frequent reaction was to hide or to flee, if necessary abandoning their booty in their haste: a man who had shot and taken a buck in Rockingham Forest in December 1278 and was carrying it home in the middle of the night dropped it and fled as soon as he realised that he had been seen by a forester; two men found carrying a buck in a wood in Inglewood Forest at about the same date behaved in exactly the

---

[72] PRO, E. 32/76, m. 9.

[73] PRO, E. 32/161, m. 9.

[74] Parker, 'Some Stories of Deer-Stealers', p. 16; PRO, E. 32/30, m. 13 (see also m. 5); E. 32/132, m. 6d.

[75] Jean R. Birrell, 'Forest Law and the Peasantry in the Later Thirteenth Century', in P. Coss and S. Lloyd (eds.) *Thirteenth Century England*, II, (Woodbridge, 1988), pp. 154–8.

[76] Barbara Hanawalt makes the point that the forest laws created the first officers with a regular patrolling function and 'beat'; 'Men's Games, King's Deer; Poaching in Medieval England', *Journal of Renaissance Studies*, 18 (1988), p. 176.

same way; so did three men seen carrying a sack in Sudborough in 1246, and so, too, did many others.[77] The venison might be picked up by the foresters, or might be lost for good. Two brothers who hid when they saw a woodward in Cannock Forest in 1285 were said to have been too frightened to return to recover their deer, which was eventually consumed by pigs.[78] So great was 'the climate of fear' generated by the processes of forest law that even innocent bystanders fled or hid rather than be discovered in suspicious circumstances. This was a strategy that was not always successful; the unfortunate Henry son of Bence, found hiding under a bush near a doe with its throat cut in Nassington Wood, Rockingham Forest, in 1209, 'laid long in prison' before being released, his innocence eventually accepted.[79]

Flight was not, however, the only option for a poacher who realised that he had been seen. A common alternative was to offer a bribe, and the need to bribe discoverers, not only foresters but interested passers-by, who seem routinely to have expected their cut, was an occupational hazard of poaching. The bribe was sometimes of cash, but it perhaps more often took the convenient – and obviously highly acceptable – form of a share in the venison: two men who came upon a poacher in the act of skinning a deer in Rockingham Forest in 1275 each went away with a share; two unfortunate poachers discovered skinning a hind they had killed in Inglewood Forest had to share it with no fewer than three armed men who saw them.[80] Foresters represented a greater threat, though they might still be bribed: a parker who found two poachers skinning a hind in Pickering Forest in October 1331 'took a bribe to allow them to carry it away';[81] a forester who found two peasant poachers with a dead roe deer in Alrewas Hay, Cannock Forest, in the 1250s, took not only the venison but the not inconsiderable sum of 3s.[82]

But, in the end, many peasant poachers had to surrender to the foresters who found them, and this they seem to have done without a struggle, or rather without the sort of struggle which gets into the record because it led to the injury or even death of one of the parties concerned. Not for the peasantry the bravado and aggression typical of many poachers from higher up the social scale, who were emboldened not only by the company of their fellows and the weapons they habitually carried but by a quite different

[77] PRO, E. 32/76, m. 10; Parker, 'Some Stories of Deer-Stealers', p. 11 (see also p. 14); *Select Pleas*, ed. Turner, p. 84 (see also pp. 57, 36).
[78] PRO, E. 32/188, m. 7d.
[79] This case (from *Select Pleas*, ed. Turner, p. 3) is quoted by C.R. Young (*Royal Forests*, p. 107), from whom I have taken the phrase 'climate of fear'. For other similar cases, see Parker, 'Some Stories of Deer-Stealers', pp. 28–9.
[80] PRO, E. 32/76, m. 9; Parker, 'Some Stories of Deer-Stealers', p. 17. See also PRO, E. 32/187, m. 6.
[81] *Honor and Forest of Pickering*, ed. Turton, II, p. 97.
[82] PRO, E. 32/187, m. 5.

ethos.[83] Nor do peasants in these circumstances seem to have gone in for the demonstrative gestures which were a feature of the poaching of some non-peasant gangs, which is not to say that peasants lacked their own means of showing hostility to forest law.[84]

V

In their motives for poaching, and in the way they disposed of their booty, peasant poachers were both like and unlike their social superiors. The prime aim of the peasant poacher, clearly, was to lay hands on some precious venison. They remained, in a sense, subsistence hunters, whose over-riding motive was the desire for venison and, to a lesser degree, deer skins, whether to consume or to sell. In a wholly unremarkable incident, which must have been replicated in every forest on a regular basis, two men snared a deer in the Forest of Dean, took it back to the house of the father of one of them, and there it was eaten.[85] Venison must always have been a welcome addition to a poor man's table, but, like their social superiors, peasants had a sense of occasion, and felt that fresh venison added lustre to their festive meals. Often, a deer was hunted with a specific celebratory meal in mind: sometime prior to 1255, the two sons of a certain Sweyn, together with a local wood-ward, took a beast in Rockingham Forest and carried it to the house of Walter Bate of Pilton, where it was eaten at Walter's wedding; similarly, the hind killed by Hugh Tredgold and Adam, son of Agnes of Langrigg, in Inglewood in 1268, was carried back to Adam's house and eaten at his wedding feast.[86] Christmas was another occasion for feasting at all levels of society, and it is tempting to see an incident which occurred in the Forest of Dean on Christmas Eve, 1273, in this context: the local foresters caught two men – brothers – in the act of carrying, in the direction of Gloucester, under cover of night, half a doe they had bought from a Littledean man who had earlier snared it.[87]

However, there was a lot of meat on a carcass, and there were obvious dangers in having venison lying around too long; in any case, peasants, like their social superiors, seem to have enjoyed being in a position to make gifts. Whatever the reasons, once a carcass had successfully been smuggled home,

---

[83] For some typical arrests, without recorded struggle, see *New Forest Documents*, nos. 457, 458, 459. For violent encounters between foresters and non-peasant poachers, see Young, *Royal Forests*, p. 81; Hanawalt, 'Men's Games', pp. 188–91; Birrell, 'Who Poached the King's Deer?', pp. 15–16.

[84] For example, selective non-cooperation with special inquisitions (as well, of course, as by poaching).

[85] PRO, E. 32/30, m. 15.

[86] *Select Pleas*, ed. Turner, pp. 36, 112; Parker, 'Some Stories of Deer-Stealers', p. 10.

[87] PRO, E. 32/30, m. 13. See also E. 32/72, m. 4.

it was often shared out: the charcoal burner from Geddington who found a
dead buck in Rockingham Forest in 1250 sent parts of it to two fellow-
villagers as soon as he had got it safely home (a gift they had cause to rue,
as all three ended up in prison); a hind which strayed into a croft in Scalby
(Yorks.) in 1311 was killed by three men who included the croft's owner;
next, it was carried to the house of the absent vicar, where one of them was
employed, and where it was skinned; the vicar's maidservant then seems to
have taken over; she took some for herself, gave some to a friend, a laundress
of nearby Newby, and sent the rest out to the vicar's ploughmen for their
lunch.[88] Often, perhaps especially when a straying deer had been taken close
to a settlement, no doubt with some publicity, venison was more widely
distributed; when, in the autumn of 1275, two men from Sneinton, in Sherwood Forest, found a doe dead in one of the village fields, they seized it
and used it to make gifts 'throughout the vill' (*exheinias per villam*).[89] It is
difficult not to detect pleasure here in the ability to distribute largess, even
if a desire to involve and implicate their fellow-villagers may also have entered
into their calculations.

In one striking way, however, peasants behaved differently when it came
to disposing of poached venison. They were quite immune to the unwritten
taboo on selling venison which inhibited the gentry and aristocracy, though
it must be said that some regular poachers from higher up the social scale
disposed of venison in ways which came pretty close to selling it. For a truly
poor man, the income from the sale of a carcass might be more precious
than the meat itself and, in any case, no one could live off a diet of venison
alone. References to the sale of poached venison by peasants are so frequent
as to suggest that this was the motive for much peasant poaching. Venison
was sometimes disposed of to receivers, who were a common feature of
forest villages; this 'passive crime', interestingly, was one in which women
participated; Gillian, daughter of Roger le Dunte, of Minstead, was described
in 1315 as receiver of John Salandryn of Otterford 'and others', whilst it was
a Rose Glade of Arnold who had supplied a man caught in possession of
venison in Sherwood Forest in 1272.[90]

Some poached venison was sold direct to local residents, often a cleric,
known to be ready to pay for it with, we may presume, no questions asked.[91]
Some was taken to a nearby town large enough to provide a market and a

[88] *Select Pleas*, ed. Turner, p. 33; *Honor and Forest of Pickering*, ed. Turton, II, pp. 106–7.
[89] *Sherwood Forest Book*, p. 133.
[90] *New Forest Documents*, no. 451; *Sherwood Forest Book*, p. 113. For women receivers, see
   B.A. Hanawalt, *Crime and Conflict in English Communities 1300–48* (London, 1979), p.
   264.
[91] For a series of clerics ready to purchase poached venison, see PRO, E. 32/76, mm, 9–13
   (1286 eyre for Rockingham Forest).

welcome degree of anonymity. Venison from Rockingham Forest was sold in Northampton and Stamford, from the New Forest in Southampton and Winchester and from Sherwood Forest in Nottingham, to quote but a few examples of this widespread practice.[92] By its very nature, the scale of such a clandestine trade is difficult to assess; no doubt, in any case, it varied from place to place and over time. It seems to have been a persistent, if perhaps small-scale, phenomenon in the case of the New Forest, where individuals were regularly amerced for disposing of small quantities in the vicinity: half a young hind was sold for 2s. 6d. in Southampton on one occasion, a buck was sold to the rector of Minstead for 3s. 6d. on another, and so on.[93] In the case of the Forest of Dean, an exceptionally large forest, well stocked with deer and with relatively easy access to such towns as Bristol and Monmouth, there was a regular and systematic export of venison, along with other woodland produce, from a string of little ports along the estuary of the river Severn, on a scale that really takes it beyond the scope of this article.[94]

VI

So there is ample evidence of a rich tradition of peasant deer poaching in forest villages. The poachers whose exploits have been described were clearly a disparate group about whom it is difficult to generalise. At one end of the scale were the opportunists who kept their eyes and ears open for any chance to obtain some venison – beasts wounded by other hunters, strays, victims of dogs or wolves – both scavenging and taking advantage of the profligacy of the aristocratic hunt. The habit of such opportunistic 'poaching' was probably widespread among forest villagers. As we have seen, it involved groups of men and women, acting, as it were, spontaneously, close to their holdings or village, as well as the many men who habitually worked in or crossed the forest, among whom it was perhaps almost second nature, at least for the hardier or rasher among them, to keep a watch for any venison which might come their way.

At the other end of the scale were the men for whom poaching was probably a way of life. The latter were a significant, if elusive, group. It would be interesting to know to what extent men who braved forest law to poach deer also hunted – or poached – lesser beasts in a way which our

<hr>

[92] PRO, E. 32/249, m. 3; E. 32/68; *New Forest Documents*, nos. 447, 236, 235, 237; *Sherwood Forest Book*, p. 113.
[93] *New Forest Documents*, no. 447.
[94] PRO, E. 32/29, mm. 4d–6; E. 32/30, mm. 5d–6. See also, Birrell, 'Who Poached the King's Deer?', p. 20.

records do not reveal. It seems highly likely that they did, and that the activities revealed by the forest eyre were only a small part of a wider picture. However that may be, specific individuals occur and recur in the court records over several years, and many of them are, in any case, described as 'habitual offenders'. Fathers passed on their skills to their sons, and, as many of the examples quoted above have shown, fathers, sons and brothers often hunted together. Three brothers poached together in the Forest of Chute in the 1270s and were received by their father, from whom they had no doubt learned their trade; three men poaching together in Kinver Forest (Staffs.) in 1250 all shared the same surname.[95] Close male relatives started with the advantage of knowing each other well, and perhaps also felt better able to trust each other in what was, after all, a dangerous enterprise, which could have disastrous results for all involved. Occasionally, we see the same surname recur over decades, suggesting the existence of little poaching dynasties. The Welps of Brigstock, for example, appear at three successive eyres for the Forest of Rockingham: a Peter played a dubious role in an incident in 1253, presented at the 1255 eyre;[96] two Welps appear at the 1272 eyre; Robert was found in Brigstock Park with a trap in February 1264 and Peter was one of a large and regular poaching gang operating in the years before the eyre;[97] lastly, a Peter, son of Peter, was presented at the 1286 eyre for poaching with associates from Brigstock and other local villages in 1274.[98]

Small gangs of peasant poachers, comprising men from one or more neighbouring forest villages, also existed,[99] though it must be admitted that it is often difficult to identify or place socially all the members of a given group; many such gangs seem to have gravitated round leaders from above the peasantry, and therefore escape the strict limits of this study. However, they, like the many humble servants who poached on their own or in the company of their masters, are a phenomenon worthy of further study. It was more characteristic of truly peasant poachers to operate alone or with a single companion, not forgetting, of course, the invaluable dog. This is in marked contrast with men from higher up the social scale, who preferred to hunt in company – in the case of barons with their friends, households and numerous hangers-on, in the case of lesser men with shifting groups of confederates; for them, however highly they valued the end-product of venison, much of the point, not to say pleasure, of the activity lay in the sport enjoyed in the company of friends.

[95] PRO, E. 32/101, m. 10d; E. 32/187, m. 7. For pairs of brothers, see *ibid.*, m. 6; E. 32/72, mm. 6d, 7. For some fathers poaching with sons, see E. 32/76, m. 9; E. 32/132, m. 8.
[96] *Select Pleas*, ed. Turner, p. 106.
[97] PRO, E. 32/72, mm. 4d, 5.
[98] PRO, E. 32/76, m. 9d.
[99] Birrell, 'Who Poached the King's Deer?', p. 21.

Whether hunting alone or in company, peasant poachers tended to come from the immediate vicinity of the scene of their exploits, in which they again differed from their social superiors. Certainly, knightly and baronial poachers hunted in the forests which were nearest to their home or homes, but they were men who were always on the move and, to a degree, the whole country was their chosen hunting ground. They visited friends in good hunting country, and characteristically enlivened their frequent journeys through a forest by stopping off to hunt, with or without permission. This was not part of the experience of the much more territorially bound peasant poacher, and it is rare to find one straying far from home.

The scale of peasant poaching is something we can only guess at, given that many poachers identified at forest eyres were alleged to be habitual offenders, and given that we have no way of knowing how many offenders escaped detection altogether. But peasant poachers appear in every forest eyre, and it seems likely that they were present in most, perhaps all, forest villages. How they were regarded by their fellow-villagers, indeed what tensions were created in forest villages by the various aspects of forest law, are difficult questions, on which our records throw a little light, but which there is not space to discuss here. Foresters made sweeping assertions, often complaining that specific villages were nests of poachers; the example of Langley, in the New Forest, where 'all the men of the vill' snared deer, has already been quoted; at the 1286 eyre for Cannock Forest, it was alleged that Hulle of Bromley was a frequent offender 'along with others from the same place'.[100] Though there is obviously an element of exaggeration here, such claims would appear to reveal a feeling of exasperation on the part of the foresters in the face of what they saw as a serious problem. And, whilst an analysis of the eyre rolls for any forest suggests that certain villages – such as Colwick, Carlton and, above all, Woodborough, in Sherwood Forest, and Brigstock in Rockingham Forest – produced more than their fair share of poachers,[101] few forest villages seem never to have produced any.

We are not well informed about how peasant poachers saw themselves or how they felt about their activities. We have no peasant equivalent of the literature extolling the joys of the chase among the upper classes,[102] and, in any case, peasant methods were designed to be effective and discreet, rather than protracted and 'sporting'. One can only guess the extent to which peasants, too, whatever their motives and whatever the danger incurred, took pride and pleasure in their skills.

---

[100] PRO, E. 32/188, m. 6.
[101] For Colwick, Carlton and Woodborough, see PRO, E. 32/132, mm. 4–8; for Brigstock, see E. 32/72, mm. 4–7; E. 32/76, mm. 9–13.
[102] The point is well made in Hay, 'Poaching and the Game Laws', pp. 201–2.

5

The growth of London in the medieval English economy

PAMELA NIGHTINGALE

I T IS widely recognised that the phenomenal growth of London from the late sixteenth century contributed to the development of the modern English economy.[1] But there is less agreement about the extent to which this growth had medieval origins, even though London's share of England's assessed lay wealth grew conspicuously from 2 per cent in 1334 to 8.9 per cent in 1515.[2] Earlier historians explained London's apparent exception to the general picture of urban decline in the fifteenth century by the city's geographical advantages and political status which made its continuing expansion seem inevitable.[3] However, the recent topographical researches of Dr Derek Keene and his colleagues have led them to conclude that, far from being an exception to the general pattern of urban decline, London suffered from the same demographic trends which affected other medieval towns.[4] Most historians have been persuaded by Dr Keene's deductions from the Cheapside evidence that London reached the peak of its medieval population, which he estimates at between 80,000 to 100,000, at about 1300, that it then declined, and that, despite a period of increased commercial activity from

---

[1] F.J. Fisher, 'London as an "Engine of Economic Growth"', and 'The Development of London as a Centre of Conspicuous Consumption', in P. J. Corfield and N.B. Harte (eds.), *London and the English Economy, 1500–1700* (London, 1990), pp. 185–98, 105–18; E.A. Wrigley, 'A Simple Model of London's Importance in Changing English Society and Economy', *Past and Present*, 37 (1967), pp. 44–70.

[2] R.S. Schofield, 'The Geographical Distribution of Wealth in England, 1334–1649', *Econ. Hist. Rev.*, 2nd ser., 18 (1965), p. 508.

[3] M. Postan, 'The Fifteenth Century', *Econ. Hist. Rev.*, 9 (1938–9), p. 163; Fisher, 'London as an "Engine of Growth"', p. 195. Capitals which are also ports have always been conspicuous for their growth: J. de Vries, *European Urbanisation, 1500–1800* (London, 1984), p. 141.

[4] D. Keene, 'A New Study of London before the Great Fire', *Urban Hist. Yearbook*, 1984, pp. 18–19; D. Keene, 'Medieval London and its Region', *London Jl*, 14 (1989), p. 101.

the last quarter of the fourteenth century until the 1420s,[5] the city did not recover its former size until about 1600.

Dr Keene accounts for London's growth before 1300 by the two customary explanations that the city grew with the national population, and that its emergence as the centre of government meant that the purchasing power of the royal court moved away from the fairs and was concentrated in London at the end of the thirteenth century.[6] He explains its subsequent decline by the demographic crisis which followed the great famine of 1315–17 and by the later impact of the plague.[7] These findings have stimulated new research and thinking about the impact which a city of 80,000 to 100,000 would have had on the medieval English economy,[8] but they leave unanswered the question how, if London shrank to half that size in the 1370s, it could still greatly increase its share of the kingdom's wealth by 1515. The quantity of surviving topographical evidence has meant that the studies on which this new interpretation is based have been restricted hitherto to relatively small areas of the city. It is, therefore, important that a demographic deduction which was initially put forward in the most cautious way and which depends on some unknown factors should still be seen as speculative. It has to be tested within the wider context of the city's commercial fortunes, its changing economic structure and its relationship with the national economy.

It seems clear from the records of taxation that London's position in the national economy altered in the century after 1180. The aids and tallages of the eight richest provincial towns expressed as a percentage of London's came to 125 per cent in 1176–7, but 175 per cent in 1213–14.[9] Even more striking is the evidence of the twentieth levied on movables in 1269, which more closely reflects commercial wealth. This shows that the assessments of the eight richest provincial towns had increased to 285 per cent of London's.[10] It seems from this evidence that London was growing from the end of the twelfth century at a much slower rate than the chief provincial towns,

[5] D. Keene, 'New Study of London', p. 18.

[6] T.F. Tout, 'The Beginnings of the Modern Capital: London and Westminster in the Fourteenth Century', in his *Collected Papers* (Manchester, 1932–4), pp. 249–75; G.A. Williams, *Medieval London: From Commune to Capital*, 2nd edn (London, 1970), pp. 107–9; Keene, 'Medieval London and its Region', p. 102.

[7] Keene, 'New Study of London', p. 18; Keene, 'Medieval London and its Region', p. 101; D. Keene, 'Shops and Shopping in Medieval London', in L. Grant (ed.), *Medieval Art, Architecture, and Archaeology in London* (London, 1990), p. 42.

[8] B.M.S. Campbell, 'Towards an Agricultural Geography of Medieval England', *Agric. Hist. Rev.*, 36 (1988), p. 90; D.F. Harrison, 'Bridges and Economic Development, 1300–1800', *Econ. Hist. Rev.*, 2nd ser., 45 (1992), p. 254.

[9] M. Biddle (ed.), *Winchester in the Early Middle Ages* (Winchester Studies, I, Oxford, 1976), p. 500. Eight towns have been chosen to permit useful comparisons with the later tax records which do not cover all towns.

[10] J.F. Hadwin, 'The Medieval Lay Subsidies and Economic History', *Econ. Hist. Rev.*, 2nd ser., 36 (1983), p. 217 (table III).

and therefore did not automatically grow proportionately with the kingdom's wealth and population. The reason for this can be found in the new direction taken by the chief export trade. In 1203–4 King John's tax on movables shows that the eastern ports, led by Boston, were each attracting almost as much commercial wealth as London because they were nearer the main wool-growing regions and were better placed to export wool to Flanders.[11] In 1280 London exported only a quarter of the national total.[12] The Flemings, who were the chief exporters, also used the eastern ports to reach a wide market for their cloth by selling it at the nearby fairs. They had every incentive to avoid London because it was situated far from the best wool- and corn-growing region, and from the late eleventh century the citizens had imposed restrictions on alien merchants to protect their own retail and distributive trade.[13] During the thirteenth century London also experienced greater competition from the newly 'planted' as well as the older provincial towns, whose trade was stimulated by the growing population and a buoyant money supply.[14]

How, then, can one account for the reversal of these trends and the sudden growth of London which becomes apparent at the end of the thirteenth century? It is unlikely that the more settled residence of the court at Westminster was the chief reason. The twenty-three records which identify where the crown bought spices between 1220 and 1270 show that the majority of purchases were already made in the city.[15] Since the early twelfth century the crown had used the king's chamberlain of London to buy most of its luxuries there because it was the chief market for these imports.[16] London's early domination of the luxury trade is explained by its function as an entrepot commanding a deep hinterland, and by its proximity to the Rhine which was then the major route to the Mediterranean. Along the Rhine flowed luxuries from the East as well as the silver which fed London's

[11] London paid 16.8 per cent, Boston 15.7 per cent, Southampton 14.3 per cent, Lincoln 13.3 per cent and Lynn 13.1 per cent: N.S.B. Gras, *The Early English Customs System* (Cambridge, Mass., 1918), pp. 221–2.

[12] E.M. Carus-Wilson and O. Coleman, *England's Export Trade, 1275–1547* (Oxford, 1963), p. 36.

[13] T.H. Lloyd, *The English Wool Trade in the Middle Ages* (Cambridge, 1977), p. 55; M. Bateson, 'A London Municipal Collection of the Reign of John', *Eng. Hist. Rev.*, 17 (1902), pp. 480–511, 707–30.

[14] M. Beresford, *New Towns of the Middle Ages: Town Plantation in England, Wales and Gascony* (London, 1967), pp. 87, 89, 303 (table X).

[15] London accounted for ten, and its outport, Sandwich, for two, compared with five at the fairs. See the present writer's *A Medieval Mercantile Community: The Grocers' Company and the Politics and Trade of London, 1000–1485* (New Haven and London, 1995), pp. 75–7. Four other purchases were made at Southampton, and one each at York and Winchester.

[16] Bateson, 'London Municipal Collection', pp. 495–9. In 1157 London sent spices to supply the court in Lincoln: *Pipe Roll 3 Henry II* p. 113.

mint and ensured the city's early dominance as the financial centre of the kingdom.[17]

If one has to identify the crucial time when the concentration of royal and aristocratic demand made a vital difference to London's economy it would be when the rival royal centre of Winchester began to decline in Stephen's reign.[18] Winchester's importance had grown after 1066 because of its closeness to Southampton, the most convenient port for Normandy.[19] But by 1180 new supplies of German silver were passing through the London mint and expanding the economy after a period of monetary contraction which had closed many provincial mints.[20] With the exchequer at Westminster and with the royal treasury there by the end of the twelfth century,[21] London accumulated the governmental and legal business which made it also the unrivalled centre of aristocratic consumption.[22]

Inevitably the Italians and Cahorsins who imported Mediterranean luxuries were drawn to London. But their principal object was to finance by their imports their purchases of wool, and it was the wool trade which was promoting national economic growth and increasing the supply of coin. Big landowners probably supplied only about one third of the national wool exports,[23] and much of the money from sales was spent at the increased number of local markets or in the provincial towns.[24] Even at their height in 1285–6 the court's purchases in London amounted to less than £9,500.[25] This was small compared with the estimated £600,000 of coin circulating in that

---

[17] *Laws of the Kings of England*, ed. and trans. A.J. Robertson (Cambridge, 1925), p. 73; D.M. Metcalf, 'Continuity and Change in English Monetary History, c. 973–1086: part I', *Brit. Numismatic Jl*, 100 (1980), pp. 32–3.

[18] Biddle (ed.) *Winchester in the Early Middle Ages*, pp. 489–90.

[19] *Ibid.*, pp. 438, 470–2.

[20] P. Nightingale, '"The King's Profit": Trends in English Mint and Monetary Policy in the Eleventh and Twelfth Centuries', in N.J. Mayhew and P. Spufford (eds.), *Later Medieval Mints: Organisation, Administration and Techniques* (British Archaeological Reports, International Series, no. 389, Oxford, 1988), pp. 61, 63, 66, 69–71.

[21] N.J. Mayhew, 'From Regional to Central Minting, 1158–1464', in, C.E. Challis (ed.), *A New History of the Royal Mint* (Cambridge, 1992), p. 106; R.A. Brown, '"The Treasury" of the Later Twelfth Century', in J. Conway Davies (ed.), *Studies Presented to Sir Hilary Jenkinson* (1957), pp. 35–49; T.F. Tout, *Chapters in the Administrative History of Medieval England*, 6 vols. (Manchester, 1920–33), I, pp. 96–9.

[22] F.M. Stenton, 'Norman London, an Essay', in D.M. Stenton (ed.), *Preparatory to Anglo-Saxon England* (Oxford, 1970), pp. 54–5; *The Chronicle of Richard of Devizes, 1189–92*, ed. J.T. Appleby (London, 1963), p. 65.

[23] A.R. Bridbury, 'Before the Black Death', *Econ. Hist. Rev.*, 2nd ser., 30 (1977), p. 398. Small parcels of wool from peasants' stocks provided most of the wool levy in 1338–9: W.M. Ormrod, 'The Crown and the English Economy, 1290–1348', in B.M.S. Campbell (ed.), *Before the Black Death: Studies in the 'Crisis' of the Early Fourteenth Century* (Manchester, 1991), p. 177.

[24] R.H. Britnell, *The Commercialisation of English Society 1000–1500* (Cambridge, 1993), p. 125.

[25] Public Record Office, E.101/352/3.

period.[26] In 1300–1 the Wardrobe's purchases in London were less than £4,000, whereas the city's wool exports alone were worth over £88,000 that year.[27]

It was the diversion of wool exports from the eastern ports which most obviously increased London's share of national wealth at the end of the thirteenth century. This change began from 1270, not for economic reasons but as a consequence of political events. The first was the expulsion of the Flemings in 1270 which progressively ended their visits to England, leaving the Italians as the major purchasers of wool.[28] To pay for their increased exports the Italians had to import more, and they began to speculate in sea-borne cargoes of alum and dyes, as well as increasing their sales of luxuries in London.[29] When the Flemings ceased to visit them, the fairs rapidly began to decline.[30] It is likely that from 1270 more Flemish cloth was being brought by intermediaries to London,[31] and the crafts which used alien imports, and the London merchants who dealt in them, began to organise themselves more strongly from about this time.[32]

A greater stimulus was given to these developments by the king's interference in the wool trade from 1294 as a preliminary to war against France.[33] Although the Italians always sold their imports in London, until 1295 they had continued to buy most of their wool at the fairs and to ship it from Boston or Hull. But the outbreak of the war encouraged piracy in the North Sea and increased the cost and danger to shipping. It became cheaper and safer to send it by land to London for the short journey by convoy across

[26] M. Prestwich, 'Edward I's Monetary Policies and their Consequences', *Econ. Hist. Rev.*, 2nd ser., 22 (1969), p. 407; N. Mayhew, 'Money and Prices in England from Henry II to Edward III', *Agric. Hist. Rev.*, 35 (1987), p. 125 (table 1).

[27] Carus-Wilson and Coleman, *England's Export Trade*, p. 40. T.H. Lloyd estimates the average value of each sack to have been £8 and the total value of wool exports at that time as averaging £316,712 a year: 'Overseas Trade and the English Money Supply in the Fourteenth Century', in N. J. Mayhew (ed.), *Edwardian Monetary Affairs, 1279–1344* (Brit. Arch. Reports, no. 36, Oxford, 1977), p. 101 (table 2). The Great Wardrobe's purchases in London subsequently sank even more: Williams, *Medieval London*, p. 155 (table C.1). Alien merchants alone were importing £22,301 of general merchandise in 1304–5: T.H. Lloyd, *Alien Merchants in England in the High Middle Ages* (Brighton, 1982), p. 219 (table A I.9).

[28] Lloyd, *Wool Trade*, ch. 2.

[29] R.S. Lopez, 'Majorcans and Genoese on the North-Sea Route in the Thirteenth Century', *Revue belge de philologie et d'histoire*, 29 (1951), pp. 1163–71.

[30] D. Keene, *Survey of Medieval Winchester*, 2 vols. (Winchester Studies, 2, Oxford, 1985), I, pp. 119–21.

[31] In 1276, after a temporary restoration of commercial relations, about a hundred Flemish merchants, compared with fifty Londoners, were fined for selling cloth which did not meet the assize: E.M. Veale, '"The Great Twelve": Mistery and Fraternity in Thirteenth-Century London', *Bull. Inst. Hist. Research*, 64 (1991), pp. 255–6.

[32] *Ibid.*, pp. 247, 251, 253, 256, 259.

[33] Lloyd, *Wool Trade*, pp. 80–2.

the Channel.[34] London's share of wool exports rose to 38.6 per cent in 1295 and went on rising to 54 per cent by 1314, at the expense of the provincial ports and the fairs.[35] Although the booming demand for shops in Cheapside, and the appearance there of wardrobes for the nobility, indicate that the decline of the fairs encouraged the upper classes to increase their purchases in London, the volume of imports could only have been absorbed if they were also being distributed by Londoners to the provinces.[36]

In 1285 Edward I forced the Londoners to admit to citizenship any alien of good repute who desired it. This, though, did not bring about any important change in London's economy because they had not been excluded from citizenship before.[37] The Londoners knew that their prosperity depended on the aliens using their port. They were not generally hostile to them provided they did not challenge their retail and distributive trade. But in 1303 it was endangered when the king granted the *Carta Mercatoria* to alien merchants in return for higher duties on their exports of wool. The charter allowed the aliens to deal with non-freemen, and to sell spices and mercery by retail. Immediately alien imports into the city increased, probably at the expense of the Londoners' trade.[38] However, the growth in the number of active pepperers from 54 in the 1290s to 101 in the 1310s suggests that not all Londoners suffered as a consequence.

In fact the higher duty which the aliens paid on their wool encouraged Londoners to increase their own exports.[39] They invested the proceeds overseas in imports which gave them the profits from a double trade.[40] But the limited demand for luxurious imports meant that silver flowed into England bringing inflation as well as commercial expansion.[41] The greater concentration of foreign trade in London increased its proportion of national wealth from 2.1 per cent in 1294 to 3.5 per cent in 1307.[42] Even more striking was its gain at the expense of the eight richest provincial towns. Whereas in 1269

[34] *Ibid.*, pp. 81–2, 140; Carus-Wilson and Coleman, *England's Export Trade*, p. 39.

[35] Carus-Wilson and Coleman, *England's Export Trade*, pp. 38–42.

[36] Keene, 'Medieval London and its Region', p. 102; Lloyd, *Alien Merchants*, p. 219 (table A I.9).

[37] Prof. Williams explains much of London's growth in this period by the operation of the monarchy, particularly its free-trade policy: Williams, *Medieval London*, pp. 107–10. Dr Lloyd estimates that the denizen imports were almost as large as the alien imports: 'Overseas Trade and the English Money Supply', p. 102, table 2.

[38] Lloyd, *Alien Merchants*, pp. 211–19 (tables A I.1–9).

[39] Carus-Wilson and Coleman, *England's Export Trade*, p. 41.

[40] Williams, *Medieval London*, p. 150 (table A.3). Note the increase of wool exports by the distributive trades.

[41] Lloyd, 'Overseas Trade and the English Money Supply', p. 103.

[42] Calculated from J.F. Willard, 'The Taxes upon Movables of the Reign of Edward I', *Eng. Hist. Rev.*, 28 (1913), pp. 519, 521; J.F. Willard, 'The Taxes upon Movables of the Reign of Edward II', *Eng. Hist. Rev.*, 29 (1914), p. 319.

they had paid 285 per cent of the tax paid by London, in 1304 they paid only 173.6 per cent and in 1312 93.7 per cent.[43]

There is no doubt that these were booming years for London's economy. But how certain is it that this growth in wealth produced a population of 80,000–100,000? If the concentration of the wool trade in the city caused the boom, it must be remembered that at its height it involved little more than half the wool exported through London in 1353–4 and 1361–2. The same was also true of imports.[44] Inevitably these proportions were reflected in the level of London's retail and distributive trade which relied on its imports. It would seem that the economic base of the city was smaller in 1300 than in the 1370s, when cloth exports were also helping to support a population of about 45,000.[45]

Dr Keene's high estimate of the population c. 1300 is based on his conclusion that the demand for Cheapside property in that period was not matched again until 1600. What happened in Cheapside is not disputed, although later developments do suggest that the amalgamation of shops did not necessarily mean a smaller labour force.[46] However, his estimate of the whole city's population c. 1300 crucially depends on the hypothesis that the density of building and population in Cheapside then bore the same relation to the rest of the city as it did in 1600. Only if this were true would London's population in 1300 have been about the size of Florence. His alternative interpretation was that the density of building and population in the city in 1300 might have fallen off much more sharply from the centre towards the limit of the urban area than it did in 1600.[47]

There is in fact evidence for the latter interpretation in his study of the Walbrook area. Large properties like Bucklersbury were a feature there until the later fourteenth century when the grocers began the same process of subdividing them which had happened earlier in Cheapside. There is evidence of an expansion of business particularly between the 1360s and the 1380s when rentals in the Poultry area rose while the Blunt mansion was subdivided into a row of tenements;[48] also, two churches were rebuilt and much enlarged in the 1420s and 1440s because the number of parishioners

[43] Hadwin, 'Lay Subsidies', p. 217 (table III).
[44] Carus-Wilson and Coleman, *England's Export Trade*, pp. 40, 47, 48. The highest value of alien imports to London at the beginning of the fourteenth century was £26,526 in 1307–8, but in 1371 they reached a peak of £69,160: Lloyd, *Alien Merchants*, p. 219 (table A I.9); T.H. Lloyd, *England and the German Hanse, 1157–1611* (Cambridge, 1991), pp. 98–9 (table 3).
[45] Calculated at about twice the number who paid the poll tax of 1377.
[46] See n. 124 below.
[47] Keene, 'New Study of London', p. 20.
[48] D. Keene, 'The Walbrook Study: A Summary Report and Appendix' (typescript, Inst. Hist. Research, London, 1987), pp. 5, 8, 13, 15, 20.

had grown.[49] It would seem that the Walbrook area was not so densely settled in 1300 as it was in the fifteenth century, and it is therefore most unlikely that its population in 1300 was equal to that of 1600.[50] If this was true of Walbrook it was probably true of other areas of the city which had a different function from the luxury retailers of Cheapside. A large block of property near the Tower was owned by one man before 1285. Ten years later it had two houses and the Wool and Stone Quays on it. But from the 1320s shops and more houses appeared on the quays, and the neighbouring property was owned by rich merchants.[51] This development obviously owed much to the growth of London's wool trade. It appears that the pattern of growth and decline was no more uniform throughout all areas of the medieval city than it was in its later history.[52]

The research project, 'Feeding the City', has made deductions about the population of London while it has also reduced to 4 million the estimate of national population *c.* 1300. The poll tax of 1377 indicates that London's population was about 1.7 per cent of the national total, but it is likely that it would have been only 1.5 per cent in 1300.[53] This suggests that London's population in about 1300 would have been no more than 60,000.[54] There can be no doubt that London's region was capable of feeding a much larger city, but the evidence does not show that it was actually doing so. The authors conclude that a city of 100,000 would have required provisioning from an area which extended almost to the Wash and along the coast of Sussex and southern Kent.[55] But there is no evidence of any regular corn trade between East Anglia and London, and even the possible exception of

---

[49] *Ibid.*, p. 5.

[50] After its growth in the late fourteenth century Walbrook began to grow rapidly again from 1550: Keene, 'Walbrook Study', p. 20. This shows that the level of population in 1300 cannot be straightforwardly equated with that of 1600 – the equation on which the estimate of 80,000 to 100,000 in 1300 depends.

[51] T. Dyson, 'The Topographical Development of the Custom-House Area', *Trans. London and Middlesex Arch. Soc.*, 26 (1975), pp. 111–12.

[52] R. Finlay and B. Shearer, 'Population Growth and Suburban Expansion', in A.L. Beir and R. Finlay (eds.), *London, 1500–1700: The Making of the Metropolis* (London, 1986), pp. 42–3.

[53] B.M.S. Campbell, J.A. Galloway, D. Keene and M. Murphy, *A Medieval Capital and its Grain Supply: Agrarian Production and Distribution in the London Region c.1300* (Institute of British Geographers, Historical Geography Research Series, no. 30, London, 1993), pp. 44–5.

[54] *Ibid.*, p. 45. On p. 11 the authors arrive at an alternative higher figure of 'well over 70,000', by estimating London's size in 1300 from its share of the taxation of 1334 and the poll tax figures for 1377. Both would give too high a figure for 1300 because London was always richer per head of population than other towns, and by 1377 the restructuring of the national economy after the plague had increased its share of the population beyond the proportion it enjoyed in 1300, as the authors themselves recognise on p. 44.

[55] *Ibid.*, pp. 76–7, where they conclude that a city of 100,000 would have required provisioning beyond the isoplath of 6.3 pence marked on figure 7, p. 61.

Yarmouth relates to the 1350s.[56] East Anglia and southern Kent and Sussex are far more likely in 1300 to have been supplying the cities of Flanders with food.[57]

London was not large enough in 1300 to bring about any significant improvement in medieval agriculture.[58] One could also deduce that it was not drawing on the wide provisioning area which was theoretically available to it because its own population was no higher than 60,000. Furthermore, in contrast with what happened in the fifteenth century, it seems that London had not accumulated enough of the kingdom's trade and population to prevent its share of national wealth declining in the years before the Black Death.[59] The data produced by the project supports the topographical evidence from Cheapside in indicating a sharp reduction in the city's demand during the 1320s.[60] This is shown by a fall in that decade of 20 per cent in the value of the arable land which it is assumed was feeding London. The possibility that this reflects a similar reduction of the city's population is supported by a fall of 24 per cent in the number of London's pepperers and spicers who were active in that decade.[61]

The convergence of these three pieces of evidence suggests that the values of the same land in the period 1375–99 might also indicate the trend of the city's population. The decline in the average value of the arable land from 5d. in 1285–1312 to 3½d. in 1375–99, when adjusted for inflation, implies that the population of the city may have been about 30 per cent higher in 1300 than in 1377 when the poll tax suggests it was about 45,000.[62] This deduction, too, would indicate a population in 1300 of no more than 60,000. Another rough calculation which points in the same direction is suggested by the 12,400 corpses estimated to have been buried in the emergency graveyards opened in 1348. The manner in which the victims were buried does not suggest overwhelming numbers. Since it is generally agreed that London's population in 1348 was lower than it had been in 1300, the oft-quoted figure of 50,000 burials in West Smithfield alone looks excessive even in relation to Dr

---

[56] *Ibid.*, pp. 69–70.

[57] *Ibid.*, pp. 181–2, 68.

[58] *Ibid.*, pp. 182–3.

[59] See the evidence of national taxation at n. 69 below.

[60] *Centre for Metropolitan History: Annual Report, 1988–9* (Inst. Hist. Research, London), p. 8.

[61] Nightingale, *Medieval Mercantile Community*, app. A. They fell from 101 in the first decade to 77 in the second (all subsequent references to the number of pepperers and grocers are to this appendix).

[62] Project Report, 'Feeding the City: London's Impact on the Agrarian Economy of Southern England, *c.* 1250–1400', in *The Annual Report for the Centre for Metropolitan History, 1991–2* (Inst. Hist. Research, London), p. 9 (table 1).

Keene's estimates of total population, and is best regarded as an exaggerated fiction.[63] Even if the number of burials is inflated from the estimated 12,400 by almost a third to 18,000 to allow for corpses buried in churchyards and for people who may have fled the city, a death-rate such as that for Westminster of about 40 per cent[64] would mean that the population before the plague was no higher than 45,000 – close to Ekwall's and Professor Williams' estimate from the number of taxpayers.[65] The drop of about 20 per cent in the 1320s would then mean that the population *c.* 1300 would have been about 55,000–60,000, which is the likely size of London at the beginning of the sixteenth century.[66]

If London was roughly the size in 1500 that it was in 1300, how would this accord with the evidence from Cheapside that there was no recovery in the later Middle Ages to the level of 1300? It seems that for three decades much of the city might have shared with Westminster the sharp decline of the 1320s and a depression which lasted to the immediate aftermath of the Black Death.[67] The number of active pepperers did not equal that of the second decade of the century until the 1340s, and it saw no sustained expansion until the 1360s.[68] At the same time the city's share of the kingdom's wealth sank from 3.5 per cent in 1307 to 2.1 per cent in 1315, and it continued close to that lower figure until the tax assessment was frozen in 1334.[69] Since the city's commercial wealth had already fallen in 1315, before the effect of the great famine could be felt, the explanation for its fall, like that for its previous growth, can be found in the fortunes of the wool trade.

[63] D. Hawkins, 'The Black Death and the New London Cemeteries of 1348', *Antiquity*, 64 (1990), pp. 637–42. For a recent statement of the contrary view, see R.H. Britnell, 'The Black Death in English Towns', *Urban Hist.*, 21 (1994), pp. 198–9, 204–5.

[64] G. Rosser, *Medieval Westminster, 1200–1540* (Oxford, 1989), pp. 170–1. The death-rate for the London pepperers was 34 per cent, but their housing would have been of a higher standard than the average, and one must assume a higher death-rate among the poorer classes. The evidence also indicates that the pepperers did not leave the city, which suggests the estimate of 18,000 deaths is too high.

[65] E. Ekwall, *Two Early London Subsidy Rolls* (Lund, 1951), pp. 71–81; Williams, *Medieval London*, p. 317.

[66] Keene, 'Medieval London and its Region', p. 107.

[67] Rosser, *Medieval Westminster*, pp. 169–70.

[68] Although the total number recovered, it was inflated by the newcomers who replaced those who died in 1348–9. There was no real recovery until the 1350s.

[69] Willard, 'Taxes on Movables of Edward II', pp. 320–1; J.F. Willard, 'The Taxes on Movables of the Reign of Edward III', *Eng. Hist. Rev.*, 30 (1915), pp. 72–3. The exceptionably low figure of 0.7 per cent for the twentieth of 1327 can be explained by the political upheavals that year in London which brought about the deposition of Edward II and which deterred alien merchants from visiting the city: Hadwin, 'Lay Subsidies', p. 217 (table III); Lloyd, *Alien Merchants*, p. 219 (table A 1.9).

In 1315–16 there was a sudden drop in the amount of wool exported nationally, and exports did not recover their former level until 1338–9.[70] The fall was caused by the outbreak of war between France and Flanders, but it was perpetuated by civil war in Flanders until 1329.[71] London was able to maintain its share of this declining trade because of the political developments which created the oversea wool staple, initially at St Omer, in 1313.[72] This helped to perpetuate the funnelling of wool exports through the city which had begun in 1295.[73] But the effects of the famine of 1315–17 on the price of food and the dislocation of the agrarian economy in many areas,[74] combined with the low output of the mints, can only have depressed the demand for all but the most essential goods.[75] In 1321 London's weavers declared that the number of looms there had fallen from 300 to 80.[76] The fall in the city's population is therefore most easily explained by the reduction of its retail and distributive trade, particularly in the luxuries of Cheapside. Unemployment accounts for the Londoners' violence in the revolution which deposed Edward II and for their insistence on the restoration of the franchise as the price for supporting Isabella and Mortimer.[77] But that was an inadequate remedy. From 1334 prices generally slumped as the money supply continued to fall.[78] This meant that the landowning class had even less money to buy London's imports and manufactures.[79] On the eve of the Black Death, when the king's diversion of the wool trade had created a new monetary crisis, there was little sign of an economic recovery.

Why, then, should any part of the city's economy improve after the 1340s if it did not do so in Cheapside? The answer lies in the structural change caused by the redistribution of incomes which followed the plague. Landowners' incomes diminished still more as the loss of population inflated wages while the demand for food fell. But these trends combined to increase the spending power of peasants and artisans, which altered the pattern of

---

[70] Carus-Wilson and Coleman, *England's Export Trade*, pp. 42–5, 124.

[71] Lloyd, *Wool Trade*, pp. 125–6.

[72] *Ibid*, pp. 101–7.

[73] Carus-Wilson and Coleman, *England's Export Trade*, pp. 41–3.

[74] R.M. Smith, 'Demographic Developments in Rural England, 1300–48: A Survey', in Campbell (ed.), *Before the Black Death*, pp. 37–52.

[75] Lloyd, 'Overseas Trade and the English Money Supply', pp. 105–9; M. Mate, 'High Prices in Early Fourteenth-Century England: Causes and Consequences', *Econ. Hist. Rev.*, 2nd ser., 28 (1973), pp. 1–16.

[76] *Munimenta Gildhallae Londoniensis: Liber Custumarum*, ed. H.T. Riley, 3 vols. in 4 (Rolls Series, no. 12, London, 1859–62), II(1), p. 421.

[77] Williams, *Medieval London*, ch. 12.

[78] W.M. Ormrod, 'The Crown and the English Economy, 1290–1348', in Campbell (ed.), *Before the Black Death*, pp. 182–3.

[79] Bridbury, 'Before the Black Death', pp. 403–8.

demand at the same time that English woollens became more competitive overseas and encouraged investment in their manufacture.[80] Recovery was assisted by rising wool exports in the 1350s[81] and by a comparable surge in the output of the mints.[82] The English cloth industry expanded and brought employment and new immigrants to the towns. More importantly it enabled London's distributive trade to escape from its former dependence on luxury imports and to supply the provincial market with raw materials and imports such as linens as well as its own manufactures.[83]

The restructuring of London's economy from 1350, which integrated it much more into the national economy, was aided by the king's suspension of the franchise in 1357. It remained suspended for twenty-six years. In 1353 the oversea wool staple was also abandoned and Englishmen were forbidden to export wool until 1357.[84] As a consequence provincial dealers flocked to London to sell wool to the aliens. Its wool exports rose to their greatest volume with 52.5 per cent of the national total in 1353–4, and alien imports soared.[85] But the re-establishment of an oversea wool staple more or less permanently at Calais from 1361 cut the aliens' share of exports and allowed London's staplers to establish a dominant share of the imports of dyes and alum from Bruges. Between the 1360s and 1390s the numbers active in London's grocery trade, which dealt in these imports, more than doubled to 263.[86]

Many of the newcomers were provincial merchants who saw in the suspension of the franchise their chance to export wool through London and also found dyes and alum the most profitable return trade. The emptying of houses by the plague made it easy for them to buy property anywhere in the city. The grocers' new demand for shops in the Walbrook area[87] reflects

[80] J.H. Munro, 'Industrial Transformations in the North-West European Textile Trades, c. 1290–c. 1340: Economic Progress or Economic Crisis?', in Campbell (ed.), *Before the Black Death*, pp. 114–15, 133–9; Britnell, *Commercialisation of English Society*, pp. 168–70; J. Hatcher, 'England in the Aftermath of the Black Death', *Past and Present*, 144 (1994), especially pp. 25–35.

[81] Carus-Wilson and Coleman, *England's Export Trade*, p. 122.

[82] Challis (ed.), *New History of the Mint*, p. 680.

[83] Compare E.A. Wrigley's view that the secret of urban growth lay in the awakening of rural interest in urban products, which in London's case were essential imports: 'City and Country in the Past. A Sharp Divide or a Continuum?', *Past and Present*, 64, no. 154 (1991), p. 117.

[84] Lloyd, *Wool Trade*, pp. 205–9.

[85] Carus-Wilson and Coleman, *England's Export Trade*, pp. 48, 124; alien imports into London reached 73 per cent of the national total in 1371–2: Lloyd, *England and the German Hanse*, pp. 98–9 (table 3).

[86] There were 114 active in the 1360s and 263 in the 1390s. The pepperers changed their name to grocers to indicate the new character of their trade: *A Facsimile of the First Volume of the MS. Archives of the Worshipful Company of Grocers of the City of London*. A.D. 1345–1463, ed. J.A. Kingdon, 2 vols. (London, 1883–6), I, pp. 45–7.

[87] Keene, 'Walbrook Study', pp. 13–14.

only part of their activities. The riverside parishes were most convenient for the wool exporters, and properties near the city's gates gave the distributive traders more room for carts and storage than the pepperers' old quarter near Cheapside. These preferences could explain the falling rents in Sopers Lane.[88] In the 1370s and 1380s grocers were to be found in thirty-five parishes.[89]

The greater concentration of the wool trade in the city from 1350, and the establishment of the staple at Calais earned profits which built up the Londoners' mercantile capital and financial power. This gave them increased weight in the national political conflicts of Richard II's reign and won the restoration of London's franchise in 1377, and again in 1383.[90] Its operation meant that citizens had the choice of distributing imports to the provinces themselves, as the grocers did on their journeys to buy wool, or they could follow the policy of the mercers and oblige the provincial merchants to go to them in London.[91] This encouraged provincial chapmen to buy the mercers' imported linens by selling them English woollens in London. The direction of cloth exports through London gained strength from the 1370s as the reduced output of coin, which followed declining wool exports, made merchants more reliant on credit and barter.[92] In these conditions the city's superior reserves of mercantile capital began to tell. The Statute-Staple certificates indicate that a rising proportion of debts were enrolled in London. Its share increased from 33.6 per cent of the national total in the 1360s to 53 per cent in the 1390s, and then to 63 per cent in the recessionary first decade of the fifteenth century, while those of York and Hull declined.[93] A similar pattern appears in London's cloth exports. Whereas they had been only 18 per cent of Bristol's in 1366–7, in the 1370s they increased to 50 per cent or more.[94] When London's figures are next available in 1401–2, they show it dominated the trade with 51 per cent of national exports.[95]

Did this greater concentration of wealth and trade bring also a growing population? The doubling of the grocers' numbers in the second half of the fourteenth century and their rise to a peak of 386 in the 1420s suggests that

---

[88] Keene, 'New Study of London', p. 18.
[89] Evidence gathered from wills and the city's records.
[90] P. Nightingale, 'Capitalists, Crafts, and Constitutional Change in Late Fourteenth-Century London', *Past and Present*, 124 (1989), pp. 22, 31–2.
[91] H.J. Creaton, 'The Wardens' Accounts of the Mercers' Company of London' (Univ. of London MPhil thesis, 1977), pp. 369–70.
[92] P. Nightingale, 'Monetary Contraction and Mercantile Credit in Later Medieval England', *Econ. Hist. Rev.*, 2nd ser., 43 (1990), p. 567.
[93] J. Kermode, 'Medieval Indebtedness: The Regions versus London', in N. Rogers (ed.), *England in the Fifteenth Century: Proceedings of the 1992 Harlaxton Symposium* (Stamford, 1994), pp. 72–88, especially table 1.2, p. 85.
[94] Carus-Wilson and Coleman, *England's Export Trade*, pp. 77–9.
[95] *Ibid.*, pp. 77, 89.

it did. So, too, does the division of Farringdon Ward in 1394 which was granted because of the increase of its population.[96] Trades expanded out of Cheapside or moved to areas better suited to their needs. One group of drapers moved from the Stocks to Basinghall Street where Bakewell Hall was built as the principal cloth market.[97] The numbers in the Drapers' Company jumped from 96 in 1413 to 169 in 1424, and by 1493 they had reached 243.[98] The mercers, who founded their company in 1347 with 107 men in Cheapside,[99] had in 1474–5 109 men in sixteen wards of the city who were rich enough to have goods or land worth £100, and they were almost certainly by then more numerous, as well as richer, than the grocers.[100] Many tailors moved into Fleet Street to be near their customers in the Inns of Court, while the number of masters and apprentices doubled between 1425 and 1465, and the number of alien immigrants who practised the trade also grew.[101] Even the goldsmiths, who had been confined by their charter of 1327 to Cheapside, overflowed by the end of the fifteenth century into several other areas of the city,[102] as, too, did the pewterers, who drifted closer to the river as their numbers rose from 30 in 1348 to 100 in 1457.[103] The cutlers moved their chief quarter from West Cheap to Vintry Ward by 1401,[104] and the haberdashers expanded from the neighbourhood of St Paul's to other areas, including a concentration near London Bridge.[105] New breweries were established on the riverbank c. 1480.[106] What happened in Cheapside was therefore not a reflection of all the other areas of the city.

[96] *Calendar of Letter-Books of the City of London: Letter Book H*, ed. R.R. Sharpe (London, 1907), pp. 129–31.

[97] Keene, 'Walbrook Study', p. 7. In Winchester the migration of trades, which began in the twelfth century, appears to be characteristic of 'a period of expansion and prosperity': Biddle (ed.), *Winchester in the Early Middle Ages*, p. 439.

[98] Keene, 'Walbrook Study', pp. 7, 13; A.H. Johnson, *The History of the Worshipful Company of the Drapers of London*, 5 vols. (Oxford, 1914–22), I, pp. 105, 147.

[99] Creaton, 'Wardens' Accounts of the Mercers' Company', I, p. 145.

[100] *Acts of Court of the Mercers' Company, 1453–1527*, ed. L. Lyell and F.D. Watney (Cambridge, 1936), pp. 78–9, 84.

[101] M.P. Davies, 'The Tailors of London and their Guild, c. 1300–1500' (Univ. of Oxford DPhil, 1994), pp. 164, 170–9, 187, 197, 219–20.

[102] T.F. Reddaway, 'The London Goldsmiths c. 1500', *Trans. Royal Hist. Soc.* 5th ser., 12 (1962), pp. 50–3. Large numbers of alien immigrants also worked in the trade in the fifteenth century. In 1469, 113 of them were at work: T.F. Reddaway and L.E.M. Walker, *The Early History of the Goldsmiths' Company, 1327–1509* (London, 1975), p. 120.

[103] R.F. Homer, 'The Medieval Pewterers of London, c. 1190–1457', *Trans. London and Middlesex Arch. Soc.*, 36 (1985), pp. 144, 146.

[104] C. Welch, *The History of the Cutlers' Company of London*, 2 vols. (London, 1916–23), I, pp. 38–40, 159, 162.

[105] I.W. Archer, *The History of the Haberdashers' Company* (Chichester, 1991), pp. 10–11.

[106] M. Carlin, 'St Botolph, Aldgate: The Historical Gazeteer of London before the Great Fire' (typescript, Inst. Hist. Research, London, 1987), pp. 2, 8.

London achieved this growth despite being challenged by other ports and the reviving fairs. Bristol, and, most of all, Southampton, were rivals for its cloth trade. In the 1430s and 1440s the Genoese took over Southampton as their entrepot and demonstrated how useless was London's franchise if the city could be bypassed. The merchants of Southampton set up their own distributive trade and they drew to the port cloth which would otherwise have gone to London.[107] The Londoners passed the Hosting Act in 1439 to compel the Italians to observe the urban franchises. Although the rules were strictly enforced in London, they were not in Southampton, and therefore London lost more trade to its rival.[108]

London's commercial ascendancy was saved from this new threat partly, again, by war. Bristol was temporarily denied its lucrative market in Gascony when the French reconquered it.[109] Similarly merchants from the eastern ports suffered from the struggles against the Hansards.[110] Again, naval warfare favoured London as the nearest port to the continent, and the Merchant Adventurers were able to dominate cloth exports by organising armed convoys for their ships. But the economic recession throughout Europe also played a crucial part in the middle of the century. Lack of coin cut the foreign demand for English cloth and also for the luxury imports sold in England by the Italians.[111] Interest rates rose, and with them the cost of credit.[112] Many Italian firms relied on credit to buy their cloth in England, and when credit became tighter they had to reduce their purchases.[113] Once again the greater capital and credit available in London worked against Southampton and its share of exports fell.[114]

A pattern also becomes visible in the 1440s and 1450s of increasing numbers of provincial chapmen carrying cloth by road to London and returning with imports to sell to their local communities. In more prosperous times they could trade in the provincial towns and in fairs. But the contraction of money and credit, and the diminishing trade of the provincial ports, drew them to London where they could barter their cloth for its imports. Some

[107] A. Ruddock, *Italian Merchants and Shipping in Southampton, 1270–1600* (Southampton Rec. Ser., Southampton, 1951), pp. 88–9.

[108] *Ibid.*, pp. 157–9; Carus-Wilson and Coleman, *England's Export Trade*, pp. 95–7.

[109] E. Carus-Wilson, *Medieval Merchant Venturers* (London, 1954), pp. 10, 45–9.

[110] M. Postan, 'The Economic and Political Relations of England and the Hanse (1400–1475)', in E. Power and M. Postan (eds.), *Studies in English Trade in the Fifteenth Century* (London, 1933), pp. 134–8.

[111] Britnell, *Commercialisation of English Society*, pp. 182–3.

[112] The Grocers' Company obtained 10.4 per cent for their money in 1447–8, but 15 per cent in 1456–7: *Facsimile of the First Volume*, pp. 295, 367.

[113] W. Childs, '"To Oure Losse and Hindraunce": English Credit to Alien Merchants in the Mid-Fifteenth Century', in J. Kermode (ed.), *Enterprise and Individuals* (Stroud, 1991), pp. 68–98.

[114] Carus-Wilson and Coleman, *England's Export Trade*, pp. 98–101.

of London's companies assisted this diversion of trade there by forbidding their members to go to the fairs.[115] The appearance of aldermen among the haberdashers and merchant tailors from 1470 speaks of the growing prosperity of these trades because of their cloth exports and the wider internal market they supplied.[116]

Sharper competition in a recession meant that London's industries gained from the lower cost of transporting their raw materials, their easier access to credit and the concentration of the distributive and export trade in the city. Cloth manufacturing and finishing provided new employment as provincial dyers and fullers found it harder to compete.[117] About 3,000 cap makers were reportedly working in London and its immediate neighbourhood in 1441.[118] Local cloth markets increased.[119] There was a guild of dyers in 1471, and of fullers in 1480.[120] Other trades, like the salters, rose in prosperity through their dealings in cloth,[121] while the chandlers prospered from the increase in London's imports of salt in the later fifteenth century.[122] Growing imports of iron and tin suggest that the metal workers increased their production, and London's craftsmen monopolised the export of pewter.[123] The pressure to cut costs directly swelled London's population, as it did in the sixteenth century, by masters using more unpaid apprentices in trades which did not demand a high degree of manual skills.[124] A petition to open a new grammar school next to the Mercers' Hall in 1447 explained

[115] *Facsimile of the First Volume*, pp. 139, 145, 157, 161; *Acts of Court of the Mercers' Company*, pp. 100, 115–16, 138–9, 158–9.

[116] A.B. Beaven, *The Aldermen of the City of London*, 2 vols. (London, 1908–13), I, p. 330; Archer, *History of the Haberdashers' Company*, pp. 16, 20–3; Davies, 'Tailors of London', p. 112.

[117] Among the goods the mercers dealt in were 'fine woollen cloth of London-making . . . scarlets and cloth in grain', i.e. the most expensive cloths: Creaton, 'Wardens' Accounts of the Mercers' Company', II, pp. 150–3. London monopolised the most expensive dyeing with grain: W.R. Childs, *Anglo-Castilian Trade in the Later Middle Ages* (Manchester, 1978) p. 80.

[118] Archer, *History of the Haberdashers' Company*, p. 9.

[119] Project Report on 'Before the Bank', in *Centre for Metropolitan History: Annual Report*, 1991–2 (Inst. Hist. Research, London), p. 15.

[120] Childs, *Anglo-Castilian Trade*, p. 80; *Cal. Pat. Rolls, 1467–77*, p. 236; *Cal. Pat. Rolls, 1476–85*, p. 221.

[121] A.R. Bridbury, *England and the Salt Trade in the Later Middle Ages* (Oxford, 1955), pp. 146–8; the salters paid the eighth highest contribution in the city towards a royal loan in 1488: *Acts of Court of the Mercers' Company*, pp. 188–9.

[122] Bridbury, *Salt Trade*, pp. 171–2; *Calendar of Letter-Books of the City of London: Letter Book L*, ed. R.R. Sharpe (London, 1912), p. 211.

[123] W.R. Childs, 'England's Iron Trade in the Fifteenth Century', *Econ. Hist. Rev.*, 2nd ser., 35 (1981), p. 27; the ironmongers produced seven aldermen in the fifteenth century: Beaven, *Aldermen*, I, 330. They also paid the ninth highest contribution in the city's grant to the king in 1488: *Acts of Court of the Mercers' Company*, pp. 188–9; J. Hatcher, *English Tin Production and Trade before 1550* (Oxford, 1973), pp. 33, 119–20, 138–44.

[124] This policy was also followed in the sixteenth century: S. Rappaport, *Worlds within Worlds: Structures of Life in Sixteenth-Century London* (Cambridge, 1989), pp. 104–10.

that it was to meet the needs of the 'grete multitude of younge peple, not oonly borne and brought forth in the same Citee, but also of many other parties of this lond'.[125] These developments meant that the structure of London's employment became more capitalistic. At the end of the century there were larger shops and fewer independent masters, but a greater number of employees.[126] Although opportunities for enfranchised servants diminished, lack of alternative employment in the provinces encouraged them to move out to the suburbs. The threat of cheap competition from the western suburbs and from Southwark haunted the city's companies as these areas filled up with poor immigrants, many of them aliens, and growing numbers of prostitutes.[127]

It therefore seems that, despite its early growth in population of up to 60,000 which London reached in about 1300, it recovered from its subsequent decline in two main periods, the 1350s and 1360s, and the last decades of the fifteenth century. By 1500 it had again about 60,000 inhabitants. But the significant fact is that, whereas possibly one in sixty-six people had lived in London in 1300,[128] one in forty probably did so in 1500 – an increased concentration which helps to account for its greater share of national wealth.[129] This did not come about naturally. Initially it had political rather than economic causes because the diversion of the wool trade from the eastern ports was caused by war and by a royal policy which created the oversea staples. These factors also operated in the Londoners' favour in the second half of the fourteenth century to preserve their domination of the wool trade and to direct the imports of raw materials for the cloth industry through their hands. War in the later fifteenth century also interrupted Bristol's trade with Gascony and that of the eastern ports with the Baltic, leaving London to dominate exports to the remaining German market.

---

[125] *Rotuli Parliamentorum*, 6 vols. (London, 1783), V, p. 137.

[126] Keene, 'Shops and Shopping in Medieval London', p. 43.

[127] K. McDonnell, *Medieval London Suburbs* (Chichester, 1978), pp. 124–6. In 1456 the city tried to curb suburban competition by charging double fees for apprentices in Southwark: 'Journals of the Court of Common Council' (City of London Record Office), VII, fol. 54. In 1483 growing numbers of prostitutes were reportedly walking about the streets of the city and the suburbs: *Calendar of Letter-Book L*. p. 206. There are signs that Southwark was growing by the end of the fifteenth century, while even the poor area outside Aldgate had recovered by 1530 the density of building it enjoyed in 1300, that is, several decades ahead of Cheapside: Carlin, 'St Botolph, Aldgate', pp. 2, 7–8, 12.

[128] Calculated from the new estimate of a national population of 4 million.

[129] Dr Keene, working with an estimate for the national population of 5 million in 1300 and of 100,000 in London, suggested one in fifty lived in London in 1300, and about the same, or one in forty in 1500: 'Medieval London and its Region', pp. 100 and app. A. Calculating from a city of 100,000 in 1300 and a national population of 4 million, the figure would be one in forty, and from a city of 80,000, one in fifty – not a significant enough difference from the figures for 1500 to explain London's increased share of wealth and its marked expansion in the sixteenth century.

Economic forces worked partly through London's financial power which influenced royal policy over the staple and the franchise.[130] The franchise had mixed effects on its development, inhibiting alien trade but concentrating the distribution of imports in the Londoners' own hands. The plague, when combined with the high money supply of the 1350s and 1360s, stimulated and restructured demand. Even in the fifteenth century London had no difficulty in finding supplies of labour provided it had employment to offer. Its former emphasis on the retailing of luxuries was replaced by the distribution of more essential imports, and by its own manufactures, which met the needs of a more prosperous peasantry. In contrast with its decline during the depression of the early fourteenth century, once the oversea staple had concentrated trade and mercantile capital in London and the plague had restructured the economy, recessions worked to its advantage because it had the resources to withstand them more successfully than its provincial rivals. Immigrants searching for work were thereby drained from the provinces, and apprentices particularly were drawn from the impoverished north.[131] When the money supply recovered, first in the middle of the fourteenth century and then at the end of the fifteenth, London's trade recovered with it. But the decline of the provincial towns meant that by 1500 London had a greater concentration of population and wealth than in 1300 and it could expand at a far higher rate. Thus two of the great afflictions of the late medieval economy, plague and the shortage of coin, worked with royal policy and warfare to foster the conditions which made possible London's later extraordinary growth.

---

[130] For the importance of institutions in modifying economic growth, see S.A. Epstein, 'Town and Country: Economy and Institutions in Late Medieval Italy', *Econ. Hist. Rev.*, 2nd ser., 46 (1993), pp. 453–77.

[131] S. Thrupp, *The Merchant Class of Medieval London* (Chicago, 1948), pp. 211 (table 20), 389–92; A.J. Pollard, *North-Eastern England during the Wars of the Roses: Lay Society War and Politics, 1450–1500* (Oxford, 1990), pp. 71–80. Increased numbers were driven from the land in the later fifteenth century by the conversion of arable to pasture: A.F. Butcher, 'The Origins of Romney Freemen, 1433–1523', *Econ. Hist. Rev.*, 2nd ser., 27 (1974), pp. 16–27.

6

The bankruptcy of the Scali of Florence in England, 1326–1328

EDMUND FRYDE

I

A FOURTEENTH-CENTURY Italian merchant in financial difficulties considered a deliberate, sudden bankruptcy as one of the possible solutions to his problems.[1] The purpose of such a move would be to conceal as large a proportion of his assets as was practicable and to ensure for himself a not unprosperous future. There was always a risk of surprising reactions from the victims and political complications could add to the perils of the unscrupulous bankrupt. The public authorities had naturally to intervene and to impose some sort of orderly liquidation of business breakdowns, which might otherwise escalate and spread widespread ruin. All these features can be illustrated from the story of the English branches of the Scali. Their bankruptcy, and that of the Pulci and Rembertini some twenty years earlier, involved the interventions of the royal council and the chancery. The records produced by the resultant official proceedings throw interesting light on an early stage of international banking in western Europe, before the evolution of more uniform types of business documents and of standardised methods of attesting financial liabilities.

The ruthless unscrupulousness of these bankruptcies is well illustrated by what the Frescobaldi of Florence tried to do in Gascony in 1311. The outlines of this story are well known.[2] However, none of the existing accounts

---

[1] All the references to unpublished sources are to documents preserved at the Public Record Office (hereafter PRO).

[2] A. Sapori, *La compagnia dei Frescobaldi in Inghilterra* (Florence, 1947); *Gascon Rolls, 1307–1317*, ed. Y. Renouard (London, 1962); Y. Renouard, 'I Frescobaldi in Guyenne (1307–1322)', *Archivio Storico Italiano*, 122 (1964), pp. 459–70, reprinted in his *Études d'histoire médiévale* (Paris, 1968), II (no. xv, pp. 1059–68); R.W. Kaeuper, 'The Frescobaldi of Florence and the English Crown', *University of Nebraska Studies in Medieval and Renaissance History*, 10 (1973), pp. 41–95.

spell out all the details.[3] The Frescobaldi were under dire pressure. Their position as the principal bankers of King Edward II had exposed them to relentless hostility of Edward's political opponents, the Lords Ordainers, who were trying to cripple him financially by ruining his chief financiers. Also they had made enemies among business rivals in England. Anticipating imminent arrest and sequestration of all their assets, they tried to organise pre-emptive action. The head of the firm, Amerigo de' Frescobaldi, and his brother Bettino had managed to get away to Bruges and from there they tried to direct operations for the rescue of their assets. Amerigo was the titular constable of Bordeaux and controlled most of the revenues of Gascony, where he was represented by his deputy, Ugolino Ugolini, and three other associates. From Bruges he directed these men to prepare their escape to Flanders. In the meantime Ugolini was to ignore all royal orders for making payments and to avoid all other disbursements except on direct instructions of Amerigo. He was to assemble all the money and valuables that could be scraped together, in order to remove all this treasure outside the king's territories. Furthermore, the Gascon branch of the Frescobaldi was to acquire up to 1,000 tuns of wine, equivalent to about 8,500 hectolitres.[4] If they could not avoid paying in advance, they were to arrange assignments on Gascon revenues in the hands of the various local Gascon receivers, as Ugolini was still their official superior. These assignments would, of course, be worthless, as they were sure to be cancelled after the flight of Ugolini and his associates from Gascony. Nor would the defrauded creditors have had any remedy, as all the wine was to be shipped with all speed to Flanders as soon as it had been acquired. In order to make sure of the purchase of as much wine as possible, Ugolini was to offer very high prices, even up to double its real value, in the safe knowledge that nothing would ever be paid for it. Things turned out otherwise. The bearer of Amerigo's letter was intercepted outside Bordeaux by English officials. Ugolini and his three Italian factors were arrested and all their valuables and goods were seized.[5]

The bankruptcy of the Scali can also be usefully compared with another case of fraudulent default by the Buonaccorsi of Florence, in 1342. This is again an exceptionally well-documented story. Giovanni Villani, the famous

---

[3] My chief source for the instructions of the head of the Frescobaldi to his agents in Gascony about how to carry out a fraudulent bankruptcy consists of Exchequer, Treasury of the Receipt, Diplomatic Documents, E.30/1557, no.2. I owe my knowledge of this document to the kindness of Dr Pierre Chaplais. It has been partly published by E. Bond in *Archaeologia*, 28 (1840), pp. 250–3.

[4] Calculation of Renouard *Etudes d'histoire médiévale*, II, p. 1065 n. 9.

[5] The account of the royal officials who superseded Ugolini and arrested him and his agents is published in *Gascon Rolls, 1307–1317*, appendix II, pp. 546–67. It includes (on p. 560) a summary of Amerigo de' Frescobaldi's ill-fated letter to his Gascon agents and details of expenses incurred in arresting them and keeping them in various castles.

Florentine chronicler, was one of the chief partners of the Buonaccorsi and the considerable modern literature on him has thrown much light on his business activities.[6] In the first days of June 1342 the partners and agents of the Buonaccorsi suddenly fled from Florence, Avignon and Naples.[7] A complaint of the Neapolitan creditors at Florence started bankruptcy proceedings against them. Their creditors consisted almost entirely of people who had entrusted deposits to their bank.[8] A large number of Florentine firms were in difficulties and on the verge of bankruptcy at that time, but contemporaries at Florence treated the action of the Buonaccorsi as much more fraudulent than that of the other companies. Henceforth the partners of the Buonaccorsi were regarded with exceptional distrust, which was probably justified.[9] Giovanni Villani tried to give a version of events in his chronicle that deliberately obscures the truth.[10] Like the other Florentine bankers, the Buonaccorsi supported the setting up at Florence, early in September 1342, of a military dictatorship by Walter de Brienne. The new government, without annulling the proceedings in bankruptcy against them, effectively suspended all further legal actions against their partners for nearly a year.[11] They were resumed only in October 1343, after the violent overthrow of Walter's dictatorship.

The Scali were one of the oldest Florentine mercantile and banking companies. The company's existence can be traced back to the first quarter of the thirteenth century.[12] On the eve of its sudden collapse on 4 August 1326,[13] it was generally considered to be the most important Florentine commercial and banking firm. One impressive illustration of the scale of its activities comes from the papal archives. In the years 1321–4 Pope John XXII transmit-

---

[6] See especially M. Luzzati, 'Ricerche sulle attività mercantili e sul fallimento di Giovanni Villani', *Bulletino dell' Istituto Storico Italiano per il Medio Evo e Archivo Muratoriano*, 81 (1969), and M. Luzzati, *Giovanni Villani e la Compagnia dei Buonaccorsi* (Istituto della Enciclopedia Italiano, Rome, 1971).

[7] Luzzati, *Giovanni Villani*, pp. 48, 67.

[8] *Ibid.*, p. 35.

[9] *Ibid.*, pp. 55, 59: 'Ignoriamo. . . in che misura i soci Buonaccorsi fossero riusciti a sottrare ai creditori beni immobili e capitali liquidi: i sospetti di fraudolenza nei loro confronti erano stati tuttavia cosi numerosi e tanto accanito era stato l'assedio della *multitudo creditorum*.'

[10] This is one of the most convincing conclusions of Luzzati's book. See especially p. 55: 'fu proprio questo, cioè un implicito sospetto di fraudolenza, che il Villani cercò di nascondere'.

[11] *Ibid.* pp. 48–55.

[12] Their firm has never been the subject of a separate study. There is a summary of known information about them in Y. Renouard, *Recherches sur les compagnies commerciales et bancaires utilisées par les papes d'Avignon avant le Grand Schisme* (Paris, 1942), pp. 8–10. There is a list of its associates and factors mentioned in the papal archives between 1317 and 1326 in Y. Renouard, 'Le compagnie commerciali fiorentine del Trecento' (originally published in 1938), in his *Etudes d'histoire médiévale*, I, pp. 541–3.

[13] A. Sapori, *Studi di storia economica (secoli XIII–XIV–XV)*, I, 3rd edn (Florence, 1955), p. 393 n. 2.

ted to the papal legate in charge of military operations in Lombardy the enormous total of 560,000 florins. There were some transports of money under military escorts, but the bulk of the funds were transmitted by Florentine banks. The share of the Scali was 22 per cent of the total sum (125,000 florins). It is, however, worth stressing that the Scali were not used for making papal transfers to Italy after November 1324, though other Florentine firms continued to be employed for this purpose.[14] Perhaps the papal financial officials, who had means of being exceptionally well informed, began to have reasons for distrusting the solidity of the Scali. According to Giovanni Villani, who is a reliable source on such matters, the total liabilities of the Scali after their bankruptcy amounted to 400,000 florins.[15] This would surpass slightly the yearly revenue of Edward II in 1323.[16]

The years 1326–7 were exceptionally difficult for all the leading Florentine bankers. They were the chief political backers of Duke Charles of Calabria, the lord of Florence. His regime lasted nineteen months from the spring of 1326 to his sudden death on 14 November 1327. It was a very expensive government, financed by high taxes, but in his constant need for ready cash Charles anticipated his future revenues by heavy borrowing from the Florentine banking companies.[17] This seems to have been one of the causes of the downfall of the Scali, and their collapse in turn worsened the general crisis of the Florentine economy. Villani called the bankruptcy of the Scali in the late summer of 1326 a worse disaster than even the crushing defeat of the Florentines by a Pisan army in the previous year.[18] Thus, Florentine business at Genoa came to a standstill as the enraged creditors of the Scali seized the goods of the other Florentine merchants. Three leading Florentine companies had to pay the Genoese claimants 11,700 florins to end this intolerable situation.[19] The credit of all the Florentine banks was suddenly in doubt. Pope John XXII in a panic suspended altogether the employment of

---

[14] Y. Renouard, *Les relations des papes d'Avignon et des compagnies commerciales et bancaires de 1316 à 1378* (Paris, 1941), pp. 172–4.

[15] Renouard, *Recherches*, p. 9.

[16] I am assuming that 400,000 florins of Florence corresponded in 1326 to 100,000 marks sterling, at the rate of exchange of 3s. 3d. to a florin. This is the rate in the record of the proceedings about the bankruptcy of the Scali (Chancery Miscellanea, C.47/13, no. 3). The revenue of Edward II was estimated in January 1324 at £60,549. Cf. N. Fryde, *The Tyranny and Fall of Edward II, 1321–1326* (Cambridge, 1979), p. 97.

[17] G. Yver, *Le commerce et les marchands dans l'Italie méridionale au XIIIe et au XIVe siècle* (Paris, 1903), pp. 314–17; B. Barbadoro, *Le finanze della repubblica fiorentina* (Florence, 1929), pp. 541–59; R. Barducci, 'Politica e speculazione finanziaria a Firenze dopo la crisi del primo trecento (1343–1358)', *Archivio Storico Italiano*, 137 (1979), pp. 203–4. I owe thanks to my friend, Prof. Louis Green, for valuable advice about these events.

[18] Renouard, *Relations des papes*, p. 81, citing *Croniche di Giovanni, Matteo e Filippo Villani secondo le migliori stampe e corredate di note filologiche e storiche*, Biblioteca classica italiana, secolo XIV (Trieste, 1857), X, p. 4.

[19] Renouard, *Recherches*, p. 9.

banking firms for the transfer of funds to the papal army in Lombardy and only changed his mind two years later after a direct transport of 60,000 florins under an escort of papal officials had been partly plundered near Pavia.[20]

The liquidation of the Scali dragged on for many years at Florence. In 1329 the official syndics in charge of their assets were trying to dispose of the valuable properties of one of the partners.[21] As late as 1343 the Scali were still trying to recover some of the money due from their own debtors and, like the Buonaccorsi, sought for a time the help of Walter de Brienne's dictatorship, though they ultimately turned against him. The Scali and their close associates, the Amieri, continued thereafter to be of some importance in Florentine politics.[22] Their Florentine creditors received ultimately 44 per cent of what was owed to them.[23]

II

The main sources for the study of the proceedings in bankruptcy against the London branch of the Scali are two formal records drawn up by the officials of the royal chancery. There must have once existed other informal records containing very complex calculations lying behind the final settlement. The lengthier of the two formal documents is contained today in Chancery Miscellanea, C.47/13, no. 3. It summarises the entire proceedings from August 1326 to the carrying out of the final awards to the creditors, completed by February 1328.[24] The other record is C.47/13, no. 4. It is a partial list of claims submitted to the chancery. It omits three undoubtedly English claimants. It also omits two German claims which were dealt with separately on privileged terms and were settled by payments made on 20 September 1327.[25] Our C.47/13, no. 4, may have been drawn up after that date. It does include notes of the scaling down of some of the claims and must have been drawn up after the completion of detailed accounting.

Neither of these records tells us what was the origin of the debts owed by the Scali to the creditors of the London branch. Presumably some had arisen out of sums of money entrusted to the Scali in order that they might transfer them to foreign countries. This was probably the origin of the exchange transactions that will be discussed later in greater detail. The rest,

[20] Renouard, *Relations des papes*, p. 171.
[21] *I libri di commercio dei Peruzzi*, ed. A. Sapori (Milan, 1934), pp. 54, 357.
[22] Luzzati, *Giovanni Villani*, pp. 57–8; A Sapori, *La crisi delle compagnie mercantili dei Bardi e dei Peruzzi* (Florence, 1926), pp. 151, 158 and n.1.
[23] Renouard, *Recherches*, pp. 9–10.
[24] *Cal. Close Rolls 1327–30*, p. 368.
[25] *Ibid.*, p. 223.

no doubt, consisted of interest-bearing deposits entrusted to the Scali, though there is no information about the terms on which they were held by this Florentine bank.

News of the impending collapse of the Scali must have travelled fast, as within sixteen days of their bankruptcy in Florence (4 August 1326) Edward II ordered remedial measures in England. On 20 August he instructed all sheriffs to arrest the agents and the goods of the Scali and to hold inquiries into the debts owed to their firm,

> the king having learned that the said society is dissolved and the merchants thereof dispersed and that such merchants, staying in London and elsewhere in the realm, who are held to the king and certain merchants and others in the realm in diverse sums of money propose to leave the realm privily with their goods and to defraud the king and the said merchants and others of such debts.[26]

This charge of fraudulent intent was common form in cases of bankruptcy and one cannot tell whether it was justified in this particular instance.

The head of the English branch of the Scali had gone abroad in 1325,[27] leaving behind only two senior factors. These men, Landus Omodei and Cerbius Tenchini, were not partners of their firm and this was cited as the ground for their ultimate release in February 1328, as they could not be held personally responsible.[28] One may be justified in suspecting that, already in 1325, the London branch was preparing for a possible bankruptcy in the near future.

In the autumn of 1326 the royal council was in charge of dealing with the affairs of the Scali. Nothing is heard at this stage of the role of the chancery. On 13 September the council directed that all the sequestrated money and goods of the Scali should be entrusted to the other leading Florentine firms active in England, the Bardi and the Peruzzi. They agreed to keep those assets until such time as the king might set on foot judicial proceedings. At this point it was envisaged that the creditors would be summoned 'to make their prosecution before certain of his justices to be deputed for this purpose'. An association of creditors had been formed, headed by John de Pinibus, archdeacon of Bazas, attorney of one of the cardinals who had suffered losses. On their surety the two factors of the bankrupt company, Omodei and Tenchini, were provisionally released and

---

[26] *Cal. Fine Rolls, 1319–27*, p. 409.

[27] *Cal. Pat. Rolls, 1324–7*, p. 106.

[28] *Cal. Pat. Rolls, 1327–30*, p. 233: 'Discharge of the arrest and the bail of Cerbius Tenchini and Landus Omodei, proctors and servants of the society of the Scali of Florence, . . . as it appears that they were not partners of the same.'

were allowed to move freely in the realm, but were prohibited from leaving the country.[29]

The revolution that put an end to the rule of Edward II in September–October 1326 nullified most of these initial arrangements.[30] The sheriffs of London failed to deliver to the Bardi and the Peruzzi the assets of the Scali. This was just as well, as the house of the Bardi in the city of London had been plundered in October. Both firms had been bankers of the hated Despensers and were in temporary eclipse.[31]

Proceedings in bankruptcy were resumed in February 1327. The creditors included a powerful group of cardinals and this might have been the chief reason why the English government was anxious to settle this business speedily. The lord mayor of London was ordered to deliver the goods and other assets of the Scali into the hands of the attorneys of this syndicate of creditors.[32] It is now that the royal chancery was entrusted with supervising the liquidation of the Scali and we hear no more of proceedings before the royal justices. The resultant records never mention whether the chancellor himself was involved in this case. It is more probable that the hearings took place before the keeper of the chancery rolls and its senior clerks. It is noticeable that the mandates which under the great seal gave effect to the various decisions that were reached gradually, as the case proceeded, did not require any further authorization and have no notes of warranty. The chancery was now in exclusive control.[33]

All creditors were invited to present their claims at the chancery on 15 June 1327. It was ascertained that the assets of the English branch of the Scali available for distribution to the claimants amounted to £459.[34] What followed is not explained in the two formal records that alone are available but can be reconstructed to some extent through a series of calculations. The total claims amounted to £2,420 12s. 3d.[35] Two German claims were accorded privileged treatment (50 per cent of debts paid), as will be discussed more fully presently. The rest were satisfied at the rate of about 19 per cent of each claim, though there are slight variations, one small creditor receiving, for example, 20 per cent.[36] How that percentage of 19 per cent

---

[29] *Cal. Close Rolls, 1323–7*, p. 607 and PRO, C.47/13, no. 3.
[30] Queen Isabella landed in Suffolk on 24 September 1326. Cf. Fryde, *Tyranny and Fall*, p. 185.
[31] *Ibid.*, pp. 193–4, 214.
[32] *Cal. Close Rolls 1327–30*, p. 40 (25 February 1327), and C.47/13, no. 3.
[33] This is quite clear from the record of the proceedings: *ibid.*
[34] *Ibid.*
[35] *Ibid.*
[36] Elias de Burgo received £3 14s. 3d. on a claim of £19 7s. 6d. (C.47/13, nos. 3 and 4). However, he was the servant of Archdeacon John de Pinibus, who appears to have been the head of the syndicate of creditors.

was arrived at can be satisfactorily demonstrated, as £459 (the total assets) amount to just over 19 per cent of £2,420 12s. 3d.

The treatment of the two German claims is puzzling. They amounted to £360 and the claimants, by the unanimous assent of the other creditors, received £180 (50 per cent) on 20 September 1327. The payments were made by the Scali at Lincoln. The debts were attested by two bonds issued by the agents of the Scali at Antwerp in Brabant. There is no mention of payments being due in England,[37] although, as these two debts were payable in the English sterling currency, this is possible. One of the Germans was the attorney of Liffard Clippyng. This was the name of an important family of Hanseatic merchants from Dortmund.[38]

A guess might be hazarded for the privileged treatment of these two claimants. Perhaps they were threatening separate legal actions which might have delayed considerably the final settlement and might have encouraged other continental creditors of the Scali to present demands in London. Be that as it may, these Germans secured more than twice the percentage allowed to the other creditors (50 per cent as opposed to 19 per cent).

In order to establish how this large payment was made possible one can put forward only a number of hypotheses. We know that £362 4s. 8d. were actually distributed to the remaining creditors.[39] With the addition of £180 we get a total of £542 4s. 8d., a sum considerably in excess of the £459 already available for distribution. However, it can be calculated that the accounting at the chancery revealed that the claims submitted by the creditors surpassed by £172 14s., the amount that was really owed to them. Some claimants had failed to disclose that they had secured partial repayments. In some other cases the records of the Scali revealed a smaller debt than the amount claimed by a creditor.[40] This excess of claims over genuine debts may have provided some room for the more generous treatment of the two Germans. It is nowhere explained where this additional money came from (over and above the bankruptcy fund of £459). Perhaps the Scali managed to raise some more money by borrowing from some of the creditors who had made excessive claims but were anxious to pacify the two German claimants.

Except possibly for the two German debts, all the claims presented to the chancery appear to have arisen out of liabilities incurred by the English branch of the Scali. Their factors were asked in each case whether they

37 C.47/13, no. 3; *Cal. Close Rolls 1327–30*, p. 223.
38 Cf. E.B. Fryde, 'Financial Resources of Edward III in the Netherlands, 1337–40', in Fryde, *Studies in Medieval Trade and Finance* (London, 1983), no. VII, pp. 1125–6.
39 C.47/13, no. 3.
40 The evidence is in C.47/13, no. 4. For some of the details see below.

admitted the claim and whether the debt was still outstanding. In a number of cases they alleged in reply that a part of the debt had been repaid. The chancery examined the evidence and, in six cases, after accepting the proofs offered by the Scali, reduced the debts.[41] The whole operation was completed by February 1328.[42]

One of the most interesting features of these proceedings in chancery is the wide variety of proofs presented by the creditors. The situation was similar to what had happened some twenty years earlier after the English representatives of the Pulci and Rembertini had absconded from this country in January 1306.[43]

The most common type of evidence presented by the creditors of the Scali were holograph letters written at London in the hand of Landus Omodei, the senior factor at their London branch, and sealed with the seal of Scali. An alternative consisted of letters obligatory written at London and sealed with the seal of their society. A slightly different variant appears among the claims submitted against the Pulci and Rembertini. This was a letter written in London under the seal of one of the merchants of their company, binding both himself and the society.[44] Lastly, among the evidence presented by the creditors of the Scali, was a notarial act drawn up in London obliging their society.[45]

Transactions where obligations incurred in one currency were repayable in a different kind of coinage were a frequent feature of Italian business dealings. They might arise out of genuine transfers of money from one country to another. All the cases recorded in the proceedings concerning the Pulci and Rembertini and the Scali were probably of this kind. But exchange transactions could be used merely to conceal interest charges under the cover of differing exchange rates.

A loan repayable in a different currency might be recorded in some sort of formal instrument such as a notarial act or a bond under the seal of the borrower.[46] The claims against the Scali included both these types of documents. The notarial act mentioned a moment ago concerned an exchange transaction. To cite another variant, formal letters obligatory sealed by the Scali were presented by the attorney of Cardinal Raymond Guilhem de Fargues, who claimed 2,430 florins of Florence and 15d. sterling as the

[41] *Ibid.*, nos. 3 and 4.
[42] *Cal. Close Rolls 1327–30*, p. 368.
[43] *Cal. Pat. Rolls 1301–7*, p. 412.
[44] Exchequer, King's Remembrancer, Accounts Various, E.101/127/5, no. 19.
[45] C.47/13, no. 4: 'per publicum instrumentum scriptum et publicatum manu Ugochionis Sensii de Ficulino apostolica auctoritate notarii'. It is mentioned in C.47/13, no. 3 that it was drawn up in London.
[46] R. de Roover, *L'évolution de la lettre de change, XIVe – XVIII siècles* (Paris, 1953), pp. 38–40.

exchange value of 600 marks sterling (*pro precio et cambio sexcentarum marca-rum sterlingorum*).[47] If the associates or correspondents of the original borrower had to be instructed to repay the loan in another currency and in a different locality, this could be done through an informal letter duplicating some of the contents of the formal notarial act or of sealed bond. Such a letter of payment (*lettera di pagamento*) ultimately evolved into the type of special document that we call a bill of exchange.[48] The statements of the claimants against the Pulci and Rembertini and against the Scali are not detailed enough to show whether they were presenting fully developed bills of exchange. The earliest such document of which we have the full text dates from 1339,[49] but this happens to be merely the earliest survivor of what was by then a well-established type of business instrument.[50] Most probably the documents connected with the two bankruptcies were variants of a less technically developed letter of payment directing the reimbursement of a debt incurred in a different currency from the one used in repayment. Thus, one of the creditors of the Pulci and Rembertini, Bettino Boiamonti of Lucca, claimed that their society owed him 426 marks, 9s. 4d. sterling 'pur change de deners qe lour compaignons de Provyns eussent a la foyre de Provyns Lan de Grace 1305 pur rendre a Londres 9 Decembre lan avantdit'.[51]

Italian merchants often relied on their account books as a sufficient record of transactions between themselves. Thus, the head of the Scali in London, involved in a dispute with another Florentine merchant, claimed in August 1324 that 'it was usual amongst the alien merchants of the realm, in the case of loans and other financial transactions between them, for memoranda thereof to be made in their papers on both sides, stating the amount, the cause and the term of payment without any bond being made between them'.[52] In 1314 the officials of the English royal exchequer accepted the statements in the account books of Antonio Pessagno, the king's Genoese banker, as a basis for the certificate of loans and repayments that they sent to King Edward II, as the exchequer itself lacked a record of comparable completeness.[53]

---

[47] C.47/13, no. 3.

[48] De Roover, *Evolution de la lettre de change*, pp. 38–40. See also F. Melis, *Documenti per la storia economica dei secoli XIII-XVI* (Florence, 1972), pp. 88–9.

[49] Published in an English translation by R.S. Lopez and I.W. Raymond, *Medieval Trade in the Mediterranean World* (London, 1955), p. 231.

[50] Cf. De Roover, *Evolution de la lettre de change*, p. 40, discussing a case in 1330, 'année pour laquelle, d'après d'autres sources, cette évolution s'était déjà accomplie'.

[51] Exchequer Miscellanea, E. 163/3, no. 2.

[52] *Cal. Pat. Rolls, 1324–7*, p. 68.

[53] N. Fryde, 'Antonio Pessagno of Genoa, King's Merchant of Edward II of England', *Studi in memoria di Federigo Melis*, 5 vols. (Florence, 1978), II, p. 178.

The evidence of the records of the Scali was cited several times in the proceedings in chancery about their bankruptcy. The attorney of Cardinals Luca Fieschi and John Caetani invoked jointly three bills written by Landus Omodei sealed with the seal of the Scali and also 'the books of the said society'.[54] Antonio Usodimare of Genoa claimed £200 on the evidence of the books and papers of the company (*ut apparet per libros et papiras dicte societatis de Scalis*).[55] These records could also be invoked by the merchants themselves to substantiate their counter claims. Thus, Archdeacon John de Pinibus, attorney of Cardinal Raymond de Fargues, presented a claim for 165 marks. The Scali retorted that they had repaid £50 out of this debt. John resolutely denied this. Landus Omodei of the Scali was able to show that this payment was attested by two available records (*in papiro suo et in quadam littera manu ipsius Johannis scripta*). The chancery accepted the statement of Landus.[56] Antonio Usodimare of Genoa as attorney of Leonellus de Marinis of Genoa demanded £178 in accordance with letters sealed with the company seal (*per litteras sigillatas sigillo dicte societatis*). But the chancery scaled this down to £125. 6s. 8d. *per papiras* which must refer to the records of the Scali.[57]

The claimants included attorneys of four cardinals. John de Pinibus, archdeacon of Bazas, acted for Cardinal Raymond Guilhem de Fargues, cardinal deacon of St Maria Nuova, whose chaplain he was.[58] Cardinal Raymond had been promoted in 1310 by his uncle, Pope Clement V, and lived until 1346. He was out of favour under Clement's successors and was chiefly preoccupied with administering his revenues.[59] He had benefices in England[60] and his dealings with the Scali may have originated in the need to transfer to France his English income. His claims had originally amounted to £510 but the Scali were able to prove that they had repaid him £116 13s. 4d. on two different deposits. Even after this reduction he still received the largest single payment (£75 3s. 2d.), though the next big claimants, a pair of Italian merchants, were not far behind (£71 18s. 6d.)[61] The way in which

---

[54] C.47/13, no. 4: 'per libros dicte societatis'.

[55] *Ibid*.

[56] C.47/13, nos. 3 and 4.

[57] *Ibid*.

[58] *Accounts Rendered by Papal Collectors in England, 1317–1378*, ed. W.E. Lunt and E.B. Graves (Philadelphia, 1968), p. 53.

[59] B. Guillemain, *La cour pontificale d'Avignon (1309–1376): étude d'une société* (Paris, 1962), pp. 193, 212–13.

[60] *Accounts Rendered by Papal Collectors*, p. 80 (York diocese); *Calendar of Memoranda Rolls (Exchequer), Michaelmas 1326 – Michaelmas 1327*, ed. R.E. Latham (HMSO, London, 1968), no. 1750 (Chichester diocese). He was dean of Salisbury in 1317. Cf. R.M. Haines, *The Church and Politics in Fourteenth Century England: The Career of Adam Orleton, c. 1275–1345* (Cambridge, 1978), p. 17.

[61] C.47/13, nos. 3 and 4.

Raymond's attorney tried at first to secure more than was due to his master suggests that they may have been rather unscrupulous churchmen.

Luca Fieschi, a member of an illustrious Genoese family which had produced two popes in the thirteenth century, was cardinal deacon of St Maria in Via Lata, from 1300 to 1336.[62] He had been repeatedly entrusted with political missions, including one to England in 1317–18.[63] On that occasion he had been captured and robbed by men acting in collusion with Thomas, earl of Lancaster. In compensation Edward gave Fieschi a pension.[64] His deposit with the Scali of £60 may have originated out of this or out of the revenues of his English benefices.[65] John Caetani, cardinal deacon of St Teodoro, was cardinal from 1316 to 1335.[66] He was related to the great Roman family to which had belonged Pope Boniface VIII. He served as papal legate to England in 1327. He had numerous preferments in this country, including the positions of archdeacon of Coventry and of a canon of Lincoln.[67] He was claiming £118 17s. 1d., using the same attorney (Thomas de Luco) as Luca Fieschi.[68] The fourth cardinal, called simply Cardinal 'Avynon',[69] has defied all my attempts at identification.[70] His claim, after a slight reduction of £3, amounted to £100 6s. 8d. His attorney, Peter Baurelli, acted in conjunction with John de Pinibus.[71] Lastly, Arnaud de Fabrica, likewise represented by John de Pinibus, is probably to be identified with a man of that name who was a clerk (*scriptor litterarum secretarum*) of the papal chamber.[72] He claimed £43 1s. 8d.[73] A claim by Elias de Burgo, a servant of John de Pinibus, for £19 7s. 6d. has been mentioned earlier on. Altogether this group connected with the papal court claimed £734 19s. 7d.

---

[62] Guillemain, *La cour pontificale*, p. 212.

[63] *Ibid.*, p. 185 n. 11 and p. 310; J.R. Maddicott, *Thomas of Lancaster, 1307–1322* (Oxford, 1970), pp. 204–6.

[64] N. Fryde, 'Antonio Pessagno', p. 164.

[65] He was a canon of Lichfield (*Cal. Memoranda Rolls*, no. 354) and held at least one other English benefice (*Cal. Pat. Rolls 1324–7*, p. 119).

[66] Guillemain, *La cour pontificale*, p. 190 n. 56. He was closely related to the other great Roman family of the Orsini (*ibid.* and p. 191 n. 61).

[67] *Calendar and Register of Adam de Orelton, Bishop of Worcester, 1327–33*, ed. R.M. Haines (Worcs. Hist. Soc., 1979), cf. index, *sub nomine*; *Cal. Pat. Rolls, 1330–4*, p. 243.

[68] C.47/13, nos. 3 and 4.

[69] C.47/13, no. 3.

[70] The problem arises from the fact that after the death of his nephew, Cardinal Jacques de Via in 1317, Pope John XXII did not appoint a successor to the bishopric. The cardinal of Avignon was presumably the prelate who was adminstering the bishopric in 1326–7. Cf. Guillemain, *La cour pontificale*, pp. 158, 212 n. 167, 501.

[71] C.47/13, nos. 3 and 4.

[72] Guillemain, *La cour pontificale*, p. 296 and n. 106.

[73] C.47/13, no. 4. His original deposit consisted of '220 French gold florins with a lamb (*agni aurei*)'.

As might be expected, Italian merchants presented the largest total of claims, amounting to £1,033 3s. 6d.[74] Italian banking firms dealt habitually with businessmen from many different Italian cities. The list of the creditors of the London branch of the Scali included men from Florence, Lucca and Genoa. The Lucchese group claimed £333 6s. 8d. Two partners, of whom one was Silvester Ricci of Florence, were the second largest claimants after Cardinal Raymond de Fargues. The Ricci were one of the more important Florentine families. Silvester and his partner claimed £374 10s. 2d. and recovered £71 18s. 6d. Their attorney was Antonio Usodimare of Genoa, who also claimed £125 6s. 8d. for another Genoese, Leonellus de Marinis, as well as £200 for himself. Unlike these other Italians, Antonio is well known to English historians. In the previous decade he had been associated with Antonio Pessagno.[75] In 1337–41 he was the acting constable of Bordeaux, deputising for his relative, Nicholas Usodimare.[76]

The claims of English creditors formed a much more modest group amounting, at most, to £103. There were four of them, though it is not certain that Magister Robert Lowell (claim of forty marks) was an Englishman, as Antonio Usodimare acted as his attorney.[77] Gilbert de la Bruere (claim of £25) is probably identical with the canon of York of that name.[78] I have been unable to discover anything about Richard de Hamiseldene (claim of £10 3s. 4d.). John Charlton, who claimed £41, was a London mercer and an important civic politician. He had been mayor of the wool staple in 1318–23 and again in 1326. Though a supporter of Edward II, and exiled for a while from London after Edward's downfall, he was again an influential citizen a few months later.[79]

It would be anachronistic to regard the settlement of the bankruptcy of the Scali by the chancery as an example of the exercise by that department of equitable jurisdiction. Such things lay in distant future. The chancery had been brought into the proceedings as an act of state, because important creditors were involved.[80] After the bankruptcy of the Pulci and Rembertini, it was the royal council that tried to produce a settlement to satisfy the claims of notables like the earl of Hereford, Lady Isabella de Vescy and Guy Ferre,

---

[74] All the claims mentioned in this paragraph are listed in C.47/13, nos. 3 and 4.
[75] N. Fryde, 'Antonio Pessagno', p. 163.
[76] T.F. Tout, *Chapters in the Adminstrative History of Medieval England*, 6 vols. (Manchester, 1920–33), VI, p. 68.
[77] C.47/13, no. 4.
[78] *Cal. Pat. Rolls, 1324–7*, p. 68.
[79] G.A. Williams, *Medieval London: From Commune to Capital* (London, 1963), pp. 280, 285, 294, 297, 300.
[80] See the wise comments of B. Wilkinson in 'The Chancery', in J.F. Willard, W.A. Morris, J.R. Strayer and W.H. Dunham (eds.), *The English Government at Work, 1327–1336*, 3 vols. (Cambridge, Mass., 1940–50), I, pp. 188–95.

royal seneschal in Gascony.[81] In 1326, likewise, the council was initially in charge of the proceedings against the Scali and it was only after the revolution of October 1326 that the chancery was brought in to settle this affair. Besides, one must not stress too much the difference between the royal council and the chancery. In routine administrative proceedings the chancellor and his senior assistants often formed the effective core of the royal council.[82]

Once the chancery had been entrusted with the business of the Scali, it produced a very workmanlike settlement. It carried out careful hearings, treated all the parties in a fair, judicious way and enforced a settlement that was as just as the circumstances permitted. It drew up and preserved a permanent record of its decisions. This was presumably kept henceforth among the chancery files[83] and hence it is found today among the Chancery Miscellanea at the Public Record Office.

[81] Chancery Miscellanea, C.47/13/1, no. 25. The record starts; 'Accorde et par le consaille [le] Roy.'
[82] Wilkinson, 'The Chancery', pp. 194–5.
[83] There is a hole for filing in the longer of the two records, C.47/13, no. 3.

7

The English export trade in cloth in the fourteenth century

WENDY CHILDS

THE FORTUNES of England's cloth industry and trade in the thirteenth and fourteenth centuries have long been a matter of interest and, thirty years ago, Edward Miller contributed to the debate an essential, wide-ranging and careful article,[1] whose value is demonstrated by the frequency of its citation. With Miller, most historians would probably accept that England's industry declined or at best failed to expand in the thirteenth century, that this had much to do with competition from Flemish imports, that certainly some urban centres were in difficulty while some country areas grew. Many would probably also agree with Anthony Bridbury who, with his usual invigorating criticism of all earlier discussions,[2] emphasised the absence of secure figures, and the fact that evidence can be read in several ways. However, without doubt the evidence assembled over the years shows that whatever the industry's difficulties, it was far from dead in the early fourteenth century.[3] Continuing high imports of mordants and dyestuffs, especially of woad,[4] the crown's willingness to support groups with an interest in home industry (as in the prohibition of the export of teasels and fullers earth in 1326 at the behest of Londoners)[5] and the tightening of the cloth assize (which may have been meant to hamper foreign competition), all suggest growth before 1347. In his article Miller also identified the diversity of English products,

---

[1] E. Miller, 'The Fortunes of the English Textile Industry during the Thirteenth Century', *Econ. Hist. Rev.*, 2nd ser., 18 (1965), pp. 64–82.

[2] A.R. Bridbury, *Medieval English Clothmaking: An Economic Survey* (London, 1982).

[3] Miller, 'Fortunes', pp. 77–9.

[4] E.M. Carus-Wilson, 'La guède française en Angleterre: un grand commerce du moyen âge', *Revue du Nord*, 35 (1953), pp. 89ff.

[5] This was an event important enough to be recorded in chronicles as well as municipal records: *Calendar of Letter Books of the City of London: Letter Book E*, ed. R.R. Sharpe (London, 1903), pp. 210–11; *The Anonimalle Chronicle 1307 to 1334; from Brotherton Collection MS 29*, ed. W.R. Childs and J. Taylor (Yorks. Arch. Soc. Rec. Ser., no. 147, 1991).

and suggested that the cheaper cloths available indicated that England was responding to market difficulties by falling back on 'slump' products.[6] Recently debate has focussed again on the topic of the range of products, and John Munro and Patrick Chorley have seen cheap cloth less as a slump product than as an indication of an international 'mass market' in the thirteenth century.[7] This market was certainly changing in 1300–40, which would put further pressures on producers, but England's industry was over the worst by then and dealt very successfully with changes in the later fourteenth century.

The range of English cloths on the late thirteenth-century international market can be established from several sources, as the example of Spain illustrates.[8] A price-fixing list from the Spanish *cortes* in 1268 covered at least forty-six separate types of cloth, in four broad price bands. Only four types of English cloth were mentioned, but they spread across the spectrum. The top group of scarlets and coloureds included two English types: Lincoln scarlet (second only to scarlet from Montpellier and priced above scarlet of Ghent), and best English grained cloth (sixth equal with Ghent coloured cloth). English black (equal with says of Ypres and Bruges) was at the bottom of the second group. English *pardo* (a grey or brown colour, probably a russet cloth) came very low in the third group, which included serges, biffas and the cheaper cloths of Bruges, Douai, Valenciennes, St Omer, and one local cloth (burel of Avila). The fourth group was mainly of local Spanish cloth (*panno desta tierra*), with specific mention of *cardenos, viados*, blankets, frieze and says, variously of Avila, Segovia, Zamora and Navarre.[9] A late thirteenth-century tariff list for northern Spanish ports noted only one English cloth, in the second of its three tax categories; below the scarlets and coloured cloths of Ghent and Ypres, English stamfords (*estanfortes Danglaterra tintos o per tenir*) were included with biffas, and cloths of St Omer,

[6] Miller, 'Fortunes', pp. 77–80.
[7] P. Chorley, 'The Cloth Exports of Flanders and Northern France during the Thirteenth Century: A Luxury Trade?', *Econ. Hist. Rev.*, 2nd ser., 40 (1987), pp. 349–79. And see particularly J.H. Munro, 'Industrial Transformations in the North-West European Textile Trades, *c.* 1290–*c.* 1340: Economic Progress or Economic Crisis?', in B.M.S. Campbell (ed.), *Before the Black Death: Studies in the 'Crisis' of the Early Fourteenth Century*, (Manchester, 1991), pp. 110–48.
[8] For context for these remarks see W.R. Childs, *Anglo-Castilian Trade in the Later Middle Ages* (Manchester, 1978), pp. 77–8; P. Chorley, 'English Cloth Exports during the Thirteenth and Early Fourteenth Centuries: The Continental Evidence', *Hist. Research*, 61 (1988), pp. 1–10.
[9] *Cortes de los antiguos reinos de León y de Castilla*, 5 vols. (Publicadas por la Real Academia de la Historia, Madrid, 1883–1903), I, pp. 65–8. Prices break naturally into four bands; a top group at £1 to £2 5s. the *vara*, a second at 10s. to 12s. 6d., a third at 5s. to 9s., a fourth at 4d. to 4s.

Tournai and Bruges.[10] Fragmentary customs accounts for San Sebastian and Fuenterrabía in 1293–4, however, show three sorts of English cloth, still across the spectrum: six pieces were black and at 250 maravedís each were fairly expensive, but not in the top category; four pieces were of cheaper white cloth at 140 maravedís; and one piece of narrow red say was unpriced.[11] This sort of evidence shows a reasonably broad production, but overall suggests a limited amount exported in the late thirteenth century, in line with traditional explanations of Flemish competition. Naturally, evidence for domestic commerce suggests a much wider choice. Half a dozen of 108 towns in a thirteenth-century metrical list were known for their woollen cloths: scarlet of Lincoln, hauberge of Stamford, blanket of Blyth, burnet of Beverley, russet of Colchester, chalons of Guildford,[12] and the appointment of an ulnager at London in 1315 indicates that the 'normal' commercial range of woollen cloth known to the king's clerks was wadmal, Heydok, Mendips, kerseys, Louth says, worsted of Norwich, Ireland and Causton, other says and scarlets, and all kinds of cloth of Lincoln, Essex, Norfolk, Suffolk, Kent, Stamford, Beverley, St Osith, Devon and Cornwall.[13] Some of this undoubtedly went abroad through London, a murage grant for which in 1317 listed dyed English cloth, russet and scarlet coming to London to be sold, and bales of cloth coming to London for export.[14]

A source mentioned but not fully exploited in examinations of the industry's output is the series of particular customs accounts, which have the advantage of showing in much more detail the balance and range of cloth which England actually put into Europe at the beginning of the fourteenth century. Customs accounts cannot in general be said to have been ignored by historians of the cloth trade. Published figures from the final audited and enrolled accounts for wool and cloth exports are readily available and underpin our understanding of the major changes in England's overseas trade.[15] They have also been used for the wine trade, and a number of the particular

[10] A. Castro, 'Unos aranceles de aduanas del siglo XIII', *Revista de Filología Española*, 8 (1921), p. 10.

[11] M. Gaibrois Riaña de Ballesteros, *Historia del Reinado de Sancho IV*, 3 vols. (Madrid, 1922–9), I, appendix, pp. iiiff. The material on cloth has been summarised by M. Gual Camarena, 'El comercio de telas en el siglo XIII hispano', *Anuario de Historia Económic y Social*, 1 (1968), pp. 85–106. The amounts of English cloth were small, but trade was upset this year by various Anglo-French and Hispano-Gascon conflicts. In that sense, it was exceptional (*pace* Chorley, 'English Cloth Exports', p. 6, n. 13).

[12] *English Historical Documents, 1189–1327*, ed. H. Rothwell (London, 1975), no. 230, pp. 881–4.

[13] *Calendar of Letter Books*, E, pp. 53–4, 57.

[14] *Ibid.*, p. 65.

[15] E.M. Carus-Wilson and O. Coleman, *England's Export Trade, 1275–1547* (Oxford, 1963). Dr Lloyd has recently published the audited figures for the period 1303 to 1337: T.H. Lloyd, *Alien Merchants in England in the High Middle Ages* (Brighton, 1982) appendix 1.

accounts have also been published.[16] Yet the detailed accounts, for goods other than wool, are not as freely used for the early fourteenth century as they might be, because they have a number of shortcomings, and are less full than those of the fifteenth century. In the early fourteenth century they were still part of a new and experimental system, not yet properly covering all areas, not yet homogeneous, not yet tightly supervised, and covering only alien trade. Nonetheless, they are more focussed, more consistently supervised and survive better than the ulnage accounts,[17] and add valuable detail to our knowledge of the patterns and order of magnitude of England's international trade. They deserve closer examination.

I

In 1303 the crown negotiated payment of customs from all alien merchants in return for the commercial freedoms listed in the grant known as the *Carta Mercatoria*. The merchants agreed to pay extra duties by the unit on wool, wool fells, hides, wine, wax and cloth, and by the value on all other imports and exports. Collectors were set up alongside those for the old wool duties and kept detailed records of merchants, goods and sometimes ships. They brought their rolls to the exchequer for auditing, where the documents were checked and, once accepted, the totals of tax collected were recorded in the enrolled accounts. When this had been done, of course, the detailed accounts quickly lost their value, and many have been lost over the centuries, but a reasonable number survive for the period from 1303 to 1311 (at which date the tax was suspended by the baronial opponents of Edward II), and again for the 1320s (after it had been reinstated by a triumphant Edward II after the battle of Boroughbridge in 1322).[18] Unfortunately survivals are rare for the 1330s and 1340s, which means we cannot see how alien exports were running in the 1340s immediately before the introduction of the new duty

---

[16] M.K. James, *Studies in the Medieval Wine Trade*, ed. E.M. Veale (Oxford, 1971); N.S.B. Gras, *The Early English Customs System* (Cambridge, Mass., 1918); *The Overseas Trade of Bristol in the Later Middle Ages*, ed. E.M. Carus-Wilson (Bristol Rec. Society, no. 7, 1937); *The Customs Accounts of Hull, 1453–1490*, ed. W.R. Childs (Yorks. Arch. Soc. Rec. Ser., no. 144, 1986); *The Overseas Trade of London: Exchequer Customs Accounts 1480–1*, ed. H.S. Cobb (London Rec. Soc., no. 27, 1990).

[17] The strengths and weaknesses of the ulnage system are examined in E.M. Carus-Wilson, 'The Aulnage Accounts: A Criticism', *Econ. Hist. Rev.*, 2 (1929), pp. 114–23, reprinted in *Medieval Merchant Venturers* 2nd edn (London, 1967), pp. 279–91; Bridbury, *English Clothmaking*, ch. 5.

[18] Full year or partial accounts survive for Hull (1303–9, 1310–11, 1324–5), Boston (1303, 1308–10, 1326–7, 1333–4), Lynn (1303–7, 1308–9, 1322–7), Yarmouth (1309–11, 1324–7, 1331–2), Ipswich (1304–5, 1308–9, 1323–7), London (1306–8, 1310–11), Sandwich (1303–4, 1307–8, 1326–8), Southampton (1308–11, 1322–3), Devon (1323–6) and Bristol (1303–9, 1323–7).

in 1347, by which both aliens and Englishmen were taxed, but they provide interesting information for the earlier decades, and points of comparison for the end of the century.

Always bearing in mind that we see alien trade only, from an examination of the customs accounts four things immediately stand out. First, the scale of exports was clearly higher than appears from the audited and enrolled accounts; secondly, the range of products was considerable; thirdly, regional differences (only to be expected) were clearly visible; fourthly, channels were still open to all the continental markets served in the previous centuries. Some cloth exported was recorded as cloth of assize, taxed by the piece, and thus appears also in the enrolled accounts. The standard cloth on which duty was charged for imports by 1303 was the cloth of assize of two yards wide as laid down in the regulations of 1197, with subsequent exemptions and changes, which permitted widths of seven quarters and six quarters for some cloths. Although length was not specified, customary lengths of twenty-four yards and twenty-six yards had been acknowledged, and in 1328 length would be set at twenty-six yards for coloured cloth and twenty-eight yards for rays. It is likely that, for customs purposes, a similar standard was applied to domestic cloth exports.[19] Such cloths of assize (whatever the precise measure used) were exported from all the cloth-exporting ports in modest numbers, except Yarmouth and Ipswich. Annual totals reached some 300 to 700 cloths between 1303 and 1308, and over 700 cloths in 1322–3 (Table 7.1).

Boston was the busiest port, with an average export of almost 160 ungrained cloths a year up to 1308. London came next with an average of over 100 in those years, but its exports were more erratic, at 354 in 1303–4, but only 28 in 1306–7. Hull was third busiest with an average of 80 cloths a year up to 1309. Bristol was a steady exporter at a lower level, but numbers reached 78 in 1307–8. Lynn and Sandwich rarely exported over 40 in any year, except that in 1322–3 Sandwich exported 377, possibly acting as an outport for London. In addition, scarlets and grained cloths were also exported. Again Boston was the main centre, and at times aliens there exported more scarlets than they imported. Over 100 scarlets and 22 half-grained cloths were exported in 1303, 48 scarlets in 1308–9, but only 21 in 1309–10. In other ports where scarlets appeared (Hull, Lynn, London, Bristol) exports were rarely more than half a dozen a year. The records

---

[19] In 1328 further regulations would specify length for the first time, at twenty-six yards for coloured and twenty-eight yards for rayed cloth before shrinkage. The problem of regulations for domestic cloth is discussed by Bridbury, *English Clothmaking*, appendix A, and P. Chorley, 'The English Assize of Cloth: A Note', *Bull. Inst. Hist. Research*, 59 (1986), pp. 125–30.

Table 7.1 *Total recorded number of cloths of assize exported (including scarlets)*

Year		Year		Year		Year		Year	
1303	445	1322–3	706	1331–2	13+	1340–1	0	1349–50	128
1303–4	504	1323–4	54	1332–3	11+	1341–2	7	1350–1	79
1304–5	692	1324–5	71	1333–4	12	1342–3	0	1351–2	118
1305–6	386	1325–6	118	1334–5	7	1343–4	0	1352–3	266
1306–7	307	1326–7	75	1335–6	57	1344–5	0	1353–4	708
1307–8	381	1327–8	46	1336–7	14	1345–6	—	1354–5	504
1308–9	234	1328–9	97	1337–8	10	1346–7	—	1355–6	881
1309–10	77	1329–30	40+	1338–9	1	1347–8	368	1356–7	1,640
1310–11	93	1330–1	26+	1339–40	21	1348–9	217	1357–8	2,095

Source: Lloyd, *Alien Merchants*, app. C; PRO, E.356/9,10; Carus-Wilson and Coleman (eds.), *England's Export Trade*, pp. 75–6.

suggest a strong continuing specialism at Lincoln. Scarlets exported from London in 1306–7 and 1308–9 were specifically noted as from Lincoln, and it is likely that the high level of exports from Boston reflects its proximity.

These figures make the English trade look meagre, but the collectors seem to have interpreted the cloth of assize fairly strictly. Much other cloth was exported taxed by value. The detailed particular accounts amplify the picture, and illustrate England's ability to produce a whole range of cloths which alien merchants were confident of selling in international markets. They took Beverley cloths, blanket, worsteds, says and says of worsted (sometimes called serges and serges of worsted), Louth says, frieze, wadmal, kersey, bluet, brunet, russets from east and west,[20] Mendips, *grisancos*, Irish and Welsh cloth. A great deal of the cloth was exported simply as 'English cloth' (*pannus anglicanus*), the precise nature of which is never made clear. It is more than simply descriptive to distinguish English cloth from foreign, and probably refers to a width distinctive to many English cloths, different from that of the assize but not too far off, perhaps of six or seven quarters.[21] A valuation at Hull in 1324–5 of two of these cloths at £4 each was similar to valuations given to pieces of cloth amounting to the equivalent of a cloth of assize in 1304–5 and 1305–6.[22] This makes it unlikely that they were narrow (strait) cloths, which by later definition were only half the width of a cloth of assize.

The value of the information is best demonstrated by looking at each port in turn, a process by which the regional differences also clearly appear. In the north, Hull was at this stage a moderate exporter, not yet able to draw on York's textile industry, which was limited before the 1330s.[23] Exports were mainly of cloths of assize and scarlets, and the value of other cloth was low, at £15 to £30 a year.[24] The most important named variety was Louth say, with 300 ells worth £10 10s. 0d. sent out in 1305–6, and 59 pieces

[20] Few russets were recorded through Ipswich and London: for the relatively quiet level of Colchester activity at this time see R.H. Britnell, *Growth and Decline in Colchester, 1300–1525* (Cambridge, 1986), pp. 13–21.

[21] Even within accepted conventions widths could vary: a fifteenth-century inquiry showed narrow cloths in Devon being made to various widths between 27 and 32½ inches. W.R. Childs, 'Devon's Overseas Trade in the Later Middle Ages', in M. Duffy, S. Fisher, B. Greenhill, D. J. Starkey, J. Youings (eds.) *The New Maritime History of Devon, I: From Early Times to the Late Eighteenth Century* (Exeter, 1992), p. 79.

[22] In 1304–5 six pieces of cloth were valued at £4, then the value was erased and the cloth customed as the equivalent of one and one eighth of a full cloth; in 1305–6 two pieces of bluet and one of russet were similarly valued together at £4 then charged as one cloth of assize: PRO, E.122/55/19, 20.

[23] Unfortunately no detailed accounts survive for Newcastle. For York's development, see J. Bartlett, 'The Expansion and Decline of York in the Later Middle Ages', *Econ. Hist. Rev.*, 2nd ser., 12 (1959–60), pp. 17–33; E. Miller, 'Medieval York', *VCH Yorks: The City of York*, pp. 43–4, 87.

[24] PRO, E.122/6/1; 55/11, 19, 20; 56/2, 14, 26; 57/2.

worth £92 exported in 1306–7. This relatively cheap cloth was loaded on an Italian galley, which had ventured far up the east coast. Most cloth was probably coloured, but two of the seventeen pieces which were valued at £20 14s. 0d. in 1304–5 were stated to be white, and ten pieces of white and russet cloth (worth £4) were exported in 1307–8. Russet cloth was also exported in 1305–6 when two pieces of bluet and one of russet were customed together as the equivalent of one cloth of assize; in that year, alongside 91 cloths of assize and 6 scarlets, 150 ells of wadmal (£2 5s. 0d.) and 6 pieces of Irish cloth (£2 8s.0d.) were also sent abroad. In 1307–8, alongside 102 cloths of assize and 5 scarlets, 6 pieces of worsted (£2 5s. 0d.) and 19 pieces of other unspecified cloth worth £29 5s. 0d. were exported; further says of worsted (£4) went out in 1310–11; and when the petty custom was again charged after 1322, we also see in Hull 'English cloth' worth £21 exported in 1324–5.

At Boston we have fewer accounts, but enough to see that the pattern was markedly different.[25] Not only was Boston the leading exporter of both scarlets and cloths of assize (as shown above), but only Lynn approached it as an exporter of cloth by value. Unfortunately at both ports cloth values were often included in aggregate totals for cargoes, so exact figures elude us, but it is still possible to see exports within a minimum–maximum band. The leading export at both ports was 'English cloth', followed at some distance by worsteds, but both ports fielded quite a range. In Boston in 1303 total exports of cloth were worth between £1,313 and £2,267, between 32 and 50 per cent of the value of the port's exports (excluding wool). 'English cloth' separately valued was worth £1,130, and it was included in mixed cargoes worth another £649, making a possible maximum value near £1,779; worsteds were similarly valued at between £143 and £287, says of worsted were valued at £5 to £12, strait cloths at £9, Irish cloth at £10 to £15, blanket and coverlets at £12 to £25; and cloth of Beverley at £4. The next surviving accounts, for 1308–9 and 1309–10, show a decline in both range and value, but both are short accounts, and the proportion of cloth in the export values remained constant. In ten months in 1308–9 'English cloth' was worth a minimum of £623 and a possible maximum of £1,028, and worsted somewhere between £20 and £30, between 38 and 62 per cent of export values; in two months alone in 1309–10 Beverley cloth was worth £6, 'English cloth' between £253 and £356 and worsted between £193 and £245, making between 43 and 58 per cent of total values. Not much had changed by the 1320s. In 1326–7 alongside twenty-nine and a half scarlets, 'English cloth' was valued at £636 to £1,007, worsteds at £57 to £98 and Beverley cloth at

25 PRO, E.122/5/7, printed in Gras, *Early English Customs System*, pp. 273–88; E.122/6/2, 8, 19, 22; E.122/7/1.

£36 to £60, again making 45 to 67 per cent of alien export values. A rare later account for a half year in 1334 shows that by then the maximum value of 'English cloth' was only £65 and exports of says were valued at only £1 10s.0d. This was at most a maximum of 24 per cent of alien export values, and suggests a considerable decline, but this was part of a general decline in recorded alien trade, and drawing any conclusions from isolated short accounts is always dangerous.

At Lynn, just across the Wash, exports were much lower in the 1300s, but as at Boston 'English cloth' predominated. Lynn's exports came to rival Boston's in the 1320s.[26] In 1303 there were exports of one Lincoln scarlet, says, blanket, and 'English cloth' worth a maximum of £177, far below Boston's total. In 1303–4 a similar mixture and five Beverley cloths were still low at a maximum of £128, but the following years were somewhat higher. In 1305–6 separately valued 'English cloth' (£43 10s. 0d.) and worsted (£4) were low but they also occurred in mixed cargoes with a value of £887; in 1305–6 'English cloth' separately valued was worth £411, and small amounts of red cloth (*pannus rubeus*) and says appeared together with 'English cloth' in mixed cargoes worth up to £788. In 1306–7 most cloth was valued separately; 'English cloth' was again the main export (£240) with blanket, *pannus rubeus*, worsted and says coming to £134. In 1308–9 small amounts of says and Beverley cloths were exported. By 1322 exports had increased, but they declined subsequently. In 1322–3 'English cloth' was worth between £980 and £1,037, worsteds between £143 and £148, says of worsteds alone were worth £21 and says were part of a mixed cargo worth £17. The following year 'English cloth' was worth £617, worsteds £276 and says of worsted only £2. In 1324–5 'English cloth' was worth £300, worsted £63, says of worsted £13 and says £20; a mixed cargo of says and 'English cloth' was worth £15 and cloth called 'Beauvier' was valued at £10. In 1325–6 'English cloth' was valued at £177 10s. 0d., worsted at £20 15s. 0d., and says of worsted at £22 6s. 0d. Over these years the proportion of cloth in the overall export values of the port dropped from a minimum of 62 per cent, to 44, 37, then 19 per cent in the face of rising ale exports.

At Yarmouth the survival of accounts is less good, but enough to show that the pattern again varied.[27] Here worsteds were much more important. Although these might be a relative newcomer to the English cloth making industry,[28] they were clearly already important in the exports of the Wash

---

[26] PRO, E.122/93/2, 3, 4, 17, 18, 24, 28. Of these, E.122/93/17 is printed in *The Making of King's Lynn*, ed. D. Owen (Oxford, 1984) no. 406, pp. 341–9.

[27] PRO, E.122/148/13, 27, 30, 31.

[28] G.A. Williams, *Medieval London: From Commune to Capital* (London, 1963), pp. 136–40; A.F. Sutton, 'The Early Linen and Worsted Industry of Norfolk and the Evolution of the London Mercers' Company', *Norfolk Arch.*, 40 (1989), p. 201.

and East Anglian ports, and would grow further to peak in 1357–8.[29] In two
months alone in 1310 worsted worth £42 was exported along with cloth *que
dicant blanket* worth £5. In the following full year worsted was worth £613,
blanket £135, frieze £100, a small amount of wadmal £3 5s. 0d. and unspecified cloth only £54. The total amounted to at least £902, 34 per cent of
export values. After 1322 the records suggest decline: between 1324 and 1326
all exports were described as 'English cloth', and were worth between £419
and £424. Whether worsteds really disappeared or were for some reason
included in 'English cloth' is not clear.

At Ipswich, where we might expect to find reference to the well-known
Colchester russets, we find none exported by name, and indeed, little alien
interest in cloth.[30] Particular accounts for 1304–5 and 1308–9 show no cloth
exports at all. Cloth was more important in the 1320s, but interest fluctuated.
In 1324–5 'English cloth' alone was valued at £212, and 'English cloth' with
worsted at £18; in 1325–6 the exports were lower with 'English cloth' alone
worth £90, and 'English cloth' with worsted worth a further £50 10s. 0d.;
in 1326–7 again no cloth exports were registered; but in 1331–2 exports
revived with 'English cloth' valued at between £173 and £179 and worsteds
at £7.

Worsteds were also drawn into London trade, and formed an integral part
of the trade of the London mercers, a considerable number of whom had
Norfolk backgrounds.[31] Some of the worsted fed into London was exported
but in amounts more modest than at Lynn or Yarmouth, and as part of a
greater variety of other cloths. London accounts are few and short, but they
suggest that London already offered the greatest range of cloths, even if it
was not yet the dominant port it later became.[32] In half a year in 1307–8
values reached at least £144 with a possible maximum of £334, and in four
months in the following year were somewhere between a minimum of £430
and a maximum of £816, making up somewhere between 30 and 56 per
cent of the miscellaneous export values recorded in those months. In the
first account worsted was worth between £15 and about £77, says of worsted
were worth £67, serge was worth between £17 and £39 and a small cargo
of mixed serge, blanket and bluet was valued at £7. 'English cloth' was
worth between £21 and £121. Two scarlets were exported in valued cargoes,

---

[29] Then exports reached over 26,000 pieces: A. Beardwood, *Alien Merchants in England,
1350 to 1377: Their Legal and Economic Position* (Cambridge, Mass., 1931), Appendix c,
p. 177.

[30] PRO, E.122/52/38; E.122/50/8, 12, 13, 17, 19. If this drop in russets reflects the move
from cheap cloths suggested by Munro and Chorley, producers were nevertheless able to
increase the sale of russets later in the century. For further changes see Britnell, *Growth
and Decline*, pp. 58–60, 163–5.

[31] Sutton, 'Early Linen and Worsted Industry', pp. 203–6.

[32] PRO, E.122/68/22; E.122/69/2, 5; E.122/157/4.

and it is of some interest that one of these, described as a Lincoln scarlet, was valued individually at £16 13s. 4d. This sharply contrasts with the value of 'English cloth' and cloth of assize at £4 or less. In 1307–8 a similar pattern is clear. As well as seven cloths of assize and two scarlets, 'English cloth' was worth between £38 and £185, worsted between £73 and £228, serge between £3 and £52. Louth says (recorded as serges) were again important and worth between £185 and £270, serge of worsted was worth £5, Irish serge £5 and a mixed cargo of bluet, chalons and coverlets £1. *Stamyn' ad religiosos* worth £12 10s. 0d. that year were probably early examples of later 'monks' cloths'. Again scarlets were highly valued. Individual Lincoln cloths were valued at £14 and £13 10s. 0d., and ten ells of English scarlet were valued at £4. In a somewhat damaged account for 1310–11, just before the tax was suspended, the same range shows: 'English cloth', worsted, serge, serges said to be of worsted and of Lincoln, coverlets and blankets, worth altogether between £201 and £471. Unfortunately no accounts survive to suggest what was happening to the alien cloth trade in London from the 1320s.

In the south-east and in Southampton exports other than cloths of assize were fewer. Among the small amounts which were exported, however, blanket seems more important, and kerseys appear. Sandwich apparently exported only cloths of assize, except for twenty-two pieces of blanket in 1327–8.[33] Exports of cloths of assize were particularly high there in 1322–3 at 377, when Winchelsea also exported 84.[34] At Dover a small amount of worsteds, serges and kerseys worth altogether £16 17s. 8d. were exported in 1303–4. At Southampton small amounts of valued cloth trickled through:[35] blanket worth £10 13s. 4d., twenty yards of woollen cloth, and thirty ells of coloured cloth in 1308–9; six remnants of woollen cloth worth £16 13s. 4d. the following year; and blanket worth £14 11s. 8d. and other woollen cloths in 1310–11. In 1322–3 alongside fifty-three cloths of assize, aliens exported 'English cloth' worth £23 3s. 4d., blanket worth £17 and worsted worth £7 10s. 0d.

In the south-west in the 1320s cloth was proportionately more important in exports.[36] No accounts survive before 1322 – perhaps none were drawn up – but certainly cloth of Devon and Cornwall was already produced and known in commercial markets, as in London in 1315.[37] In 1323–4, from

---

[33] PRO, E.122/124/11, 13, 18, 29, 30. The first two of these are printed in Gras, *Early English Customs System*, pp. 272–3, 333–46.

[34] Lloyd, *Alien Merchants*, pp. 220, 222.

[35] PRO, E.122/136/8, 17, 21, 27, 29. The first of these is printed in Gras, *Early English Customs System*, pp. 360–73.

[36] PRO, E.122/40/7a, 7b, printed in Gras, *Early English Customs System*, pp. 394–7.

[37] *Calendar of Letter Books, E*, pp. 53–4.

Table 7.2 *Totals of valued cloth exports, 1303–27*

Date	Min.–max. value (£)	Date	Min.–max. value (£)
1303	1,367–2,178	1309–10	515–620
1303–4	82–145	1310–11	1,134–1,411
1304–5	71–958	1322–3	1,194–1,273
1305–6	429–1,219	1323–4	1,015–1,027
1306–7	594–780	1324–5	753–793
1307–8	349–785	1325–6	786–789
1308–9	676–1,188	1326–7	760–1,170

Source: PRO, E.122 *passim*, 1303–27. For ports included each year see n. 18 above.

'Exemouth', aliens took russets, Mendips, and *grisancos* worth £120 (66 per cent of export values), and Plymouth exported a cargo of cloth and fish worth £12. In the following year *grisancos* and russets worth £46 went through 'Exemouth' and Teignmouth; and in 1325–6 *grisancos* worth £122 were shipped through 'Exemouth' (100 per cent of export values). Just as with other cloths, it is difficult to define the *grisancos*. They were undoubtedly grey cloths, not of high quality, and they or russets (also usually grey cloths)[38] may have been the English *pardo* cloth known in Castile.

At Bristol another pattern appears; nothing but cloth of assize was registered.[39] Whether this is a real pattern, or a quirk of local recording is not clear, but it is a pattern which continued through the late fourteenth century. Moreover, in those later accounts only whole cloths or half-cloths were registered in Bristol at a time when all other ports were registering irregular yardage. It suggests that Bristol collectors had early adopted the custom of converting varied cloths to cloths of assize, and moreover converting to the nearest half-cloth, effectively disguising any possible variety. The only exceptions were small amounts of Irish cloth valued at £2 13s. 4d. in 1304–5 and £27 in 1325–6, and (in the later period) Welsh cloth.

As far as scale is concerned, the accounts show that exports were much higher than normally suggested. Alongside exports of several hundreds of cloths of assize, even our incomplete records of alien trade show other cloth valued often at over £1,000 a year (Table 7.2). If we had accounts for Boston, Lynn and London in the same years we might easily find this rose to £2,000 a year. If English-owned cloth could be added, the sum would be higher. However, turning the value into equivalent cloths of assize for comparison is not easy, as the cloth is often valued in aggregate, and sizes were never

[38] Britnell, *Growth and Decline*, pp. 55–7, provides a full description of russets as made in Essex.

[39] PRO, E.122/15/1 (printed in Gras, *Early English Customs System*, pp. 347–60), 3, 4 (both printed in Carus-Wilson, *Overseas Trade of Bristol*, pp. 168–79).

stated. The single valuation we have of 'English cloths' at £4 each[40] suggests alien exports might be the equivalent of another 250 to 500 cloths a year, but valuations at Lynn by the ell suggest it could be nearly double that. This is still a drop in the ocean compared with the value of the wool trade, and small beer compared with imports of foreign cloth, but locally it could be very important. In Devon where there was little wool trade cloth exports were a major currency earner. In 1323–4 cloth exports valued at £120 were clearly more valuable than tin exports at £61.[41] Even in Boston with its huge wool exports, further trade worth up to £1,000, 50 per cent of non-wool values, meant welcome work for local craftsmen.

Some further observations about scale must be made. First the accounts seem to indicate a decline (or further decline) in the late 1320s, and a decline of cloths of assize on the enrolled accounts seems to confirm this,[42] but the lack of detailed accounts between then and 1347 makes it impossible to trace the full extent. Moreover, this does not necessarily mean an overall decline in England's cloth trade at that time. Here, two points might be made. First, the cloth of assize was redefined in 1328, and the drop in recorded numbers in the enrolled accounts may be partly due to changes in recording practice. Certainly the nil returns for the 1340s sit oddly with the return of 368 for 1347–8, but equally clearly alien trade was lower in 1347–53 with exports of some 80 to 400 cloths a year compared with 300 to 700 in the earlier period. Second, this is a time when alien trade was generally dropping, but denizen trade was rising. The English hold on the wool trade increased from about one third in the late thirteenth century to somewhere between two-thirds and three-quarters in the early fourteenth century, even before the royal manipulations of the trade gave English merchants their near monopoly. Moreover, the increasing English role in the wine trade, dating precisely to the decade of the 1320s, and provoking in 1330 a government inquiry into the loss of alien wine duties, seems to be entirely due to commercial competitiveness. There is no reason to suppose the cloth trade was different from other trades. We know Englishmen such as Simon Swanland were deeply involved in the import trade;[43] others were equally likely to be interested in the export trade. The increasing English wine trade probably also stimulated the English merchants' interest in cloth as a return cargo. The wine trade already drew many English ships; in 1307–8 for instance some 316 of the 624 ships at Bordeaux were English, capable of carrying 31,652 tuns of

[40] PRO, E.122/56/26. See also n. 22 above.
[41] Childs, 'Devon's Overseas Trade', p. 79.
[42] Lloyd, *Alien Merchants*, appendix 1; PRO, E.356/9, 10.
[43] *Cal. Close Rolls, 1313–18*, p. 496; *Cal. Pat. Rolls, 1317–21*, p. 390.

wine.[44] Herring and corn were major cargoes for Gascony, but Gascony was also a consumer of English cloth, not only from Bristol, but from ports all round the coast.[45] The crown's decision to tax cloth exports in 1347 indicates growth and visibility, and if aliens were fading then denizens must have been strengthening their hold. This is borne out by the evidence for 1347–53, the first years of the new cloth tax, when English merchants were handling 90 per cent of exports. Their share may well have been similar in the early 1340s and even 1330s, and if their share in the 1320s approached this, England's exports could be significantly higher than the documents record.

A further point to bear in mind is the varied supply of cloth. At the cheaper end worsteds were increasing, and many other cloths in the cheaper range remained available. Whether we see these as the 'mass market' goods of Munro and Chorley or the 'slump products' of Miller, it is clear that, when English merchants of the 1340s and 1350s were seeking to expand their European markets, they were not by any means starting from scratch. English cloths of many types were still known all over Europe and gave a firm basis for commercial response to changing demand. Merchants could choose cloth to match their markets from producers in the eastern counties or the west, expensively and cheaply, from Lincoln scarlets, through cloths of Beverley, russets, blankets, says, worsteds and above all 'English cloth', whatever exactly that encompassed.

A further value of the accounts is that they indicate where alien merchants drew their main supplies. The cloths known by name on the continent in the thirteenth century had been from the east coast, and Lincoln, Louth and Beverley cloths were still visible by name in the customs accounts as shown above.[46] While it is still often stated that the English cloth industry moved from east to west (although few would now suggest that this had anything to do with the fulling mill), alien exports of cloth did not reflect this. Comparing their exports of cloths of assize over the century, we can see that in the 1300s Boston was the port they used most, followed by London, then Hull, Bristol, Sandwich and Southampton. In the 1360s London and Boston changed places, Hull remained in third place and Southampton took over from Bristol in fourth place. By the 1400s London had greatly increased its lead, and because it became the Italian centre Southampton jumped to

---

[44] PRO, E.101/162/1, 5. Of the ships fifty-four were from Yarmouth, eighty-eight from other eastern ports, fifteen from London, eighty-four from the south-east and south coast, and eighty-six from the south-west. Bristol and the Bristol Channel ports sent only ten ships, but Bristol was also served by ships from Weymouth and Gascony.

[45] See cloth export licences in 1364 to pay for Bordeaux wines, n. 65 below.

[46] The unnamed English cloth found on foreign tariff lists might be the *pannus anglicanus* found in eastern ports, or cloths of assize, or the various cloths from the south-west. The *pardo* in Spain is likely to be grey cloth such as *grisancos* or russets.

second place, but Boston still came third, Yarmouth and Ipswich together overtook Hull, and Exeter overtook Bristol. As far as alien merchants were concerned they dealt in the west as well as the east. However, although Bristol was a major exporter of cloth of assize, it never reached more than fourth place, and the east coast ports and London were, and remained, their main buying markets. Alien activity of course reflected not simply English production areas, but also the commercial weight of Bruges and the other Low Country entrepots, and even merchants from Iberia and Italy linked their English trade with Flanders. Moreover, cloth made in the west of England was easily transported to eastern ports for export. Nonetheless, the continued alien use of the eastern ports is still a point worth emphasising, since alien activity provides one of the few direct comparisons between the customs accounts for the beginning and the end of the century. When denizen trade is also taxed after the imposition of the cloth tax of 1347, Bristol's true importance is revealed; but if its early trade was already dominated by its own merchants to the extent it was later, its importance must already have been high.[47] Thus all we may see then is a change in the quality of recorded information, not a shift of location.

Finally, the customs accounts also indicate which markets English cloth could reach, at least in so far as this is reflected in the nationality of the alien exporter or shipmaster. Spaniards and Italians (among whose early records reference to English cloth is mostly found)[48] continued to buy. Their interest in Bruges made Southampton, Sandwich and even the eastern ports of England more convenient than Bristol.[49] Andres Perez of Burgos traded mainly in London, but exported thirty-three cloths of assize, five and a half cloths in part grain, and three coverlets worth £2 6s. 0d. from Boston in 1303; on the same ship Don Garsea of Burgos exported twenty cloths of assize, one scarlet, half a cloth in part grain, and English cloth worth £7.[50] Italians shipped cloth as well as wool from east coast ports and the substantial cargo of Louth say loaded in Hull in 1307 for Gerard Nerle of Florence on the galley of Andali de Nigro indicates cheaper English cloth could still reach Italy.[51] Merchants from northern areas were naturally more regular exporters. In Hull's relatively modest trade Norwegian merchants were noticeable, exporting twenty-six cloths of assize, and English cloth and wor-

[47] The apparent sharp change of location once English trade was also taxed is shown visually in M. Bonney, 'The English Medieval Wool and Cloth Trade: New Approaches for the Local Historian', *The Local Historian*, 22 (1992), pp. 33–4, charts 4 and 6.
[48] Chorley, 'English Cloth Exports', pp. 1–10.
[49] They had shipped cloths of Stamford, Beverley, York, Louth, Lincoln and Northampton from the east coast in 1272: Childs, *Anglo-Castilian Trade*, p. 77.
[50] Gras, *Early English Customs System*, p. 281.
[51] PRO, E.122/56/2.

sted worth £31 between 1306 and 1311, but most of Hull's cloth export there was handled by Low Country merchants or German merchants shipping on Baltic ships from Lübeck, Hamburg and Rostok. At Boston, apart from the Burgos exporters in 1303, all cloth exporters seem to be Germans or Low Country men. In 1303, some of the biggest shipments were on ships with masters from Lübeck and Rostok, which loaded between 33 and 55 per cent of the total cloth exports. Other ships, with masters from Harderwijk, or Zutfen, also carried exports for men of Lübeck, Greifswald and Osnabrück, indicating further German interest. Across the Wash, at Lynn, men of Westphalia joined those of Hamburg and Lübeck, but the Hansard boycott of Lynn, although incomplete, left much of the cloth to men and merchants of the Low Countries and Friesland to 1311.[52] The boycott also probably partly explains why Lynn was more important than Hull for Norwegian and Gotland merchants, who took steady amounts of English cloth northwards. Yarmouth worsteds were spread in similar eastwards directions, but not directly by Norwegians. Hansard ships at Yarmouth were more often from Hamburg than from Lübeck, and rather more ships of Sluys and Bruges came for worsteds. Ships and merchants also came from Friesland, and more northern French activity is visible there, from Dunkerque, Abbeville and Barfleur. London accounts do not record ships, which makes identification more difficult, but they show German, Low Country, French and Gascon merchants as we would expect. Surnames of St Omer, Paris, Guisnes and Cologne suggest some of the origins. At Sandwich, more exporters came from Bayonne and Spain, and in the far west French and Gascon merchants dominated. At Exeter in 1323–4 they took all exports;[53] and at Bristol, after 1303, when cloth was exported by William de Gaunt (Ghent) and Henry de Chalons whose names suggest a Low Country and northern French interest, merchants from the far west of Europe predominated. Some were merchants of Coutances, La Réole and Poitou, but most were from Bordeaux and Bayonne. The only exception to this was a small Portuguese shipment of one and a half cloths in 1308–9.[54] Although the end-user is never specified, the accounts show that exports by merchants from Norway to Italy kept the channels open for English cloth to spread as widely in the early four-

---

[52] Lloyd, *Alien Merchants*, p. 142; T.H. Lloyd, *England and the German Hanse, 1157–1611* (Cambridge, 1991), pp. 38–9, 42–3.

[53] PRO, E.122/40/7a, 7b, as in Gras, *Early English Customs System*, pp. 395–7.

[54] PRO, E.122/ 5/1: three Portuguese ships unloaded cargo worth £272 16s. 5d., but loaded only 1½ cloths, and lead and tin worth £13 4s. It seems that the Portuguese themselves were not positively seeking cloth, although English cloth had been used in Portugal at least since 1253 (Chorley, 'English Cloth Exports', p. 4 n.8). It would be tempting to see the rest of the cargo space as filled with cloth exported by Bristol merchants.

teenth century as it had in the thirteenth century and would in the fifteenth century.

II

The detailed accounts of 1303 to the 1330s thus provide us with considerably more depth of information on the scale, range and markets of the early fourteenth-century trade. The fuller information on the range and balance of goods exported in the early fourteenth century is also important in any assessment of how England responded to the perceived change in European markets which took place over the fourteenth century. There is, of course, little question about the general change in the scale of English exports in this period. Even if the exports of the early century were higher than recorded, they were still far below the exports of the end of the century. The fast increase from the 1360s is obvious. Alien exports reached at least 6,000 cloths a year in the early 1390s and 10,000 to 12,000 by the end of the decade. Total recorded exports reached 40,000 cloths of assize a year, and were certainly somewhat higher, since the methods of collection and recording underestimated the total trade. Worsteds were still separately listed; and despite the general directive that collectors should take proportional customs after the rate from every other cloth beyond or within the assize,[55] kerseys were not included permanently before 1390;[56] some ports continued to value rather than convert straits and dozens throughout the 1390s;[57] and certain other cloths always remained goods for valuation. The rise shows that the English read their markets well, and the later particular accounts show what they chose, and how it compared with earlier exports.

Munro and Chorley see the period 1300 to 1340 as crucial for a major change in the European cloth trade and production, partly as routes became riskier and cheaper cloths could no longer stand rising transport and handling costs over long distances.[58] The theoretical economic arguments explaining such a change have been developed by Munro, who examines transaction-cost, comparative-advantage and demographic real-income models, all of which have strength in particular places at particular times. Technical changes and fashion demands also encouraged the move to fulled

[55] *Cal. Pat. Rolls, 1345–8*, p. 276.
[56] Carus-Wilson and Coleman, *England's Export Trade*, pp. 14–15, 199–200.
[57] For instance, Devon's straits and dozens, the equivalent of some 700 broadcloths, were not included in the totals. Although worsteds had declined, the figures in Carus-Wilson and Coleman probably underestimate the remains of that trade too: Childs, 'Devon's overseas trade', p.79; Carus-Wilson and Coleman, *England's Export Trade*, p. 199 n. 5.
[58] Chorley, 'Cloth Exports of Flanders', pp. 349–79; Munro, 'Industrial Transformations', pp. 110–48.

woollen cloth – in Flemish terms the move from dry to greased products, and in English terms from worsteds to woollens. Wheel-spun yarn could be produced much faster and cheaper, but was less regular. The irregularities, however, could be obscured in fulled cloth, and also, if cloth was to be fulled, then plain tabby weaving, the cheapest construction, was the best to use. While decreasing costs for yarn and construction partly offset the more expensive finishing processes, fulled broadcloth nonetheless remained at the top end of the market. Fashion interacted with technical changes. Elaborate dagging was much easier to produce in non-fraying fulled cloth, and as dagging became easier it became more fashionable, and encouraged yet more purchases of fulled cloth. Did exports move decisively from cheaper cloths, from 'mass market' or 'slump' products to more luxurious cloths, as in continental Europe? On the surface it seems they did. There was certainly a great increase in the export of broadcloth of assize, and a sharp decline by the end of the century, in both proportion and number in worsteds.[59] The evidence for such a change is not confined to documents. The increasing use of true woollen cloth is confirmed quite clearly by the textiles found in London excavations, analysed and beautifully illustrated in a recent publication from the Museum of London.[60] Twill weaves (among which fall most of the worsteds) declined over the fourteenth century, and tabby weaves (the weave of the broadcloth) increased from 204 out of 403 finds (51 per cent) in the early fourteenth century to 498 out of 558 (89 per cent) at its end. Among the remaining worsteds were some very fine examples indeed; and among the few kermes-dyed cloths, the later fourteenth century examples were finer than those of the early century. Although it is not at all easy to equate documented names with physical survivals, the illustrations and descriptions of these finds help us appreciate what some of the cloths would have looked like, and illustrate the variety within the overall change to woollen cloths. Most were now tabby-woven and many were fulled, but types and patterns still varied considerably, and checked, striped or banded cloths (rays) were less heavily fulled to preserve the force of their patterns.[61]

Through shared tastes and fashions, but above all through markets to which it exported, England was bound to be directly affected by changes in Europe. Our clearest indications of positive ordering come from the fifteenth century, when a merchant of Toulouse sent snippets of his last buys to his

[59] Carus-Wilson and Coleman, *England's Export Trade*, pp. 199–200.
[60] E. Crowfoot, F. Pritchard and K. Staniland (eds.), *Medieval Finds from Excavations in London, IV: Textiles and Clothing, c.1150–c.1450* (HMSO, London, 1992), pp. 27 (table 1), 41–5. Comment on dagging will be found at pp. 194–8.
[61] Crowfoot, Pritchard and Staniland (eds.), *Medieval Finds*, pp. 44–5, 50, 52.

agent for matching in 1458,[62] and when a Spanish merchant ordered specific styles from his partner in London in 1470,[63] but no doubt similar practices took place earlier. Of course not all merchants got it right every time, and a number of cloths remained unsold on the voyage of the *Trinity* of Bristol to Huelva and Oran in 1480–1,[64] but the increasing exports, especially from the 1350s, suggest that English producers and merchants at this period were reading their markets correctly from Iberia to Poland. As always a range of sources illustrate what they sent. In 1364 licences of exemption from the Calais staple show permitted exports not only of 3,640 cloths of assize, but also of cheaper cloths, packs of western and Colchester cloth, Devon straits called 'backes', cogware, worsteds (from Hull, Boston and Yarmouth), Welsh russets and Mendips (from Bristol) and packs of Irish cloth (from Fowey).[65] Cloths supplied to the king of Navarre at the turn of the century show a range of qualities reflected in prices ranging between 24s. and 60s. the *codo* as well as a huge variety of colours.[66] Cloths were still distinctive enough to carry their names with them: and in Cracow in 1414 burgesses could still buy Beverley cloth (in green) as well as English grey and white.[67] Such sources are often best on colours and patterns, but the customs accounts still have much to offer on general balance.

England continued to export scarlet cloths and half-grained cloths, a continuation of the earlier luxury trade. Lincoln scarlets had been some of the best in Europe, and continued to clothe royalty in the fifteenth century, but total exports in the late fourteenth century were still only around fifty a year, lower than at Boston in 1303, and even in the fifteenth century were still modest. London rather than Boston became the main port of exit, but her exports were well under 100 a year in the 1470s; and although frequently over 100 in the 1480s, still averaged only 96. Exports of half-grained cloths were somewhat higher,[68] but overall the percentage of real luxury cloths to

[62] P. Wolffe, 'Three Samples of English Fifteenth Century Cloth', in N.B. Harte and K.G. Ponting (eds.), *Cloth and Clothing in Medieval Europe: Essays in Memory of Professor E.M. Carus-Wilson* (London, 1983), pp. 120–5.

[63] *Cal. Close Rolls, 1468–76*, no. 709, pp. 191–4. The transcript there of the Castilian text is incomplete and should include 'papeles': Childs, *Anglo-Castilian Trade*, p. 79.

[64] T.F. Reddaway and A.A. Ruddock (eds.), 'The Accounts of John Balsall, Purser of the Trinity of Bristol, 1480–1', *Camden Miscellany XXIII* (Camden Soc., 4th ser., no. 7, 1969).

[65] *Cal. Pat. Rolls, 1361–4*, pp. 477–8, 480, 485, 491–2, 495–7, 500, 507–8, 510–11, 514–15, 517, 521–2, 524; *Cal. Pat. Rolls, 1364–7*, pp. 1, 11, 13, 15, 16–17, 21, 32–3, 35–6, 47–50, 52, 56, 59, 61, 81–2, 84, 86.

[66] Childs, *Anglo-Castilian Trade*, pp. 79–83. Purchases for the Navarrese royal household also suggest that the cloths sent to Iberia were pricier than they had been in the thirteenth century, since none of the imported cheap cloth at 10s. the *codo* came from England.

[67] F.W. Carter, *Trade and Urban Development in Poland: An Economic Geography of Cracow from its Origins to 1795* (Cambridge, 1994), p. 147.

[68] Castilians took over half London's export of scarlets in the 1470s and 1480s and a third of half-grained cloths, Childs, *Anglo-Castilian Trade*, pp. 81–2.

other exports was low, possibly lower than in the early fourteenth century.

On broadcloths, the enrolled accounts alone are still misleading, but particular customs accounts continue to show the range and balance in each port.[69] They would repay considerably fuller analysis than there is room for here, but samples round the coast will illustrate the possibilities in the late fourteenth century. Little was now called 'English cloth', much was described simply as *pannus*, but not all cloth was broadcloth, and not all broadcloth was exported as whole cloths. Hull measured broadcloth to the nearest eighth, suggesting a variety of lengths; it also exported strait cloth by the ell (6,809 ells in 1383–4, equivalent to about 170 full cloths), a few beds of worsted, some Irish cloth and occasionally motley and russet cloth.[70] Lynn exported more whole broadcloths, but also broad and strait cloths in dozens and pieces. Her collectors also recorded some cloths as unfulled, some straits as fulled, alongside white cloths, kerseys, strait cloths called 'damdukes', chalons and worsteds.[71] Boston's exports were also mainly of broadcloth, perhaps still reflecting major urban suppliers, but other cloths were not negligible. In 1365–6 exports of 2,350 broadcloths were accompanied by narrow cloths and worsteds, a few chalons and some Irish cloth, worth altogether at least £442 and possibly nearer £697.[72] Yarmouth was different. In 1388 fewer than fifty whole cloths were customed, but other woollen cloth, presumably in short lengths, worth at least £812 was exported, along with narrow cloths, kerseys and chalons. The main export, however, was worsted valued at least at £1,052. In Yarmouth that year textile exports worth over £2,000 went abroad quite apart from the cloths of assize recorded on the enrolled accounts. In the 1390s the pattern was similar: some worsteds were described as fulled or as linen worsteds, and mantle cloth (*pannus mantellinus*) and rolls of beaver cloth appeared.[73] The variety at London in 1389 suggests its growing catchment area. It exported Welsh and Irish cloth, York coverlets, cloth of Guildford and Coventry, worsteds and says of single, half-double and double widths. Most exports were of unspecified woollen cloth, again in irregular yardage suggesting trade in pieces larger or smaller

---

[69] They may now pose the new problem of silent inclusions and subsequent loss of detail. Kerseys were assessed at three to the broadcloth; dozens and strait dozens at two and four to the cloth respectively. Poundage accounts at this period have the further advantage of providing valuations of broadcloth as well as others.

[70] PRO, E.122/59/1, 8, 19; E.122/159/11.

[71] PRO, E.122/94/14, printed in Gras, *Early English Customs System*, pp. 526–53.

[72] PRO, E.122/7/10.

[73] PRO, E.122/149/22, 27, 28. It is not possible to check how many were translated into cloths of assize since the duties at Yarmouth were farmed and no cloth accounts were rendered at the exchequer.

than the standard cloth. Some was narrow cloth, and there were also scarlet cloths, manufactured caps and hose.[74]

In the south, at Southampton, the main export was broadcloth, still with irregular yardage, but more scarlets also appeared, destined for Italy. Worsted beds, especially from Winchester, Guildford cloths and a steady export of Irish mantles and falding are also recorded.[75] The Devon ports, like Yarmouth, illustrate the problem of using enrolled totals. From 1,000 cloths a year in the 1360s Devon's exports dropped to only 300 a year in the 1390s, but between 73 and 83 per cent of Devon's exports were narrow cloths handled as short lengths (dozens), none of which were included in the returns of cloth exports. If allowance is made for these, then Devon exports still ran at the equivalent of 1,000 broadcloths a year.[76] In the west Bristol's trade looks like that of the early period: the collectors registered exports only as regular whole or half cloths of assize, except for Irish, Welsh and frieze cloth. Even the surviving poundage account registered only whole broadcloths.[77]

Clearly there were still exports at the cheaper end of the range, but were they, nonetheless, more expensive cloths than those exported earlier? A comparison of prices is essential but difficult. Ideally they should come from the same type of source, and customs accounts with valuations look promising. Valuations were formally the purchase prices as attested by written documents or sworn statements of the merchants,[78] and were made at the same point (on leaving the country). Merchants might be tempted to undervalue their goods, but for exports English collectors would know the likely values of English purchases. In the early fourteenth century such valuations were probably near the market price, but by the fifteenth century valuations of common and bulk commodities had often become conventionalised. However, the late fourteenth-century cloth valuations still range widely, which suggests a continued link with the market and the possibility of comparison with early fourteenth-century valuations. They are not perfect, but possible to use.

In the first part of the century prices at the ports ranged from about 2½d. an ell for narrow cloths to about 13s. a yard for grained broadcloths (Table 7.3). In London, Lincoln scarlets were valued at £13 10s. £14 and

---

[74] PRO, E.122/71/13.

[75] PRO, E.122/138/11, 16, 20.

[76] Childs, 'Devon's Overseas Trade', p. 79.

[77] PRO, E.122/17/6 (for 1402).

[78] At Hull in 1324–5 the collectors specifically recorded that prices were *per iuramentum*: PRO, E.122/56/26.

Table 7.3 Cloth prices in the customs accounts of the early fourteenth century[a]

Cloth type	Hull[b]	Lynn[c]	London[d]	Devon[e]
			Prices	
Lincoln scarlet: cloth		7s.	£13 10s.–£16 13s. 4d.	
English scarlet: ell	15s.–£1 15s. 6d.		8s.	
Cloth: piece	£4			
'English cloth': cloth				
piece		2s.–2s. 5d.[f]	13s. 4d.–£1 17s. 6d.	
ell		9¼d.–10d.		
'English cloth called blankets': ell				£1 8s. 10d.
Red (rubeus): cloth		£4		
ell		4s.		
Grey and russet: cloth	8s.			
White and russet: piece				
Says: piece		8s.–12s.	10s.–14s. 9d.[g]	
ell		2¼d.		
of Louth: piece	£1 11s. 1d.			
ell	8¾d.			
Says of worsted: piece	7s.–8s.			
Worsted: piece		9s.	10s.–11s. 10d.	
ell		3¼d.–4d.	10s.–£1 10s. 0d.[h]	
Irish: piece	8s.			
Wadmal: ell	3¼d.			

[a] Only a few prices are available since the value of goods (including cloth) is frequently aggregated in this period. Lynn collectors seem to use 20 ells to the cloth.

[b] PRO, E.122/55/19, 20; 6/1; 56/14, 26 (1304–24).

[c] PRO, E.122/93/3, 28 (1303–7, 1325–6).

[d] PRO, E.122/68/22; 69/2 (1306–8).

[e] PRO, E.122/40/7b (1324–5).

[f] Once 1s., and once 2s. 7d.

[g] Once given as £1 4s.

[h] This wide range of valuations suggests that some were double width, but not so specified.

£16 13s. 4d. each (about 10s. to 13s. a yard),[79] and English scarlet at 8s. the ell; 'English cloth' was valued at 13s. 4d. to £1 17s. 6d. the piece, worsted at 10s. to £1 10s. the piece, and says at 10s. to 14s. 9d. the piece, but prices per ell cannot be estimated since the size of the pieces were unrecorded. At Hull fewer prices can be disentangled but they ranged through unspecified wool cloth at 15s. to £1 15s. 6d. the piece, Irish cloth at only 8s. the piece, worsteds at 7s. to 8s. the piece, Louth says at £1 11s. the piece and at 8½d. the ell, and wadmal at 3½d. the ell. Two full 'English cloths' in 1324–5 were valued at £4 each.[80] Boston offers no individual prices, but at Lynn more prices were given by the standard ell. Here English scarlet was valued at 7s. the ell; 'English cloth' normally varied between 2s. and 2s. 5d. the ell; red cloth (*pannus rubeus*) was 4s. the ell and £4 the full cloth; blanket was usually 9½d. or 10d. the ell; says 8s. to 12s. the piece, and 2½d. the ell; and in the 1320s worsted was valued at 3½d. to 4½d. an ell.

At the end of the century it was still possible to buy cloth at about 2½d. a yard, which, allowing for inflation in the later period, indicates that England had not forsaken the cheaper end of the market altogether (Table 7.4). At the top end of the market valuations seem to have fallen, suggesting either declining quality or more efficient production, or a combination of both. There was still scarlet valued at 10s. 10d. the ell, but also at 6s. 8d. the ell, and half-grained cloth was valued at 4s. to 8s. the ell. Broadcloth valuations indicate a very wide range, and some differences between ports. There was a tendency for the highest-valued cloths to go through London and Southampton where Italians might export them, for Yarmouth and Hull to export some of the cheapest and for Bristol to handle a narrower range of medium-priced cloths for Iberia and Gascony.[81] Full cloths were mainly valued at £1 to £2 14s. each (about 9¼d. to 2s. the yard), but sometimes as high as £5 13s. 4d. (about 4s. 4d. the yard and as expensive as half-grained cloth). Coventry, Guildford and white Kent cloths exported from London were at the cheaper end, valued at £1 to £1 4s. each (somewhat under 1s. the yard if they held twenty-six yards). Narrow cloths, like the broadcloths,

---

[79] Measurements can never be exact, but for purposes of comparison, I have assumed that the full cloth contained twenty-six yards according to the assize of 1328, which was probably meant to give twenty-four usable yards after shrinking. It is possible, of course, that some cloths did not comply with the statutes, but overall the general price range is probably not too badly distorted by a few variations. At times the collectors measured by the ell, and at Hull and Lynn seem to have used twenty ells to the cloth. The English ell was one and a quarter yards, thus suggesting a cloth of about twenty-five yards.

[80] PRO, E.122/56/26. Unfortunately the accounts for Hull also make it clear that the piece was not a standard size; once six pieces were customed as the equivalent of one and one eighth of a full cloth, and once as two and a half full cloths.

[81] Again a word of warning: it is always possible that the valuations at this date were beginning to owe something to the local conventions of the ports, but the variations must also indicate some continued reflection of the actual range of qualities and prices.

Table 7.4 Cloth prices in a sample of customs accounts of the late fourteenth century[a]

Cloth type	Prices					
	Hull[b]	Lynn[c]	Yarmouth[d]	London[e]	Southampton[f]	Bristol[k]
Scarlet: ell				6s. 8d.–10s. 10d.		
Half-grain: ell				4s.–8s.		
Broadcloth: whole	£1–£1 15s. 0d.	£1 15s.–£2 6s.	£1–£2	£1 4s.[h]–£2 10s.	£1 10s.–£2 14s.[i]	£1 8s.–£1 17s.
ell				1s. 1d.–3s.		
Dozens: piece	4d.–1s. 9d.	15s.–19s.	10s.–15s. 8d.			14s.–17s.
Straits: ell			5s.–6s. 8d.	4d.–1s.		
Dozen straits: piece						
Guildford: cloth				£1 1s.–£1 4s.		
White Kent: cloth				£1 4s.		
Coventry: cloth				£1–£1 2s.		
ell				1s. 0d.–1s. 1d.		
Kerseys: piece	3s. 4d.–4s. 4d.	3s. 4d.–4s. 4d.	3s. 4d.–4s. 9d.	4s.–5s.	10s.	
Blanket: ell				1s.		
Says: piece			4s.–4s. 6d.	4s. 6d.–6s. 0d.[j]		
half-double				12s. 0d.–18s. 4d.		
worsteds: piece				5s.	6s.	
half-double				10s.–18s.		
double				17s.		
ell				2s. 4d.		

fulled	3s. 4d.–5s.
linen	4s.–5s. 4d.
Frieze: cloth	£1
Beaver	
broad: roll	£1
strait: roll	13s. 4d.
Irish: ell	1s. 1d.–1s. 5d. [h]
yard	5d.–8½d.
falding: yard	11½d.–1s. 6d.
Welsh: cloth	
piece of 3 dozens	£1 6s. 8d.–£1 10s.
dozens	£1 6s. 8d.–£1 8s.
ell	10s. 11d.
straits: ell	6d.–8d.
	4d.–5d.

[a] Within the table the most frequent price range is given. There are no available prices for Boston. The unit is the cloth, unless otherwise stated. Where the collectors have recorded prices by the ell or yard, these have also been noted in the table. The assize of 1328 and subsequent statutes specified twenty-six yards to the cloth at this date. The English ell was normally 1.25 English yards, but it is not clear what rate of conversion per cloth the London collectors were using. At Hull the collectors seem to use twenty ells to the cloth (PRO, E.122/59/11).

[b] PRO, E.122/59/1, 8, 19;159/11 (1383–99).

[c] PRO, E.122/94/14 (1392–3).

[d] PRO, E.122/149/22, 27, 28 (1388–93).

[e] PRO, E.122/71/13 (1389).

[f] PRO, E.122/38/11, 16, 20 (1383–92).

[g] PRO, E.122/17/6 (1402).

[h] Occasionally as high as £5 13s. 4d. the cloth and 6s. the ell.

[i] Occasionally as high as £4 10s. 0d. the cloth.

[j] Occasionally at 8s. 6d. and 9s. 0d. the piece.

[k] Once at 7d. the ell.

spanned a considerable range being valued at 4d. to 1s. 9d. the ell. Blanket (valued at 1s. the ell), the Irish cloth sold through London (valued at 1s. 1d. to 1s. 5d. the ell) and the Irish falding at Southampton (valued at 11½d. to 1s. 6d. the ell) look like medium-quality cloths; but other Irish cloth at Southampton and Welsh cloths (usually valued at 6d. to 8d. the ell) were definitely at the cheaper end of production. Worsteds are more difficult to place, as they were valued by the piece of unspecified length, and widths were also often unspecified. Pieces of single worsted were valued at 4s. to 6s., of half-double at 10s. to 18s. and double at 17s.; single says were normally valued at 4s. 6d. to 6s. the piece, and half-doubles at 12s. to 18s. 4d. the piece. Only occasionally was worsted valued by the ell and then double worsted at 2s. 4d. the ell was clearly not a cheap cloth. Apart from the lower end of the Irish and Welsh production, kerseys were now the cheap cloths, usually running at between 3s. 4d. and 5s. each, about 2¼d. to 3¼d. the yard, if each held the statutory 18 yards.[82]

In the main, such prices were not cheap, but, allowing for inflation, some cannot have been far from those of the early century. They indicate that England had not moved wholeheartedly up market, despite the drop in the cheaper worsted exports. Producers had successfully responded to the demand for woollens, and had settled mainly for the middling bracket which clearly sold well in northern markets, but kerseys and some straits at 2½d., 4d. and 5d. the ell could take the place of worsteds, says and wadmal at 2½d. to 3½d. the ell in the earlier period, even if fewer were sent to the more distant Mediterranean markets. A full analysis of the surviving accounts, although fraught with difficulties of measurement, could probably provide a clearer picture of the balance of the cheaper and more expensive cloths in England's exports.

The customs accounts thus contribute something to several points in the debate on the fortunes of the cloth industry, although they settle few arguments. They reflect the decisions of individual cloth traders, coping with changing conditions, and indicate once more the complexities historians have to absorb within statements of general trends. In the matter of decline during the thirteenth century, the accounts warn about overestimating the extent of decay. In the matter of urban decline, they suggest that Lincoln, Beverley and Louth continued to export their distinctive cloths well into the fourteenth century, and Boston's strength as a cloth exporter through to the 1320s suggests that her traditionally urban hinterland was still producing

---

[82] An alternative method of comparison, taking the contemporary convention of three kerseys as the equivalent of one cloth of assize, also demonstates the cheapness of kersey. With kerseys at 3s. 4d. to 5s. each, the value of the notional equivalent cloth of assize would be only 10s. to 15s., the equivalent of 4½d. to 6¼d. a running yard of six quarters wide.

steadily. Whether the cloths termed simply 'English' were mainly urban or country cloths, which had always encompassed both rough homespun and commercial products, is unclear. In the matter of a possible shift from east to west for English production areas, the activity of alien shippers suggests little change. It is probably on the matter of the range and change in products that the particular accounts have most to offer. They cannot, of course, clarify what changes took place before 1303. Whether exports between then and the 1330s reflect long-established tradition or recent moves to a 'slump product' is impossible to tell, but they provide the best survey we have of actual exports in that period, and they have much to offer on the possible later changes. For whatever mixture of technical change, fashion and economic pressures, the cloth used in and exported from England changed over the century. That continental markets changed sometime between 1300 and 1340 seems well established, and such change undoubtedly added further stress to old centres forced to shift products; but English industry seems to have been well placed to manage change in that period, and to cope with further economic pressures after the Black Death. English historians tend to emphasis the general rise in the standard of living after the Black Death, with more people of middling income able to buy more goods including cloth of middling sort. Continental historians tend to emphasise the increasing gap between rich and poor, which boosted the move to luxury products. England's response of an increased export of broadcloth and declining export of worsteds in the second half of the fourteenth century fits with the notion that the structure of demand on the continent was changing. But these changes were late, well after 1340, and, moreover, the customs accounts as well as other sources show that makers also kept going with cheaper cloths, albeit different types. Kerseys, straits, 'damdukes', Devon 'backes' and russets, for which they found markets, particularly in northern Europe, replaced the worsteds, says and wadmal of the early century. The prices, valuations and exact balance of exports need more investigation, but the customs accounts suggest that England produced a considerable range throughout the fourteenth century. We might argue for steady responsive adaptation, almost 'business as usual' within a changing technical world, rather than for a radical shift of product in England. But then as all historians trying to cope with the complex picture of European trends in the cloth industry have always acknowledged, within overall trends there was always room for diversity in response to local opportunities and pressures.

8

A medieval tax haven: Berwick upon Tweed and the English crown, 1333–1461

ANTHONY TUCK

O N 20 July 1333, Edward III received the surrender of the town of Berwick upon Tweed. The town had been in Scottish hands since 1318, but with the renewal of Anglo-Scottish warfare in 1332 its recovery became one of Edward III's main aims. The English laid siege to the town in early April 1333, and on 15 and 16 July the English commander entered into agreements with the commander of the garrison and the warden of the town that if the town were not relieved by 19 July it would be surrendered to the English. The Scottish relieving force was defeated by Edward III at Halidon Hill, two miles north-west of the town, on 19 July, and the following day the town capitulated.[1]

The surrender, however, was not unconditional. Under the terms of the agreements made on 15 and 16 July, all the inhabitants of the town who did not wish to enter the allegiance of the English king were free to leave with their families and possessions, while those who were prepared to give their fealty to Edward III were permitted to remain in the town and peacefully reside there. Furthermore, the burgesses of the town were guaranteed 'all their franchises, usages, laws and customs had and used in the time of king Alexander (III)', and their property in the town was to be held in accordance with the law of Scotland.[2]

These terms were generous, and were to be cited several times over the next half-century by the burgesses of the town in face of attempts by the

---

[1] For a discussion of the Anglo-Scottish war of 1333–5, see R.A. Nicholson, *Edward III and the Scots* (Oxford, 1965). Of the older historians of Berwick, J. Scott, *Berwick upon Tweed* (London, 1888), ch. 4, offers the best account of the English recapture of the town. Although the town became administratively part of Northumberland in 1888, it is not covered by Northumberland County History Committee, *A History of Northumberland*, 15 vols. (Newcastle upon Tyne and London, 1893–1940).

[2] *Rotuli Scotiae*, ed. D. Macpherson, J. Caley and W. Illingworth, 2 vols. (Rec. Comm., London, 1814–19) (hereafter *Rot. Scot.*), I, pp. 253–4.

English government to extend English fiscal measures to the town. There was no suggestion at the time of surrender that the town was to be annexed to the realm of England; indeed, in the months following the surrender Edward established an administration in the town which was intended to have jurisdiction over all those parts of Scotland which were already in the English allegiance or which the king hoped soon would be. When Edward Balliol, during his brief and contested reign as king of Scots, handed over to Edward III the whole of Lothian together with Dumfriesshire, Kirkcudbrightshire, Roxburghshire, Selkirkshire, Peeblesshire and Berwickshire, Berwick was intended to be the adminstrative centre for 'English' Scotland, and the Berwick chamberlain's accounts show officials from these counties accounting to him so long as their lands remained in the English allegiance. They were designated 'the king's land beyond the Tweed', to distinguish 'English' Scotland from the realm of England.[3]

The implementation of the surrender agreement, however, was to prove less than straightforward. After Robert I had taken the town from the English in 1318, some of those who had held property there and owed allegiance to the English crown were ejected, and they or their descendants now expected to be restored. Over the two years following the English recapture of the town, Edward III made several grants in favour of such Englishmen, and those who had benefited from Robert I's ejection of Englishmen now found their tenements and messuages forfeited and restored to those who had held them during the earlier period of English occupation.[4] On 4 June 1336 Edward III confirmed the charter which Edward I had granted to the burgesses of the town in 1302,[5] and it seems that the English government construed the occupation of the town 1333 as the re-establishment, in legal terms at least, of English rule first imposed by Edward I in 1296 and merely interrupted by Robert I's seizure of the town in 1318.

Notwithstanding the guarantees to those residents of the town at the time of its surrender to Edward III, the English king soon declared his intention of encouraging Englishmen to settle in the town. On 2 August 1333 he sent letters to nineteen towns in England, urging English merchants to go to Berwick, where they would be offered burgages and 'large and sufficient

---

[3] *Ibid.*, I, pp. 255–6. The establishment and development of the English administration in the town is dealt with in B.L. Atkinson, 'Berwick upon Tweed in the Wars of Edward III' (Univ. of Leeds MA thesis, 1959). For the cession of land by Edward Balliol, see Nicholson, *Edward III*, pp. 160–2. The text of the document of cession is given in *Rymer's Foedera (1066–1383)*, ed. A. Clarke, F. Holbrooke and J. Caley, 4 vols. in 7 (Rec. Comm., London, 1816–69), II(2), p. 888.

[4] *Rot. Scot.*, I, pp. 272–3, 335–6.

[5] *Ibid.*, I, pp. 428–9.

privileges and liberties'.[6] The continued prosperity of the town was an important consideration behind the policy of inviting English merchants to settle in Berwick, but so was security. The loyalty of those inhabitants who had remained in the town after its surrender evidently could not be taken for granted. In April 1335, for instance, Edward ordered twenty 'suspicious persons' to be removed from Berwick and lodged in various castles in Northumberland. Some of these were persons of substance in the town, such as Christopher de Coloigne, a German-born burgess who may have been related to James of Coloigne whose sympathies evidently lay with the Scottish cause and who had forfeited his commercial base at the 'White Hall' in 1334. Christopher petitioned for his release on the ground that he had done no wrong and his detention was contrary to the surrender agreement. Both he and the others detained with him were released in October 1335 on condition that they did not go to Berwick or Scotland.[7] Scottish monks and friars in Berwick also aroused Edward's suspicions, and he ordered them to be removed and replaced with English religious who might be expected by their preaching to encourage loyalty to the English king.[8] A substantial presence in the town of both merchants and religious from England would go some way towards ensuring the loyalty of the town to Edward III.

Throughout the 128 years of English occupation that followed the town's surrender in 1333 its main importance to the English crown was as a garrison town and supply base for armies advancing further into Scotland.[9] Yet both Edward III and his successors were concerned to ensure that the town retained a substantial civilian community which could if need be contribute to the defence of the town and which would ensure its economic viability. Grants of messuages in the town contained a clause requiring the grantee to keep the property in good repair and either live there himself or ensure that the inhabitant was an Englishman, and residence in the town was a condition of enjoying the mercantile privileges guaranteed to the burgesses.[10]

Under Scottish rule the town had enjoyed a high degree of prosperity and economic importance as the main centre for Scottish overseas trade, with

[6] *Ibid.*, I, p. 258. The towns to which letters were sent included London, Bristol, Newcastle, Southampton, York, Norwich and Lincoln.

[7] *Ibid.*, I, pp. 335, 388; *Northern Petitions Illustrative of Life in Berwick, Cumbria and Durham in the Fourteenth Century*, ed. C.M. Fraser (Surtees Soc., no. 194, Durham, 1981), pp. 86–7. For the Coloigne family, see D. Ditchburn, 'Trade with Northern Europe, 1297–1540', in M. Lynch, M. Spearman and G. Stell (eds.), *The Scottish Medieval Town* (Edinburgh, 1988), p. 162.

[8] *Chronicon de Lanercost, 1201–1346*, ed. J. Stevenson (Maitland Club, Edinburgh, 1839), p. 275.

[9] Beryl Atkinson argued that its importance as a victualling base should not be exaggerated, pointing out that English armies operating in Scotland were often victualled from Newcastle: Atkinson, 'Berwick upon Tweed', pp. 112–13.

[10] E.g. *Rot. Scot.*, I, pp. 384, 400–1, 642, 820–1.

wool as the dominant commodity. One of the country's principal mints was established there, and rents and property prices were high. Indeed, the Lanercost chronicler described the town as a 'second Alexandria' on account of its populousness and its commercial activity.[11] The re-occupation of the town by the English after 1333 and its role as a military base necessarily involved some degree of change and reorientation for the town's economy.[12] The establishment of an English garrison in the town brought in income in the form of soldiers' wages, in so far as they were spent locally, and expenditure on repairs to the castle and other fortifications. Neither of these sources of income should be exaggerated: soldiers' wages were not always paid regularly, and in the years between 1333 and 1355 only small sums were spent on the repair of the castle and the fortification of the town.[13] Perhaps the English occupation of substantial parts of south-east Scotland after 1334 lulled the English government into a false sense of security, for a survey in 1344 found evidence of considerable deterioration.[14] However, the temporary recapture of the town, though not the castle, by the Scots over the winter of 1355–6 jolted the government into more substantial expenditure over the following ten years.[15] The renewal of Anglo-Scottish warfare in Richard II's reign, and the substantial reduction by 1377 in the area of English-held land in Scotland, produced another increase in expenditure, with over £1,500 being spent on repairs at Berwick during the reign.[16] By the latter part of Richard II's reign, the keeper of Berwick and the East March received £3,000 in time of peace and £12,000 in time of war, though how much of this found its way into the hands of merchants, victuallers and craftsmen at Berwick remains largely conjecture.[17]

The commerce of the town perhaps underwent less reorientation than might have been expected as a result of its recapture by the English in 1333.[18] Under Scottish rule Berwick had been the outlet for wool, woolfells and hides from a wide area of southern Scotland, including no doubt the border

[11] *Chron. de Lanercost*, p. 185; W.B. Stevenson, 'The Monastic Presence: Berwick in the Twelfth and Thirteenth Centuries', in Lynch, Spearman and Stell (eds.), *Scottish Medieval Town*, pp. 99–115, and especially p. 113; I. Stewart, 'Scottish Mints', in R.A.G. Carson (ed.), *Mints, Dies and Currency: Essays Dedicated to the Memory of Albert Baldwin* (London, 1971), pp. 165–273, especially pp. 172–3, 183.
[12] Ditchburn, 'Trade with Northern Europe', p. 162.
[13] For a general survey of the economic impact of militarisation, see J.A. Tuck, 'War and Society in the Medieval North', *Northern Hist.*, 21 (1985), pp. 33–52. For repairs to Berwick Castle, 1333–55, see R.A. Brown, H.M. Colvin and A.J. Taylor, *The History of the King's Works*, 6 vols. (London, 1963–82), II, pp. 566–7.
[14] Brown, Colvin and Taylor, *History of the King's Works*, II, p. 567.
[15] *Ibid.*, II, pp. 567–8.
[16] *Ibid.*, II, pp. 568–9.
[17] R.L. Storey, 'Wardens of the Marches of England towards Scotland', *Eng. Hist. Rev.*, 72 (1957), pp. 602–3; Tuck, 'War and Society', pp. 44–5.
[18] Ditchburn, 'Trade with Northern Europe', p. 162.

abbeys of Dryburgh, Jedburgh, Kelso and Melrose,[19] but it is not entirely
true that with its fall to the English it was immediately cut off from its
'natural hinterland'.[20] For some years after 1333 much of this hinterland –
including the four abbeys – was under English control, and, as will be
argued, the favourable fiscal regime at Berwick ensured the continued shipment of Scottish wool through the port, even when the Scots had recaptured
most of their lost territory.

The customs accounts suggest that Berwick did not undergo a permanent
dislocation of its commercial life after the English reconquest. Customs
accounts survive for the period from 1327 to 1333, when the town was under
Scottish rule, and for the years from the capture of the town until Michaelmas
1342, though not in a continuous sequence. The customs at Berwick, as at
all other ports under the jurisdiction of the English crown, were farmed
from 1343 to 1351, and an account survives only for the last year of this
period, Michaelmas 1350–1, when the customs were demised to a syndicate
headed by John Malewyn.[21] From Michaelmas 1351, however, a virtually
continuous sequence of enrolled accounts survives until shortly before the
Scots regained the town in 1461.[22] Precise comparison between the figures
for 1327–33 and those for the years between 1333 and 1342 is difficult,
because the surviving accounts cover sometimes more and sometimes less
than a year, and there is a gap between August 1329 and June 1330 when
the customs officials did not render an account, as well as gaps in the years
after the English reconquest.[23] However, it is clear that wool exports fell
sharply in the years immediately after 1333.[24] In the seventeen months from

---

[19] A. Stevenson, 'Trade with the South, 1070–1513', in Lynch, Spearman and Stell (eds.),
     Scottish Medieval Town, pp. 182, 185.
[20] Ditchburn, 'Trade with Northern Europe', p. 162.
[21] E.B. Fryde, 'The English Farmers of the Customs, 1343–51', in Fryde, *Studies in Medieval
     Trade and Finance* (London, 1983), no. X, pp. 1–17; *The Exchequer Rolls of Scotland*, ed.
     J. Stuart, G. Burnett *et al.*, 23 vols. (Edinburgh, 1878–1908), I, pp. 97–8, 173–4, 319–
     20, 370–1, 419–20; Stevenson, 'Trade with the South', p. 191; Public Record Office
     (hereafter PRO), Customs Accounts, E. 122/193/8, 9 (1335–6, 1341–2). The Berwick
     customs were farmed for £1,200 in 1350–1, though the farmers were unable to levy that
     amount 'on account of divers impediments': PRO, Enrolled Customs Accounts, E.356/8,
     mm. 45–6; *Cal. Close Rolls, 1348–54*, pp. 274, 425.
[22] PRO, Customs Accounts, E.122/3/1, 13 (1390–1, 1394–5); Enrolled Customs Accounts,
     E.356/8, mm. 45–47d. (1333–79); E.356/14, mm. 58, 58d. (1379–99); E.356/18, mm.
     46, 46d. (1399–1432); E.356/19, mm. 42, 42d. (1432–47); E.356/20, m. 59 (1447–57).
[23] There are no enrolled accounts for the period from 27 July 1335 to 26 February 1339,
     but the period from October 1335 to July 1336 is covered by collectors' accounts: PRO,
     E.122/193/8. The cocket was closed between 30 November 1338 and 26 February 1339:
     PRO, E.356/8, m. 45.
[24] In calculating wool exports from Berwick the sack is taken as weighing 364 lb and 240
     woolfells are taken as the equivalent of one sack. As in England, the 'long two hundred'
     (i.e. 240) woolfells were customed at the same rate as a sack of wool, and the recorded
     totals for woolfells are converted to sacks at this rate. This follows the method of E.M.

June 1330 to November 1331, 3,753 sacks were exported, while in the nine-teen months for which accounts survive between Michaelmas 1334 and the end of July 1336 only 1,922 sacks were exported, a decline of nearly one half. A slight recovery is apparent by 1340, with 1,525 sacks being exported between Michaelmas 1340 and 22 March 1341, but for the year from Michaelmas 1341 to Michaelmas 1342 only 1,082 sacks were exported, still well below the level prevailing during the last years of Scottish occupation.[25]

The political dislocation, and the disruption within the mercantile com-munity brought about by the forfeitures and deportations discussed above, played some part in the decline of wool exports, but other factors were probably at work too. Demand for wool in Flanders had been notably high between 1329 and 1333, partly because of the return of settled political conditions there, and exports of English wool rose sharply in these years.[26] The export trade in wool from Berwick was sensitive to changes in the level of industrial activity in Flanders as well as changes in the political allegiance of the town, and the decline in exports after 1333 is not necessarily the result of the town being cut off from its natural hinterland. Indeed, much of that hinterland was under English control until the 1340s. Edward III's manipulation of the wool trade for diplomatic and fiscal purposes from 1336 onwards may explain the uncertain nature of the recovery in the trade at Berwick even after the disruptive effects of the English recapture of the town had lost much of their force. The export of wool through Berwick was banned from 11 February 1337 until 6 January 1338, when it was lifted by petition of the burgesses, who complained of the impoverishment of the town, but they were permitted to export only to England. Not until 12 May 1338 were they permitted to resume exports overseas. Exports were banned and the cocket seal closed again between 30 November 1338 and 26 February 1339.[27]

The continued viability of Berwick as a centre for the export of wool, woolfells and hides no doubt owed much to the maintenance of Scottish, rather than the imposition of English, levels of customs duty there after 1333. The continuance of the Scottish rate of half a mark (6s. 8d.), described in the enrolled accounts as the 'Ancient Custom', was implicit in the con-firmation to the burgesses of Berwick at the English reconquest that they

Carus-Wilson and O. Coleman, *England's Export Trade, 1275–1547* (Oxford, 1963), pp. 13–14. Berwick was excluded from their tables (cf. *ibid.*, p. 177) as it was also excluded from those compiled by H.L. Gray in E. Power and M.M. Postan (eds.), *Studies in English Trade in the Fifteenth Century* (London, 1933), pp. 321–60.
[25] PRO, E.122/193/9; E.356/8, m. 45.
[26] Carus-Wilson and Coleman, *England's Export Trade*, pp. 44–5; T.H. Lloyd, *The English Wool Trade in the Middle Ages* (Cambridge, 1977), pp. 123–4.
[27] E.B. Fryde, 'Parliament and the French War, 1336–40', in Fryde, *Studies*, no. V, p. 257; *Rot. Scot.*, I, pp. 482–3, 518–19, 531, 533; PRO, E.356/8, m. 45.

could enjoy the liberties they had had in the time of Alexander III. It is not clear when the customs duty on wool was first levied in Scotland, but it may well have been in the late 1270s, following the imposition in 1275 of the 'Great Custom' of 6s. 8d. per sack on wool exported from English ports.[28]

As long as English and Scottish rates remained the same, Berwick enjoyed no competitive advantage against other ports either in England or in Scotland. But within two years of the English recapture of the town Edward III had begun the process of increasing the duty on wool to finance his wars with Scotland and, from 1337, with France. This process was to take the total export duty on each sack of wool to 26s. 8d. in 1336 and eventually to 46s. 8d., but these enhanced rates were not imposed at Berwick.[29] The difference which now emerged between the level of duty on wool exported through English ports and the level of duty which the burgesses of Berwick believed should be levied on wool exported through their town was to become the major issue in contention between the town and the English crown. As duties in England rose rapidly, so the incentive to take wool to Berwick increased, especially that grown in Northumberland. The lifting in May 1338 of the ban on exporting wool through Berwick was accompanied by a prohibition on the taking of English wool to the town, but the prohibition was ineffective and the ban was reimposed in the following November 'because many English merchants are taking wool to Berwick to be exported to avoid duties levied within England'.[30] The ban was probably intended to be a warning rather than a permanent measure. When it was lifted, in February 1339, Berwick merchants were able to resume the export of Scottish wool at the traditional duty of 6s. 8d. per sack,[31] but the export of English wool through Berwick was still forbidden. The prohibition still proved ineffective, however, and over the following four years the collectors of customs at Berwick received orders on several occasions to seize English wool found there.[32]

Although the English government was never prepared to allow the unrestricted export of English wool through Berwick, the difficulty of enforcing a complete ban led to a series of temporary concessions to the merchants over the next fifty years. These concessions were generally represented as favours to the merchants, to relieve the poverty of the town. Between 1341 and January 1343, for example, they were licensed to export 1,000 sacks of

---

[28] *Exchequer Rolls*, I, p. xcix; Stevenson, 'Trade with the South', p. 187; A.A.M. Duncan, *Scotland: The Making of the Kingdom* (Edinburgh, 1975), pp. 603–4.

[29] Carus-Wilson and Coleman, *England's Export Trade*, pp. 194–6.

[30] *Rot. Scot.*, I, pp. 518, 531, 533, 547, 558; PRO, E.356/8, m. 45.

[31] *Ibid.*, I, p. 558; PRO, E.356/8, m. 45.

[32] *Ibid.*, I, p. 598, 605; *Cal. Pat. Rolls, 1338–40*, pp. 380–1; *Cal. Pat. Rolls, 1343–5*, pp. 174, 575; *Cal. Pat. Rolls, 1345–8*, pp. 117, 455, 462.

Northumbrian wool at a duty of 13s. 4d. per sack.[33] In January 1343 this was extended to a general power to export Northumbrian wool at the prevailing English rate of 46s. 8d. per sack. This was accompanied by a proclamation requiring Northumbrian growers to send their wool to Berwick until Midsummer, 'so that merchants may have greater occasion to go to that town'. Berwick was in effect to become the Northumbrian wool staple, and this may account for the fact that no wool was customed at Newcastle between January 1343 and the farming of the customs at Michaelmas.[34] The farming of the customs was soon followed by another concession to the Berwick merchants whereby they were licensed to export 200 sacks of English wool paying duty of only 6s. 8d. per sack, the same rate that was imposed on wool of Scottish growth. Similar licences, for 1,000 sacks, were granted in the 1370s and 1380s. The difficulties of enforcing the limits on the purchase of Northumbrian wool under such licences were obvious, and there is evidence both for the abuse of the licences and for misrepresentation of the origin of wool.[35]

The renewal of war between England and Scotland in 1345, culminating in the capture of David II at the battle of Neville's Cross in the following year, led to a temporary disruption of the wool trade through Berwick, but when conditions returned to normal in 1347 Edward III sought to double the customs duty on Scottish wool exported through Berwick, from half a mark (6s. 8d.) to one mark (13s. 4d.) per sack, and then to 26s. 8d. in February 1348.[36] The burgesses of Berwick, however, argued that this was contrary to the terms agreed when Berwick was surrendered in 1333, that they were impoverished by high customs duties and that the increased duties had caused many merchants to leave the town. The king backed down, and restored the export duty on Scottish wool to its traditional level of 6s. 8d., though wool grown in Teviotdale and other places in the English allegiance was still to pay a duty of 26s. 8d.[37] This was a significant victory for the mercantile community of Berwick, and apart from temporary increases in duties to pay for repairs to the walls of the town in the mid-1350s[38] the burgesses continued to enjoy their traditional fiscal privileges for another decade. The embargo on wool exports from all ports within the allegiance of the English king which was imposed between Michaelmas 1352 and

[33] *Rot. Scot.*, I, p. 632.
[34] *Ibid.*, I, p. 635; *Cal. Close Rolls, 1343–6*, p. 86; Carus-Wilson and Coleman, *England's Export Trade*, p. 46.
[35] *Rot. Scot.*, I, pp. 642, 805, 961, 981, II, p. 76; PRO, E.356/8, mm. 47, 47d.; E.356/14, mm. 58, 58d.
[36] *Calendar of Documents Relating to Scotland*, ed. J. Bain, 4 vols. (Scottish Rec. Publications, Edinburgh, 1881–8), III, no. 1524, pp. 278–9.
[37] *Rot. Scot.*, I, p. 690.
[38] *Ibid.*, I, pp. 765, 773.

1 August 1353 to prepare for the establishment of a home staple gave rise to a protest from the merchants of Berwick, but after the lifting of the embargo the wool trade at Berwick enjoyed several years of stability. The average shipment of wool from the town between 1353 and 1361 – years when the trade proceeded without interruption of any kind – amounted to 1,342 sacks per year.[39] This was still less than the annual average in the last years of Scottish control, and the period was one in which English wool exports as a whole reached a high level. More wool, however, was being exported through Berwick than through Newcastle in these years, and although the wool exported through Berwick is invariably described in the customs accounts as of Scottish growth (*de crescentia Scocie*), it is possible that some wool from Northumberland found its way to Berwick in defiance of the ban.[40]

The return of David II to Scotland in 1357 under the Treaty of Berwick, however, led to renewed pressure on Berwick's fiscal privileges from the English government. Under the terms of the Treaty, the Scots had to pay a ransom of 100,000 marks (£66,666 13s. 4d) for David, and to raise the money customs duties in Scotland were doubled in 1357; they were trebled in the autumn of 1358, and quadrupled in 1368.[41] Berwick now enjoyed a fiscal advantage against Scottish as well as English ports: customs duties were lower in the town than in any other port in either kingdom. This was not a situation which the English government was prepared to tolerate for long, and on 1 March 1361 the English government issued an order increasing the duty on Scottish wool exported through Berwick to 20s. per sack, the level that now prevailed in Scottish ports. The order made it clear that the increase was a response to the increased duty levied in Scotland, arguing (in a way that might have been intended to cut the ground from under the burgesses of Berwick) that 'the town of Berwick ought to be ruled by the laws and customs of the realm of Scotland, and has hitherto been so ruled'.[42] The ban on the export of English wool through Berwick was again imposed, in face of evidence that the duty of 50s. per sack imposed in Newcastle was encouraging 'the greater part of the English wool grown in divers counties'

[39] PRO, E.356/8, mm. 45, 45d.; *Northern Petitions*, pp. 52–3; Lloyd, *English Wool Trade*, pp. 205–6.
[40] Carus-Wilson and Coleman, *England's Export Trade*, pp. 47–8; PRO, E.356/8, mm. 45, 45d. The mercantile community of Newcastle was well aware of the advantages of exporting through Berwick: *Rotuli Parliamentorum*, 6 vols. (Rec. Comm., London, 1783) (hereafter *Rot. Parl.*), II, p. 178.
[41] *Rymer's Foedera*, III(1), pp. 372–4; *Exchequer Rolls*, II, pp. xl–xli; R. Nicholson, *Scotland: The Later Middle Ages* (Edinburgh, 1974), pp. 165–6, 176.
[42] *Cal. Fine Rolls, 1356–68*, p. 153; PRO, E.356/8, m. 46.

to be taken to Berwick 'in order to defraud the king of his due custom and subsidy'.[43]

The burgesses of Berwick, however, were determined to resist the increase, and in November 1362 the English government reduced the duty to 13s. 4d., half of which was to go 'to the relief of the burgesses', for the king had noted the damage done to the town 'by pestilence as well as other adversities'. The concession was to last for three years, and no English wool was to be exported at the concessionary rate.[44] Perhaps the burgesses were content with this compromise: the wool trade remained buoyant, with an average of 1,694 sacks being exported annually between November 1362 and September 1366.[45] This was, again, a higher figure than that for Newcastle, though it is perhaps significant that in the short period when the duty at Berwick stood at 20s. Newcastle's export trade in wool enjoyed a temporary boom.[46] From 1363 onwards, however, Berwick had a competitive advantage over Scottish as well as English ports, and there is evidence that the export of Scottish wool through Berwick was having a damaging effect on customs revenue at towns in south-east Scotland, especially Haddington, which was said in 1370 to 'be far from the March these days'.[47] Wool growers in the Borders evidently found it more convenient, as well as fiscally more attractive, to take their wool to Berwick rather than Haddington. In February 1370 David II sought to stem the flow of Scottish wool to Berwick by granting a charter to the burgh of Dunbar with the right to have the seal of the cocket at the port of Belhaven and collect customs duties there.[48] David also sought to attract English and Teviotdale wool to Scottish ports. The monks of Melrose were granted a special concession to ship wool from Edinburgh at a duty of 13s. 4d per sack during the triple duty regime and 20s. per sack when the duties were quadrupled in 136, presumably to encourage them to take their wool there rather than to Berwick.[49] So far as English wool was concerned, even a duty of 26s. 8d. was substantially less than that imposed in English ports, and throughout the period from 1357 until 1377 when the Scots stopped paying instalments on David II's ransom, merchants from Edinburgh and Haddington, and sometimes those from Linlithgow and North Berwick, were licensed to buy English wool and ship it at a duty of 6s. 8d. or 13s. 4d. per sack. Indeed in 1372–3 1,172 sacks of English wool

[43] Ibid., p. 153.
[44] Rot. Scot., I, p. 867; PRO, E. 356/8, mm. 46, 46d.
[45] PRO, E. 356/8, mm. 46, 46d.
[46] Carus-Wilson and Coleman (eds.), England's Export Trade, p. 48.
[47] The Register of the Great Seal of Scotland, ed. J.M. Thomson and J.B. Paul, 9 vols. (Scot. RO, Edinburgh, 1882–1912), I, no. 340, p. 119.
[48] Ibid.
[49] Exchequer Rolls, II, pp. lxxxvii–lxxxviii, 89, 91, 127, 202, 233, 275, 311.

were exported through Haddington and Dunbar, representing a loss to the
English crown of £2,930. Much of this wool may have been Northumbrian,
and, together with competition from Berwick, may explain the low levels of
wool exports from Newcastle in these years.[50]

Following the quadrupling of Scottish customs duties, Edward again tried
to raise the duty on Scottish wool exported through Berwick, and over 1,000
sacks of wool were exported through Berwick at a duty of 26s. 8d. per sack
in 1372. In December 1372, however, Edward had to reverse his policy and
reduce the duty on Scottish wool exported by merchants resident in Berwick
to the traditional level of 6s. 8d. per sack, while at the same time maintaining
the duty at 26s. 8d. on wool grown in those parts of Scotland which were
still within the English allegiance.[51] This was followed in 1373 by a licence
to the Berwick merchants to purchase 1,000 sacks of wool in Northumberland and export them to Calais or elsewhere at a duty of 26s. 8d. per sack.
The whole episode represented another victory for the Berwick merchants'
determination to maintain their privilege of exporting Scottish wool paying
only the traditional duty of 6s. 8d. per sack.[52] This policy was formalised
by an ordinance of Richard II's government promulgated on 29 November
1377 by which the burgesses of Berwick were granted the right to export
Scottish wool at 6s. 8d. per sack and wool grown in Teviotdale at 13s. 4d.
per sack. The problem of the export of Northumbrian wool through Berwick
was to be solved by a geographical compromise under which the Berwick
merchants were permitted to export wool grown in Northumberland between
the Tweed and the Coquet at a duty of 26s. 8d. per sack.[53] The right to
export at these rates was limited to those burgesses who were resident in
the town, and although the ordinance was intended to bring some stability
to the wool export trade at Berwick, its implementation did not prove free
from difficulty. As early as August 1379 the English government had evidently
heard rumours that non-resident merchants were buying wool in Northumberland and exporting it through Berwick, and in May of the following year
the government alleged that Berwick merchants were buying wool more
widely in Northumberland than allowed by the ordinance.[54]

Furthermore, the Anglo-Scottish war of 1384–9 disrupted the wool trade
through Berwick. No wool was customed at Berwick between 2 June and 10

---

[50] *Ibid.*, II, pp. 119–20, 193–4, 372, 379–80, 398–9; Carus-Wilson and Coleman, *England's
Export Trade*, pp. 49–51. In the parliament of April 1379 the Commons complained about
the quantity of wool grown in the northern counties that was being 'taken into Scotland
without paying any custom or subsidy to the king': *Rot. Parl.*, III, p. 63.

[51] *Rot. Scot.*, I, pp. 947, 953; PRO, E. 356/8, m. 46d. The enhanced duty was imposed
between 2 November 1371 and 12 December 1372.

[52] *Rot. Scot.*, I, p. 961; PRO, E. 356/8, m. 47. A premium of 19d. per sack was levied if
the wool was taken anywhere but to Calais.

[53] *Rot. Scot.*, II, pp. 4–5; PRO, E. 356/8, m. 47d.

[54] *Rot. Scot.*, II, pp. 17, 23.

November 1384, and in December 1385 the king granted the merchants of the town, as a special concession, the right to buy 1,000 sacks of wool from the whole of Northumberland and export it paying 13s. 4d. duty per sack rather than the 26s. 8d. duty levied under the 1377 ordinance on wool grown between Tweed and Coquet. The war of 1384–9 resulted in the loss to the English of virtually the whole of Teviotdale, and exports of wool described in the accounts as grown in Teviotdale and customed at the rate of 13s. 4d. per sack dwindled to the point of insignificance after 1390.[55] Nonetheless, the customs duties laid down in 1377 continued to be imposed throughout Richard II's reign; they were confirmed in 1392 and renewed by Henry IV on 16 November 1399. This renewal was evidently confirmed by parliament, and in an attempt to avoid misrepresentation it was accompanied by a requirement that buyers and sellers should agree indentures specifying 'the true origin of the wool and its quantity'. The loss of Teviotdale, however, undermined the tripartite scale of duties, for it is probable (though impossible to prove) that wool grown in Teviotdale, and particularly by the border abbeys, was now being exported through Berwick as wool of Scottish growth, paying duty at the rate of 6s. 8d. per sack.[56] The tripartite scale was confirmed again on 10 November 1404, but the burgesses of Berwick were now becoming dissatisfied with it. In 1410 they petitioned parliament asking for a unified tariff of 13s. 4d. per sack to be imposed on wool of whatever growth. They complained that the tripartite scale had given rise to ambiguities, and they reminded the king that Richard II had given them licence to ship 1,000 sacks of Northumbrian wool at 13s. 4d. per sack some years earlier. Their request was accompanied by their now-familiar complaints about the risk of depopulation if their wishes were not met. Henry IV accepted their petition, and on 8 May 1410 granted a unified rate of duty of 13s. 4d. per sack, to last for three years. In fact it proved permanent, being renewed for ten years at the accession of Henry V in 1413, for six years in 1422 at Henry VI's accession, and for eight years in 1426.[57]

---

[55] For the Anglo-Scottish war, see A. Grant, 'The Otterburn War from the Scottish Point of View', in A. Tuck and A. Goodman (eds.), *War and Border Societies in the Middle Ages* (London, 1992), pp. 30–64. The fluctuations in the wool trade in these years, and the decline in the export of wool described as grown in Teviotdale, are apparent from the enrolled customs accounts of 1385–99: PRO, E. 356/14, mm. 58, 58d. See also *Rot. Scot.*, II, pp. 76, 96, 100–1, 106.

[56] PRO, E. 356/14, mm. 58, 58d.; E. 356/18, m. 46; *Rot. Scot.*, II, pp. 17, 151–2, 206; *Cal. Close Rolls, 1389–92*, p. 465; *Proceedings and Ordinances of the Privy Council (1386–1542)*, ed. N.H. Nicolas, 7 vols. (Rec. Comm., London, 1834–7), II, pp. 126–7.

[57] PRO, E. 356/18, mm. 46, 46d.; *Northern Petitions*, pp. 55–8. In a petition to the council about this time the community of Berwick asked not only for a unified duty of 13s. 4d. a sack but also for this rate to be abated by 6s. 8d. a sack 'during pleasure, which would draw many merchants to the town'. The council did not agree: *Cal. Documents Relating to Scotland*, IV, no. 835, p. 168. In 1422 the concession was accompanied by a request that the wool should be shipped only to Middelburg or Bruges, but in 1426 the burgesses

In seeking a single rate of duty on all wool exported through Berwick, the burgesses were abandoning their long-held commitment to the 'ancient custom' of 6s. 8d. per sack on Scottish wool, though at 13s. 4d. per sack the Berwick merchants were still able to undercut Scottish ports such as Haddington and Dunbar in exporting wool of Scottish growth. Furthermore, in so far as much of the wool now described as Scottish was grown in Teviotdale, and had been customed at 13s. 4d. per sack when Teviotdale was English, the position was not in practice greatly altered. But perhaps the most important reason for the merchants' wish to have a unified tariff was the advantage it gave them in purchasing wool in north Northumberland. The previous duty of 26s. 8d. per sack mày have encouraged many growers in north Northumberland to take their wool to Scotland for export, as the Commons had complained in 1379. The Scottish crown continued to allow English wool to be exported through Scottish ports at a preferential duty of 6s. 8d. per sack, and the decline in the value of Scottish money compared with English from the late 1370s onwards made export though Scottish ports even more attractive to English growers: in 1393, for example, the Scottish parliament fixed the value of the English noble (6s. 8d.) at 9s. 6d. Scots, and thus the Scottish duty of 6s. 8d. on English wool represented a charge of no more than 4s. 10d. to English growers.[58]

These changes in the rates of duty imposed on wool exported through Berwick have to be seen, however, against the background of a steady decline in the quantity of wool exported through the town. Between 1371 and 1385 an average of 671 sacks per year were exported. With the outbreak of the Anglo-Scottish war exports fell to an annual average of 362 sacks, recovering somewhat in the last years of Richard II's reign (1391–1400) to an average of 540 sacks per year. In the first three decades of the fifteenth century, however, the average fell to only 316 sacks per year over the twenty-six years from 1404 to 1432.[59] Competition from Scotland may have played a part in the decline of Berwick's exports, but the main reason was almost certainly a general decline in wool exports, which affected all English ports in this

complained that the king of Scots had placed an embargo on the purchase of Scottish wool by Berwick merchants and asked for the right to buy wool from Northumberland north of the Blyth rather than the Coquet and freedom to ship it where they liked. The former request was refused, the latter granted: *Rot. Parl.*, IV, pp. 309–10; *Rot. Scot.*, II, p. 256.

[58] *Exchequer Rolls*, IV, pp. cxxi-cxxv, 78, 114; *Acts of the Parliaments of Scotland*, ed. T. Thomson and C. Innes, 12 vols. (Rec. Comm., Edinburgh, 1814–75), I, p. 569; I.H. Stewart, *The Scottish Coinage* (London, 1955), pp. 35–42. After the grant of the unified tariff the enrolled accounts cease to indicate the source of wool exported through Berwick. It is thus impossible to judge whether Scotland or Northumberland was the more important source after 1410. Merchants were unable to buy Scottish wool in the 1420s, as they alleged in their petition of 1426.

[59] PRO, E.356/8, mm. 47, 47d.; E.356/14, mm. 58, 58d.

decade and which marks the beginning of the long-term decline in the export of raw wool from England to the Low Countries. Throughout the fourteenth century the merchants of Berwick had successfully asserted their right to levy only the 'ancient custom' on wool, but by the 1370s market forces were beginning to undermine the trade which had long been the basis of the prosperity of the town's mercantile community.

Although the wool tax was perhaps the most significant and the most contentious of the fiscal measures imposed by the government of Edward III, the tax on each barrel of wine imported into England (tunnage) and the tax on general merchandise exported from English ports (poundage) also became an issue in the crown's relationship with the mercantile community of Berwick. These levies originated during the campaigns of 1345–7 in France, and were granted with the consent of merchants to finance the arming of ships to suppress piracy. They were levied again from time to time between 1350 and 1372 with the consent of the merchants or the citizens and burgesses in parliament, but from 1373 onwards they were imposed regularly with the consent of the whole of the Commons in parliament.[60] There is no evidence that these duties were levied in Berwick before 1382,[61] but on 25 May in that year Richard II's government issued a commission for the collection of tunnage and poundage in the town.[62] On 16 February 1383, however, the crown ordered the collection to be suspended. The writ ordering the suspension makes the point that Berwick lay outside the bounds and limits of the kingdom, and that the men of the town did not come to parliament; therefore they were not to be burdened with a subsidy agreed by parliament.[63] No doubt a protest from the mercantile community of Berwick lay behind the government's reversal of policy, and the community was in effect asserting the principle of no taxation without representation. Their victory, however, did not prove permanent: tunnage and poundage were imposed again in 1389 and 1390, and between 1397 and 1403. However, no commissions to levy the duty are enrolled after 1403, and it was not levied again in Berwick, so it appears, until 1449. The sporadic nature of the imposition of these duties in Berwick suggests a certain unease on the government's part about extending taxes granted by parliament to a town which was not represented there and which had long been recognised as

---

[60] G.L. Harriss, *King, Parliament and Public Finance in Medieval England to 1369* (Oxford, 1975), pp. 459–65; N.S.B. Gras, *The Early English Customs System* (Cambridge, Mass., 1918), pp. 81–2.

[61] There is no entry for Berwick on the enrolled accounts for the subsidy on wine and on merchandise levied in 1372–3 and 1378 (PRO, E.356/13) and no commission enrolled on the fine rolls ordering the collection of the subsidy in the town.

[62] *Cal. Fine Rolls, 1377–83*, p. 299.

[63] *Rot. Scot.*, II, p. 48.

situated outside the realm. The potential revenue from tunnage and poundage at Berwick was not substantial. The surviving account for these duties
in 1389–90 notes that no wine was brought into the town during the period
of the account, and the subsidy on general merchandise amounted to only
£28 14s. 2d.[64]

Since Berwick did not send members to the English parliament until
after its reconquest by the English in 1482, lay subsidies granted by the
Commons in the English parliament were not levied in the town, and,
unlike tunnage and poundage, there is no evidence that the English
crown ever attempted to levy the lay subsidy there. Nor is there much
evidence for the levying of locally negotiated subsidies similar to those
imposed from time to time in Wales and Cheshire. The merchants of
Berwick granted Edward III a subsidy in 1340–1, but little is known of
the details, and it may have been an extraordinary subsidy on wool
rather than a levy on the movable goods of the Berwick community.[65]
The lay inhabitants of Berwick were, it appears, exempt from the levies
of fifteenths and tenths which were imposed upon lay communities within
the realm. The position of the clergy in Berwick was probably similar.
The re-establishment of English rule in the town in 1333 entailed no
change in ecclesiastical jurisdiction. The town remained within the diocese
of St Andrews, and the convocation of the Province of York made no
attempt to levy clerical subsidies in the town. After the outbreak of the
Great Schism in 1378, the bishop of Durham exercised spiritual jurisdiction in the town, but again there is no evidence that clerical taxes granted
by the northern convocation were extended to Berwick's clergy, or that
the clergy were ever summoned to attend the northern convocation.[66]

[64] An account survives for the collection of tunnage and poundage, including the tax on
cloth, 'in the East March' from 24 August 1389 to 2 February 1390: PRO, E. 122/3/12,
and see also *Cal. Documents Relating to Scotland*, V, no. 864, p. 275; *Cal. Pat. Rolls,
1388–93*, p. 86. There is, however, no entry for Berwick on the enrolled accounts of the
collection of subsidies in this period: PRO, E.356/15. Further commissions to levy the
subsidies are to be found in *Cal. Fine Rolls, 1391–9*, pp. 205–6, and *Cal. Fine Rolls,
1399–1405*, pp. 121–2, 226–8. The commission to levy tunnage and poundage in 1449
is enrolled on the fine rolls: *Cal. Fine Rolls, 1445–52*, pp. 136, 191–3. The grant of taxes
in the February parliament of 1449, on which this commission is based, was not to be
held to the prejudice of Berwick in respect of the customs and subsidy on wool, but such
a clause was excluded from the grant of tunnage and poundage: *Rot. Parl.*, V, pp. 142–4.
[65] P. Morgan, *War and Society in Medieval Cheshire* (Chetham Soc., 3rd ser., no. 34, Manchester, 1987), pp. 124–35. For the levying of subsidies in Wales and Cheshire in Richard
II's reign, see PRO, Exchequer Issue Rolls, E.403/536, m. 12; E.403/532, m. 16;
Receivers' and Ministers' Accounts, S.C.6/1215/6–8; S.C.6/1222/6, 7. The evidence for
the subsidy granted by Berwick merchants in 1340–1 is PRO, E.356/8, m. 45.
[66] *Register of Thomas Langley, Bishop of Durham, 1406–1437*, ed. R.L. Storey, 6 vols. (Surtees
Soc., nos. 164, 166, 169–70, 177, 182, Durham, 1956–70), I, nos. 96, 210, pp. 85–9,
162–4, V, no. 1383, pp. 99–100. The commission to exercise spiritual jurisdiction was
revoked following the ending of the Schism: *ibid.*, V, no. 1506, pp. 169–70.

The political principles underlying Berwick's fiscal privileges are, however, more complex than the 1383 concession implies. Customs duties on wool, woolfells and hides were levied in Wales at the rates prevailing in England and accounted for by the chamberlain of the exchequer of Carmarthen, even though no part of Wales elected representatives to the Commons in parliament.[67] In the fifteenth century the crown sought to extend the lay subsidy to the bishopric of Durham, but was met with resistance by Bishops Langley and Neville and by Prior Wessington.[68] Their opposition was grounded not on the principle of representation in parliament (an argument which made more of an appeal to the Wessington family's distinguished descendant in a land unknown to him),[69] but rather on the ancient liberties of the bishopric.[70] Similarly, the Berwick burgesses' objection to the imposition of higher customs duties in the town was based on the right of the burgesses to enjoy the liberties and customs they had had in the time of Alexander III rather than on the fact that they did not send representatives to the English parliament. Although the crown took notice of the argument about representation in 1383, the exemption of Berwick from customs duties on wool at English levels was grounded even as late as 1449 on grants of privileges by the king's ancestors. The issue of representation was one amongst a number of arguments which the burgesses of Berwick used to defend their fiscal privileges, but both in Berwick and elsewhere the specific liberties granted by charter to a particular community were perhaps more persuasive in the fourteenth and fifteenth centuries than arguments to do with representation in parliament.

Berwick's privileges, however, perhaps owed as much to practical considerations as to political principles. From time to time, as we have seen, the English crown sought to extend the scope of the customs duties levied in Berwick and to raise the duty on wool, woolfells and hides beyond the

[67] E.A. Lewis, 'A Contribution to the Commercial History of Medieval Wales', *Y Cymmrodor*, 24 (1913), pp. 86–188.

[68] The parish tax of 1374 was imposed on Durham as well as the rest of the realm, but not on Berwick. It was said, however, to have been granted by the men of the liberty of Durham voluntarily (*mera et spontanea voluntate*), and was not to be held to their prejudice in future: *Rot. Parl.*, II, p. 461. The tax of 6d. and 1s. levied in the bishopric in 1437 was again stated to be a freewill offering, not in any way to be prejudicial to their liberties. This concession was enrolled on the Durham chancery rolls immediately before the collection in the bishopric of the tax of 6d. and 1s. granted in 1450: PRO, Durham, 3/44, m. 12. These precedents were also noted by Prior Wessington: *Historiae Dunelmensis Scriptores Tres*, ed. J. Raine (Surtees Soc., no. 9, Durham, 1839), appendix no. ccxxviii, p. cclxx.

[69] George Washington's descent from Prior Wessington's family is discussed by R.B. Dobson, *Durham Priory, 1400–1450* (Cambridge, 1973), p. 89 n. 3. The connection is commemorated on a plaque outside the south door of the nave of Durham Cathedral.

[70] PRO, Durham 3/44, m. 12; *Historiae Dunelmensis Scriptores Tres*, appendix no. ccxxviii, p. cclxx; G. Lapsley, *The County Palatine of Durham* (New York, 1900), pp. 116–18.

'ancient custom' of Alexander III, but were met with resistance from the mercantile community of the town. The success of this resistance owes something, no doubt, to the strength of the political principles on which it was grounded, but also to the effectiveness of the community of Berwick as a pressure group. Although they were not represented in the English parliament, the burgesses of Berwick were able to make their wishes known both to parliament and to the council by petition and perhaps – though there is no documentary evidence for this – through the good offices of the nobles who held office as captains of Berwick and wardens of the East March.[71] There is little sign that the interests of the Berwick merchants were popular with the Commons in parliament: indeed, in the fifteenth century parliament evidently lobbied against Berwick's privilege of exporting wool free of the Staple, which went back at least to the Ordinance of 1377. The renewal of the unified tariff in 1422 was accompanied by a condition that the wool should be exported to Middelburg or Bruges, but the Berwick merchants successfully petitioned against this restriction in 1425 and it was rescinded. Thereafter, parliamentary enactments on the Staple were generally accompanied by a clause saving the privilege of Berwick merchants to export wool wherever they wished.[72] The small quantity and comparatively poor quality of English wool shipped through Berwick perhaps served to limit criticism of Berwick's privileged position. The real reason, however, for the success of the Berwick merchants in defending their fiscal privileges lay in the military and strategic – and perhaps psychological – importance of the town to the English government as a bastion of English power on the northern border.[73] Although Berwick never attained the same military and commercial importance as Calais, and although much less money was spent on the town than was poured into Calais, both were military bases obtained by conquest which Edward III and his successors were determined to retain in English hands.

Although primarily, as we have seen, a garrison town and supply base, the English crown had an interest in ensuring the continued prosperity of the town's mercantile community. This was partly for military reasons: although there was friction from time to time between the civilian community and the military government of the town,[74] the civilian community was

---

[71] E.g. *Northern Petitions*, pp. 7–91.

[72] *Rot. Parl.*, III, pp. 429, 661, IV, pp. 250, 309–10, 358–60; *Statutes of the Realm (1101– 1713)*, ed. A. Luders, T.E. Tomlins, J. France, W.E. Taunton and J. Raithby, 11 vols. (Rec. Comm., London, 1808–28), II, pp. 112, 254; *Northern Petitions*, pp. 57–8; J.H. Munro, *Wool, Cloth and Gold: The Struggle for Bullion in Anglo-Burgundian Trade, 1340– 1478* (Toronto, 1972), pp. 56, 86, 120.

[73] Atkinson, 'Berwick upon Tweed', pp. 112–13. She makes the important point that Edward III also needed to ensure that the town was denied to the Scots.

[74] *Rot. Scot.*, I, pp. 613–15, 641–2, 930, II, p. 87.

expected to play a part in the defence of the town and income from the customs revenue was occasionally earmarked for the repair of the town's defences.[75] Perhaps more significantly, from the 1350s onwards part of the fee payable to the captain of Berwick – often a member of the Percy family – was assigned on the customs at Berwick, and both the Percies themselves and the English exchequer had an interest in ensuring that the export trade from Berwick flourished at least to the level that allowed the fee to be collected from the customs.[76]

In their dealings with the English crown, the burgesses of Berwick made much of the arguments about depopulation and decay of trade. In 1348, for example, following the raising of duty on Scottish wool exported through the town, the burgesses argued that many men had left the town as a consequence. In the next year, the mayor and burgesses wrote a plaintive letter to Edward III claiming that they had 'often shown the king and council the misfortunes and perils of their town, daily hoping that some remedy may be sent for their salvation, but they have found no relief and are now abandoned and forgotten'.[77] Nine years later, in 1358, the crown attempted to stop depopulation in the town by confiscating property and rents held by burgesses who left the town to live elsewhere, and in 1362, when duty on Scottish wool was reduced from 20s. to 13s. 4d., the king noted the damage done to the town 'by pestilence'.[78] In 1371, the poverty and depopulation of the town were given as reasons for conceding that the duty on Scottish wool should return to its ancient level of 6s. 8d. per sack, and this argument was repeated several times in the fifteenth century.[79]

Fear of depopulation and decay of trade were powerful weapons for the mercantile community of Berwick to use in their dealings with the crown, yet the validity of their arguments requires examination. Before the plague of 1348–9 there is little evidence of depopulation within the town. The chamberlain's accounts record the forfeiture of property by those who had been granted tenements of the town by Robert I, but show equally that those who forfeited were replaced by Englishmen.[80] After the Black Death, however, the position worsened. The plague itself had an immediate impact on the burgesses, and intensified their sense of insecurity. In the petition which the mayor and burgesses sent to Edward III in 1349 they declared

---

[75] *Ibid.*, I, pp. 613, 765, 773, II, p. 77
[76] PRO, E. 122/3/3(2); E.356/8, mm. 46d., 47; *Cal. Documents Relating to Scotland*, V, no. 837, p. 272.
[77] *Rot. Scot.*, I, pp. 724–5; *Cal. Documents Relating to Scotland*, V, no. 810, pp. 269–70.
[78] *Rot. Scot.*, I, pp. 820–1, 867.
[79] *Ibid.*, I, p. 944; *Cal. Close Rolls. 1389–92*, p. 465; PRO, E.356/18, m. 46; *Cal. Documents Relating to Scotland*, IV, no. 835, p. 168; *Northern Petitions*, pp. 55–8.
[80] PRO, Berwick Chamberlain's Accounts, S.C.6/951/1, 2 (1335–6, 1341–2).

that 'the Scots are greatly cheered by the pestilence', which had evidently not yet reached Scotland. This gloomy assessment is strikingly borne out by the chronicler Henry Knighton, who recorded that as news of the plague in England reached Scotland the Scots adopted a new oath, 'Be the foul deth of Engelond', and assembled an army in Selkirk Forest to invade their plague-stricken southern neighbour. No sooner had the army mustered, however, than it too was struck down with plague and the invasion plan abandoned.[81]

The pleas of misfortune and poverty which the burgesses of Berwick put forward in their petitions to the English crown were designed, of course, to gain political and fiscal concessions, and their generalisations should not necessarily be taken at face value. The exposed position of Berwick, and the threat of attack and possible recapture by the Scots, acted as a disincentive to live in the town: in 1358, for instance, the government attempted to stop depopulation in the town following the temporary Scottish recapture in 1355–6 by declaring that burgesses who went to live elsewhere would have their property in the town confiscated.[82] The accounts of the chamberlain of Berwick, the official responsible for the collection of rents and other dues from the civilian population of the town, suggest some depopulation from the 1360s onwards. No accounts survive for the years between 1349 and 1363, but the account for Easter 1363 to Easter 1364 records that many rents and profits could not be levied 'because of lack of tenants and other causes'. The more detailed accounts for August 1369 to August 1371 and August 1373 to August 1375 record some waste tenements in all the streets of the town, with most in the area of the town known as La Nesse, where a third of the tenements were vacant. The accounts for 1373–4 suggest that 40 out of 124 burgages in the town were vacant, a sufficiently high figure to give some credence to complaints of depopulation, but perhaps explicable more in terms of the general fall in population after the outbreaks of plague between 1348 and 1369 than a substantial exodus from Berwick itself.[83]

The fall in the population of the town, especially in the last three decades of the fourteenth century, and its evident vulnerability, were thus real problems. The crown needed to sustain the mercantile community of the town and to ensure that the basis of its prosperity, the trade in wool, was not fatally damaged by the imposition of customs duties that would destroy its competitive position against both Newcastle and the ports of south-east Scot-

---

[81] *Cal. Documents Relating to Scotland*, V, no. 810, pp. 269–70; *Chronicon Henrici Knighton*, ed. J.R. Lumby, 2 vols. (Rolls Ser., no. 92, London, 1889–95), I, pp. 62–3.

[82] *Rot. Scot.*, II, pp. 820–1.

[83] *Cal. Documents Relating to Scotland*, IV, nos. 21, 135, 177, pp. 5–7, 30–1, 41; PRO, S.C.6/951/4–8 (1363–4, 1369–70, 1370–1, 1373–4, 1374–5).

land. The fiscal privileges of Berwick were essential to its survival as a bastion of English power, and the mercantile community of the town made the most of this in putting pressure on the English government to maintain the liberties granted to their predecessors by Alexander III.

9

Taxation and communities in late medieval England

CHRISTOPHER DYER

T HIS ESSAY has two purposes: first to investigate how English villages and towns organised their direct taxes after 1334, when the government gave them the task of assessing their own contributions; and secondly, of using that information to explore medieval attitudes towards hierarchy and social responsibility.[1]

The concept of community presents historians with many dilemmas and uncertainties. On the one hand it has a solid, institutional significance which need not cause much difficulty. When the community of the vill was charged with some rent payment or public function (repairing a bridge, for example) we can be sure that we are observing practical self-government. Likewise in a town the *communitas* was sometimes assigned a specific constitutional role, such as the election of officials, even though there were doubts about methods of representation. The word 'community' also carries with it a whole range of imprecise meanings: it implies a sharing of values among its members, and a collective sense of purpose; or it might refer to the interactions between people which made them mutually dependent, and led them to co-operate. Such issues of mentality or everyday social contact are difficult to define and analyse

[1] The author is grateful for the assistance of archivists in various record offices, in particular to the staff of Essex Record Office and of the National Register of Archives. Valuable advice was given by Dr R.W. Hoyle. Dr R.M. Smith gave me access to transcripts of the poll taxes in advance of publication. I am grateful to Dr C.C. Fenwick and Dr R.S. Schofield for permission to use information from their doctoral theses. This subject is an appropriate one for this volume because of Edward Miller's distinguished contributions to the subject of public finance and its effect on the medieval economy and society, notably in chapter 6 of M.M. Postan, E.E. Rich and E. Miller (eds.), *Cambridge Economic History of Europe*, III (Cambridge, 1963), and chapter 8 of C.M. Cipolla (ed.), *The Fontana Economic History of Europe*, I (London, 1972).

historically.[2] Nonetheless, it has been assumed that in the case of villages, and to a lesser extent towns, at some early period communities were strong and cohesive, and that they were threatened by economic and social change. The demise of communities is sometimes attributed to the increase in social differentiation in the early modern period, or to the corrosive effects of the market in the thirteenth century, or it is associated with the redistribution of landed resources after the Black Death of 1348–9.[3] Historians of religion argue that the spiritual community of the parish reached a peak in the fifteenth and early sixteenth centuries, and was destroyed by the Reformation and individualistic puritanism.[4]

The 'decline of community' may be no more than a historical cliché and sceptics doubt whether society was ever socially cohesive or as imbued with a collective mentality as some historians wish to think. Perhaps the communal ceremonies and rituals, most highly developed in towns, were shams, organised by the elite, to give divided places a semblance of unity.[5]

The records of direct taxation have been used to define the social and economic context within which communities functioned. The tax quotas of the lay subsidy fixed in 1334, the poll taxes of 1377–81 and the new subsidy of 1524–5 enable towns to be put in ranking order, and then for their changing fortunes over the long term to be compared, thus

---

[2] For rural communities, see H.M. Cam, 'The Community of the Vill', in V. Ruffer and A.J. Taylor (eds.), *Medieval Studies Presented to Rose Graham* (Oxford, 1950), pp. 1–14; W.O. Ault, 'The Vill in Medieval England', *Proceedings of the American Philosophical Society*, 126 (1982), pp. 188–211; C. Dyer, 'The English Medieval Village Community and its Decline', *Journal of British Studies*, 33 (1994), pp. 407–29. For towns, A.G. Rosser, 'The Essence of Medieval Urban Communities: The Vill of Westminster 1200–1450', and C. Phythian-Adams, 'Ceremony and the Citizen: The Communal Year at Coventry 1450–1550', in R. Holt and G. Rosser (eds.), *The Medieval Town. A Reader in English Urban History, 1200–1540* (London, 1990), pp. 216–37, 238–64; S. Reynolds, *An Introduction to the History of English Medieval Towns* (Oxford, 1977), pp. 171–7; B.R. McRee, 'Peacemaking and its Limits in Late Medieval Norwich', *English Historical Review*, 109 (1994), pp. 831–66.

[3] K. Wrightson, *English Society 1580–1680* (London, 1982), pp. 39–65, 180–2; M.K. McIntosh, *Autonomy and Community: The Royal Manor of Havering, 1200–1500* (Cambridge, 1986), pp. 176–8; Z. Razi, 'Family, Land and the Village Community in Later Medieval England', in T.H. Aston (ed.), *Landlords, Peasants and Politics in Medieval England* (Cambridge, 1987), pp. 360–93.

[4] R. Hutton, *The Rise and Fall of Merry England. The Ritual Year, 1400–1700* (Oxford, 1994), pp. 69–110.

[5] For scepticism on rural communities, R.M. Smith, '"Modernisation" and the Corporate Medieval Village Community in England: Some Sceptical Reflections', in A.R.H. Baker and D. Gregory (eds.), *Explorations in Historical Geography* (Cambridge, 1984), pp. 140–79; for doubts about urban unity, R.H. Hilton, *English and French Towns in Feudal Society: A Comparative Study* (Cambridge, 1992), pp. 105–51.

testing theories of 'urban decline'.[6] The same records for villages (together
with the ninth of 1340–1 and the parish tax of 1428) allow us to see
which places contracted or even were completely deserted in the period
of demographic decline.[7] Broad shifts in regional wealth, showing for
example the rise in prosperity of those areas most active in the cloth
industry, have emerged from systematic comparisons of the 1334 assessments or the poll taxes with the subsidies of the early sixteenth century.[8]
The lists of names of taxpayers for the thirteenth- and fourteenth-century
lay subsidies, usually with an assessment of the value of movable goods,
more rarely with details of the goods valued, have provided material for
studies of agricultural practice, market orientation and migration.[9] They
have been used to indicate wealth or poverty, and to assess hardship
occasioned by rents and taxes.[10] The poll taxes give information about
occupations and employment, as well as marriage and family structure.[11]
Wage earning is also recorded in the taxes of the 1520s, together with

---

[6] W.G. Hoskins, *Local History in England*, 3rd edn (London, 1984), pp. 275–80; A.D.
Dyer, *Decline and Growth in English Towns, 1400–1640* (London, 1991). The latter work
contains bibliographical details of the attempts, initiated by A.R. Bridbury, to use the
proportion of tax paid by towns to resolve the 'urban decline' controversy, pp. 77–8. For
local studies of towns using tax evidence, see T.R. Slater, 'The Urban Hierarchy in
Medieval Staffordshire', *Journal of Historical Geography*, 11 (1985), pp. 115–37; R.B.
Dobson, 'Yorkshire Towns in the Late Fourteenth Century', *Publications of the Thoresby
Society*, 59 (1983), pp. 1–21.

[7] M.W. Beresford, 'A Review of Historical Research (to 1968)', in M.W. Beresford and
J.G. Hurst (eds.), *Deserted Medieval Villages. Studies* (London, 1971), pp. 6–40; A.R.H.
Baker, 'Evidence in the *Nonarum Inquisitiones* of Contracting Arable Land in England in
the Early Fourteenth Century', *Economic History Review*, 2nd ser., 19 (1966), pp. 518–32.

[8] R.S. Schofield, 'The Geographical Distribution of Wealth in England, 1334–1649', in
R. Floud (ed.), *Essays in Quantitative Economic History* (Oxford, 1974), pp. 79–106;
H.C. Darby (ed.), *A New Historical Geography of England before 1600* (Cambridge, 1976),
pp. 137–45, 162–3, 189–96; H.C. Darby, R.E. Glasscock, J. Sheail and G.R. Versey, 'The
Changing Geographical Distribution of Wealth in England: 1066–1334–1525', *Journal of
Historical Geography*, 5 (1979), pp. 247–62.

[9] M.M. Postan, 'Village Livestock in the Thirteenth Century', in M.M. Postan, *Essays on
Medieval Agriculture and General Problems of the Medieval Economy* (Cambridge, 1973),
pp. 214–48; K. Biddick, 'Missing Links: Taxable Wealth, Markets and Stratification among
Medieval English Peasants', *Journal of Interdisciplinary History*, 18 (1987), pp. 277–98;
P. McClure, 'Patterns of Migration in the Late Middle Ages: The Evidence of English
Place-Name Surnames', *Economic History Review*, 2nd ser., 32 (1979), pp. 167–82.

[10] B.F. Harvey, 'The Population Trend in England between 1300 and 1348', *Transactions
of the Royal Historical Society*, 5th ser., 16 (1966), p. 28; J.R. Maddicott, *The English
Peasantry and the Demands of the Crown* (Past and Present Supplement, 1, 1975).

[11] R.H. Hilton, 'Some Social and Economic Evidence in Late Medieval English Tax Returns',
in R.H. Hilton, *Class Conflict and the Crisis of Feudalism* (London, 1985), pp. 253–67;
P.J.P. Goldberg, 'Urban Identity and the Poll Tax of 1377, 1379, and 1381', *Economic
History Review*, 2nd ser., 43 (1990), pp. 194–216; R.M. Smith, 'Hypothèses sur la nup-
tialité en Angleterre aux XIIIe–XVIe siècles', *Annales: Economies, Sociétés, Civilisations*, 38
(1983), pp. 107–36; L.R. Poos, *A Rural Society after the Black Death: Essex 1350–1525*
(Cambridge, 1991), pp. 22–31, 148–56, 185–8.

data for wealth and status of individuals, settlements and regions.[12] Taxation throws light on ideas, both those of the authorities who devised the fiscal machinery, and those of the taxpayers, who often co-operated with the system, or who revealed their views of government policies by evading and hindering some taxes, threatening rebellion and more rarely taking up arms.[13] All historical work on taxation has to take into account the formalised nature of the records, and the corruption and inefficiency involved in their production, which may invalidate any conclusion based on them.

I

The form of direct taxation considered here, the lay subsidy, developed in the period 1275–1332.[14] It was based on the principle that every household's movable goods should be valued, and a proportion of that value (fixed in different years at a ninth, tenth, twelfth, fifteenth or other fraction) was payable in tax. In line with legal restraints, and the need to treat taxpayers reasonably, goods such as foodstuffs for home consumption, and means of livelihood, such as ploughs, were excluded from the calculations, and those whose total fell below a limit – often 10s. – were exempt.[15] The taxes were assessed and collected by local officials, who used a good deal of discretion by adjusting from tax to tax the goods that they chose to value, the values that they applied and the exemption limits. The taxpayers had devices for concealment and persuasion. The effects of the grass roots implementation of the tax can be observed in the tendency for subsidies set at different fractions to produce not dissimilar totals, so that the 'ninth' of 1297 yielded £32,900, while the 'tenth and fifteenth' of 1332 netted £32,400.[16] There seems to have been a tacit agreement to exclude a growing proportion of the less prosperous. In Worcestershire, for example, the number contributing to the subsidies

---

[12] J.C.K. Cornwall, *Wealth and Society in Early Sixteenth Century England* (London, 1988).

[13] G.L. Harriss, *King, Parliament, and Public Finance in Medieval England to 1369* (Oxford, 1975), pp. 313–55; E. Miller, 'War, Taxation and the English Economy in the Late Thirteenth and Early Fourteenth Centuries', in J.M. Winter (ed.), *War and Economic Development: Essays in Memory of David Joslin* (Cambridge, 1975), pp. 11–31; W.M. Ormrod, 'The Peasants' Revolt and the Government of England', *Journal of British Studies*, 29 (1990), pp. 1–30.

[14] J.F. Willard, *Parliamentary Taxes on Personal Property 1290 to 1334. A Study in Mediaeval English Financial Administration* (Cambridge, Mass., 1934).

[15] *Ibid.*, pp. 77–81, 87–92.

[16] J.F. Hadwin, 'The Medieval Lay Subsidies and Economic History', *Economic History Review*, 2nd ser., 36 (1983), pp. 200–17.

of 1275 and 1327 fell from 7,373 to 4,644.[17] No known demographic decline could explain such a shrinkage.[18]

Concessions to the taxpayers, and the use of local people as administrators, presumably help to explain the relatively smooth passage of these subsidies. These were troubled times, with bad harvests and famine, and more general economic recession; the frequent taxes, especially in the 1330s, coincided with other fiscal measures, such as purveyance and heavy indirect levies, which meant that the taxpayers really suffered, yet they grumbled, protested against specific cases of corruption, but in the end paid up, and the exchequer records show that the government received a remarkably high proportion of the amount expected. In contemporary France, taxes met with some violent opposition and were not gathered with the same efficiency.[19]

Complaints about corruption surrounding the 1332 subsidy led the government in 1334 to institute a new policy. Instead of the laborious and fallible assessment of each taxpayer by the subtaxers, leading to the compilation of the detailed name-by-name lists so valuable to historians, each taxpaying vill negotiated a lump sum somewhat greater than the total paid in 1332, supposedly therefore representing a 'tenth and a fifteenth' (the higher rate of a tenth being paid by royal demesnes and some boroughs). The details of assessment and collection were to be the responsibility of the communities. Henceforth the administration of the tax for the government became much easier – every time that parliament granted a 'fifteenth' every vill collected its quota, and the state could rely on the delivery of a global total of between £34,000 and £37,000.[20] The system worked so well that it continued in use into the seventeenth century with surprisingly little adjustment – there was some relief for individual vills after the Black Death, and others had their quotas reduced or temporarily removed after they had suffered at the hands of Scottish

[17] *Lay Subsidy Roll for the County of Worcester, 1 Edward III*, ed. F.J. Eld (Worcestershire Historical Society, 1895), p. iv.

[18] Z. Razi, *Life, Marriage and Death in a Medieval Parish: Economy, Society and Demography in Halesowen 1270–1400* (Cambridge, 1980), pp. 39–41.

[19] Maddicott, *English Peasantry*, pp. 12–47; W.M. Ormrod, 'The Crown and the English Economy, 1290–1348', in B.M.S. Campbell (ed.), *Before the Black Death. Studies in the 'Crisis' of the Early Fourteenth Century* (Manchester, 1991), pp. 151–9; J.B. Henneman, *Royal Taxation in Fourteenth-Century France. The Development of War Financing* (Princeton, N.J., 1971).

[20] Willard, *Parliamentary Taxes*, pp. 11–13; *The Lay Subsidy of 1334*, ed. R.E. Glasscock (British Academy Records of Social and Economy History, new ser., 2, 1975), pp. xiii–xxiv; Ormrod, 'Crown and the English Economy', p. 153.

or French raids, or from inundations by the sea.[21] General abatements in 1433 and 1446 diminished the overall total by £6,000, and this was often distributed variably to take note of local circumstances.[22] Apart from the quotas and later abatements, historians are left with little detailed documentation, and the central government neither collected nor preserved lists of individual taxpayers. Such lists reappeared with the new subsidies under the Tudors, but even then the old 'fifteenth' continued to be collected alongside the fiscal experiments.[23]

There are enough fragments of evidence to suggest that after 1334 the communities, freed from such guidelines as the minimum assessment of 10s., spread the tax burden more widely. When the government gathered complaints against officials in Lincolnshire in 1341, they were told of wealthy taxpayers (including an ex-sheriff of the county) who would not contribute to their village's quota. As tax collector, Peter Maundeville of Beelsby in four successive subsidies in the late 1330s exempted both himself and his brother, Robert, who was the richest man in the village.[24]

The most direct evidence for a regressive tendency comes from Kent, which continued to tax individuals, on the basis of hundreds rather than vills.[25] The number of taxpayers rose from 11,000 in 1334 to 17,000 in 1338 and there were still 15,000 in 1373.[26] The increase was achieved partly by reducing the lower limit of assessment at which tax was paid, a move already apparent in 1334 when in some hundreds the old 10s. limit was observed, but in Blackford hundred twenty-six people whose goods were valued at 5s. were expected to pay the fifteenth at 4d. each. It is sometimes said that such extensions of the tax included the poor, but people assessed at 5s. were probably in possession of animals and goods worth much more than this, and should really be regarded as

---

[21] S. Dowell, *A History of Taxation and Taxes in England*, 4 vols. (London, 1884), I, pp. 95–101, 121–3; K.J. Allison, 'The Lost Villages of Norfolk', *Norfolk Archaeology*, 31 (1955), pp. 130–1.

[22] Dowell, *History of Taxation*, I, pp. 126–7; D. Dymond and R. Virgoe, 'The Reduced Population and Wealth of Early Fifteenth-Century Suffolk', *Proceedings of the Suffolk Institute of Archaeology and History*, 36 (1988), pp. 73–100.

[23] R.W. Hoyle, 'Resistance and Manipulation in Early Tudor Taxation: Some Evidence from the North', *Archives*, 20 (1993), pp. 158–76; R.W. Hoyle, 'Crown, Parliament and Taxation in Sixteenth-Century England', *English Historical Review*, 109 (1994), pp. 1174–96.

[24] Maddicott, *English Peasantry*, pp. 51–2; *The 1341 Royal Inquest in Lincolnshire*, ed. B.M. McLane (Lincoln Record Society, 78, 1988), pp. 54, 55.

[25] Maddicott, *English Peasantry*, p. 51; 'The Kent Lay Subsidy of 1334–5', ed. C.W. Chalklin and H.A. Hanley, in *Documents Illustrative of Medieval Kentish Society*, ed. F.R.H. Du Boulay (Kent Archaeological Society, Records Publications, 18, 1964), pp. 58–172.

[26] 'Kent Lay Subsidy', ed. Chalklin and Hanley, p. 58; C.C. Fenwick, 'The English Poll Taxes of 1377, 1379 and 1381' (Univ. of London PhD thesis, 1983), pp. 20–2.

belonging to a middling category. Kent contained at least 30,000 house-holds in the 1330s, so the inclusion of 11,000 or even 17,000 still left the main body of wage earners and smallholders exempt.[27] Nonetheless, if Kent was typical, its tax documents would support the view that after 1334 the burden was shifting towards the less well off. This would not, however, tell us precisely about the way in which communities elsewhere in England treated their new powers, because the vill did not serve as the unit of taxation in Kent.

Another clue to attitudes towards the distribution of taxation is provided in 1377–81 by the poll taxes, and in particular the third and last levy of 1380–1.[28] The first poll tax of 1377 required 4d. from everyone, excluding the very poor, but including young servants and children over the age of fourteen who would not have been taxed under any previous system. For the second poll tax, a schedule was provided for the seriously wealthy (gentry, farmers, franklins and merchants, for example) to pay at higher rates, but the great majority of the population were still expected to pay a flat rate of 4d. Neither of these taxes gave much scope for the local elites to exercise any power or influence over the assessment. But the third tax provided that the 'sufficient . . . shall aid the lesser' within the understanding that each village should return a total of 1s. per person, everyone over the age of fifteen being expected to pay. The detailed lists allow us to see the extent to which the communities shared the burden equitably. To take ten villages in Gloucestershire's Bradley hundred as a sample, we find that in three places the government's recommendations were ignored, and everyone paid 1s. – for example at Shipton, people described variously as cultivators (*cultores*), shepherds, labourers and servants all paid the same even though they must have had very unequal resources.[29] However, in the majority of villages some effort was made to help the wage earners, often at the level of individual households. At Hampnett the 'sufficient' peasant Roger de Morton and his wife paid 3s. 4d. and their two servants Robert and Nicholas contributed 4d. each, so that the household as a whole paid 4s. In other cases the village shared out the payment, as at Whittington where a clearly opulent cultivator and his wife paid 6s., a shepherd and his wife 3s. 6d. and two other households 2s. each, while a number of labourers and servants, and others described as 'impotent' were let off with payments ranging

[27] The estimates of Kent's population depend on the 1377 poll tax total of 56,557: R.B. Dobson, *The Peasants' Revolt of 1381*, 2nd edn (London, 1983), p. 56.

[28] The details of the poll tax come from Fenwick, 'English Poll Taxes'.

[29] The information on the Gloucestershire poll taxes come from an edition being prepared by C.C. Fenwick and R.M. Smith for publication by the British Academy, and I am grateful for Dr Smith's willingness to lend me this material in advance of publication.

from 4d. for a single person to 1s. 6d. for a married couple. In the thirteen villages of Hinckford hundred in Essex, the sharing out of the poll tax was carried out in a similarly inconsistent fashion.[30] Three made no attempt at all to fulfil the expectations of the government, and everyone paid 1s.; in the remainder efforts to help the poorer inhabitants resulted in a minority of the more substantial taxpayers contributing 1s. 3d. or 1s. 6d. each, while their poorer neighbours were charged with 4d., 6d. or 8d., which can scarcely have reflected accurately real disparities in wealth.

But the poll tax was a rather special case – new, much resented and giving little responsibility to the local worthies who normally decided who should be taxed. Their main contribution to equitable assessment is apparent to us only in the absence of many teenage children and females. The concealment of potential payers, or connivance at their evasion, cut out of the taxable population those who received payment mainly in kind in the households of their parents and employers.

II

We are fortunately not entirely dependent for information about post-1334 taxes on the evidence of complaints against corrupt officials, the Kentish records or the analogy of the third poll tax, because a few tax lists have survived from the period 1334–1513 which give us a precious sample of actual tax-paying practice from which tentative conclusions can be drawn.

Let us begin with the towns, which exercised much control over their tax arrangements before 1334, and have preserved in their own archives records of assessments for the royal subsidies, for the early fourteenth-century tallages, and of levies for loans to the crown, or for public works. Shifts in policy produced some remarkable changes in the numbers of contributors in very short periods. The authorities at Shrewsbury clearly showed themselves to be very flexible and indeed inconsistent in their allocation of payments, so that in the subsidy lists there were 112 taxpayers in 1297, 402 in 1304 and 286 in 1332;[31] at Colchester 518 people contributed to a tallage in 1312–13, whereas 388 paid the tax in 1301 and 127 in 1327.[32] Neither the levy of 1301 nor that of 1312–13 had a minimum payment fixed by the government. The sudden increase in

[30] C. Oman, *The Great Revolt of 1381* (Oxford, 1906), pp. 167–82.
[31] *The Wealth of Shrewsbury in the Early Fourteenth Century*, ed. D. and R. Cromarty (Shropshire Archaeological and Historical Society, 1993), pp. 28–32.
[32] *VCH Essex*, IX, p. 29; R.H. Britnell, *Growth and Decline in Colchester, 1300–1525* (Cambridge, 1986), p. 16; *The Medieval Essex Community*, ed. J.C. Ward (Essex Record Office: Essex Historical Documents, 1, 1983), pp. 16–17.

taxpayers at Grimsby between 1327 and 1332 – from forty-eight to seventy-nine – has plausibly been explained in terms of that town's response to the change of rate from a twentieth in 1327 to a tenth in the later levy, but other towns tackled the same problem in different ways, often drawing on the same number or even smaller numbers of tax-payers.[33] The townspeople were aware of these manipulations of the system, and complained – in early fourteenth-century Norwich and York the rulers (called 'the bailiffs and the rich' at Norwich) were accused of unfairness; at York they were said to have exempted themselves and made wage earners contribute.[34]

Given the instincts already apparent in the period before 1334, when the central government exercised some restrictions on the municipal authorities, it comes as no surprise that as restraints were removed the numbers of taxpayers rose and groups previously exempt were expected to pay. In the subsidy of 1332, 305 people contributed to Winchester's tax, compared with 463 in 1430, even though the city's population was falling; Dunwich experienced even steeper decline, yet 158 taxpayers could still be found in 1420, and 173 in 1429–30, compared with only 35 in 1327 – in the early fourteenth century only one in twelve households were included, but a century later a majority paid.[35] The 73 taxpayers of Leicester in 1332 had grown to 455 in 1336, 463 in 1348 and apparently 456 (though the list contains some alterations so the total is uncertain) in 1354, after the first plague.[36] Coventry, unlike these other towns, was growing in the late fourteenth and early fifteenth centuries, but probably not at a sufficient rate to explain the multiplication in taxpayers, from 200 in the 1327 subsidy to 578 for a loan to the crown in 1430, which seems to have been administered in the same fashion as a subsidy. A Coventry statement of 1451 about a levy to pay for fortifications pays lip service to the need to spare the poor, but defined that group sufficiently narrowly to expect labourers with a wage of 4d. per day to contribute 1d. or 2d.[37]

In fact when we analyse the Coventry list of 1430 we find that only two people paid less than 1s. 0d. and about a third contributed 1s. 0d. to 1s. 11d., much the same proportion as in 1327. Elsewhere, however,

---

[33] S.H. Rigby, *Medieval Grimsby: Growth and Decline* (Hull, 1993), pp. 24–5.

[34] McRee, 'Peacemaking and its Limits', p. 846; Hilton, *English and French Towns*, p. 137.

[35] D. Keene, *Survey of Medieval Winchester*, 2 vols. (Winchester Studies, 2, Oxford, 1985), I, pp. 403, 406; *The Bailiffs' Minute Book of Dunwich, 1404–30*, ed. M. Bailey (Suffolk Record Society, 14, 1992), pp. 102–4, 138–48.

[36] *Records of the Borough of Leicester*, ed. M. Bateson, 7 vols. (London, 1901), II, pp. 34–40, 74, 93–9; *Wealth of Shrewsbury*, ed. Cromarty and Cromarty, p. 28.

[37] *The Coventry Leet Book*, ed. M.D. Harris (Early English Text Society, 134, 135, 138, 146, London, 1907–13), pp. 66, 122–9, 258.

the whole tax system looks decidedly regressive with large numbers of very small payments – at Leicester and Dunwich (in 1336 and 1429–30 respectively) about a third of the payments were below 6d., while the rich do not seem to have paid their fair share.[38] At Winchester in 1332 eight people paid £1 or more, accounting for a third of the total of money, while in 1430 six payers of £1 or more produced only 13 per cent of the city's total and no less than 133 assessments were at 4d. or 2d.[39] The Coventry tax of 1327 appears very contrived, with exactly 200 payers, a very small proportion of the total of at least a thousand households.[40] But the merchants made a substantial contribution, with twenty-six wealthier people (14 per cent of the taxed total) paying 10s. or more, compared with thirty (5 per cent) in the same category in 1430, when Coventry was twice as populous, its economy was booming, and fortunes were being made in the cloth trade.

III

Taxation records for villages and small towns are very rare, and no systematic attempt has been made to find them and analyse them until now. Those that have been discovered are shown in Table 9.1, and after they have been analysed, their testimony can be checked and supplemented by occasional references to the levying of subsidies in other sources, such as manorial accounts, wills and legal disputes brought before seigniorial and royal courts.

The small sample of five tax lists cover a narrow date range concentrated at the end of our period. Their geographical spread extends from south Herefordshire to central Essex, and includes a large village with an urban core at Writtle, a failed borough at Newborough, which was founded with 101 burgages in 1263 but reverted to a rural economy by the time of the tax list, and mainly agrarian settlements at Walford, West Horndon and Emberton.[41] Horndon, Writtle, Newborough and Walford all belong to regions of dispersed settlement, and the Writtle list is

[38] The Dunwich tax in 1327: S.H.A.H.[ervey] (ed.), *Suffolk in 1327 being a Subsidy Return* (Suffolk Green Books, 9, Woodbridge, 1906), p. 221. In 1327 the wealthiest five paid 37 per cent of the total; in 1429–30 the leading four contributed 17 per cent.

[39] Keene, *Medieval Winchester*, pp. 402–7.

[40] 'Subsidy Roll for Warwickshire for 1327', ed. W.F. Carter and E.A. Fry, *Transactions of the Midland Record Society*, 6 (1902), pp. 7–8; on Coventry's population *The Early Records of Medieval Coventry*, ed. P.R. Coss (British Academy Records of Social and Economic History, new series, 11, London, 1986), p. 366; C. Phythian-Adams, *Desolation of a City: Coventry and the Urban Crisis of the Late Middle Ages* (Cambridge, 1979), pp. 33–5.

[41] K.C. Newton, *The Manor of Writtle* (London, 1970); D. Palliser, *The Staffordshire Landscape* (London, 1976), pp. 149, 151; *VCH Bucks.*, IV, pp. 338–43.

Table 9.1 *Local assessments for the lay subsidy*

Place	County	Date	Basis for assessment	No. of payments[a]	Total
Emberton	Buckinghamshire	1512–13	Land and goods	51	£3 2s. 0d.
Newborough & Hoar Cross	Staffordshire	1450	Land	83	£1 3s. 8d.
Walford & Howle	Herefordshire	1486–7	Land (some goods)	52	£2 5s. 0d.
West Horndon[b] & Childerditch	Essex	c. 1500	Land	18	£2 4s. 9d.
Writle[c]	Essex	c. 1500	Land (some goods)	226	£12 6s. 0½d.

[a] This means in most cases the number of taxpayers, but see text on Writle.

[b] There are two other similar lists for the vill, c.1512 and a later date, Essex RO, D/DP 08/2, 3.

[c] There is another, similar list, dated c. 1490, Essex RO, D/DP 07/2.

Sources: Emberton: *Early Taxation Returns*, ed. A. C. Chibnall (Buckinghamshire Record Society, XIV, 1967), pp. 108–9; Newborough: British Library, Stowe 880, fos. 4–5; Walford: Gloucestershire Record Office, D33/356; West Horndon: Essex Record Office, D/DP 08/1; Writle: Essex Record Office D/DP 07/1.

divided into ten sections corresponding to the hamlets of its parish. The complexities of the local settlement patterns is indicated by the fact that three of the lists cover more than one vill – Newborough was taxed with Hoar Cross, Walford with Howle, and West Horndon with Childerditch. Emberton was (and is) a more conventional nucleated midland village, but it was linked with its neighbour of Petsoe, which was deserted during the later Middle Ages.[42] We would expect the Herefordshire and Staffordshire places in particular to have had a more pastoral economy than the others, though even in the case of the open-field village of Emberton, a large pasture lay nearby on the site of Petsoe.

The quotas fixed in 1334 had been based on the then well-established tradition of taxing movable goods. All of our five vills had moved to using land for assessing payment. At West Horndon taxpayers/tenants are named, and the acreages are given, or the holding is identified: 'The gate hows with Strapylls' for example. At Walford there are occasional references to charges on holdings: 'The mille in the woode', but in most cases the tenant or taxpayer is named. At Writtle in *c.* 1500 the original list gives the names of 131 taxpayers, and the rest of the entries refer to holdings only – 'Of the tenement of Blaches', for example, or the holding is identified by reference to a *former* tenant. In later use of the list, however, names of taxpayers have been added in the margin, indicating that most of the holdings were in the hands of separate individuals. For the purposes of counting taxpayers, the document is clearly unsatisfactory – a number of tenements may have been engrossed into the hands of a single tenant, whereas others may have been shared by a group. Indeed at Emberton the latter practice is confirmed by reference to two holdings being held by a named individual 'and his coparceners'. The historian can only count tax contributions and hope that the multiple holdings and the sharing of holdings will cancel out one another.

The Emberton list makes an explicit division between thirty names who were assessed 'by land', and another thirty 'by goods', though nine names appear on both lists. However, the method by which goods were being assessed does not seem to have been continuing the traditions of the early fourteenth-century subsidies, as most of the taxpayers were charged with a few pence, and they look like token payments by relatively poor households. Goods are not mentioned in the other lists explicitly, but individuals are sometimes named without any reference to land, and the sums are as paltry as those found at Emberton. A likely group of assessments on goods at Writtle is found in the section of the list devoted to the small borough

---

[42] Beresford and Hurst (eds.), *Deserted Medieval Villages*, p. 184.

identified as the 'Forum de Writtell' in c. 1490 and 'Breg Stret' in c. 1500, which included eight small payments from people with no named holding.

If the tax was charged on tenements rather than individuals, as appears to have been partially the case in some of our villages, does that mean that the whole tax system had fossilised and was becoming more artificial? Such a development might be implied by the heading of the earliest of the West Horndon lists: 'The tax boke of Westhorndon with the hamlet of Chylderdych in the kyngys progenetors dayes', which appears to be a record of the 'traditional' allocation of payments, written in Henry VIII's reign but recording earlier arrangements. The list itself, however, does not suggest such extreme formalisation, as it contains many alterations – the manor's own contribution, for example, had been changed from 13s. 4d. to 10s. and then again to 6s. 8d. It appears that although in some cases the tax was being levied on tenements rather than individuals, payments had not atrophied into routine charges unrelated to the value of land or the circumstances of the tenant.

Though they were produced in such diverse villages and in varying ways, the tax lists tell a consistent story about the strategy for gathering money. The numbers of taxpayers were evidently large, greater than before 1334, which is all the more remarkable in view of the drop in population during the intervening period. Indeed, instead of a fraction of households being eligible for tax in the early fourteenth century – in the region of a third – our lists must account for a majority.[43] The extra numbers were made up by dipping into the ranks of society previously exempt, so we find many payments below 6d. (Table 9.2). At Newborough, twenty-five paid 1d., and at Emberton, there were four contributions of 1d. and fifteen of 2d. The types of people brought into the tax net are indicated by such entries as: 'Of Rauff Fenton for a cotage at Brigge End, 1d.' in the Newborough list, together with tenants of burgages, which after the failure of the borough were simply small landholdings containing about three acres. In a survey of Agardsley, the manor to which Newborough belonged, compiled in 1415, twenty-three of the forty-four named tenants held four acres or less, and many of their successors must have been among the taxpayers of 1450.[44] The Writtle lists of c. 1490 and c. 1500 include payments for many smallholdings, a garden for example, or a single croft. Tenements as small as three acres, four acres and six acres paid 1d., 2d. and 2d. respectively at West Horndon. Lists also include payments by subtenants, again of apparently minor parcels

---

[43] On the proportion of households contributing to subsidies, see Ormrod, 'Crown and the English Economy', p. 156.
[44] Public Record Office (hereafter PRO), DL 42/4; for the size of burgages, M. Bateson, 'The Laws of Breteuil', *English Historical Review*, 16 (1901), p. 334.

Table 9.2 *Analysis of local assessments*

Place	Date	over 5s. 0d.	Assessments (and percentages)			Total
			2s.–4s. 11d.	1s.–1s. 11d.	11d., or below	
Emberton	1512–13	4 (8%)	5 (10%)	7 (14%)	35 (69%)	51 (100%)
Newborough	1450	0	0	5 (6%)	78 (94%)	83 (100%)
Walford	1486–7	0	5 (10%)	10 (19%)	36 (69%)	52 (100%)[a]
West Horndon	c. 1500	4 (22%)	1 (6%)	2 (11%)	11 (61%)	18 (100%)
Writtle	c. 1500	12 (5%)	10 (4%)	38 (17%)	166 (74%)	226 (100%)

[a] One entry is illegible.
Source: see Table 9.1.

of land, like the 1d. contributed at Newborough 'Of Roger Drury tenant to Nicholas Agard'. As the Writtle taxpayers included the inhabitants of the small borough the list tells us about their occupations: weavers, a glover, dyer, fuller and thatcher, with other craftsmen living in the nearby hamlets, including a fuller, shoemaker, smith, butcher and glover. Some of these may have been quite prosperous, though such artisans would often not have paid tax before 1334, and certainly not those pursuing such unremunerative trades as thatching.

The inclusion of substantial numbers of 'new' taxpayers from among the smallholders, wage earners and poorer artisans is not, however, complemented by the comprehensive evasion of tax burdens by the wealthy. Newborough was a rather special case, with two very substantial landholders (their predecessors were credited with almost 400 acres and 100 acres respectively in the survey of 1415) who escaped with tax assessments of 16d. each. The highest payment in that vill was 19d., but apparent evasion in 1450 evidently continued a tradition, as the wealthiest taxpayer in 1327 contributed only 2s.[45] The whole vill paid so little tax that the four highest payers in 1450 were contributing almost a quarter of the quota. Unless the whole place was chronically poverty-stricken throughout the period, we must conclude that the leading taxpayers benefited from a generous underassessment made in the early fourteenth century that was perpetuated by the 1334 quotas. In the other cases where we can make comparisons, the better-off villagers seem to have been paying a higher proportion of the tax burden in the decades around 1500 than their predecessors had done in the early fourteenth century. At Writtle the twelve largest assessments accounted for 45 per cent of the total in c. 1500, compared with 25 per cent in 1327. The four wealthiest West Horndon people paid 74 per cent in c. 1500, compared with 61 per cent in 1327, and at Emberton whereas the four highest contributors provided about a third of the total (35 per cent) in 1332, their four equivalents in 1512–13 paid 48 per cent.[46]

Now we would be better able to put these figures in perspective if we could reconstruct the changes in the social structure and economy of the villages in the 120 to 180 years that separated the tax assessments. The places were certainly subject to the general tendencies of the period – the drop in population; the amalgamation of holdings; the leasing of demesnes; the decline in profits from arable cultivation, and conversion to pasture; the

[45] 'The Exchequer Subsidy Roll of A.D. 1327', ed G. Wrottesley (Staffordshire Historical Collections, VII, London, 1886), p. 231.
[46] Medieval Essex Community, ed. Ward, pp. 85–7, 95; Early Taxation Returns, ed. Chibnall, pp. 86–8.

scarcity of labour and rise in wages. Writtle's population fell by two-thirds;[47] the hamlet of Petsoe adjoining Emberton was abandoned and its site turned into a pasture; and the engrossing of previously separate holdings is well attested in the Newborough survey of 1415. But we do not have the detailed documentation, such as an exactly contemporary manorial survey, which would allow us to check on the realism of the tax assessments. There are indications that the West Horndon contributions reflected the hierarchy of wealth, because we are given acreages of holdings in some cases, and an advantage was evidently given to the poorer taxpayers, as they paid sums equivalent to ½d. per acre or less, whereas the larger holdings were charged between ½d. and 1d. per acre. We can also compare our tax lists with the new assessments based on land, goods and wages for the military survey and subsidies of 1522–5. The editor of the Emberton list has pointed out the close correlation between the 1512–13 payments and the land valuations made for the 1522 military survey, and it appears that the earlier tax was assessed at about 1s. in the pound, so that land worth £14 annually paid 13s. 4d. in tax, and a small tenement valued at 10s. per year was assessed at 6d.[48] Comparison between the upper band of taxpayers in our village lists and those compiled under the government's rules in 1524–5 produces varied results which are summarised in Table 9.3. These seem to confirm our suspicion that at Newborough there had been a gross underassessment both of the whole settlement and its leading inhabitants in the early fourteenth century, and in 1525 this was put right, and the two wealthier payers contributed 40s. and 20s. compared with 16d. each by their predecessors in 1450. There may have been a similar, though less extreme, story at Walford. In two other villages, however, in the local assessments the wealthier minority paid a higher proportion than in the new subsidy of the 1520s regulated by the central government.

How typical are our village tax lists? The emphasis on tenements and land as the basis for taxation gives a misleading impression, judging from Schofield's study of disputes over taxation in the period 1485–1547.[49] He found that eighteen villages and towns were using either traditional tenements, or fresh valuations of land, as in our lists, but there were more, twenty-five in all, where goods and chattels were valued, and three which used both land and goods in combination. In the north of England assessment by goods and chattels meant in practice that the tax was levied on

[47] Newton, *Writtle*, pp. 79–82; L.R. Poos, 'The Rural Population of Essex in the Later Middle Ages', *Economic History Review*, 2nd ser., 38 (1985), pp. 515–30.

[48] *Early Taxation Returns*, ed. Chibnall, pp. xvi–xvii.

[49] R.S. Schofield, 'Parliamentary Lay Taxation, 1485–1547' (Univ. of Cambridge PhD thesis, 1963), pp. 81–98.

Table 9.3 *Local assessments compared with the subsidies of 1524–5*

Village	Date of list	Total in money	Percentage paid by top four	Date of subsidy	Total in money	Percentage paid by top four
Emberton	1512–13	£3 2s. 0d.	48	1524	£2 10s. 2d.	39
Newborough	1450	£1 3s. 8d.	24	1525	£6 16s. 6d.	59
Walford	1486–7	£2 5s. 0d.	30	1524	£3 11s. 2d.	46
West Horndon	c. 1500	£2 4s. 9d.	74	1524	£1 0s. 2d.	67
Writtle	c. 1500	£12 6s. 0½d.	45[a]	1524	£33 15s. 10d.	60[r]

[a] In the case of Writtle, the twelve highest assessments have been used.
Sources: see Table 9.1; for the subsidies *Subsidy Roll for the County of Buckingham Anno 1524*, ed. A. C. Chibnall and A. Vere Woodman (Buckinghamshire Record Society, 8, 1950), p. 75; PRO, E.179 177/18, 117/98, 108/151.

animals.[50] This procedure was not confined to the north, as Schofield showed that at Godalming in Surrey in 1488 cattle were taxed at 1d. each, horses at 2d., pigs at ½d. and sheep at five for a penny. A midland example from the early fifteenth century is Quinton (Warws.) where the tax contribution of the manor was disputed when a new lord took over in 1430.[51] The tenants alleged that 'time out of mind' the manor had supplied 10s. 0d. to the village quota of £5 8s. 11d. The lord claimed that as he owned twenty-one beasts he owed to the tax only 7s. 0d., as 4d. per beast was the prevailing tax charge: 'according to the price of the avers of the whole vill'. The twenty-four tenants of 1430 could have mustered perhaps 150 cattle and horses,[52] and tax was presumably charged on sheep as well, but as the demesne had none, its liability was not mentioned. Such a system would have involved a tenant with two yardlands paying 4s. on a likely total of a dozen larger animals, with extra for a flock of fifty or so sheep, while a poor cottager with a cow would have contributed 4d.

Those vills which used animals as their main means of assessing taxes have left no detailed documents which can be compared with the surviving lists. This is presumably because animals could have been counted without written records, and if a list was made it would have been immediately redundant after the money had been collected. We can presume that such a tax assessment would have been not dissimilar from those based on land, with the largest active cultivators, such as the demesne farmers, responsible for a high proportion of the total, and the usual tail of smallholders paying a few pence.

The general tendency of the post-1334 tax system to include the poor is indicated by bequests in wills to help taxpayers. For example, in 1434, John Beneyt of Thornham Magna in Suffolk left money 'to be expended on the tax of the fifteenth of the poor of the vill', and the category of people needing help is stated explicitly in the will of John Barton of Holme near Newark in Nottinghamshire, who in 1490 required his executors to pay for all paupers of the village of North Muskham assessed at 4d. and below in the taxes granted in the two years after his death.[53]

---

[50] M.L. Bush, '"Up for the Commonweal": The Significance of Tax Grievances in the English Rebellion of 1536', *English Historical Review*, 106 (1991), pp. 299–300; Hoyle, 'Resistance and Manipulation', p. 159. Livestock had figured prominently, but not exclusively, in the valuations of movables before 1334.

[51] Magdalen College, Oxford, 35/9.

[52] *Ibid.*, 35/5, gives a list of animals and pasture rents in 1473 – the rural economy here may not have changed radically over the forty years.

[53] Suffolk Record Office (Bury St Edmunds Branch), IC500/2/9, fol. 1; *Testamenta Eboracensia*, ed. J. Raine, IV (Surtees Society, LIII, Durham, 1869), pp. 61–2.

IV

If we are to draw conclusions about the social attitudes that lay behind the assessments, we must consider the methods by which taxation was administered within the vill, and identify those with most influence on decision making. The surviving lists have come down to us through the archives of manorial lords – the two Essex lists, for example, form part of the papers of the Petre family of Ingatestone. The Emberton and Newborough documents were both copied into notebooks kept by local gentry. One of the West Horndon lists states that it shows the tax 'set . . . by Richard fitz Lewys knyght', the lord of the manor at the time. The lords' interest is obvious, as they usually paid the largest contribution, and would have had a major voice in the whole process. But as the Quinton dispute in 1430 shows, the lord and the villagers had separate interests, and the ultimate responsibility lay with the vill and not the manor, hence the failure of almost all tax lists to survive. Archive keeping was not normally associated with the self-government of the vill, which depended on oral deliberations and decisions preserved by memory. Whoever wrote the surviving lists – parish clergy seem the most likely – they had no model to follow, as the lists appear in different forms, on sheets of paper, in rolls and small books, and are arranged and worded according to no set formula. Their hurried and sometimes barely legible handwriting, and lack of dates, show that these were informal working notes, not intended for long-term reference, and certainly not for posterity.

The village or town seems to have organised its own tax affairs, involving the lord on occasions, though as the West Horndon case shows, the lord might play a dominant role. Schofield's work again reveals the administrative machinery of the vill, sometimes delegating the task to a few officials, or sometimes holding general meetings. The evidence given to the Star Chamber in 1541 concerning the administration of the tenth and fifteenth at the small Oxfordshire market town of Burford preserves the memory of earlier practices, as witnesses agreed that they were describing 'theyre olde and auncyent usage'.[54] This consisted of the bailiffs gathering as many as a hundred townspeople into the common hall, where a bill was written, containing the names of the taxpayers and their obligations. The rule was followed that the tax on houses should be assessed at the rate of a penny in every shilling of rent. The bill was then given to the two constables who were responsible for collecting the money. In villages the churchwardens

---

[54] *The Burford Records. A Study in Minor Town Government*, ed. R.H. Gretton (Oxford, 1920), pp. 661–5.

seem to have played an important role in organising taxation, perhaps with the same functions as the Burford bailiffs. This is indicated by a plea of debt in the manor court of Stoneleigh (Warws.) in 1434 when William Halley claimed that the two churchwardens had wrongly detained 7s. 6d. 'for the collection of a tenth and fifteenth'.[55] The administrative role of the church-wardens is strongly implied by a Suffolk will of 1434 which left money to pay for the fifteenth, but in a year when no tax was levied, the money should be spent on ornaments for the church.[56] The function of the constables as tax collectors is confirmed by payments of the manor's contributions to the constables of the vill, as happened for example at Loudham in Suffolk in 1416–17.[57]

Taxation, like the other administrative functions of the village, lay in the hands of the wealthier and more experienced inhabitants, a local and low-key version of the 'better and wiser part' beloved of medieval political theorists. The decisions would be made by the same people, mostly peasants with medium to large holdings of land, who deliberated in the courts as chief pledges, jurors and affeerers, who administered the manor as reeves, bailiffs and haywards, and who managed the affairs of the parish church as church-wardens. As in these other tasks they would make self-interested judgements, but would need to take into account wider public opinion, as a too blatant bias towards the larger landholders might lead to troublesome frictions and non-cooperation, as occurred at Burford and in the other recorded disputes.

Tax collection happened only when parliament granted a 'tenth and fif-teenth', frequently during the active phases of the Hundred Years War, but irregularly at other times. But the vill had financial responsibilities continuously, and references in wills linking the payment of taxes to poor relief and church expenses hint at a common fund or at least interconnected funds. This supposition is strengthened by the tendency for the sums col-lected in our local lists to exceed the amount owed to the exchequer. Emberton, for example, after the abatements of 1433 and 1446, was expected to fulfil a quota of £2 15s. 4d., yet in 1512–13 the local assessors expected to raise £3 2s. 0d. Perhaps this was a protection against shortfalls from non-payment, but it is possible that the surplus was deliberately designed for charitable work or other village uses.[58]

---

55 Shakespeare Birthplace Trust Record Office, Stratford-upon-Avon, DR 18/3.
56 Suffolk Record Office (Bury St Edmunds Branch), IC500/2/9, fol. 1.
57 Suffolk Record Office (Ipswich Branch), HD 1538/295/8.
58 On the 'common box' see Dyer, 'Medieval Village Community', pp. 415–16; on Emberton, *Early Taxation Returns*, ed. Chibnall, p. 101.

V

The changes in the tax system in the fourteenth and fifteenth centuries presumably resulted from a combination of economic developments, affecting the capacity of people to pay, and shifts in attitude by the village and town elites who were in charge of the assessments. We seem to be observing a difference in approach between villages and towns, with the latter in the vanguard of the extension of taxation to as many wage earners and cottagers as possible, while the rural elites in some places continued to pay a large share. Perhaps the more open public life of villages made blatant evasion more difficult to conceal, and the social climate must have been influenced by regular face to face contact between rich and poor.

The general tendency to make many of the less affluent pay taxes deserves an explanation. This could be taken as a reflection of economic reality. Whereas the cottagers and wage earners of the early fourteenth century were really poor, judging from all calculations of real wages, their successors in the late fourteenth and fifteenth centuries were well able to afford a few pence in tax – a contribution of 8d. to the 1332 subsidy was near to an unskilled worker's wages for a week, while a labourer in *c.* 1500 could have earned that sum in two days.[59] One might see in the requirement that the poorer sections of society should pay taxes a reflection of that resentment against high-earning and idle labourers expressed with such strength of feeling in the legislation and literature of the late fourteenth century, which led to village and urban elites, for example, into participating in the enforcement of the Statute of Labourers.[60] The poll tax was partly inspired by the idea that the supposedly new rich wage earners should no longer escape their obligations. While that view may have come from the upper classes in parliament and government, rather than the better-off peasants in the villages, we have seen that villagers showed little enthusiasm for sharing the burden of the third poll tax. However, the move to include more urban wage earners in the subsidy is well documented before 1348–9, and even before 1334, and so the tendency cannot be associated entirely with the scarce labour and high wages of the post-Black Death period.[61]

The village and town notables evidently thought that all members of a community should make some contribution, however small. The sums of 1d. and 2d. were mere tokens; even when added together to make 2s. or 3s.

---

[59] D.L. Farmer, 'Prices and Wages', in *AHEW*, II, pp. 760–80; D.L. Farmer, 'Prices and Wages, 1350–1500, in: *AHEW*, III, pp. 467–94.

[60] L.R. Poos, 'The Social Context of Statute of Labourers Enforcement', *Law and History Review*, 1 (1983), pp. 27–52.

[61] See p. 175 above.

they did little to shift the burden from the major taxpayers. The same principle, that everyone should give something, can be seen in the finances of the church. At Blunham in Bedfordshire, for example, a large parish containing about a hundred households, tithes were collected from 136 men and 48 women in 1520, and while the miller paid 10s. 10½d. and the better-off cultivators 5s. or 6s., we find 30 individuals, who apparently lacked even a garden or poultry, contributing personal tithes of 1d. or 2d. each.[62] The oblations given to the church on major feast days fall into the same category, in which everyone was expected to put a coin on the plate. In the manorial accounts of the thirteenth and fourteenth centuries the lords of manors can often be found providing their farm servants with money for this purpose.[63]

While we can presume that these modest payments caused no great hardship for wage earners after 1349, can the same be said for those burdened with more substantial sums? Taxpayers grumbled about subsidies when they came in continuous succession in the 1370s and 1440s, but were stirred to revolt only by experimental new taxes in 1381, 1489, 1497 and 1525.[64] The 10s. or so paid by the higher rank of taxpayers would have been an irritation, but perhaps the middling groups were the most adversely affected: those with ten or twenty acres of land, would have felt the squeeze of reduced prices of grain after 1375, and would sometimes have had to pay increased wages. Their contribution of 18d. or 2s. may have been hard for them to find in bad years.

VI

The following generalisations can be made about late medieval communities. Management of their own tax affairs was an important function of self-government and helped to make the payments more acceptable. In larger towns the burden was shifted from the wealthy to the less affluent, causing friction, and making us doubt the social unity that the town governments proclaimed. In the countryside, the story is more complicated. The small-holders were expected to make at least a token contribution everywhere. In

---

[62] *Hundreds, Manors, Parishes and the Church. A Selection of Early Documents for Bedfordshire*, ed. J.J. Thompson (Publications of the Bedfordshire Historical Record Society, LXIX, 1990), pp. 124–44; *VCH Beds.*, III, p. 233.

[63] E.g. Bodleian Library, Oxford, Suffolk roll no. 21, account of Mildenhall in 1323–4, in which 3s. 6d. was spent on the oblations of the *famuli* at Christmas, Easter and the Assumption.

[64] M. Bush, 'Tax Reform and Rebellion in Early Tudor England', *History*, 76 (1991), pp. 379–400; Hoyle, 'Resistance and Manipulation'; G.W. Bernard, *War, Taxation and Rebellion in Early Tudor England. Henry VIII, Wolsey and the Amicable Grant of 1525* (Brighton, 1986).

some places the leading villagers paid a significant proportion of the quota though there were also examples of avoidance. We have seen that taxation was linked with other aspects of the community's activities, including the distribution of charity, and we must suppose that the tax payments were connected with a web of neighbourly co-operation, and a belief that the better off should help the poor. But these relationships and attitudes could also involve patronage, deference, pressure on the poor from the wealthy and other features of a stratified society.

10

Peasants and the collapse of the manorial economy on some Ramsey Abbey estates

AMBROSE RAFTIS

F OR ECONOMIC historians the end to the age of serfdom has usually been associated with the collapse of the direct exploitation of the demense around 1400 along with the fleeing and eventual disappearance of serfs and serfdom. However, recent scholarship has found it increasingly difficult to obtain a clear picture of the rationale behind the lord's decisions at this time.[1] Could it be that peasant tenant decisions were more operative in these changes than we have hitherto acknowledged? Certainly, major advances in the study of tenants over the hundred years after the Black Death now point in this direction.[2] This essay attempts to add focus to such research.

In a forthcoming study entitled *Peasant Economic Development within the English Manorial System*, it has been possible to trace the economic role of main customary tenants on some estates of Ramsey Abbey over the greater part of the fourteenth century. This study will carry the investigation one step farther and present the decision-making structure involving main customary tenants during the collapse of some Ramsey manorial economies around 1400.

The general features of the methodology employed for this study will not be surprising in so far as the investigation will reveal further examples of interplay between uniformities and the breakdown of uniformities. The major tradition of manorial studies that began some hundred years ago was especially attracted by manorial customaries from the thirteenth century where, as today with accounting practices, uniformity was the primary organisational principle. Tenurial obligations were neatly summarised according to the size of the tenurial unit and all other tenants holding units of the

---

[1] See, for example, J.M.W. Bean, 'Landlords', in *AHEW*, III, pp. 526–86.
[2] J.A. Tuck, E. Miller, R.H. Britnell, E. King, C.C. Dyer, D.H. Owen, P.D.A. Harvey, M. Mate and H.S.A. Fox, 'Tenant Farming and Tenant Farmers', in *AHEW*, III, pp. 587–743.

same size. Virgaters, for example, owed the same obligations as the tenant at the head of the list; subdivisions of the virgate, such as semi-virgates and cotlands, were presented in the same fashion. The whole thrust of manorial economics over the past hundred years, following analyses that began with the customaries of Ramsey Abbey,[3] was projected from this pattern of uniformity of tenure and customary obligation.

Another tradition of scholarship that has grown over the past generation can be usefully depicted as an attack on uniformities in every aspect of the manorial economic tradition. A summary of this scholarship could in fact well begin as long ago as R.H. Hilton's shift of emphasis away from fields to crop courses and furlongs[4] and could bring us up to the emphasis upon local decision making by Mavis Mate and M.P. Hogan.[5] The following essay represents a further addition to the scores of studies that now may be included in this more recent tradition of scholarship.

I

In order to establish the context for the transformation that would occur *c*. 1400 the ongoing organisation must first be clearly depicted. This is in fact made readily possible by the survival of detailed tenurial lists for Ramsey manors during the last quarter of the fourteenth century. Such records reveal that the number of work service tenures remained fairly stable over the relatively prosperous years of the 1370s and 1380s. Tenurial arrangements varied even among the contiguous manors that are cited as examples here. But comparisons of work service holdings after a twenty-year span indicate the relative stability:

Work service tenement units

Abbots Ripton   1375/6:   21 virgates, 10 half-virgates, 1 three-quarter-virgate, 1 quarter-virgate

                  1394/5:   20 virgates, 7 half-virgates, 1 quarter-virgate, 2 cotlands

Upwood   1371/2:   11 virgates, 7 half-virgates, 1 quarter-virgate, 13 cotlands

---

[3] 'The classical picture of the manorial order . . . was to no small extent created on the basis of the material from the Ramsey cartulary.' E.A. Kosminsky, *Studies in the Agrarian History of England in the Thirteenth Century*, ed. R.H. Hilton, trans. Ruth Kisch (New York, 1956), p. 118.

[4] R.H. Hilton, 'Medieval Agrarian History', in *VCH Leics.*, II, esp. pp. 155ff.

[5] Mavis Mate, 'Agrarian Economy after the Black Death: The Manors of Canterbury Cathedral Priory: 1348–1391', *Econ. Hist. Rev.*, 2nd ser., 38 (1984), pp. 341–54; M.P. Hogan, 'Clays, *Culturae* and the Cultivator's Wisdom: Management Efficiency at Fourteenth-Century Wistow', *Agric. Hist. Rev.*, 36 (1988), pp. 117–32.

Wistow	1392/3:	1 one-and-a-half-virgates, 9 virgates, 11 half-virgates, 1 quarter-virgate, 5 cotlands
	1368/9:	8 virgates, 11 half-virgates, 4 three-quarter virgates, 3 quarter-virgates, 1 eighth-virgate, 1 cotland, 2 half-cotlands, 4 hidemanlands
	1388/9:	6 virgates, 17 half-virgates, 4 three-quarter-virgates, 3 quarter-virgates, 1 cotland, 3 hidemanlands

Something of the same stability can be seen from the total numbers of work services owed for each of these years:

Number of works owed

Abbots Ripton	1375/6: 5,030	1394/5: 4,137
Upwood	1371/2: 3,270	1392/3: 3,000
Wistow	1368/9: 3,626	1388/9: 3,463

Apparently, then, even after the demographic cataclysm of the Black Death and its sequels, the administration of these estates had preserved a facade of uniformity. But this facade fades rapidly when one peers behind it to the actual scene 'on the ground'. Here one becomes aware that the first priority of the lord was to keep land occupied and various compromises would be effected to this purpose. There was adequate peasant demand for Ramsey land at this time to guarantee the occupancy of the land but the terms of this occupancy were clearly not all dictated by the lord. During the good harvest years of the 1380s a higher percentage of owed *opera* was employed rather than being sold, but there is no evidence for an increase of lands held for services. Rather, the lord intensified sowing on the same acreage.[6] The long-term trend was actually towards wealthier customary tenants extending control over more customary lands, whether these were or were not paying work services. This did not mean that the peasant tenant found land owing work or office services more attractive than land for which services could be commuted in the short term (*ad censum*) or the long term (*ad arrentatum*). Rather, it was a parcel arrangement whereby the peasant extracted concessions from the lord's administrators before he took land for work services or for offices.

The Abbots Ripton arrangement for the year 1375/6 may be taken as a simplified example. The six official duties, as the text describes them, of beadle and ploughmen each received one half-virgate free from obligations and another half-virgate with work services commuted for that year. That is

[6] J.A. Raftis, *The Estates of Ramsey Abbey: A Study in Economic Growth and Organization* (Toronto, 1957), p. 261.

to say, none of these six held land for services (*ad opera*). Earlier in the century such official duties were rewarded only by the commutation of services for one half-virgate. Eight of the wealthier tenants who took one virgate each for services were conceded a further half-virgate for a yearly commutation to cash payment. The wealthiest tenants were able to gain special deals. Philip Ladde held one half-virgate as ploughman, one half-virgate for yearly commutation and one virgate for long-term commutation. A wealthy newcomer, William Jurdon, held one half-virgate by a yearly commutation and two and a quarter virgates by long-term commutation.

Again, it is useful to note how simple calculations of numbers without reference to names leaves a false impression of continuity. Listed below are the total numbers of tenants (A), along with the total number of same tenant family names (B) and the number of individuals with a service bearing tenement (C). These listings indicate that service bearing units are spread throughout most of the families. The number of such tenants is also remarkably stable for the two comparable dates.

		A	B	C		A	B	C
Abbots Ripton	1375/6:	44	35	35	1394/5:	40	32	31
Upwood	1371/2:	35	31	23	1392/3:	34	33	26
Wistow	1368/9:	47	38	32	1388/9:	45	35	32

The actual tenurial arrangements that have been illustrated above for Abbots Ripton can serve to make us aware of the many ways by which customary tenants could vary in their wealth and therefore in their capacity to exploit opportunities offered by the manor. Attention is also drawn to the fact that uniform listing of holdings fails to report directly on the 'bundle of resources' in wood, meadow and pasture available to that tenement, on the number of buildings on the messuage, the capital value of the holding in its current condition, the size of the family labour resources and so forth. Listing only the one tenant accountable for the unit of property greatly facilitated the accounting procedure.

The fact that tenants held properties in various combinations of service and money rents is also suggestive of a bargaining process between administrators and individuals. Nevertheless, rent listings are only the tip of the iceberg. Even for holdings by service, there could be various concessions by seasonal sale of work, as has been noted elsewhere[7] from earlier in the fourteenth century. Given that the sale price of works had remained the same from the thirteenth century, such sales could be benign arrangements. Lands that were let for yearly or long-term commutation would vary in value

---

[7] J.A. Raftis, *Peasant Economic Development* (forthcoming), ch. 3.

because of the state of the capital on the property. This was observable from the thirteenth century in the range of entry fines for units of the same size. No doubt this was the reason why larger tenants were not attracted to undervalued smallholdings as the century moved on. In any case, variations in rents by the late fourteenth century indicate a growing range of individual bargaining. At Upwood over 1385/6, for example, we have the following yearly and long-term rents:

Unit	*Rents recorded (number of units in brackets)*
virgate	24s. (1), 18s. (1), 13s. 4d. ($3\frac{1}{2}$)
half-virgate	12s. (1), 10s. (4), 6s. 8d. (2), 6s. (1)
quarter-virgate	3s. 4d. (3), 2s. (3)
cotland (2 acres)	7s. (1), 6s. 8d. (1), 6s. (1), 4s. (1), 3s. (1)
cotland (1 acre)	3s. (4), 2s. (1)

Over the fourteenth century demesne lands were leased to customary tenants in increasing amounts. By and large these leases were for fields of considerable sizes and for stable and uniform rents per acre. The units of 17 acres 3 rods, 15 acres, 12 acres, 11 acres, 10 acres and 7 acres leased in each instance to one named customary tenant and 'his associates' at Upwood over 1385/6 represent this tradition. But by this same year demesne lease prices had begun to vary considerably, especially for the smaller units. For leases from the demesne of the same manor we find the following variations. Again, we find evidence that the substantial tenants avoided such apparently undercapitalized lands. It was the smallholders Thomas Walton, John Skinner jr and Nicholas Alston who held respectively 6 acres at 6d., 4 acres at 4d. and 9 acres at 3d. in the following list:

at

    13d.:2 a $3\frac{1}{4}$ r, 1 a 3 r, 1 a
    12d.:17 a 3 r, 11 a 3 r, 11 a, 4 a 3 r, 4 a 1 r, 4 a, 2 a $3\frac{1}{4}$r
    $11\frac{1}{4}$d.:10 a
    10d.:15 a, $3\frac{1}{4}$ a 1 r
    9d.:12 a 1 r, 3 a 1 r, 3 a, $2\frac{1}{4}$ a, 2 a
    8d.:8 a, 7 a, 4 a, 6 a, 5 a, 2 a
    6d.:6 a, 3 a, $\frac{1}{2}$ a
    5d.:2 a
    4d.:4 a
    3d.:9 a

Half a dozen very small units were leased in complicated combinations of rent per acre.

Over the 1390s there began a long-term agricultural depression on the estates
of Ramsey Abbey that would ultimately bring more changes than the great
famine of the second decade of the century and the plague together with its
sequels from the mid-century. The progress of the depression can be easily
traced through manorial indebtedness. Debts could be recorded at any time
on account rolls through an inability to collect rents owing to problems of
individual tenants and more generally from a poor harvest or depressed
prices or quite simply from the ineptitude of the reeve and other officials.
Traditionally, such debts would be wiped out in a year or two. But from
the 1390s debts became a regular feature at the foot of account rolls.

The lord at first attempted to counter indebtedness by adjustments within
the complex administrative system. The decline in the demand for land
brought about more concessions in the form of increasing money rents,
whether on a yearly or more permanent basis. However, such an orderly
response failed to respond to a new phenomenon, that is the vacating of
lands in a disorderly fashion at the convenience of the tenant. This brought
about a new entry in the expense side of the account under the title 'deficit
in rents'. This entry was thought to be able to record losses too from properties let during the year. Obviously, the lord's chief administrators expected
that the regular manorial officials, that is the reeve and beadle, ought to be
able to control the situation. However, the result was an accumulation of
debts year after year under the names of former officials.

The gradual shift of responsibility to the bailiff who was often a freeman
from outside the village brought no noticeable improvement on the account
rolls. At Upwood over 1408/9, for example, the bailiff excused four individuals holding the lowest valued rental pieces of demesne 'because they
had nothing in goods'. The sum of 16s. 8d. owed by William Herying for
rental of a piece of demesne was also 'allowed', that is cancelled, since
William was no longer able to work the land. The Herying family were
numerous and well endowed with land. The example of the ailing William
shows that little or no effort was made to force other members of a family
to assume debts of relatives. When former officials continued to be pursued
for debts, as in the case of Stephen Pikeler, his son Richard simply left the
village. It is not possible to deduce that officials 'went down' with the manor.
The economic conditions of the time were the more generic causes of success
or failure. At Upwood again, for example, some debt-burdened officials such
as Alcok and Pykeler declined and disappeared, others such as Alston, Payn
and Newman acquired more land after 1400.

On the whole, the bailiffs could not bring matters under control. Most striking was the fact that substantial as well as poorer tenants abandoned tenements with impunity during any time of the year rather than at Michaelmas and often left ruinous buildings. Long-standing debts of beadles and reeves usually had to be cancelled since there was no tenant from whom the debt might be collected. The lament of the bailiff at Upwood over 1412/ 13 spelled this out: '8s 7d 1½ob are allowed from the old debt of Nicholas Alston since tenants who owed this debt are dead or have fled and left nothing that might be distrained.' Only very few are actually listed on account and court rolls as having fled from Ramsey manors over the 1390s and the following two decades. The apparent reason for this was the fact that those leaving were not major tenants and, as in the quote just given, were not even named. Such had indeed been the practice over the previous century.

More focus can be given to the piecemeal information to be found in account rolls from the extraordinary record entitled 'Book of Entry Fines'[8] of Ramsey Abbey. This volume records entries between 1398 and 1458, devoting nearly 3,900 of the 4,371 entries to land transfers. From these entries we can see tenements being unloaded whenever possible and to whoever was available. Over 3,600 of the property leases were life-leases. This active land market had virtually detached properties from the demesne economy. That is to say, in reading these many texts one cannot fail to realise that tenements owing customary service, even with the shrunken services owed by this time, are just another form of tenure on a market largely devoted to money rents. Despite continuation of the ancient form 'in bondagium', or more usually 'customary obligations' all properties moved about in the same fashion. To all intents and purposes customary land was separated from serfdom. This meant too that land was separated from traditional association with specific customary families. Indeed the consequent need to be able to trace properties rather than families was very likely the raison d'être for this collection. Rarely can one find the traditional conveyance formula 'given into the hands of the lord for the use of . . .' (*surrexit . . .*). And there is no mention at all of conveyance from father to son. Perhaps it was not thought necessary to have such conveyances in the *Liber* and they were left for the oral record. In any case, tenants from families long associated with the manor gave up lands without evidence of any particular attachment to them. The lord's priority was quite clear. As had been the case over the previous century, but only to be found when a family had

[8] E.B. DeWindt, *The Liber Gersumarum of Ramsey Abbey: A Calendar and Index of B.L. Harley MS. 445* (Toronto, 1976). The totals given in the following sentences are taken from the introduction to this study.

died out and a tenant had to be found from beyond the manor, occupancy and maintenance of capitalised tenements was the ultimate priority.

From the very beginning of this series of entries in the *Liber* many properties already had buildings in ruin. The former tenant who had failed to maintain such buildings was named but not penalised. The administration was simply happy to cancel the entry fine for a new tenant who would rebuild and maintain the property. Many of these former tenants can be identified as serfs but were not penalised for the ruinous state of their buildings. Attention is rather given to the market and to outsiders who had a demand for land that was apparently indifferent to bondaged land of even the aura of serfdom. For example, on the 22nd and 23rd of October 1399, Peter Wakyr surrendered a quarter-virgate once held by Walter Gernoun to John Chartres of St Ives and William Hacoun surrendered lands in Upwood to Nicholas Hendeson of Hemingford Grey. Very common also was marriage by a freeman to a daughter of a naif and then entry to her father's property. For example, at Wistow on 29 May 1401, Margaret daughter of John Love, naif, paid a fine to marry a freeman, Robert Ely, and on the same day Robert entered a messuage and virgate of 'servile' land held by John Love. During July of the same year, at the same village Margaret, daughter of Nicholas Martyn, naif, paid for a licence to marry a freeman, Richard son of John Baroun. John Baroun then surrendered a plot with a building together with one half-virgate of servile land to Richard and Margaret.

Undoubtedly the impersonal nature of this land market would serve to obscure the identity of villagers who were serfs. It may be significant that the scribe(s) who composed the *Liber* made an index of naifs noted in the text but all of these were from entries related to marriage. No references were ever made to either free or unfree status in the actual conveyance entries. Basic distinguishing features of the past no longer obtained. For example, we do know from account rolls that Peter Bray was a new name to Upwood and therefore presumably a freeman from outside Ramsey manors. So we are not surprised when a conveyance entry (1407/8) excuses Peter Bray from being called for official duties. But we also know that the Margarete family were old Warboys' naifs of the lord. And yet when John Margarete received two half-virgates in February of 1411 there was a long paragraph about sowing arrangements and repairs for this life-lease concluding with the sentence: 'Nor will he serve in an office of the lord against his will, but he will aid in stocking the demesne with sheep at the expense of the customaries and of the seneschal, whenever it pleases the latter.'

The *ad hoc* tenurial arrangements of an ever-opening land market hastened the dissolution of 'manorial families'. For the manorial economy on Ramsey estates was closely tied into a family economy. In the detailed thirteenth-century customaries the tenant was obviously expected to be married. Relaxation of work was allowed to wives at the time of childbirth, for example. Widows were expected to marry or to make sustenance arrangements with the family heir. Rarely were widows ordered to marry; but the 'entrance' of a tenant to a widow and her property was a common occurrence. Furthermore, tenants of smaller holdings usually implied families since the continuity of such smallhold families is well documented.[9] The reasons for family tenure are not far to seek. In this pre-modern society where variations in family size occasioned wide variations in family survival patterns, family tenure gave a greater guarantee of land occupation. Even if there was not adequate replacement of a family, the availability of husband, wife and one son or daughter ensured a workforce for the tenement and the demesne.

Family tenure would hold a basic attraction for the peasant as well. Tenants would appreciate heredity tenure and a structure that would allow all those family customs and resource arrangements that are now being studied in that active 'new' branch of historiography. One can perhaps recall how tenure by the manorial family remained as the facade behind which many variations could actually be made in forms of tenurial arrangements. And for their part, peasants were for long content to remain manorial families as long as they were able to enjoy the flexibility given by differing tenurial service and money rent arrangements.

While some families went out of existence, as indicated by the disappearance of their family name from the manor, on occasion others produced exceptional numbers of offspring and if they had the material resources could launch more than one branch of the family as tenants. Two main branches of a family with the same name were not uncommon in the early fourteenth century as study of the manor of Broughton has established.[10] Abbots Ripton showed the same phenomenon for the later fourteenth century. At this manor the following family names are to be found with two branches, and two families had even generated a further two branches, over the 1370s and 1380s: Attechurche, Bette, Jurdon, Martyn (4), Prikke, Shepherd, Smith and West (4). These branches must be distinguished from the rather larger number of family names having two branches for only a decade or less in our extant records. In the latter instances a family succession of father to son may be presumed and is indeed usually traceable through the property growth of the younger member as the other name disappears from the rolls.

[9] E.B. DeWindt, *Land and People in Holywell-cum-Needingworth* (Toronto, 1972), pp. 194–202.
[10] E. Britton, *The Community of the Vill: A Study in the History of the Family and Village Life in Fourteenth-Century England* (Toronto, 1977).

The gradual dissolution of the manorial family, or one-tenant tenure, may be seen through changes in tenurial arrangements occurring at both ends of the family structure. Branch families became more numerous and within families younger members began to appear as tenants of small units of land. Understandably, the complex mixture of demographic and economic resource factors makes these changes difficult to trace. But isolation of various groups does suggest an overall pattern. Upwood typified the most common pattern. At this manor we find, first, traditional tenurial arrangements well into the fifteenth century, that is, the demand for service lands and families with such demand not having any same surname members renting small pieces of demesne. Such were the Bigge, Galopyn, Hurre, Loveday and Wodecok families. Secondly, some families still holding in the traditional fashion began to establish several branches. The Baker, Gouler and Hering families fell into this category at Upwood. The Miles family established three substantial branches. Thirdly, a further group of families showed an increase in the number of members holding smaller units of demesne rather than in becoming major tenants. This can be seen from the following list:

Surname	Major tenant	Smaller tenant
Albyn	1	1
Aleyn	0	3
Andrew	1	2
Attewelle	1	1
Aubes	0	2
Bracer	0	2
Fraunceys	0	3
Hikkeson	1	1
Newman	1	3
Peny	1	2
Skinner	0	3
Smith	0	2
Vernoun	0	2

Wistow may be taken to represent a different pattern. As may be seen in the list below, at Wistow could be seen some multi-branch holdings with three branches in some instances and in the case of Rede as many as four. Furthermore, seven of these multi-branches had larger holdings for service, and in four of these cases tenants with the same family name held acres from the demesne. It may be recalled that none of the Upwood and Wistow families in these lists had any member with the same surname listed as holding a few pieces from the demesne prior to the 1390s. Also, Wistow still had a few families (Asplond, Attegate, Hunne, Shepherd) in the first group listed above for Upwood. The '(0)' in the following Wistow list indicates that the tenant still held a large service-bearing property. Perhaps because it was of easy access to the abbey, Wistow did in fact continue production on the demesne for a longer period than other Ramsey manors.

Surname	Major tenant	Smaller tenant
Aylmar (0)	1	1
Baroun	1	1
Blakewell	0	2
Fraunceys (0)	2	1
Hiche (0)	2	2
Notting	0	1
Outy (0)	2	2
Randolf (0)	3	0
Rede (0)	4	1
Waryn (0)	3	0
Willisson (0)	2	0
Wodekoc	1	1
Wrighte	2	0

There are many questions that our extant information does not allow us to answer. We do not know whether some families failed to have members take up small pieces of demesne simply because there were not children to do so. If there were younger members of the family, there would not always be pieces of demesne, especially from the time that the remaining demesne began to be farmed.[11] But when information is available there is an obvious tendency for more family members to become involved in the opening land market. Or, to put the point in another way, even when the family still retained service bearing holdings there was no noticeable effort to engage all members of the family in these obligations as had been the intent of the traditional manorial family tenure. Economic conditions favoured more individual peasant action.

The movement of *nativi* from their home manor provides information that complements in many respects the manorial evolution that we have been discussing above. That is to say, there is confirmation of the demographic factors assumed above, namely the large number of children in some families and the failure of replacement in others. The lord's personal interest in each and every serf provides us with this familial information.

[11] It may also be noted that there are fewer extant manorial records for Ramsey estates in the fifteenth century and where records do survive they provide less and less 'uniform' information of the traditional sort.

The provision of such personal information was new to Ramsey records. It had been the responsibility of village officials to account for the presence or absence of villagers, to keep people in tithing in the relative legal formula. From the late thirteenth century this responsibility had been left to the local jury in return for payment of a composition called *chevagium*, a fixed sum that remained the same from year to year and generation to generation in the court and account rolls.[12] In consequence, it had been rare over the previous hundred years and more for the court rolls to note anyone having left the manor without permission. The economic organisation of the manor centred about the maintenance of fully implemented customary tenure signified the day-by-day relevance of serfdom. All sorts of individuals and their families could leave, and outsiders could enter to take up customary lands, as long as the 'system' remained in place.

As has been seen, the more wealthy tenants held most of the lands owing work services as part of their larger tenurial portfolio. Such tenants would not flee the manor in order to escape service. Many, indeed, were free. Contrary to traditional interpretations, the famous 'fleeing of serfs' was not an escape from the lord's work service but first and foremost a function of the land market and secondly, the attraction of the regional economy. While numerous outsiders found Ramsey lands an attractive investment, many villeins found the manorial land market non-viable so they sought opportunities elsewhere. It was not a question of forcing the villein to return to take up lands because most often they did not have the resources to do so.

But if the villein was separated from land, he was not separated from his status and the lord sought to profit from this. There is no evidence to suggest that the lords of Ramsey had changed their legal notion of serfdom over previous centuries. Whereas earlier he may have been more often identified as villein (*villanus*), around 1400 he would be identified as a naif (*nativus*). No doubt this identification was becoming more difficult when traditional villeinage tenure could not be employed as a simple indicator of serfdom. As has been noted above, the fact that the *Liber* went to the trouble of indexing all naifs who were so identified at the time of marriages may be indicative of this problem. In any case, the lord sought to be informed of the movements of his naifs abroad so that he could acquire revenues by licensing them to be away from their home manors.

The listing of naifs who were abroad with or without licence began in court rolls around the very time of the troubled failure of the manorial economy from the late 1390s. Most often a single individual left the manor

---

[12] Raftis, *Peasant Economic Development*, ch. 3.

in the first instance, and the accumulation of names of those beyond the manor usually came from listing the children of the former resident naif. It is impossible to know whether those leaving the manor already had children since such family detail is rarely given in the first entries. But a common pattern may be discerned. Most often those leaving were not among the wealthier tenants, but held less than a virgate. And many of these ultimately had families of a size that could not easily accommodate to smaller holdings. On the other hand, many of these families had considerable competence from experience as manorial officials and they were attracted to the active market centres of the region. Of course, sons from wealthier families would sometimes follow this pattern also. The following are a few typical examples.

Wistow provides us with a good body of information. Excluding six singular surnames, there were sixty-one individuals listed as being abroad between 1400 and the early 1450s. The number of family members according to surname was as follows:

Asplond – 8
Attegate – 5
Baron – 2
Bronnote – 2
Catelyn – 3
Fraunceys – 4
Gouler – 3
Hyche – 7
Love – 2
Outy – 17
Rede – 4
Waryn – 4

For the most part, family relationships are clearly noted. For example, Thomas Asplond (alias ploughwright), who went first to Warboys in 1400 and to Sutton in 1410, had four sons (Peter, John, Reginald, William). All of these sons were still in Sutton (Cambs.) by the 1440s. Thomas' father John can be traced giving up a quarter-virgate c. 1400 that he had held earlier along with a half-virgate. The Outys represented the more wealthy families of the manor. A John Outy held two and a half virgates around 1415 and two and three-quarter virgates by the 1420s. Very likely this John was the father of a Robert Outy who left for Houghton in 1421 to become the farmer there. A Thomas Outy whose father is not clearly identified had left after 1411 and eventually appears at Hartford by 1411. Thomas was reported to have sons Robert, William and grandson William with him at Hartford while another son John was in Huntingdon. Clearly the lord retained a personal interest in these emigrants because they were not indigent and hence had a resource potential for licensing.

For the year 1446/7 the account roll entered 11s. 2d. as having been received from licences although the list given actually comes to 10s. 2d.:

John Bronnote at Upwood	12d.
Thomas Asplond with sons John and Peter at Sutton	12d.
Stephen Waryn	24d.
John son of Thomas Outy in Huntingdon	6d.
John Outy with almoner at Bury	8d.
Thomas Attegate, apprenticed as carpenter	8d.
John Hiche at Toft	12d.
John Attegate at Ramsey	40d.

Ten years later licence payments were noted from only the Asplond, Attegate and Outy families. This information about licence payments is rather exceptional since emigrants from other manors usually avoided payment.[13]

Parallel patterns are to be found in movements from other manors. Twenty-nine individuals are noted as being abroad from Upwood. Eleven of these had the surname Albyn. Nicholas Albyn, who stayed on at Upwood with a three-quarter-virgate, had children Agnes, Henry, Mariotta, Thomas and William who sought their fortunes elsewhere. Three sons are last located at King's Lynn. Richard Pykeler, who had left his father with a burden of debts from his official experience, was reported to have three sons when he died at Sutton in 1430. On the other hand, despite his father's considerable wealth in property, John Robyn left the manor in 1405 and with his sons Richard and William sought new opportunities abroad. Except for the Fraunceys family, Upwood emigrants avoided the payment of licence fees when abroad. This same phenomenon can be observed everywhere. For example, at Abbots Ripton where several members of the wealthy Martyn and Prikke families went abroad, at Broughton where the important Justice family had members abroad, at Warboys where the large and influential Berenger family had many members abroad. When we do have information, we find these scions of wealthy families at market centres and practising professions, as with the master carpenter and *medicus* from the Berenger family.

The lord's efforts to siphon revenues from the regional economy through his serfs was not a successful economic enterprise. Nevertheless, to our modern minds there is a certain ambivalence about this picture. Why did

[13] J.A. Raftis, *Tenure and Mobility: Studies in the Social History of the Medieval English Village* (Toronto, 1964), pp. 160–6.

the price of manumission elicit so little response even though it was well within the economic range of wealthy families? Why was security of tenure so little employed as an attraction to manumission?[14] Why did any serfs bother to pay licence fees at all? And surely the continued available information about the location of emigrants, especially the most successful, must have come from continued contact with the home manor. Perhaps our concept and expectations about individual freedom are anachronistic for a place and time when it was so common to wear the livery of one's retainer!

The historiography of the collapse of the manorial economy around 1400 has never been very satisfactory. It has been easy to deduce that the peasants lost the battle, that is the Peasants' Revolt, but won the war with the farming of the lord's demesne and the end of labour services. But such an explanation does little to explain fleeing of the peasantry after the demesne had been farmed. It has been easy to deduce that successful peasants were waiting in the wings to take over the lord's demesne. But why could the lord's manorial economy fail when peasants were able to succeed. Corn prices do not seem to have been decisive factors.[15] In short, fundamental changes of the late fourteenth and early fifteenth centuries cannot be explained through short-term phenomena.

Nor do traditional data about the manorial economy and serfdom over previous centuries appear to give an adequate point of departure. In a useful essay[16] John Hatcher has attempted to update this approach. But it is not easy to find a meaningful sequence from the older and generalised picture. Certainly his conclusions do not fit well with the Ramsey estate experiences related above. 'The loosening and eventual dissolution of the bonds of serfdom' were not directly related to work service and loosening of the bonds of serfdom had an evolution of its own. 'Setting of the scene for confrontation between landlords and customary tenants' and a policy forcing tenants 'to occupy lands' were peripheral to the main economic factors at work. Flexible tenancies and leaseholds did not simply 'develop rapidly' in sequence at the expense of villein tenure since service bearing properties would continue for a long time as part of a varied tenurial package.

What the Ramsey experience does underline is a long-term evolution that would only be more rapidly advanced by the economic events around 1400. The underlying reality was the fact that fewer less wealthy people could compete on the land market. Customary virgates, smallholdings and eventu-

---

[14] *Ibid.*, pp. 251–9.
[15] D.L. Farmer, 'Prices and Wages, 1350–1500', in *AHEW*, III, esp. pp. 434, 450–1.
[16] J. Hatcher, 'English Serfdom and Villeinage: Towards a Reassessment', *Past and Present*, 90 (1981), pp. 3–39.

ally even small pieces of demesne would pass into the occupation of the wealthier tenants. This was predominantly an evolution involving strictly economic adjustments as the lord sought secure revenues and tenants gradually extended their direct exploitation of manorial villeinage and demesne during the entire fourteenth century. Efficient exploitation of market opportunities would be the key to the peasant success. The fact that the main customary tenant held most of the tenements owing work service and yet was able to bargain for lease advantages changes the whole traditional 'problematic' for the later fourteenth century. The lord's revenues came to depend more and more upon an active market in land. Added to this was the interesting information that the 'fleeing serfs' recorded in Ramsey records were so often members of wealthy families who moved with impunity to find places in the regional economy of the fifteenth century.

Such strictly economic factors do not allow us to make a moral judgement in nineteenth-century fashion about this fourteenth–fifteenth century development. The poor remained largely anonymous as they would during such developments as the enclosures. For it was not the burden of work service or the badge of serfdom but declining economic opportunities that was the issue of social justice. Events around 1400 seemed to squeeze out smallholders and there is some evidence that the less wealthy families who had obtained some security by acting as officials on the lord's estates suffered from the debts on the account rolls. But this picture is not complete for the less fortunate; above all, we know practically nothing about the hiring practices of wealthy tenants.

While the material presented in this essay is new, the general thrust of the findings is not. For they point to an emphasis upon evolution that was outlined many years ago. No doubt the theme of evolution has not had the appeal of theses underlining violence in one form or another. And so, these words of Edward Miller have been neglected:

> In this sense, in the thirteenth century, twelfth-century practices were decisively reversed; but this reversal did not change the direction of economic evolution, merely the forms which that evolution assumed. The incidental profits of villein land and villein status were preserved for the peasant England that was to come; the insecurity of villein status and villein tenure made a contribution to the more flexible types of rent-contract devised in the thirteenth century and put into widespread operation in the fourteenth; and ultimately the copyholder and the leaseholder, rather than the freeholder, became the typical peasant farmer of the later Middle Ages.[17]

---

[17] E. Miller, *The Abbey and Bishopric of Ely: The Social History of an Ecclesiastical Estate from the Tenth Century to the Early Fourteenth Century* (Cambridge, 1951), p. 136.

11

The *famuli* in the later
Middle Ages

DAVID FARMER

I

ITSELF MUCH influenced by Edward Miller's study of the manors of the bishopric of Ely, Sir Michael Postan's celebrated pamphlet has remained for over forty years the only monograph devoted to the *famuli*, the staff of permanent workers on the medieval manors. Yet, as Postan realised, it was incomplete, terminating rather abruptly about 1300. 'It would also be desirable', he wrote, 'to project the history of [the] thirteenth-century study to the point at which it touches upon the great transformations of the late fourteenth and fifteenth centuries.'[1] This present essay considers, however inadequately in the space available, the survival and importance of the *famuli* in the later Middle Ages, in particular during the half-century following the most devastating outbreak of bubonic plague, the Black Death of 1348/9.

Published in an ephemeral format, and long out of print, Postan's arguments are so central to this extension of his study that they must be outlined here. Whatever the earlier function of slaves in Anglo-Saxon society, at the time of the Norman Conquest, he contended, 'they were manorial servants, permanent agricultural labourers', primarily responsible for ploughing.[2] A generation later, Domesday Book classed many of them as oxherds (*bovarii*), bordars or cottars, with the status not of slaves but of serfs, occupying smallholdings probably cut out of the demesne. During the twelfth century this change became general. In return for steering the plough, leading the team of oxen or other full-time work on the demesne, the lord excused these labourers all or most of their cash rent, released them from most of the customary labour services incumbent on the other villagers, and even helped

---

Professor Farmer completed this paper on 20 August 1994, six days before his death.
[1] M.M. Postan, *The Famulus: The Estate Labourer in the XIIth and XIIIth Centuries* (Economic History Review Supplement 2, Cambridge, 1954), p. 37.
[2] *Ibid.*, p. 6.

them cultivate their smallholdings. There was such an obvious parallel to the contemporary settlement of armed retainers in knights' fiefs and military serjeanties that Postan adopted for these service holdings the term earlier suggested by Edward Miller: manorial serjeanties, or tenure in base serjeanty.[3]

As in the higher ranks of tenure, manorial serjeanty was only an intermediate stage in the transformation from obligatory, residential service to a freer, money-based society in which the labourer paid a money rent and received a money wage. The subsequent developments, Postan insisted, were neither simultaneous nor universal. By the end of the thirteenth century, as he demonstrated, most manors paid stipends to most of their *famuli*.[4] These stipends had two elements. First, there was a small cash payment (usually a few shillings a year), or acres of sown grain (commonly one acre each of wheat and oats). The second element was the regular payment of threshed grain, such as an eight-bushel quarter of barley every ten weeks; this second element was worth much more than the first. Those paid in this way he termed stipendiary *famuli*, in contrast to the *famuli* who held manorial serjeanties or service holdings, whose reward for working on the demesne was the reduction or cancellation of their money rent and customary services. The latter category will henceforth be described more succinctly as service *famuli*.

Demesne labour forces in the thirteenth century contained both stipendiary *famuli* and service *famuli*, assisted of course by customary labour services and hired casual workers. Postan accepted that 'in many places service holdings stubbornly survived in the later Middle Ages', but elsewhere, as at Ely, they had almost disappeared by 1300.[5] Why though, at a time of labour surplus, did lords turn to stipendiaries, whose cost in money and food seems so much higher than the rent reductions and the value of customary services allowed to the holders of manorial serjeanties? Postan argued, not entirely convincingly, that the 'Saturday ploughings' of tenements held in manorial serjeanty by the demesne plough-teams (or money payments in their place) meant that there was little difference in the cost to the lord.[6] He was also a little premature in deciding that those who remained in manorial serjeanties were likely to be either the 'management' team – such as the reeve, messor, beadle, hayward, parker or woodward, with duties not so continuous as to prevent them cultivating a substantial holding – or the ploughmen, especially

---

[3] E. Miller, *The Abbey and Bishopric of Ely: The Social History of an Ecclesiastical Estate from the Tenth Century to the Early Fourteenth Century* (Cambridge, 1951), pp. 92–3.
[4] Postan, *The Famulus*, p. 27.
[5] *Ibid.*, p. 16.
[6] *Ibid.*, pp. 21–3

the plough-holders (*tenatores*) who steered the lord's ploughs. In contrast, those responsible for livestock were the more likely to be the stipendiaries.[7] This was so by the end of the fourteenth century, but not in the period of which Postan wrote, at least on the two estates most closely examined for his study and this essay.

Postan's main purpose was to demonstrate to non-specialist readers the importance of the work of the *famuli*, more significant but less known than the customary labour services owed to manorial lords. The objective here is to examine the survival of *famuli* in the recessions and depopulations of the fourteenth century and beyond, a theme which, like Postan's, is already well-known to specialists.

II

Not only is the subject too wide to be fitted comfortably into this small space, but the evidence is also too extensive to be examined comprehensively by someone living a continent and an ocean away from the primary sources.[8] So the material given most attention here is that which was available on microfilm, mainly for the manors of the bishopric of Winchester and of Glastonbury Abbey, although these great estates were not typical even of ecclesiastical properties in the fourteenth and fifteenth centuries. Whereas Professor Postan based his study largely on printed estate surveys and custumals, supplemented by some of the earliest account rolls, in default of the former this essay is grounded in the *compotus* rolls alone, and in the 'works' accounts that some of them contain. The *compoti* of some 150 manors were sampled, including forty-six from the bishopric of Winchester, nineteen from Westminster Abbey, eleven from Canterbury Cathedral Priory, eight from Glastonbury Abbey, and six from Durham Cathedral Priory, as well as others belonging to geographically scattered estates like those of Battle and Tavistock Abbeys, Worcester Cathedral Priory, the barony of Berkeley, and Merton College. The Winchester pipe roll for 1381/2 proved particularly useful, as it is more comprehensive than its fellows, in good condition, and follows immediately the Peasants' Revolt.[9] Its evidence has been compared with that from other Winchester rolls at approximately forty-year intervals:

---

[7] *Ibid.*, pp. 17–18

[8] I must record my special thanks to Dr R.H. Britnell, who most generously transcribed for me the details of the fourteenth-century Durham *famuli* and the remuneration they received, and to my colleague Prof. J.M. Hayden, who read the typescript for me and offered helpful comments.

[9] Hants RO (hereafter HRO), Eccles. 2/159388. Some of the gaps in the 'works accounts' in this roll were filled from that for 1376/7 (Eccles. 2/159384), which has these details for some northern manors which did not record them in 1381/2.

1305/6, 1341/2 and 1420/1.[10] Where they survived, accounts from roughly these dates provided data for the other manors considered here.

To define the *famuli*, though, is rather more difficult than Postan assumed. This was also a problem for the medieval accountants. The Winchester pipe rolls often list service *famuli* in with other tenants who received reductions of rent; and their granary accounts, under the heading of *Liberaciones Famulorum*, lump together the full-time stipendiaries and those paid in grain for only a few weeks work. Other accounts seem uncertain whether reeves and bailiffs should be counted among the *famuli* they supervised. In the calculations that follow, those who received rent reductions for a whole year, or grain deliveries as wages (*vadia*) for at least thirty weeks a year, are counted as full-time *famuli*, while those employed for twenty or more weeks but less than thirty are reckoned as half-time. Those working less than twenty weeks are not considered part of the permanent labour force and, save in one or two specified cases, are ignored. Blacksmiths are also omitted; though most manors list a smith among the *famuli* as either a stipendiary or a tenant in serjeanty, work on the demesne equipment was only a small part of his professional activities. A further statistical problem, not solved here, is that of uneven workloads: for example the hayward, whose work for the lord might average only a couple of hours a week, is counted as equivalent to a carter or ploughman toiling twenty times as long. *Famuli* who divided their time between two manors, like the hayward at Street and Walton, and the parker shared by Marwell and Bishopstoke, are reckoned as half-time workers at each of their manors.[11]

For some purposes, stipendiary and service *famuli* have been counted separately. The latter dwindled in numbers and distribution during the fourteenth century. By its end, save for reeves and certain other manorial managers, they are hardly to be found except on the Winchester and Glastonbury estates. In 1420/1 they still comprised some 36 per cent of the *famuli* on the bishop's manors, and 21 per cent of those on the abbey's. So rare are they elsewhere that only those on these two estates are examined separately, to show the later stages of the transformation from service *famuli* to stipendiaries.

Winchester's forty-six principal manors had 590 *famuli* in 1305/6, 515½ in 1341/2 and 499 in 1381/2.[12] During the first period the *famuli* contracted by nearly 13 per cent, but in the second by only 3 per cent even though

[10] *Ibid.*, Eccles. 2/159321, 159342, 159422.
[11] Longleat House, Glastonbury Abbey Documents (hereafter GAD) 5805, 5825, 10813, 10793.
[12] While reference is sometimes made to them, statistics from Moreton, Billingbear and Esher are not included in the tables as these manors were at farm for much of the fourteenth century. Figures from Wolvesey and Southwark are also omitted, as these were

these years included the two major outbreaks of the Black Death. On the eight Glastonbury manors for which details are available at similar dates, the *famuli* fell from 106½ at the beginning of the century to 84 in the 1340s and (on seven manors) to 59 around 1380.[13] On neither estate can the plagues be blamed as the chief cause of the declining number of *famuli*. Indeed, as we shall see, they may have helped to arrest and reverse it.

On these two estates, however, service *famuli* outnumbered the stipendiaries by a wide margin in the early fourteenth century: in 1305/6 over 60 per cent of the Winchester *famuli* and 65 per cent of those at Glastonbury held manorial serjeanties. On the Winchester manors the service *famuli* dropped to 46 per cent of the total in 1341/2, with a further slight fall to 41 per cent in 1381/2. At Glastonbury the contraction was also slow, to 59 per cent around 1341/2 and 46 per cent in 1381/2.

III

The survival of *famuli* in healthy numbers does not by itself show what proportion of the work they did on the manors that remained in hand. The 1381/2 Winchester pipe roll, however, permits some reckoning of their role on that large and conservative estate. For most manors, the pipe roll records in great detail what customary services and boon works each class of tenants had to perform, how many of these services were excused from the tenements of officials and other *famuli*, how many were lost because tenements were vacant or because the tenants lacked the ploughs and animals to perform them, how many were commuted or sold, and, at last, how many were actually used on the demesne or cancelled because the lord had no need of them. Other parts of the accounts, in the usual way, record any expenditure on hiring casual workers by the day or on piece rates. Some of the calculations that follow are based on cautious assumptions rather than exact numbers, and probably underestimate the role of the *famuli*.

Ploughing was almost entirely the responsibility of *famuli*. The Winchester accounts record how many acres were seeded on each manor, and thus how much arable was cultivated for the crops, but not how much or how often the fallow was ploughed. Here it is assumed that on the manors with a three-course rotation the fallow was equal to one half of the area sown, and that on the few manors with a two-course rotation the fallow equalled the

---

not normal manors. Minor occupations like goatherd are counted in these totals, but not in the tables.

[13] Ashcott, Glastonbury, Greinton, Longbridge Deverill, Monkton Deverill, Street and Walton. The dates of the surviving Glastonbury accounts do not coincide exactly with those of the Winchester pipe rolls.

area sown. It is also assumed that the fallow was ploughed only once. The participation of *famuli* in boon works is ignored; so is the probability that some manors still reckoned the unit of labour service and boon ploughing in unacknowledged small customary acres. On fifteen of the bishop's manors the *famuli* did all the ploughing. On only four manors – Downton, Bishopstone, Ivinghoe and Ecchinswell – did labour services and boon works account for even one quarter. Nowhere was any ploughing done by hired casual labour. Overall, the customary tenants ploughed at most 985 acres, or 8 per cent of the total. *Famuli* ploughed the remaining 92 per cent.

In harvesting, the second heaviest task of arable husbandry, *famuli* played only a supporting role. Except when they joined in the communal reap-boons, they did almost none of the work of reaping, binding and stooking. Many manors, though, hired harvesters by the day to supplement the work of the customary tenants; some, like Farnham and Droxford, relied on them entirely. Excluding the hundred or so acres of grain given to *famuli* as stipends and reaped by them, the tenants and the hired harvesters together cut about 6,770 acres of grain. Of this total, only 1,031 acres were harvested by the latter. The customary tenants thus did some 85 per cent of the work, the hired hands 15 per cent, and *famuli* almost nothing.

The other major harvest task was to carry the sheaves to the barn, or to the yard for stacking. On over a quarter of the bishop's manors there were no customary services for this work, nor were any carts hired; here the job was left entirely to *famuli*. Elsewhere virtually all the available customary services were used – perhaps more in 1381/2 than in most years, as many manors had sent their carts and horses to carry timber from Highfield to Oxford, 'for the new college built there by the lord' (*pro nouo collegio ibidem per dominum constructo*). The number of these services, though, bears little relation to the size of the arable or of the crop: while 240 may have been enough to carry in the harvest from Fonthill's 118 acres, the 55 carrying works available at Downton would certainly not have sufficed for the produce of the 180 acres there. By the yardstick of Fonthill, most manors would have been well short of the services they needed. The bishop's whole estate spent less than 20s. on hiring carts to speed the work, and it seems probable that at least half this task fell to the demesne carts and the *famuli*.

The records of hauling services (*aueragia*) again show the importance of demesne carters and their colleagues. In 1381/2 the bishop spent nothing at all on outside transport, but only fifteen of his manors had hauling services and used them – mainly those in the bailiwicks of Highclere and Bishop's Sutton. Those manors entitled to such services used them to transport less than one quarter of the grain and malt they despatched to market and to the lord's residences. Apart from some grain sold locally, and probably fetched from the granary by the buyers, the Winchester *famuli* therefore carted away all the grain from two-thirds of the manors, and three-quarters of the grain from the remainder.

The task of threshing and winnowing, however, fell chiefly to hired labourers. Seven of the manors, mainly in the Twyford bailiwick, had this done entirely by customary services, but seventeen had both the threshing and the winnowing done by workers hired by piece rates (*ad tascham*). On almost all the remainder, participation by the *famuli* consisted merely of the dairymaid (*daia*) winnowing half the grain. Calculated by value, hired workers did 76 per cent, customary services slightly more than 20 per cent, and *famuli* less than 4 per cent of the threshing and winnowing.

The shepherd, according to the thirteenth-century *Seneschaucy*, had to protect the flock from dogs and unsafe pastures, make hurdles and hedges, sleep with his watchdog in the fold with the sheep, and never go to market or the tavern without leaving a suitable deputy in his place.[14] The fourteenth-century shepherd had additional problems resulting from widespread sheep scab – sickly lambs and ewes too weak to feed them, and the chore of smearing affected animals with the concoction of tar, mercury and verdigris used to treat it. How does one count customary services, often lasting only half a day, against such a full-time job? These calculations assume that the shepherd's day was no longer than the time the customary tenant needed to wash and shear ten sheep, or make two hurdles, and that, as the 1381/2 pipe roll confirms, a penny was the appropriate payment for a day's work at either.

In that year eight manors spent in all 71s. 4½d. on paying people at piece rates to wash and shear their sheep, which was equivalent by this formula to 856½ works. The other manors used 3,262½ customary services to smarten up their flocks. In addition, the manors paid 73s. 9½d. to those who made hurdles from the lord's sticks, equivalent to 885½ works, and also used 352 customary works for this purpose. The manors also used 466 works to move sheepfolds from place to place. These operations, almost the only ones not carried out by the shepherds, total 5,822½ works.[15] On the assumptions that a shepherd's tasks every twenty-four hours amounted to only one customary work, but that he worked every day of the year, in total the eighty-eight *famuli* shepherds did the equivalent of 32,120 works in 1381/2. Even if one reckons as casual workers the sixteen men and lads who helped during lambing for some 930 days – and the pipe roll counts them

---

[14] D. Oschinsky, *Walter of Henley and Other Treatises on Estate Management and Accounting* (Oxford, 1971), p. 287.
[15] A few manors also paid small sums to outsiders for castrating the lambs.

as *famuli* – the full-time shepherds did nearly 83 per cent of the work of looking after the bishop's 29,742 sheep.

The *famuli* were inevitably less prominent in some activities, such as mowing and haymaking, and in weeding the grain, but they did most of the harrowing, all the carting of manure from the buildings to the fields, and all the fetching of building materials needed on the manors. In short, on the Winchester estate in 1381/2 they did most of the work.

IV

The overall figures cited for the number of *famuli* conceal several changes in the make-up of the permanent manorial staffs. The ploughmen became less prominent; the shepherds more so. The dairymaids often evolved into cow farmers whose status rose with their prosperity. Reeves on many estates became bailiffs, usually paid respectable cash stipends and generous allowances of wheat or money wages in their places. As ploughmen generally formed more than half of a manor's *famuli*, it is fitting to consider first the changes that affected their numbers. The most important of these factors, of course, were the amount of ploughland the lord kept in hand, to meet his needs and those of whatever markets he could supply profitably, and the availability of other labour, like customary services.

In most of England the lord's direct exploitation of demesne arable was already in decline before the start of the fourteenth century; on the Winchester manors this process actually slowed in the middle of the century as the bishop took advantage of higher grain prices.[16] Between 1305/6 and 1341/2, the area seeded on the Winchester manors dropped by 23 per cent; between 1341/2 and 1381/2, however, it fell by less than 17 per cent.[17] Early in the fourteenth century, the succession of disastrous harvests and cattle plagues had accelerated the retreat from high demesne agriculture.[18] Among the Winchester manors, Twyford cut its plough-teams from seven in 1317/18 to five and a half in 1320/1, Moreton from three to two, Downton from six and

---

[16] J.Z. Titow, *Winchester Yields: A Study in Medieval Agricultural Productivity* (Cambridge, 1972), pp. 136–44; D.L. Farmer, 'Grain Yields on the Winchester Manors in the Later Middle Ages', *Econ. Hist. Rev.*, 2nd ser., 30 (1977), p. 562.

[17] In the first half of the century many Winchester manors still counted their arable, and their labour services, by customary acres, *sicut iacent*. The 1381/2 pipe roll contains conversion factors, almost always expressed in round numbers. At Merdon, for example, it took six customary acres to equal one measured acre, but at the nearby manors of Twyford and Crawley only four and two respectively. These conversion rates seem approximate at best, and calculations based on them no better.

[18] I. Kershaw, 'The Great Famine and Agrarian Crisis in England, 1315–1322', in R.H. Hilton (ed.), *Peasants, Knights and Heretics: Studies in Medieval English Social History* (Cambridge, 1976), pp. 85–132.

Table 11.1 *Major occupations of famuli on bishopric of Winchester manors, distinguishing between service famuli (A) and stipendiary famuli (B)*

	1305/6		1341/2		1381/2		1420/1	
	A	B	A	B	A	B	A	B
(a) Labourers								
Ploughmen	217	96	142	105	99½	113½	45	71½
Carters	–	39½	–	47½	–	44½	–	25
Shepherds	33½	27	30½	39½	28	60	9	43
Dairymaids (*daie*)	–	22	–	29	–	30½	–	18¼
Cowmen	13½	10	9	6	5	16½	1	8½
Pigmen	10½	3	11	4	9½	10	2	3
Woodwards	3	–	2	–	1½	–	–	–
Totals	277½	197½	194½	231	143½	275	57	169½
(b) Managers								
Reeves	45	–	32	–	43	–	24	1
Serjeants	–	1	–	11	–	5	–	–
Haywards	22½	10	8	16½	14	6½	5	7
Beadles	7½	–	9½	–	12	–	7	–
Parkers	3	3	–	6	–	4	–	3
Warenners	–	5	2	7	–	3½	1	3
Foresters	5	–	–	–	–	–	2	1
Rent Collectors	–	–	–	–	5	–	–	–
Grangers	1	1	–	1½	–	1	–	–
Totals	84	20	51½	42	74	20	39	12

Notes: ploughmen include *carucarii*, *bovarii*, *tenatores* and *fugatores*. Shepherds include *custodes ovium*. Haywards include *messores*. Grangers include *bartonarii*.

Table 11.2 *Major occupations of famuli on Glastonbury abbey manors, distinguishing between service* famuli *(A) and stipendiary* famuli *(B)*

	1305/6		1341/2		1381/2		1420/1	
	A	B	A	B	A	B	A	B
(a) Labourers								
Ploughmen	41½	15½	29	21	17	17	3	31
Carters	–	6½	–	5	–	2	–	2
Shepherds	7	–	6	1	1	6	–	7
Dairymaids (*daie*)	–	2½	1	1	–	–	–	1
Cowmen	–	1½	1	–	–	–	–	–
Pigmen	1	2	1	3	–	1	–	2
Totals	49½	28	37	31	18	26	3	43
(b) Managers								
Reeves	8	–	8	–	6	½	6	–
Serjeants	–	–	–	–	–	–	–	2
Haywards	6	2½	–	4½	–	4	–	3
Beadles	1	–	–	–	1	–	–	–
Grangers	–	–	–	–	1	–	–	1
Parkers	–	–	–	–	–	–	–	1
Totals	15	2½	8	4½	8	4½	6	7

Notes: Ploughmen include *carucarii*, *bovarii*, *tenatores* and *fugatores*. Shepherds include *custodes ovium*. Haywards include *messores*. Grangers include *bartonarii*.

Table 11.3 Famuli on estates other than Winchester and Glastonbury, c. 1340 – c. 1380

	c. 1340						c. 1380					
	Ploughmen	Carters	Shepherds	Dair	Cowmen	Pigmen	Ploughmen	Carters	Shepherds	Dair	Cowmen	Pigmen
Canterbury Cath. (11 manors)	43	8½	12	6	7½	7½	39½	7½	16	6½	7	6
Bury St Edmunds Abbey (4 manors)	18	4	5	4	1	1	18	5	5	4	—	—
Westminster Abbey (19 manors)	91½	23½	15	18	5	11	54½	14	17½	14	6	7½
Battle Abbey & c. (5 manors)	30½	2½	13	2½	3	4	27	1	10½	4	3	3
Merton College (4 manors)	11½	5	4	4	—	2	6½	1½	2	2	—	—
Worcester Cath. (4 manors)	16	5	4½	4	—	4	15½	2	2	3	—	2
Durham Priory (6 manors)	37	10	5	7	1	5½	27	5	6	4	1	1
Berkeley Earldom (4 manors)	22	4½	2½	3	2	—	17	3	6½	3	1	—
Ramsey Abbey (5 manors)	17	7	6	—	3	5	12	6	5	—	2	5
Other (5 manors)	17	3½	10	4	1	3	15	2	7	3	1	2
Totals	303½	73½	77½	52½	23½	43	232	47	77½	49½	21	26½

Table 11.4 *Changes in demesne agriculture and staffing on Winchester manors*

	1305/6	1341/2	1381/2	1420/1
Acres seeded	10,723.5	8,235	6,870	3,253.5
Ploughmen, tenants-in-serjeanty	217	142	99.5	45.5
Ploughmen, stipendiary	96	105	113.5	71.5
Acres seeded, per ploughman	34.3	33.3	32.3	27.9
Sheep at opening Michaelmas	17,784	16,186	29,742	17,800
Shepherds, tenants-in-serjeanty	33.5	30.5	28	9
Shepherds, stipendiary	27	39.5	60	43
Sheep, per shepherd	294	231	338	342

a half in 1317/18 to six in 1320/1 and five and a half in 1325/6, and East Knoyle from six in 1317/18 to four in 1320/1, though it replaced one of them by 1325/6.[19] This trend continued: by 1331/2, twenty-one of the bishop's manors had lost at least one of their plough-teams of 1305/6, and only three – Alresford, Cheriton and Harwell – had added to them, resulting in a net loss of twenty-three teams.[20] On the Ramsey abbey manors the number of plough-teams fell drastically in the years around 1320, from thirty-eight to twenty-eight, though a couple were restored by the 1340s and a few manors actually added teams in the decades after the Black Death.[21] The eight Glastonbury manors examined here operated twenty-eight ploughs at the start of the century, and twenty-five and a half around 1340, but as almost no accounts survive for the 1320s and 1330s there may well have been a drop and subsequent recovery in those decades.

The problems of relying on tenants with intermittent labour services to look after livestock, or even on *famuli* with holdings of their own, brought other changes. Several manors, notably in the Highclere bailiwick, converted service ploughmen into stipendiaries, or gave them duties formerly done by customary tenants. The account for Bishop's Sutton in 1305/6 noted that its *famuli* had gained an oxherd 'because the oxen were kept badly by the customary tenants', and Adderbury later made the change, on the orders of the steward and bailiff, 'to care for the oxen and other beasts'. By 1341/2 all but four of the forty-eight Winchester manors had at least one plough-driver

[19] HRO, Eccles. 2/159332, 159334, 158338.
[20] *Ibid.*, Eccles. 2/159344.
[21] J.A. Raftis, *The Estates of Ramsey Abbey. A Study in Economic Growth and Organization* (Toronto, 1957), table xxviii, pp. 132–6.

(*fugator*) or oxherd to look after the plough animals.[22] All eight Glastonbury demesnes also had some stipendiary ploughmen: on most of those manors, all the plough-drivers were stipendiary, and all the plough-holders were service *famuli*.

The trend towards stipendiary ploughmen on the Winchester estates, however, went into reverse somewhat in the mid-1340s. At the beginning of the decade all five demesnes in the Taunton area had employed only stipendiaries, but Bishop's Hull and Staplegrove in 1343/4 and Holway and Poundisford the next year put all their plough-holders back into service tenements, where they remained at least until the end of the century. When Crawley added a team in 1345/6, both the new ploughmen were service *famuli*. But Bishop's Sutton, recently without any, hired a stipendiary plough-driver in the same year, and briefly added a second in the wake of the Black Death.

The consequences of the plague for manorial ploughmen seem rather muted. On the 120 manors with records from both before and after the Black Death, around 1340 there were $726\frac{1}{2}$ labourers assigned to the ploughs or, as carters, expected to work with them for part of the year. By the time of the Peasants' Revolt there were still $572\frac{1}{2}$, only 21 per cent below the earlier total. This decline is much less than any estimate of the fall in population in that period. There are obvious reasons why this contraction was modest. As the ecclesiastical estates which supply almost all the evidence were growing grain primarily for their own consumption, and the surplus they were sending to market fetched higher prices than ever before, they had good reason to persist with demesne cultivation.[23] Many, like Westminster Abbey, were loath to face the new economic realities and continued for half a century to operate as though the conditions of England before the Black Death might be magically restored.[24] The deaths of so many customary tenants, and the survivors' increasing reluctance to perform labour services, largely removed the older alternative. On many of the Winchester manors the customary tenants were obliged to do ploughing services only if they had the necessary equipment, and even virgaters and half-virgaters often did not: at Highclere in 1376/7, for example, the lord lost for this reason alone the ploughing of fifty-seven acres, and was able to use customary services to plough only fifteen.[25] So the lords either had to employ *famuli*

---

[22] The exceptions were Ashmansworth, Wargrave, Waltham St Lawrence and Bishop's Sutton.

[23] D.L. Farmer, 'Prices and Wages', in *AHEW*, III, p. 444.

[24] B. Harvey, *Westminster Abbey and its Estates in the Middle Ages* (Oxford, 1977), pp. 244–6.

[25] HRO, Eccles. 2/159384.

ploughmen to ensure their supply of labour or abandon demesne agriculture entirely.

Moreover, the powerful owners of many of these estates, helped by strict auditing and by restrictive legislation, were able to avoid paying their *famuli* significantly higher wages, and thus lacked any economic incentive to change. The very first clause of the 1351 Statute of Labourers forbade the *famuli* to take more than in 1346/7.[26] Lords could use the royal courts and their agents to compel *famuli* to stay in their employment, rather than rely on their own manorial courts to coerce footloose and rebellious tenants to do labour services. The bishops of Winchester, in particular, avoided paying more than previously until the end of the century or beyond.[27] And the shortage of customary tenants after the plague left more work to be done, and many estates found extra use for labour. Some manors tilled the land more frequently, ploughing the fallow twice during the summer to work in manure or discourage weeds, and this too kept the *famuli* busy. Often less than half, or even a third, of the labour of the demesne ploughs was spent on the lands carrying the lord's crops of that year. For example, in 1365/6 the four teams at Street ploughed some 91 acres for wheat, 52 acres for oats, ploughed 153 acres for the first tilling of the fallow (*ad warectam*) and the same 153 again for the second tilling (*rebinatio*), manured 7 acres, and ploughed the 36 acres held by the service plough-holders; only 27 per cent of the work done was on the land currently seeded for the lord.[28]

What ultimately brought about the demise of most *famuli* ploughmen was the collapse of grain prices with the good harvests of the last quarter of the fourteenth century. All estates were finding it harder to keep wages down and to silence peasant demands for the end of customary services. So most lords leased their manors to farmers, or divided the demesnes among their tenants, preferring cash rents to unprofitable agriculture. Yet, as noted before, some manors persisted with the old system, usually when their owners planned to consume most of the produce and wanted to be sure of sufficient supplies. In 1420/1, the bishop of Winchester still had twenty-five manors in hand, with 126 *famuli* described as ploughmen; this total was less than that on the same manors in 1381/2 by only half one ploughman. Around 1420, the eight Glastonbury manors studied were growing grain on about 10 per cent *more* land than forty years before, and as late as 1480/1 Street had six *famuli* described as 'akermen', cultivating 116 acres of wheat, beans and oats for the abbot. But these were exceptions.

[26] 'First, that carters, ploughmen, leaders of the plough (*fugatores*), shepherds, domestic and all other servants shall receive the liveries and wages accustomed.'
[27] Farmer, 'Prices and Wages', p. 480.
[28] GAD 5805. Plough accounts such as this are quite rare.

V

After ploughmen, the most numerous members of the *famuli* were the shepherds. On some estates their numbers increased during the fourteenth century as lords turned from arable farming to pastoral. The forty-eight Winchester manors had sixty and a half shepherds in 1305/6, tending nearly 18,000 sheep with some help from the customary tenants and lads hired for brief periods. By 1341/2, despite some reduction in the flocks, there were seventy shepherds. As noted earlier, in 1381/2 the Winchester manors had eighty-eight, guarding almost 30,000 sheep. The twenty-five manors remaining in hand in 1420/1 employed fifty-two shepherds, for some 17,400.[29]

The predominance of drained marshland on Glastonbury's western manors made their soil too wet and too valuable for sheep, but some of the abbot's eastern properties rivalled the Winchester lands in access to downland grazings. Monkton Deverill had 872 sheep at Michaelmas 1374 and 1,034 in 1420, while the Longbridge Deverill flocks increased in the same period from 428 to 846. Three manors out of the eight studied here kept no sheep, but the flocks of the others doubled in numbers. This was achieved with little increase in the number of *famuli*: around 1340, seven shepherds had looked after 1,181 sheep; eighty years later, eight shepherds sufficed for 2,535. The growth in labour efficiency – or, put differently, in the workload per shepherd – on the Glastonbury lands was therefore greater than on the bishop's, even though his shepherds on average still had slightly more sheep to guard.

On the other estates examined here, however, there seems to have been no comparable growth in sheep farming. One cannot be certain, as some manors did not record in their main accounts the size of their flocks. Thus Battle Abbey's demesne at Lullington in the 1380s (and for more than forty years afterwards) had four shepherds on the payroll, but its accounts list no sheep; Brandon in 1371/2 had three shepherds, and Worcester Cathedral Priory's demesnes at Overbury and Harvington one apiece, likewise without obvious duties.[30] The number of adult sheep on Battle's demesne at Alciston dropped from 1,577 in 1336/7 to 918 in 1380/1, and the manor lost one of its five shepherds; its fellow, Apuldram, kept both flock and *famuli*

---

[29] It should be remembered that a manor's holding of sheep varied greatly from year to year as disease ravaged the flocks, and also during a year when estates moved flocks between manors in search of seasonal pastures. These calculations of flock size must be treated cautiously.

[30] Public Record Office (hereafter PRO), S.C.6/1024/24, 1304/23; Worcester Cathedral, Dean and Chapter (hereafter WCDC), C711, C804.

unchanged. The small manor of Glynde nearby cut one of the two shepherds when its flock fell from 449 to 54.[31]

On the Durham Priory estates, Bewley advanced from one shepherd in the 1340s to three around 1380, and Wardley appointed one where there had been none before; but Ketton dropped from two to one, and Westoe lost its only one.[32] Of the Merton College manors, Woolford lost its shepherd and flock, while Leatherhead dropped from two shepherds to one between the 1340s and the mid-1370s.[33] On eleven properties of Canterbury Cathedral Priory studied, the number of adult sheep rose by barely 16 per cent between 1340 and 1380. On the nineteen manors of Westminster Abbey examined, the numbers increased from 2,500 to 3,000 sheep during the same period, and from sixteen shepherds to seventeen and a half, but their flocks were still small, only that at Todenham even approaching 400 adults in 1380.

In eastern England, nine Ramsey manors had in all 2,274 sheep in the years before the Black Death, with five shepherds to look after them; by the 1380s there were 3,326 in their flocks, but tended by only four. On all but one of these manors the number of sheep continued to rise in the ensuing decades.[34] Of the four Bury St Edmunds manors investigated, only Risby added a shepherd; by 1380, with just 74 sheep, the two shepherds at Hinderclay were clearly underemployed, and one of them had left the *famuli* by 1400. So had the Risby recruit.[35]

No more consistent picture emerges from the other manors examined. During this period both Claret and Bircham kept small flocks, each adequately tended by a single shepherd. Heytesbury's flock of 371 at Michaelmas 1341 increased to 540 at the same date in 1379, but one of the two shepherds had gone. Also in Wiltshire, Bromham in the autumn of 1376 had barely a quarter of sheep it had had in 1344; and it too lost a shepherd.[36] There are no pre-Black Death accounts from the manors of New College, but those from the last decades of the fourteenth century record only modest activity: about 600 sheep and two shepherds at Alton Barnes, around 300 at Hornchurch with one shepherd, and the same at Weedon, a shepherd

[31] East Sussex RO, Lewes (hereafter ESRO), Gage 44/1, 44/37, Glynde 1072, 1075; PRO, S.C.6/1016/7, 1017/12.

[32] Durham University Library, Durham Dean and Chapter Muniments (hereafter DDCM), Manorial Accounts: Bewley 1339/40, 1343/4, 1378/9; Wardley 1337/8, 1380/1; Ketton, 1339/40, 1343/4, 1380/1; Westoe, 1340/6, 1375/6. The sixth Durham Priory manor in Table 11.3 is Fulwell, using accounts from 1343/4 and 1379/80.

[33] Merton College, Oxford, 4396, 4418, 5721, 5730.

[34] These figures are assembled from Tables in Raftis, *Estates of Ramsey Abbey*, pp. 147–51, 202–4. The details are from different dates, only approximate to those used in the other comparisons here.

[35] Suffolk RO, Bury St Edmunds (hereafter SRO), E3/15.13/2.8, 2.19, 2.20; Joseph Regenstein Library, Chicago (hereafter Chicago), Bacon MSS 492, 507.

[36] PRO, S.C.6/838/16, 839/3, 930/17, 930/30, 1052/16, 1053/2, 1045/14, 1045/19.

with less than 200 at Heyford, and neither shepherd nor sheep at Birchanger, Takeley or Tingewick.[37] The manors in the south-west had only small flocks at that time: about 300 at Bishop Clyst, rather fewer at Werrington and Egloshaye, less than 200 at Dawlish, 70 at Ottery and 100 at Maristowe.[38] All except the last of these, though, kept a shepherd on the permanent staff.

Only the Winchester properties, therefore, show clear evidence of a major increase in the number of shepherds in the *famuli*. Occasionally a Winchester pipe roll explains why the bishop added more. The 1335/6 Fareham account attests that the tenants who used to guard the wethers did so badly and now contributed three quarters of barley a year towards the cost of a stipendiary shepherd; this formula is repeated, in shorter form, for the rest of the century.[39] Elsewhere the accounts blame the lack of customary tenants, or, as at Wargrave and Waltham St Lawrence, say that the lands of those who used to do the services were in the lord's hands.

This last must also be a main reason for the second great change among the *famuli* shepherds on the Winchester manors. At the start of the century the majority had been service *famuli*, tenants in manorial serjeanty: thirty-three and a half such, with only twenty-seven stipendiaries. By 1341/2 there were three fewer service shepherds, but twelve more stipendiaries. The 1381/2 pipe roll has the stipendiaries outnumbering the others by more than two to one. Yet even in 1420/1, when there were forty-three stipendiaries, there were still nine who held service tenements. Though the Glastonbury estates as a whole had sixteen stipendiary shepherds and only fourteen with manorial serjeanties in 1305/6, all seven on the manors studied here were service *famuli*. The Mells shepherd became a stipendiary by 1341/2, and all except one of the two at Longbridge Deverill had made the change by 1381/2. On all the manors examined from other estates, by the 1340s there was only a single service shepherd, at Heytesbury.

Two posts in the demesne staff, even on the Winchester and Glastonbury estates, were monopolised by stipendiaries throughout this period, as they had been in the thirteenth century also: those of the carter and the dairymaid. Almost every manor had a carter, and many carters on these scattered estates travelled extensively to deliver produce and other provisions to the castles and other residences of the bishop or to the abbey, as well as to fetch gear like millstones needed on the manors.[40] Such lengthy journeys could not

[37] New College, Oxford, 5825, 6389, 6059, 6281, 5875, 7006, 7090.
[38] Devon RO, Exeter (hereafter DRO Ex.), W1258/G3/2, D71/3; CR435; W1258/D42; DRO, Plymouth (hereafter DRO Plym.), 70/93; Exeter Cathedral, Dean and Chapter, 5030.
[39] HRO, Eccles. 2/159347: there was no rent allowance for the shepherd *quia est ad liber-acionem, ad quam liberi homines qui solebant custodire multones dant iij quarteria ordei quia male custodiebant.*
[40] D.L. Farmer, 'Millstones for Medieval Manors', *Agric Hist. Rev.*, 40 (1992), pp. 97–111.

easily be undertaken by someone with a holding in manorial serjeanty; moreover, during the hectic weeks of harvest the carter might also be the busiest
member of the *famuli*, and unable to tend any crop of his own. As a woman –
usually though not invariably – and probably unmarried, the *daia* (the word
here translated as dairymaid) had virtually no chance of becoming a tenant
of land. Her responsibilities are often explained in the accounts: usually she
had to make pottage for the *famuli* (as the mid-day meal), keep the fire
going and look after the poultry, do the milking and make the cheese,
winnow half the grain after threshing, probably look after the buildings of
the manorial *curia*, and perhaps make malt. At Sutton-under-Brailes in 1379/
80 the dairymaid made ninety quarters of malt, so much that the manor
had to hire someone else to do the winnowing normally required of her. At
Islip the dairymaid was also the gardener.[41] Some dairymaids needed helpers:
at Bredon in the 1380s and Werrington and Bishop Clyst in the 1390s the
famuli included a dairymaid's servant. Other manors employed additional
milkers in the summer, and Lullington had to employ a goose-girl to help
its dairymaid with the poultry.[42] Often it was the dairymaid who became
the cow farmer, renting the cows and perhaps the ewes from the lord and
selling the milk and cheese.

The forty-six main Winchester manors employed in 1381/2 some forty-four
carters and thirty dairymaids. The seventy or so other manors examined
here had around that date seventy-five carters and fifty-two dairymaids. They
were thus the most numerous of the labouring *famuli* after the ploughmen
and shepherds.

The only other common occupations were those of the cowmen and
pigmen. There were about twenty of the latter on the Winchester lands
around 1380, half of them holding in manorial serjeanty and the rest receiving the meanest stipends and liveries paid to any of the male *famuli*. The
other manors at that time employed some twenty-seven, all of them stipendiaries; whereas the number of pigmen on the Winchester lands had risen by
a third since 1341/2, elsewhere the numbers dropped by half during the
forty-year period. The bishop's manors had twenty-one or so cowmen
(including five service *famuli*) in 1381/2 – also an increase on forty years
before – while the others had twenty-four, about the same as earlier.

Though the thirteenth-century farming treatises like Walter of Henley's
Husbandry and the *Seneschaucy* distinguish sharply between the tasks of the

---

[41] Glos. RO (hereafter GRO), D1099/M31/46; Westminster Abbey Muniments (hereafter
WAM) 14792.
[42] Worcs. RO (hereafter WRO), 2636/009: 1/158/92015; DRO Ex., W1258/G3/2, D71/3;
PRO, S.C.6/1025/12.

various labourers, such specialisation was seldom present.[43] Like the customary tenants obliged to plough and sow, weed and harrow, make hay, reap and thresh, dig ditches and build fences, shear sheep and thatch ricks (and like more recent farm workers too), the members of the *famuli* needed a variety of skills. Save perhaps for the shepherds, all had to help with the harvest. In winter the carter often acted as driver of a horse plough, or led the harrow; in summer the ploughmen worked with the extra carts needed to take the sheaves to the barn. To supervise and co-ordinate these essential activities — and secure at least some of the proceeds for themselves — the lords employed a relatively large number of management officers, and these too must be examined.

VI

In the fourteenth century, the official responsible to the lord was usually a reeve, in theory elected annually from the village community or homage. But in practice this was no longer always the case. The reeve of Street was a virgater in Walton, the reeve of Kinsbourne held a quarter-virgate at Wheathampstead, and some of the Winchester reeves moved from manor to manor, as the reeve of Poundisford did to nearby Holway in 1335/6, and John Waterman from Nailsbourne to Downton about 1354/5.[44] Many certainly held office much longer than one year: William Dameme was reeve at Cheriton from Michaelmas 1343 until he died some time after Michaelmas 1387, and Robert Oldman was reeve of Cuxham from 1311 until his death from plague in 1349.[45] The majority of fourteenth-century reeves received no salary in money or grain, or any food livery except (usually) meals at the lord's expense during harvest, and small gifts of food or money, along with the other members of the *famuli*, at Christmas and Easter. Their recompense was almost entirely in the remission of part of the rent for their holding and the cancellation of most of the labour services due from it. They might also have to make good any shortfall in the manor's income if the grain harvested was less than expected, or sold for less, or if they had to pay higher wages than the Statute of Labourers and the lord's auditors permitted. That some reeves stayed so long in office suggests either that the lord could exert unusual pressure on unfree tenants to serve in such posts, or that reeves could operate successfully in the medieval black economy, with incomes from their offices much higher than the accounts record.

During the fourteenth century many lords appointed bailiffs or serjeants

[43] Oschinsky, *Walter of Henley*, pp. 264–95, 308–42.
[44] GAD 5808; Herts. RO, D/ELw/M 185.
[45] P.D.A. Harvey, *A Medieval Oxfordshire Village: Cuxham, 1240–1400* (Oxford, 1965), p. 64.

to replace their reeves, paying them with cash stipends and grain liveries, usually a bushel of wheat a week. These serjeants received no allowance of rent, and were not required to do labour services. On the Winchester manors, their role seems identical to that of the reeves. The manor and its officials were subject to the authority of a regional bailiff, himself supervised by the estate steward at Wolvesey Castle. It was clearly in the lord's power to determine his manager's status: between 1335 and 1341 the number of Winchester manors under a serjeant (*serviens*) rose from five to twelve; then, even more swiftly, the serjeants were replaced by reeves on every manor except Overton, only the Bentley serjeant keeping his post under the humbler title. This reversion to service tenure came precisely at the time when several ploughmen lost their status as stipendiaries and again had to work as holders of manorial serjeanties. By 1390 the number of serjeants had crept back to six.

Most of the Glastonbury manors also remained in the management of reeves. The majority of other estates, however, appointed serjeants, or bailiffs who acted as supervisors of individual manors rather than as regional administrators such as those at Winchester. Some, confusingly, kept the name of reeve for their officials, but paid them like serjeants with cash stipends and grain liveries or money wages in their place. Among these were four properties of Worcester Cathedral Priory and the Berkeley manor of Slimbridge; the last may have adopted this arrangement because its reeve was an outsider, presumably not entitled to a rent reduction.[46] Whatever the title of the post, the manorial managers in most places, like the labourers, had completed the transition from service tenure to stipendiary employment by the end of the fourteenth century.

This was so as well for most of the lower level of managers, the haywards or messors, the beadles and warenners. Fourteenth-century warenners and parkers seem invariably to have been stipendiaries, and beadles were usually service *famuli*, though there were a few stipendiary beadles on Canterbury manors like Adisham, Chartham and Meopham even before the Black Death. On the Winchester lands the haywards were among those who suffered the reaction in the 1340s: in 1341/2 two-thirds of the full-time haywards had been stipendiaries, but in 1381/2 less than one third were. By 1420/1 the stipendiaries were again in the majority. On the Glastonbury manors, and on all but one of the others studied, by 1380 or so all the haywards were stipendiaries. The sole exception was Heytesbury.

---

[46] Berkeley MSS, Slimbridge 30.

VII

So far only one criterion has been used to assess changes in the condition – and, indirectly, the importance – of the *famuli* in the later Middle Ages: whether they held in manorial serjeanty or were rewarded with stipends and liveries, Postan argued that it was not even certain which of these arrangements was better for them.[47] But, according to the preamble to the Witney accounts around 1380, all the customary tenants who had worked as ploughmen had become stipendiaries (receiving 2s. every winter, an acre of wheat in summer, and a quarter. of barley every ten weeks as livery) 'because it had pleased the lord because of the poverty of the people'. At nearby Adderbury, so the pipe rolls record, three ploughmen and a cowman had given back their lands into the lord's hands because of their poverty. In difficult times, the labourers themselves preferred to be stipendiaries.

One reason probably was the modest size of the holdings in return for which, as service tenants, they worked so long on the demesne. Only rarely are the *famuli* other than the reeve named, and so their holdings cannot easily be traced from records of entry fines. But the Glastonbury manors usually state the size of the tenement for which the rent was reduced, and the Winchester pipe rolls for 1376/7 and 1381/2, in listing the labour services due on almost all the manors, also make it possible in many cases to determine how large the holdings were.[48]

At the beginning of the fourteenth century the reeves on the eight Glastonbury manors studied comprised two virgaters, three half-virgaters, and three holding fardels (that is, quarter-virgates). The ploughmen were an even humbler group, with three half-virgaters, twenty-two fardel-men, and five with half-fardels or five acres apiece. All six shepherds held fardels. Around 1340 the mix was very similar, but the reeves now included four half-virgaters and one man with only six acres. One ploughman held a half-virgate, the rest having fardels. The transition to stipendiary *famuli* thinned the numbers: by 1380 or so there were only fourteen ploughmen holding in serjeanty, and only one shepherd, all being fardel-men. By 1420, on the five manors still in hand, there were three reeves with virgates, one with a fardel and one with only a cottar's plot, and two ploughmen holding fardels.

On the Winchester manors the *famuli* holding in manorial serjeanty generally had larger tenements than those at Glastonbury. Around 1380 two of the bishop's reeves each held two virgates, while eighteen had virgates and

[47] Postan, *The Famulus*, p. 20.
[48] This is not possible, however, for the many manors that imposed labour services on a *per capita* basis, irrespective of the size of the holding.

thirteen half-virgates. Those responsible for ploughing included seven virgaters, while twenty-nine held half-virgates, eleven fardels and eight cottars'
lands. Those serving as shepherds (or hiring others in their place) numbered
one virgater, nine half-virgaters, three fardel-men and two cottars.

Elsewhere, such figures are recorded for almost no service *famuli* except
some reeves, whose circumstances also varied greatly. The reeve on the
Ramsey manor of Burwell in 1307 had four holdings, totalling over fifty-nine
acres.[49] At least four of the bishopric of Worcester reeves around 1380 held
virgates – Henry Man at Bibury, Walter Calewe at Hampton Lucy, Robert
Child at Hembury and John Tylare at Stoke Episcopi.[50] There was also a
ploughman (*enche*) at Hembury holding five acres, and a hayward with the
same. On the Westminster manors in the 1370s were three reeves holding
half-virgates, at Hardwicke, Islip and Kinsbourne; the rent allowances they
received ranged from 10s. at the first to 1s. at the last, while at Aldenham a
reeve with a virgate had a reduction of about 6s. At Sutton-under-Brailes
the reeve in 1379/80 was Peter Baron, a cotman allowed 3s. 4d. and 2s.
tallage; in 1398/9 the virgater Robert Hurry ran the manor for reductions
of 6s. in his rent and 6s. of the tallage he owed.[51] On the Berkeley manor
of Ham in 1343/4 the reeve was a virgater, allowed 10s. rent; in 1381/2
another virgater as reeve had a reduction of 20s. The Hinton reeve in 1339/
40 held a half-virgate.[52] At Monkleigh in 1369/70 the reeve held a fardel,
but in 1393/4 his successor had only half that. John Gybbes, the reeve of
Dawlish in 1453/4, received allowances totalling 16s. 5½d. for his two-fardel
holding.

Of the condition of individual stipendiaries, apart from their cash income,
grain livery and minor benefits, one knows nearly nothing. The manorial
accounts almost never name them, and the student therefore cannot link
them to the villagers who paid entry fines and heriots, or who appeared
before courts. But the accounts for the Glastonbury manors of Monkton
Deverill and Walton lift a corner of the veil, at least, in the early fifteenth
century, and record the names of some of the ploughmen. Monkton Deverill
at different times in the 1410s employed as stipendiaries four men: Elias
Burdon, Richard Phelps, John Moore and Richard Eyr. Phelps worked as
second plough-holder from Michaelmas 1412 to Michaelmas 1414, with Eyr
and Burdon as plough-drivers. Of Eyr the records are otherwise silent, but
Burdon was a half-virgater and by 1420 was dead. For some years from then,
Phelps and Moore worked as plough-drivers. At that time Moore and his

[49] Raftis, *Estates of Ramsey Abbey*, p. 282.
[50] WRO, 2636/009: 1/159/920497/7, 163/92163, 166/92261, 171/924154/8.
[51] WAM 8443, 14810, 8845, 26103; GRO, D1099/M31/46, 54.
[52] Berkeley MSS, Ham 27, 48, Hinton 19.

wife Agnes had been renting for several years a cottage, a curtilage and about sixteen acres of land scattered in five small tenements, though the lord reserved some grazing for his own plough-horses. By 1426 Phelps was dead, as the account noted the loss of the rent of 4s. 6d. a year from his cottage, curtilage and thirteen acres. The following account stated that his house was in ruins, and his courtyard worthless because they were dilapidated (*pro debilitate*), but that six acres of his land had been rented for cultivation.[53] Walton's accounts continue until 1440 to record the names of its stipendiary ploughmen, but there are many gaps in the series. Most of the ploughmen held fardels – John Crosse, Henry Bosyn, Andrew Baggeworth, Robert atte Wode – but Henry Heliar, William Luyde and John King were half-virgaters. Several of the appointments were short, and there was rapid turnover. Only three of the six employed at Michaelmas 1421 had been with the *famuli* twelve months before. Two of the six on staff at Michaelmas 1428 had not been there the previous autumn.[54] Most of these men came from families well established on the manor, many of which had supplied reeves in time past. Some of these ploughmen paid the lord more money each year to be quit of labour services for their tenements than they received from him in cash stipends. One dare not generalise from so small a sample, especially as the earlier Adderbury accounts implied that villagers gave up their holdings when they became *famuli*. These two manors, at least, seem to have employed ploughmen from the better-than-middling part of the village community, though on yearly contracts, and to have housed them in their own cottages rather than in the buildings of the manorial *curia*. To judge from the number who died in office, or soon after leaving it, they were not young men; and some, at least, were married. And one must assume that they were not so busy working for the lord that they had no time to work the lands they rented.

VIII

There was great diversity not only in the size of their holdings but also in the remissions of labour dues granted to service *famuli*, and likewise in the cash incomes and liveries of the stipendiaries – so much so that, with too many uncertainties, it is impossible to construct any index of the remuneration received by the class as a whole. In arguing that it was the loan of the lord's plough-team that brought the benefits of manorial serjeanties close to the earnings of the stipendiaries, Postan probably overestimated the value of Saturday ploughings and underestimated that of the relaxation of customary

---

[53] GAD 9695, 9880, 9881, 9699, 10722.
[54] GAD 10818–21, 10789–94.

services and the reductions in rent and taxes.[55] The reeve of Kinsbourne cited above, John atte Dych, received only 1s. as a rent allowance, but services worth some 24s. were remitted. He was excused the ploughing of 7½ acres, at 5d. an acre, 5 harrowing works worth 1d. each, 121½ winter works worth ½d. each, 25½ harvest works worth 2d. each, and the marling of 17 acres valued at 6d. an acre. These are really book-keeping entries: what was more important was that the reeve gained the time to tend his own half-virgate, without having to pay the lord to have his services commuted. He was given 4d. a year in gifts at Christmas and Easter, participated in the 'reapgoose' feast at the end of harvest, which cost the lord 8d. a head, and, unusually for someone holding in serjeanty, received an acre each of wheat and oats. The total value – without any Saturday ploughing – was close to the 40s. or so a serjeant would have received, typically 13s. 4d. in stipend and six and a half quarters of wheat, then worth about 4s. a quarter.

Even though those on the abbey's manors could use the lord's team for twelve acres of ploughing during the year, the ploughmen holding quarter-virgates or less on the Winchester and Glastonbury estates were certainly worse off than the reeve of Kinsbourne. Unfortunately the accounts do not make comparable valuations of the services they were excused. Moreover, one cannot be certain that they worked as long hours as those engaged as stipendiaries. When the bishop's manors made the transition from service ploughmen to stipendiaries, or back again, the number employed was identical, which suggests a rough comparability in the main tasks they performed. But it may have been easier for the manors to demand additional work from the stipendiaries at the odd jobs for which the reeves might have had to hire others – at spreading, turning and lifting the hay or mowing the second crop, carting dung from the *curia* to the fields, digging ditches and building hedges, reaping the peas and beans or stacking the sheaves before threshing, to cite but a few tasks often mentioned as done by the *famuli*. In a rare reference to the Peasants' Revolt, the Alciston account for 1380/1 recorded that the reeve and *famuli* had to help with weeding the grain as the tenants

---

[55] Postan, *The Famulus*, pp. 21–3. He asserted (without references) that, when the Saturday plough was commuted into money payment, it was 'seldom less than six shillings and sometimes, as on a number of estates of Bishops of Winchester it was often rated at eight shillings'. I have been unable to find, in any Winchester pipe roll of the thirteenth or fourteenth centuries, or in the mid-thirteenth century custumal (British Library, MS Egerton 2418) a payment higher than 6s., and only one manor, Adderbury, which paid even that amount. The payment recorded most frequently, especially on the manors in Highclere bailiwick, is 4s. 6d.; for over a century the pipe rolls noted that it had been raised from the previous level of 3s. per ploughman on the orders of Bishop John Gervais. It was, of course, the ploughmen who provided the labour for these Saturday ploughings; while on some manors (such as Merdon) the lord paid them each a halfpenny a day for working on their day off, on others the ploughmen paid the lord to be excused this obligation.

were unwilling to work because of 'Jakke Strawe and all his meynee'.[56] At Sutton-under-Brailes the previous year a ploughman had received a reduced stipend because he did nothing else (*quia nichil facit nisi tentor caruce domini*).[57]

These were stipendiaries, but the obligations of even the service *famuli* could stretch beyond the individuals to their households: at East Knoyle, for example, the wives of the ploughmen, cowman and shepherds (all of them holding in manorial serjeanty), with the dairymaid (a stipendiary), had to milk the cows and ewes and make cheese every day, receiving for their labour the milk they collected on Sundays.[58] Yet to have the stipendiaries available throughout the week, especially to look after the demesne animals, to have them in contracts enforceable by the king's courts, and to have them work more willingly, may have been sufficient reason for most lords to abandon serjeanty tenure before the end of the fourteenth century. For their part, many of the remaining service *famuli*, like those at Witney and Adderbury, seem to have been glad to surrender their holdings in a time of uncertain yields and falling grain prices, in return for the security of regular stipends and food liveries.

The stipends the lords paid, however, varied greatly. The bishops of Winchester and their stewards were powerful enough to impose an almost uniform pay structure across their vast and scattered properties. Despite the loss of labourers in the plagues, and the disorder of 1381, until the last decade of the fourteenth century nearly all the manors paid their male *famuli* about 4s. a year in money, and a quarter of middle-value hard grain (predominantly barley) every ten weeks. The dairymaid usually received less in money, and her quarter of grain had to last for sixteen weeks. On several manors the stipendiary *famuli* were paid with acres of grain, not with money; the *famuli* had to harvest it themselves and bear the loss in an age of declining prices. At Brightwell and Harwell this practice persisted well into the fifteenth century.

No other estate restricted the earnings of the *famuli* with equal success, even when the lord had economic and juridical power comparable to that of the bishop of Winchester. On the bishopric of Worcester estates around 1380, the ploughmen received 6s. a year at Stoke Episcopi, 7s. at Hembury, 8s. at Bibury and (for a plough-holder) 13s. at Hampton Lucy. Their quarters of grain had to last longer, for twelve weeks, but were of better quality;

---

[56] Chaucer, Nun's Priest's Tale: F.N. Robinson (ed.), *The Complete Works of Geoffrey Chaucer* (Oxford, 1957), p. 205; *quia tenentes noluerunt operare propter mundum Johannis Straw* (ESRO, Gage 44/37).

[57] GRO, D 1099/M31/46.

[58] HRO, Eccles. 2/159388.

at Bibury they were entirely of wheat. On the Bury St Edmunds manor of
Hinderclay the cash stipends of the ploughmen advanced from 3s. 6d. a
year in the 1340s to 5s. 4d. in 1380/1 and 6s. 4d. in 1399/1400. On other
Bury manors like Chevington and Risby the ploughmen and others had
taken two acres of 'schepcorn' as stipend in the 1340s, but received money
by the end of the century – 10s. a year at Risby and at Chevington 13s. 4d.
in 1420/1 and 18s. by 1438/9.[59] By the 1420s the abbot of Battle paid John
Gyles, the senior ploughman at Barnhorne, 26s. 8d. a year, with a bushel
of oats and a half-bushel of beans every week; his fellow at Apuldram,
William Cardon, had 20s. a year, with a weekly bushel about three-quarters
barley and the rest wheat.[60] These payments, though, were much more than
the junior ploughmen received. At Barnhorne John Grynche's stipend was
only 6s. 8d. annually, but he ate at the lord's table during the year at a cost
to the abbot of a penny a day; it may be no accident that the manor's bailiff
was one Thomas Grynche. At Sedgebarrow and Harvington the plough-
holders received 4s. a year in the 1340s, and the plough-drivers 3s.; forty
years later Worcester Cathedral Priory paid 11s. to all ploughmen at Sedgebarrow and 10s. to those at Harvington.[61]

   The Westminster manors pursued a variety of policies. At Aldenham the
major *famuli* had received acres of grain as stipend in the 1340s, but in
1380/1 the abbot paid the carter 20s. and the two ploughmen and the shepherd 6s. each. By 1396/7 the two ploughmen were again receiving grain in
the field, but the shepherd's stipend remained unchanged and the carter
was given an additional 5s. 4d. for a tunic.[62] Several other manors including
Kelvedon, Feering and Wheathampstead were still paying some of their
famuli with acres of standing grain at the end of the fourteenth century.
Birdbrook gave its main workers acres of grain in both the 1340s and 1380s,
but by 1402/3 the ploughmen were given 10s. and the carter 13s.4d. – the
manor's serjeant claimed to have paid them even more, but the abbot's
auditors reduced sharply the figures he submitted, in two cases halving
them.[63] Bourton-on-the-Hill paid cash stipends throughout, with the payment to the carter and ploughmen rising from 5s. 6d. in the 1340s to about
14s. in the 1380s and, for the carter and plough-holder, to 16s. in the 1390s;
the shepherd's stipend, however, rose from 5s. 6d. only to 8s. and 10s. in
the later decades.[64] At Turweston – a distant but important source of the
abbey's grain – the plough-holder's stipend rose from 5s. in the 1340s to

[59] SRO, E3/15.13/2.22; 15.3/2.30, 2.35.
[60] Huntington Library, Stowe MS 578; PRO, S.C.6/1017/17.
[61] WCDC, C607, C756, C760, C804.
[62] WAM 26086, 26103, 26118.
[63] *Ibid.*, 25441, 25476, 25498.
[64] *Ibid.*, 8276, 8307, 8317.

8s. in the 1380s and 12s. in the 1390s and that of the shepherd from 4s. 6d. to 7s. and 11s.[65]

The great majority of these *famuli*, even at the end of the fourteenth century, were still of unfree status. Those without this disadvantage seem better off, but not spectacularly so. The *famuli* on the Kentish estates of Canterbury Cathedral Priory, in *gavelkind* country, were relatively well paid before the Black Death, the ploughmen at Appledore, Chartham and Ebony already receiving 8s. a year in stipend and a good grain allowance. By 1380 or so the Chartham ploughman was getting 11s. and his fellow at Ebony 10s. annually; meanwhile, the Meopham ploughman's stipend had risen from 7s. to 12s.[66] The Adisham shepherd's stipend increased from 5s. to 9s., and Chartham's from 4s. 10d. to 10s. Several of these also obtained small increases in their grain deliveries.[67]

On the manors of Durham Cathedral Priory, where serfdom withered on the vine, the carter and ploughmen at Bewley had received 7s. a year and a grain livery of wheat and peas in the 1340s; by 1378/9 they were given 12s. in cash, more wheat, and no peas. The Ketton ploughmen's stipend increased from 7s. to 12s. or 13s. 4d., again with a better livery; that of the Pittington ploughmen went from 5s. in 1339/40 to 7s. in 1344/5, 14s. in 1380/1, and 18s. or 20s in 1420/1, though without a significant change in livery. The one Wardley *famulus* named as a ploughman received 20s. in 1380/1; the ploughmen there in 1337/8 had been paid only 8s. The annual payments to the carter and senior ploughmen at Westoe rose from 7s. to 18s., though with a small drop in grain delivery.[68] And individuals on other manors might also be freemen even though their fellows were not; the 1380/1 Walton account justified a higher stipend for the plough-drivers 'because they were of free condition'.[69] Even when not recorded explicitly, this may explain why some *famuli* received substantially more than others on the same manor.

The amount and content of the grain livery given to *famuli* was more important to their condition than the money payment most received. A Winchester ploughman in the 1340s, paid 3s. or 4s. in cash and some five quarters a year of barley worth on average about 19s., obviously depended

[65] WAM 7791, 7819, 7836.
[66] The stipends on the Canterbury estates are discussed more fully in M. Mate, 'Labour and Labour Services on the Estates of Canterbury Cathedral Priory in the Fourteenth Century', *Southern Hist.*, 7 (1985), pp. 55–67.
[67] Canterbury Cathedral, Dean and Chapter (hereafter CCDC), Bedel's Rolls, Adisham 39; Appledore 34, 55; Chartham 27, 41; Ebony 46, 66; Meopham 85, 102.
[68] DDCM, Manorial Accounts: Bewley 1339/40, 1343/4, 1378/9; Ketton 1339/40, 1343/4, 1380/1; Pittington 1339/40, 1344/5, 1380/1, 1420/1; Wardley 1337/8, 1380/1; Westoe 1340/1, 1375/6.
[69] GAD 10813.

more on the latter, especially if he planned to sell what he did not consume. This balance shifted over the decades, though, as most estates gradually increased the cash stipends even as the value of grain slipped downwards. A Glastonbury shepherd at Monkton Deverill in 1411/12, given 13s. 4d. in cash and a quarter of grain every twelve weeks (worth in that average year about 17s.9d. in all) was less dependent on the movement of the market than were his neighbours on the Winchester manors in Wiltshire. It was possible, though, for a labourer to be worse off than before, despite an increase in stipend, if the market value of his grain livery dropped when prices fell.

There were certain fringe benefits common to most of the estates by the mid-fourteenth century – the daily pottage made by the dairymaid for the *famuli* out of the oatmeal set aside by the lord (usually at the rate of two bushels a head), the pairs of new gloves given to the *famuli* at harvest time, the 'reapgoose' feast at the end of harvest, the small gifts at Christmas and Easter, the harvest weeks when, on many manors, the *famuli* ate together in some extravagance at the lord's cost (*ad mensam domini*). It was, however, very rare in the fourteenth and fifteenth centuries for lords to provide substantial quantities of food outside these seasons for those who still held in serjeanty, whatever Postan's conclusions about an earlier time.[70]

Some manors provided clothes as part of the package: the bailiff of Hinderclay in 1343/4 received a fur-edged gown costing 16s. 8d. and the keeper of the key (*claviger*, presumably the man with the key to the granary) was given one without the trimmings, costing only 10s. Another Bury manor, Chevington, spent 18s. in 1420/1 on clothes for the four *famuli* ploughmen, but paid out nothing in 1438/9 because they were cast-offs from the lord's wardrobe.[71] At Glynde in 1347/8, however, the unfortunate bailiff and hayward received no money because they received clothing from the lord.[72] Some manors merely bought the cloth for the garments. Occasionally lords gave additional payments to *famuli* who had worked beyond the normal call of duty, or as inducements to work better: Bourton-on-the-Hill gave its *famuli* 2s. during the harvest of 1398 so that they would work better (*ut melius operarent*), and Hinderclay gave its shepherd an extra two bushels of grain during lambing to reward their diligence (*pro diligenti labori suo*) in the spring of 1344.[73]

Even on the Winchester manors there were finally some improvements in the remuneration of stipendiaries. Around the turn of the century, on the

---

[70] Postan, *The Famulus*, p. 23.
[71] Chicago, Bacon MSS 466; SRO, E3/15.3/2.30, 2.35.
[72] ESRO, Glynde MS 1072.
[73] WAM 8317; Chicago, Bacon MSS 466.

manors that stayed in hand, the shortage of labourers forced the bishop to allow the stipends of major *famuli* to rise to 5s. a year. When this shortage compelled him to hire freemen, he too had to pay for the privilege. At Overton, by 1420/1, he paid 8s. 4d. each in stipend to the plough-holder and to three plough-drivers who were freemen, hired for the job because there were no neifs to do it. The carter, holder of a post normally better paid, received only 5s., 'and no more because he was from the unfree'. Droxford gave its oxherd and the senior shepherd 8s. in stipend, and a few manors – Bishopstone, Alresford and Beauworth – paid one or two labouring *famuli* 6s. 8d., but, with grain liveries unchanged for a century and more, these were almost the only signs of thaw.

For Winchester's manorial managers, reeves holding in serjeanty, the freeze continued unabated. Except at Twyford, which paid its reeve 12s. in salary, the reeves seem as poorly remunerated in the early fifteenth century as in the early thirteenth – though, with the shrinking of the demesne arable and the contraction of the arable, they probably had less work to do. But on the other estates studied the manorial managers fared better. New College in the 1390s paid the bailiff of Hornchurch 40s. a year and a bushel of wheat a week, and by 1420 his stipend had reached 50s.; the bailiff at Takeley in 1396/7 received his weekly bushel and a stipend of 20s., but by 1412/13 the latter had risen to 26s. 8d.[74] Richard Greene, the bailiff at Apuldram in 1421/2, was paid 33s. 4d. and the standard wheat allowance; around the same time, Battle Abbey paid the bailiff of Lullington 26s. 8d. and the same wheat livery (except during the six harvest weeks when he fed at the lord's table), and gave the bailiff of Alciston 100s. as stipend, but without grain.[75]

By this time a further development in the monetisation of manorial salaries was already advanced. Instead of paying their managers stipends and wheat, many manors were giving them cash wages in place of the grain; some Bury manors did this even before the Black Death. Ultimately some estates extended this also to certain of the labouring *famuli*. The serjeant who ran Bocking for Canterbury Cathedral Priory in 1376/7 took 24s. in stipend for the year and 78s. in wages, the serjeant of Bromham in the same year 10s. and 52s., and the warenner of Brandon a few years before 20s. and 60s. 8d.[76] The bailiff of Maristowe, who was also the holder of the lord's plough, received 10s. in stipend and 34s. 8d. in wages, but elsewhere in Devon it was becoming common to use wages to include both pay and living allow-

---

[74] New College, Oxford, 6389, 6417, 7006, 7022.
[75] PRO, S.C.6/1017/17, 1025/23; ESRO, Gage 44/73.
[76] CCDC, Bedel's Rolls, Bocking 40; PRO, S.C.6/1045/19, 1304/35.

ance.[77] Thus the bailiffs at Bishop Clyst, Monkleigh and Werrington received only wage payments of 52s., 43s. 4d. and 39s. respectively, while Bickleigh gave wages and nothing else to its two ploughmen and cattleman at four pence a week and to its bailiff at double that rate. At Ottery the shepherd's wage was 34s. 8d. in 1385/6 and the wage of the plough-driver was 21s. 8d.[78] Strange how the most plebeian of money terms should have originated among the aristocrats of the medieval manor, while stipend once described the humblest of payments!

One can conclude, then, that the condition of the *famuli* in the later Middle Ages was inconsistent but gradually improving on those manors that remained in hand; that in most places their remuneration was assuming a more modern form; and that an increasing number were free from serfdom. At this not unsatisfactory point, however, they disappear from sight. Only two or three of the manors studied were still in hand and cultivated by *famuli* at the end of the 1450s. By then almost all manors, intact or piecemeal, had been leased to farmers. Small manors, or pieces of larger ones, could be worked by the tenant and his sons without regular help. On the larger manors, leased intact to some grandee or speculator, the *famuli* probably survived in some form. But one does not know. By the end of the fifteenth century the traditional manorial *famuli* disappear from the historian's sight.

In one sense the fading of the *famuli* hardly matters, as gone too were their economic functions as ploughmen on the arable of great estates feeding large communities, and as shepherds of their flocks. For a while, in a period one is tempted to describe as an age of bastard manorialism, the farm workers of England passed through the same social changes as their superiors, probably doing relatively better than they did. But the harsher realities of the sixteenth century were close at hand. Among the descendants of the busy, but by no means destitute, *famuli* of the later Middle Ages would be the 'sturdy beggars' of Tudor times.

---

[77] DRO Plym., 70/93.
[78] DRO Ex., W1258/G3/2; CR1132; W1258/D71/3; W1258/D42/9; DRO Plym., 70/77.

12

The great slump of the mid-fifteenth century

JOHN HATCHER

MEDIEVAL ECONOMIC and social historians are accustomed to dealing in long periods of time: often in centuries rather than decades. Indeed, it has long proved seductive to divide the half millennium from the Norman Conquest to the accession of the Tudors into just two parts: the first, running from the late eleventh century to the early fourteenth – the 'long thirteenth century' – characterised by expansion, urbanisation, commercialisation and, eventually, overpopulation; the second – 'the long fifteenth century' – characterised by retreat and retrenchment. By common consensus, tendencies developed in the first era which became progressively more favourable to landlords and injurious to the mass of the peasantry, while in that which succeeded it these tendencies were thrown into reverse, with the result that the mass of the people benefited at the expense of their social and economic superiors. Such broad brush-strokes provided an invaluable aid to understanding in the early days of the subject, when the dominant features of the medieval economic and social experience were in the process of being teased from a mass of inchoate and seemingly disparate local detail, and they have continued to serve a useful purpose when introducing new students to the discipline. But such generalities are not conducive to the detailed reconstruction and examination of the distinct phases which made up these expansive eras.

In important respects the historiography of the later Middle Ages has failed to progress far beyond the stark alternatives posed in the early 1960s by the publication of *Economic Growth: England in the Later Middle Ages*, in which A.R. Bridbury portrayed an 'astonishing record of resurgent vitality

I am grateful to Richard Britnell for making a number of helpful comments on an early draft of this paper, and for letting me read the typescript of his chapter entitled 'The Economic Context' now published in A.J. Pollard (ed.), *The Wars of the Roses* (London, 1995).

and enterprise', in direct contradiction of the long-prevailing orthodoxy of M.M. Postan's 'age of recession, arrested economic development and declining national income'.[1] The major barriers to greater consensus perhaps arise less from a lack of information, which has expanded massively in the last thirty years, than from the quest for overarching generalisations which will hold true for all or most of the leading features of English economic and social development over the whole of the timespan. With so long a period and so vast a range of items on the historical agenda, it is no wonder that diversity and contradiction appear to loom as large as uniformity and coherence. Whether it be the demonstration of success or failure, advance or decline, growth or retardation, the abundance of individuals, social strata, manors, regions, sectors, industries, trades and towns in England during the hundred and fifty years after the Black Death are sure to be able to supply many contrasting examples. Accordingly, the more that is discovered about the experiences of the later Middle Ages, the more difficult it becomes to squeeze the emergent facts into a single descriptive or explanatory framework.

Many of the abundant confrontations which litter the historiography of the later Middle Ages could undoubtedly be eased by greater definition, for as with so many historical controversies a major source of discord stems from differences in the agenda being addressed rather than from contrary judgements about identical subject matter. Thus whereas Postan's seminal article on economic contraction was concerned solely with the fifteenth century, and its main thrust was directed towards the measurement of national income and aggregate levels of settlement, output and trade, Bridbury's book dealt with the later fourteenth century as well as the fifteenth, laid emphasis upon *per caput* measures and implied that since production fell less than population it was a period of 'economic growth'. Similarly, F.R.H. Du Boulay's subsequent depiction of the later fourteenth and fifteenth centuries as an 'age of ambition, of vitality and upward social mobility' draws its strength from stimulating accounts of such matters as the greater involvement of the laity in religion and education, the flowering of vernacular literature and improved opportunities for social advancement and emulation, rather than from the quality of its economic argument.[2]

At the same time, insurmountable obstacles are not only faced by those who seek to fashion propositions applicable to the economic and social history of the whole nation. As the seemingly interminable wrangles over the fortunes of late medieval towns amply demonstrate, easy solutions cannot

---

[1] A.R. Bridbury, *Economic Growth: England in the Later Middle Ages* (London, 1962); M.M. Postan, 'The Fifteenth Century', *Econ. Hist. Rev.*, 9 (1939).

[2] F.R.H. Du Boulay, *An Age of Ambition* (London, 1970).

be found merely by selecting and studying particular sectors, nor even by the adoption of greater precision in the language in which the debate is conducted. It is not simply that we are in need of a more adequate definition of what constituted a town, or of what constituted urban prosperity or decline, nor even that we need to find some improved means of taking into account the fortunes of towns in relation to their specialisms or the regions in which they were located, or of measuring the overall trend when some towns prospered while others declined. Rather, it is that some of the prime tasks that urban historians have set themselves are virtually incapable of satisfactory completion. The difficulties of constructing a concise and accurate overview of the experiences of the urban sector of England in the one and a half or two centuries of the later Middle Ages are compounded by the fact that the fortunes of each town changed over time, as did those of the multitude of external influences which played upon them from the broader economic contexts within which they existed.

Instead of constituting an era of either economic decline or economic growth, closer examination reveals that the fourteenth and fifteenth centuries experienced a succession of subperiods each with its own distinctive characteristics. Renewed scrutiny of the first half of the fourteenth century, for example, has discerned the existence of at least three subperiods – the closing years of the long era of expansion, the series of disasters which struck arable and pastoral farming from 1315, and the quarter century or so which spanned the end of these crises and the onset of the Black Death in 1348.[3] And it has similarly been demonstrated that there were many contrasts between the third and the fourth quarters of the fourteenth century.[4] In fact, Bridbury's optimistic assessment of resurgence, vitality and economic growth fits certain decades in the later fourteenth century much better than it does the major part of the fifteenth, while Postan's gloomy sentiments might well understate the severity of the depression experienced by the nation from the 1440s to the 1470s.

There is much to be said for studying shorter periods of history in addition to the processes and sequences which spanned them. The blurring of chronology and the skipping from decade to decade in search of the most informative sources are unlikely to illuminate the distinctive features of the phases and cycles through which later medieval England passed, or the interconnections which existed between its various socio-economic sectors and strata; and

---

[3] B.M.S. Campbell (ed.), *Before the Black Death: Studies in the 'Crisis' of the Early Fourteenth Century* (Manchester, 1991); E. Miller and J. Hatcher, *Medieval England: Towns, Commerce and Crafts, 1086–1348* (London, 1995), pp. 393–429.

[4] A.R. Bridbury, 'The Black Death', *Econ. Hist. Rev.*, 2nd ser., 26 (1973); J. Hatcher, 'England in the Aftermath of the Black Death', *Past and Present*, 144 (1994).

these are precisely the matters which are in need of more light. What happened to the fortunes of, say, the generality of landlords, greater and lesser, or towns, large and small, is not to be discovered and interpreted solely by recourse to the records of landlords and towns; especially if, as is often the case in the fifteenth century, those records are patchy and partial. Much can be contributed by 'lateral' or 'functional' based study. For landlords and towns existed within a broad economic, social and political context, and inevitably their economic fortunes were influenced by the nature of that context.

Similarly, although there is broad agreement that the population of England in the early sixteenth century was at most no more than half the size it had been at its pre-Black Death peak, very little is known of the path which it actually followed over much of the intervening 200 years or more. Our understanding is also inhibited by the comparative slightness of our knowledge both of the economic impact of declining population and of economic fluctuations driven by forces independent of population movements. The works of Malthus and Ricardo are devoted primarily to the mechanisms and consequences of rising population, which was the threat which they perceived the world in which they lived was facing. Nor have historical demographers accorded the phenomenon of declining population anything like the amount of attention they have devoted to its growth, for the simple reason that substantial and prolonged population decline is a rare occurrence in the history of the western world. The possibilities exist that there may have been times during the late Middle Ages when sudden falls in the numbers of people from already depleted levels brought diseconomies rather than enhanced benefits, and that there were some major fluctuations in the level of economic activity which owed little to demographic factors.

I

Because of the strength and duration of the long-term deflationary trend there is an understandable tendency to treat the fifteenth century as a continuum, broken only by some upward movement in its closing decades. Such considerations have encouraged beliefs not only that the living standards of peasants and labourers continued to improve progressively, but that the enterprising landlord, the innovative farmer, the well-located town or the favoured industry, did not find it excessively difficult to escape virtually unscathed from the clutches of recession. The intention of this essay is to examine, primarily using research published in the last couple of decades or so, whether such optimistic sentiments are applicable to the whole period, and in particular to the middle decades of the century when an extraordinary

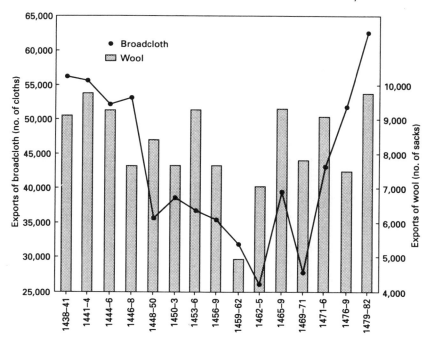

Figure 12.1   Exports of cloth and wool, 1438–82 (annual averages).
Source: M.M. Postan and E. Miller (eds.), *Cambridge Economic History of Europe*, II: *Trade and Industry in the Middle Ages*, 2nd edn (Cambridge, 1987), p. 242.

range of powerful depressive forces combined to impose an enduring and wide-ranging slump of precipitous proportions upon the long-term recessionary trend. Whereas it is apparent, when surveying the later Middle Ages as a whole, that there was growth as well as decline, and winners as well as losers, during the depths of this slump it is difficult to find many examples of growth or significant numbers of winners, and thus impossible to make a convincing case for the overall gains outweighing the pains. With scarcely an exception all available indices of production and exchange weakened, with the result that in almost all sectors of the economy substantially less was being produced, bought and sold than previously, with predictably adverse consequences for profits, employment and incomes.

Figures 12.1 and 12.2 highlight the severity of the collapse which occurred in the 1450s and 1460s in those branches of England's overseas trade which are able to be quantified; although it must be borne in mind that the civil war in addition to harming trade may well have led to some inefficiencies

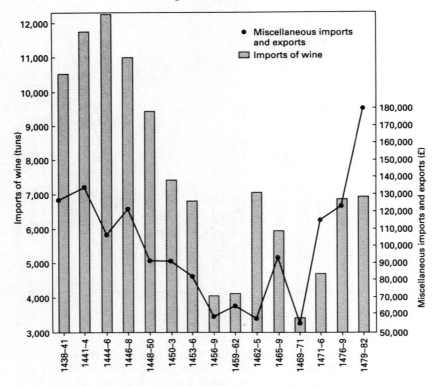

Figure 12.2   Imports of wine and imports and exports of miscellaneous merchandise, 1438–82.
Source: as for Figure 12.1.

in the collection of customs duties. The rise of England's cloth exports is one of the great success stories of the later Middle Ages, but a comparison of the average numbers of broadcloths shipped overseas between 1438 and 1448 with those shipped between 1448 and 1471 reveals a contraction of almost 40 per cent, from around 55,000 annually to only 34,000. Imports of wine fell by more than 40 per cent, from an annual average of around 11,500 tuns in 1438–48 to little more than 6,000 tuns between 1448 and 1471. Receipts from payments of poundage, which provide a partial measure of the import and export of a wide range of miscellaneous commodities subject to *ad valorem* duties, confirm the pervasive character of the slump in overseas trade by falling once again by around 40 per cent, from more than £120,000 per annum in the former period to less than £75,000 in the latter. Although exports of raw wool held up better, registering a decline of

Table 12.1 *Price indices of some major commodities, 1400–99*

	Wool	Cloth	Wheat	Barley	Oxen	Cows	Cheese
1400–9	100	—	100	100	100	100	100
1410–19	87	—	93	92	92	85	106
1420–9	81	100	86	83	98	90	109
1430–9	83	118	113	91	96	79	135
1440–9	74	114	76	64	89	74	109
1450–9	55	93	87	70	96	69	92
1460–9	78	93	86	80	100	88	73
1470–9	57	102	89	71	103	84	74
1480–9	76	128	105	85	98	91	75
1490–9	54	120	83	79	91	71	83

Sources: D.L. Farmer, 'Prices and Wages, 1350–1500', in E. Miller (ed.), *Agrarian History of England and Wales*, III: *1348–1500* (Cambridge, 1991), pp. 444, 467; J.H. Munro, 'Monetary Contraction in the Late-Medieval Low Countries, 1350–1500', in N.J. Mayhew (ed.), *Coinage in the Low Countries (880–1500)* (BAR International Series, 54, (Oxford, 1979), p. 155.

less than 15 per cent between the two periods, unlike the other commodities they had already experienced massive contraction during the agrarian crises of the 1430s; more than 40 per cent fewer sacks were exported between 1440 and 1470 than had been shipped overseas in the first three decades of the fifteenth century.

Table 12.1 shows that the decline in the quantities of commodities traded was accompanied by falls in their prices. The customs valuation placed on unfinished broadcloth was on average 20 per cent lower in the 1450s and 1460s than it had been in the preceding two decades, which meant that in value terms exports may well have declined by more than half. The price of wool, which had been falling since the beginning of the century, dropped by a further 25 per cent or more in the 1450s and, after recovering briefly in the 1460s, plunged again in the 1470s; which meant that the value of wool exports fell by more than a third. Independent estimates made by J.L. Bolton of the total value of England's overseas trade, which necessarily involve a fair bit of guesswork since not all branches of trade are adequately recorded in surviving customs accounts, suggest a decline of some 31 per cent in the value of England's imports and 34 per cent in the value of her exports when 1442–52 is compared with 1452–61.[5]

In addition to the sheer scale of the slump in overseas trade, there were a number of features which added substantially to its impact. First, its duration: in general it was not until the later 1470s that the levels of the

[5] J.L. Bolton, *The Medieval English Economy, 1150–1500* (London, 1980), p. 307.

mid-1440s were regained. Second, the instability of trade, and the violence of some of the downswings. For example, annual exports of broadcloths, which had averaged nearly 54,000 in 1446–8, plummeted to only 35,000 in the succeeding two years when fighting was resumed with France. Third, and most important, a broadly parallel but partially independent slump in the internal English economy compounded the grave damage inflicted by the frequency and severity with which her trade was disrupted by internal and external wars, state-sponsored piracy and embargoes,[6] and by the recessions which took place in the economies of her major trading partners.

There was a massive reduction in the output of coin from almost all major European mints in the 1440s and 1450s, including England's, which resulted, it is generally believed, in a widespread monetary shortage which was even more severe than the so-called 'Great Bullion Famine' of 1395–1415.[7] According to one authority, when the scarcity of money reached 'its worst point' in the early 1460s, 'the economy of Europe ground to a halt at every level, from the humblest purchases of bundles of leeks, up to the great merchants, whose galleys had to row away with goods unsold'.[8] On the other hand, it must be remembered that the money supply prior to the 'bullion famine' had been boosted by very high mintings in the 1420s and early 1430s, and that the rate at which new coins were minted, for which there are good data, is but one element in the determination of the total stock of money, for which there are not. Nonetheless, despite the tendency for some monetary historians to overstate the significance of their chosen field of study, there can be no doubt that the total stock of coin in circulation did shrink appreciably, and recent work has also suggested that, far from compensating for the fall in physical money, the supply of credit seems also to have shrunk.[9] There can be no doubt therefore that monetary factors contributed substantially to the depression of aggregate demand in the mid-fifteenth century.

Finally, the role of population movements in influencing the behaviour of the economy at this time needs to be considered, albeit briefly and superficially. The possibility remains that the impact of powerful depressive forces acting independently of population may have been accentuated by falling

---

[6] H.L. Gray, 'English Foreign Trade from 1446 to 1482', in E. Power and M.M. Postan (eds.), *Studies in English Trade in the Fifteenth Century* (London, 1933), pp. 1–38.

[7] For a review of evidence and a detailed bibliography see 'The Great Bullion Famine of the Fifteenth Century' and 'The Question of Monetary Contraction in Late Medieval Europe', in J. Day, *The Medieval Market Economy* (Oxford, 1987).

[8] P. Spufford, *Money and its Use in Medieval Europe* (Cambridge, 1988), p. 362.

[9] P. Nightingale, 'Monetary Contraction and Mercantile Credit in Later Medieval England', *Econ. Hist. Rev.*, 2nd ser., 43 (1990).

numbers. Knowledge of fifteenth-century demography remains thin, but it is becoming increasingly unlikely that for seventy-five years or more population simply stagnated at the level it had reached *c.* 1400, and recent findings are suggestive that significant falls may have occurred around and after 1450. By far the most robust evidence, but also the most difficult to relate to national mortality trends, comes from the monasteries of Christ Church Canterbury and Westminster, whose monks suffered a catastrophic decline in life-expectancy after mid-century.[10] Pointing in a similar direction is the increasing attention which is being devoted to peaks of crisis mortality in the population at large in the later fifteenth century. Studies of northern England have highlighted the severity of disease in the 1430s and in the ten years from 1475; the plague outbreak of 1479 is thought to have been particularly lethal, as is the 'sweat' of 1485.[11] Little is known about fertility, but the frequency with which historians are now observing a growing scarcity of people in the later fifteenth-century countryside, beyond that which might simply reflect a heightened unwillingness to hold land,[12] is highly suggestive of falling population levels, especially since there are also contemporaneous signs of a sharp reduction in the rate of migration from country to town, and in the numbers of inhabitants in most towns.[13]

II

A slump in the English agricultural economy ran broadly parallel with that in overseas trade, though it is not possible to date its onset as precisely since timing varied somewhat from sector to sector and region to region. It is also a matter of fine judgement to determine when the pre-existing long-term recessionary trend worsened enough to constitute a distinct phase. Nonetheless, throughout the country, by almost whatever measure might be chosen — commodity prices, rents, occupancy rates — a trough was reached within the

[10] J. Hatcher, 'Mortality in the Fifteenth Century: Some New Evidence', *Econ. Hist. Rev.*, 2nd ser., 39 (1986); B. Harvey, *Living and Dying in England, 1100–1540: The Monastic Experience* (Oxford, 1993), pp. 112–45.

[11] A.J. Pollard, *North-Eastern England during the Wars of the Roses: Lay Society, War and Politics, 1450–1500* (Oxford, 1990), pp. 46–8; P.J.P. Goldberg, 'Mortality and Economic Change in the Diocese of York, 1390–1514', *Northern History*, 24 (1986).

[12] For example, the comments by R.H. Britnell, M. Mate and H.S.A. Fox referring to eastern, south-eastern and south-western England in E. Miller (ed.), *Agrarian History of England and Wales* (hereafter *AHEW*), III: 1348–1500 (Cambridge, 1991), pp. 122–3, 619, 730.

[13] R.H. Britnell, *Growth and Decline in Colchester, 1300–1525* (Cambridge, 1986), pp. 204–5; S.H. Rigby, *Medieval Grimsby: Growth and Decline* (Hull, 1993), pp. 130–1; A. Dyer, *Decline and Growth in English Towns, 1400–1640* (London, 1991), pp. 39–40.

period from *c.* 1440 to *c.* 1470,[14] a period which also experienced a sharp contraction in the number of markets and in the amount of trade which was carried on within them.[15] This slump followed on, and was undoubtedly gravely exacerbated by, the series of natural disasters which preceded it. Long-term climatic research has suggested that the 1430s was the coldest and harshest decade experienced by England between 1100 and 1970, and it closed with a catastrophic succession of three extremely poor harvests.[16] The price of a quarter of wheat in the three years between Michaelmas 1437 and Michaelmas 1440 averaged 10s., 14s. and 8s. respectively, compared with an average price of 6s. between 1400 and 1430. In 1438 wheat yielded only 1.89 times the seed sown, allowing for tithe, which was barely half the average yield of the century after 1350, which placed it on a par with the very worst harvest on record, that of 1316.[17] As in the agrarian crises of the early fourteenth century, harvest failures were accompanied by sharply rising livestock mortality. While some regions suffered less than others the effects of the crisis were widely felt, and mortality rates of sheep and cattle soared across southern England as a result of disease and bad weather.[18] North-eastern England was very badly affected, and A.J. Pollard has recently argued that 'the economic depression of the mid-century North-East was largely the result of [the agrarian crisis of the late 1430s] and not the end point of a slow remorseless contraction'.[19]

But if the existence of the mid-century slump is widely acknowledged, the severity and pervasiveness of its impact is more contentious, and there are those who would seek to minimise it by pointing out that falling food prices and high wages were good for the majority of the population, that landlords who responded positively to the requirements of their tenants could shore up their rent rolls, and that farmers who switched from the less profitable sectors into the more profitable could prosper. The paths to success for landlords, we are told, lay in improved methods of estate manage-

---

[14] The literature is too vast to be listed in this brief survey, but for recent presentations and analyses of the evidence see E. Miller, 'Land and People', D.L. Farmer, 'Prices and Wages, 1350–1500' and the regional studies written by various contributors to chs. 2, 3 and 7 in *AHEW*, III.

[15] For a recent study of the reduction of trade in agricultural produce see R.H. Britnell, *The Commercialisation of English Society 1000–1500* (Cambridge, 1993), pp. 156–60.

[16] H.H. Lamb, *Climate: Past, Present and Future*, 2 vols. (1972–7), II, pp. 457–9, 564–5; J.Z. Titow, 'Le climat à travers les rôles de comptabilité de l'évêché de Winchester (1350–1450)', *Annales: Economies, Sociétés, Civilisations* (1970), pp. 341–2.

[17] D.L. Farmer, 'Prices and Wages', in *AHEW*, II, pp. 787–98; Farmer, 'Prices and Wages, 1350–1500', in *AHEW*, III, pp. 502–8.

[18] M.J. Stephenson, 'Wool Yields in the Medieval Economy', *Econ. Hist. Rev.*, 2nd ser., 41 (1988), pp. 383–4; M. Mate, 'Pastoral Farming in South-East England in the Fifteenth Century', *Econ. Hist. Rev.*, 2nd ser., 40 (1987), pp. 525–6.

[19] A.J. Pollard, 'The North-Eastern Economy and the Agrarian Crisis of 1438–40', *Northern History*, 25 (1989), pp. 103–4.

ment, and for farmers in specialisation as well as in diversification: in switching from rye and oats to barley and flax, from arable to pasture, and from sheep to cattle; in fattening cattle for urban markets, in rearing rabbits for their meat and fur, and in exploiting woodlands and fishponds. Indeed, if this line of argument is pushed much further it might even prove tempting to believe that those who ended up suffering at any time in the fifteenth century did so because of their own incompetence rather than the severity of the adverse economic forces which assailed them.

It is the general applicability of these optimistic sentiments which will be questioned, and it will be doubted below whether more than a small minority of incomes drawn from the profits of farming were maintained, still less enhanced in these decades. Because both the rental of land and the amount which was occupied fell, the aggregate income drawn from rent rolls must also have fallen, and if the incomes of some rentiers remained stable or increased they could only have done so because they acquired more land or enjoyed the benefits of exceptionally favourable local circumstances. It is also necessary when assessing the impact of the agrarian slump to avoid the confusion which is often allowed to arise between the total income of a lord and that part of his income which he drew from his lands; increases in the former could occur, of course, while the latter was decreasing, and the acquisition of additional manors could produce increases in the latter although the income from each manor was falling. Nor does the fact that most landlords continued to receive large landed incomes mean that those incomes were as large as they had previously been, and the fact that an estate or farm was well-run does not of itself mean that the profits it generated failed to decline.

When examining the incomes of the nobility of later medieval England K.B. McFarlane repeatedly sought to expose what he saw as the 'fallacy of the proposition that falling rents meant a poorer family', and he did so by demonstrating from the experience of a number of selected families 'how the process of accumulation offset any decline in manorial profits'.[20] Such statements drew further significance from the compelling evidence which he put forward of the decline which took place in the numbers of baronial families during the course of the fifteenth century. However, although it is demonstrably true that the wealth of some baronial and gentry families grew even during the worst storms of the century, it is demonstrably implausible that more than a handful could have done so because of the buoyancy of their estate revenues rather than through the acquisition of more assets or the growth of their non-agricultural incomes.

[20] K.B. McFarlane, *The Nobility of Later Medieval England: The Ford Lectures and Related Studies* (Oxford, 1973), p. 186 and *passim*.

Furthermore, prudent and rewarding as many of the measures taken by enterprising farmers undoubtedly were, they could have offered the majority only partial and temporary protection in a time of deepening depression. While there is abundant evidence that landlords and farmers commonly responded in a creative fashion to the difficult conditions that prevailed in traditional sectors of husbandry from the late fourteenth century onwards, and took advantage of the opportunities which arose from the new consumer demands generated by rising living standards, it is important to realise that the scale of compensation which could be offered by such innovations was limited. First, because arable and sheep farming were by far the most dominant agricultural pursuits, and were destined to remain so. Second, and no less obvious, because the scope for profitably expanding alternative activities was not open to all: it depended, among other things, upon the location, quality and resource endowment of the land in question and the demand for such products as it was capable of producing. Third, because the opportunities for doing so became increasingly restricted as the depression lengthened and deepened, and as the hitherto buoyant demand for alternative products was in turn satisfied by the substantial increases in supply which it called forth.

III

Certainly the prospects for arable farming, which was already suffering the effects of long-term decline, did not improve in the mid-fifteenth century. The average prices of wheat, rye, barley and peas in the 1440s were lower than they had been for a century, and those for oats lower than for ninety years. Moreover, these low prices were not due to bountiful yields, which might have enabled farmers to maintain their incomes by selling more. On the contrary, a comparative analysis of yields and prices in the six years between 1429 and 1434 and the eight years between 1440 and 1453 for which data are available, indicate that the sales revenue received from the produce of land devoted to wheat, barley and oats declined by between a fifth and a quarter.[21]

But it is animal husbandry which has been seen as a panacea for the hard-pressed farmer, and as the 'single venture that could be made to yield a profit throughout the [fifteenth] century'.[22] Contemporaries were in no

---

[21] The calculations have been made from data provided in Farmer, 'Prices and Wages, 1350–1500', in *AHEW*, III, pp. 431–525. The yields are derived from Winchester demesnes, but the prices are more widely based.

[22] C. Carpenter, *Locality and Polity: A Study of Warwickshire Landed Society, 1401–1499* (Cambridge, 1992), p. 181.

doubt as to its relative attractions before the onset of the slump in mid-century: the collapse of grain prices in the late fourteenth century and the persistence of low prices and high wages in the early decades of the fifteenth encouraged the conversion of arable land into pasture on a very substantial scale virtually nationwide, and it is notable that many lords continued to keep and even expand their flocks and herds long after they had abandoned arable cultivation.[23] So powerful were the forces working against concentration upon the growing of grain that animal husbandry gained ground even in the traditional arable heartlands of England, such as the Avon valley and Feldon district of Warwickshire, where in the mid-fourteenth century virtually no land at all, with the exception of common pastures and unenclosed woodland, had been designated as pasture.[24] This long-term shift of agricultural resources seems to have gathered pace in the first half of the fifteenth century as the market for wool was supported by the needs of an expanding indigenous textile industry, and the prices of meat and dairy products held up much better than those of grain.

But such evidence does not by itself demonstrate that pastoral husbandry was highly lucrative even before the mid-century slump, only that it was proving more attractive for an expanding proportion of farmers than the growing of cereals. Sheep farming was the prime pastoral activity in most regions, but the myth that it consistently produced bumper profits has been an unconscionable time dying, despite abundant evidence of rising labour costs and falling wool prices through much of the late fourteenth and fifteenth centuries.[25] In fact data from the Winchester estates reveal that the real gross income per fleece fell almost continuously in the later Middle Ages, and registered a decline of more than half between the brief post-Black Death peak of 1375–9 and the nadir reached between 1440 and 1454, when the series ends.[26] Furthermore, since the price of wool fell much faster than that of grain, the likelihood that many of those who reared sheep did so

[23] Stephenson, 'Wool Yields', p. 388; M. Bailey, 'Sand into Gold: The Foldcourse System in West Suffolk, 1200–1600' *Agric. Hist. Rev.*, 38 (1990), pp. 43–5; B.M.S. Campbell and M. Overton, 'A New Perspective on Medieval and Early Modern Agriculture: Six Centuries of Norfolk Farming', *Past and Present*, 141 (1993), pp. 77–8; *AHEW*, III, pp. 48–9, 56–9, 77–84, 115–17, 120–1, 161–70.

[24] According to the Warwickshire feet of fines between 1345 and 1355, 96 per cent of the Avon valley and Felden was arable and 4 per cent meadow; but in 1496–1500 57 per cent was designated as arable, 9 per cent as meadow, 33 per cent as pasture, and the remaining 1 per cent as woodland.

[25] M.M. Postan cautioned against accepting the hypothesis that the expansion of sheep farming compensated for the decline of arable husbandry (M.M. Postan (ed.), *The Cambridge Economic History of Europe*, I: *The Agrarian Life of the Middle Ages* (2nd edn, Cambridge, 1966), p. 591; and the case against doing so was made in much more detail in T.H. Lloyd, *The Movement of Wool Prices in Medieval England*, Economic History Review Supplements, VI (Cambridge, 1973), pp. 24–6.

[26] Stephenson, 'Wool Yields', p. 388.

because of the attractions of low labour requirements and the abundance and cheapness of pasture rather than the lure of corpulent gains is reinforced.[27]

Additionally, the increasing dependence of farmers upon sales of wool in the century after the Black Death eventually served to heighten their exposure to the slump in the wool trade when it arrived in the mid-fifteenth century. It has been calculated that the average price which an English grower received in the 1400s for a stone of wool was 4.2s.; in the 1440s it was 3.1s.; and in the 1450s it plummeted to a mere 2.3s. Nor was the collapse of wool prices a mere temporary blip: across the whole of the second half of the fifteenth century farmers received on average 25 per cent less for their wool than they had in the first half, and some 40 per cent less than they had in the first half of the preceding century.[28] In some disastrous years, such as 1452–3, 1455–6, 1459–60, 1474–7 and 1478–9, they received less than 2s. a stone if they were fortunate to be able to find a buyer at all. Such was the deterioration in the market for wool that growers often found it impossible to sell all their crop even for such nugatory recompense, and the glut some-times forced those who could afford it to store part of their crop in the hope of an upturn in demand and for fear of driving prices even lower; growers were also often forced to spend time and money searching for potential purchasers in distant places, and to give extended credit to those who would take wool off their hands.[29] Of course, these expedients were not readily available to the bulk of smaller producers who must have faced ruin.

As if sharply deteriorating market conditions and frequent outbreaks of disease were not enough, sheep farmers also appear to have suffered from a prolonged decline in the weights of fleeces which, to judge from the evidence of Winchester bishopric manors, began in the 1370s and accelerated in parallel with the slump in the wool trade; by the mid-1450s fleece weights were only half what they had been a century before.[30] The combined impact of these unfavourable influences could be disastrous: the fleeces of the sheep of Canterbury Cathedral Priory which had been sold for 4d. or 4½d. each during the early years of the fifteenth century, realised only 1½d. to 2½d. in mid-century, while those sold on behalf of the bishop of Winchester plunged in price from an average of 5.6d. between 1366 and 1380 to a mere 1.4d. in 1453.[31] Such reductions in sales revenue must have been little short

---

[27] For the price of wool relative to wheat see Lloyd, *Wool Prices*, pp. 45–51.

[28] Calculated by D.L. Farmer (*AHEW*, III, p. 467), from the 'annual means' in Lloyd, *Wool Prices*, pp. 41–4.

[29] Mate, 'Pastoral Farming', p. 527; M. Mate, 'The Occupation of the Land: Kent and Sussex', in *AHEW*, III, 121–2; J.M.W. Bean, 'Landlords', in *AHEW*, III, pp. 574–5; M. Bailey, *A Marginal Economy? East Anglian Breckland in the Later Middle Ages* (Cambridge, 1989), p. 290; Lloyd, *Wool Prices*, p. 26.

[30] Stephenson, 'Wool Yields', pp. 376–81.

[31] Mate, 'Pastoral Farming', p. 526; Stephenson, 'Wool Yields', 387–8.

of catastrophic for farmers who were not only already suffering the effects of high wages and a long-term downward drift in agricultural prices, but attempting to recover from the losses inflicted by the harvest failures and recurrent livestock epidemics of the later 1430s. The inevitable consequence was sharply falling profits for all who kept sheep and a wholesale retreat from sheep farming by landlords great and small.

The duchy of Lancaster gave up sheep farming in Pickering and on most of its Berkshire manors in the 1440s. The duke of Buckingham, who in the second quarter of the fifteenth century had maintained large flocks on his lands in Holderness, and Ralph, Lord Cromwell, who had done likewise on his manor of Tattershall (Lincs.), both abandoned their enterprises around 1450,[32] as did the Beauchamps, earls of Warwick, and the bishopric of Worcester.[33] Somewhat more favourable conditions, produced in part by the demands of the local textile industry, encouraged the duchy of Lancaster to persist for a little longer on a selection of manors in Wiltshire and Dorset, but a sorry tale of plummeting textile production, falling wool prices and a recurrent inability to dispose of clips forced a final abandonment there also in the 1460s.[34]

The accounts of Horsley manor (Glos.) for the years 1444–52 reveal that sheep farming scarcely made any profit at all for Bruton Abbey, when allowance is made for the rent which might have accrued if the pastures and meadows had been leased rather than occupied by the demesne flock. Small wonder then that by 1460 the abbey's flock and the meadows, and probably also the pastures, had been leased; though the depressed state of the trade meant that the lessee was only prepared to pay £6 13s. 4d. a year in total for them.[35] The wool produced by Syon Abbey manors in south-east England, which in the early 1440s was regularly sold to London merchants, failed to find any buyers in 1446–7, and in the following year the buyers that were found paid only 2s. 0d. a stone. For a considerable time after 1450 Syon Abbey failed to sell any wool at all, and in 1453 the accumulated clip amounting to more than ten sacks (containing over 2,600 fleeces) was handed over for disposal to a London draper. It still took many more months to sell and even then the price was a disappointing £3 6s. 8d. a sack. Understandably, the abbey gave up the unequal struggle with the market, and for the

[32] Bean, 'Landlords', pp. 574–5, 582–3; Lloyd, *Wool Prices*, pp. 24–5.
[33] C. Dyer, *Lords and Peasants in a Changing Society: The Estates of the Bishopric of Worcester, 680–1540* (Cambridge, 1980), p. 130; C Dyer, *Warwickshire Farming, 1349–c. 1520: Preparations for Agricultural Revolution* (Dugdale Society Occasional Papers, 27, Oxford, 1981), p. 16.
[34] Lloyd, *Wool Prices*, p. 26; E. Miller, 'Occupation of the Land: The Southern Counties', in *AHEW*, III, p. 151.
[35] Lloyd, *Wool Prices*, p. 26.

next two years all the wool which its flocks produced was made up into cloth for the use of its own household members.[36]

Next in importance after arable cultivation and sheep farming came cattle raising. The rewards derived from producing agricultural commodities are determined by movements in costs as well as in selling prices, and although the price of oxen moved largely in concert with that of wheat in the later Middle Ages the low labour requirements of stock rearing and cattle fattening could make them relatively more attractive. The prices of bread grains must have derived some support from the curtailment of supply as farmers cut back on their arable, but the price of meat drew positive support from a substantial rise in *per capita* demand as the diets of ordinary people improved along with their real incomes; the published price series for oxen and pigs display no tendency to fall significantly at any time in the fifteenth century.[37] Cattle rearing expanded in the opening decades of the century in very many parts of the country, and the economies of 'wood-pasture' regions with their diversity of employments and resources appear to have fared relatively better than the 'champion' arable regions of England. Increasingly, dairying and meat production took precedence over the rearing of draught animals, and the fattening of cattle to be eaten by urban consumers could prove especially lucrative, to judge from the relatively high rents that were sometimes obtained from well-located meadows and cattle pastures and the successful careers of graziers supplying captive markets on the outskirts of such towns as Birmingham, Coventry and Colchester, and in Tottenham a few miles north of London and Havering a like distance to the east.[38]

But in few, if any, regions did cattle raising thrive throughout the fifteenth century. Decline set in early in the poorly favoured East Anglican Breckland, due to the saturation of its markets for dairy products and the inherent inferiority of its pastures; and in south-eastern England, where cattle were not reared in substantial numbers and therefore were unable to offer much compensation for the increasing difficulties encountered in sheep farming, herd sizes began falling from the 1420s as did the production of cheese.[39]

---

[36] Mate, 'Pastoral Farming', p. 527.

[37] Farmer, 'Prices and Wages, 1350–1500', in *AHEW*, III, 434–5, 457.

[38] E. Miller, 'Occupation of the Land: Yorkshire and Lancashire', in *AHEW*, III, p. 48; H.S.A. Fox, 'Farming Practice and Techniques: Devon and Cornwall', in *AHEW*, III, pp. 315–19; A. Watkins, 'Cattle Grazing in the Forest of Arden in the Later Middle Ages', *Agric. Hist. Rev.*, 37 (1989), pp. 12–25; Pollard, *North-Eastern England*, pp. 36–7; Dyer, *Warwickshire Farming*, 17–21, 30–1; Britnell, *Growth and Decline in Colchester*, p. 142; D. Moss, 'The Economic Development of a Middlesex Village', *Agric. Hist. Rev.*, 27 (1980); M. McIntosh, *Autonomy and Community: The Royal Manor of Havering, 1200–1500* (Cambridge, 1986), p. 142. See also H.S.A. Fox, 'The Chronology of Enclosure and Economic Development in Medieval Devon', *Econ. Hist. Rev.*, 2nd ser., 28 (1975).

[39] Bailey, *A Marginal Economy?*, pp. 294–5; Mate, 'Pastoral Farming', pp. 527–9.

The 'boom years' for stock raising and dairying on the uplands of north-eastern England were brought to a swift end by disease and famines in the crisis years of 1438–40, and in the general economic contraction of the succeeding decades herds were reduced in size, direct management was abandoned, vaccaries remained unleased and pasture rents fell. Symptomatically, the number of cows on the prior of Durham's vaccary at Muggleswick declined from 600 in 1436 to 433 in 1446, and to 159 in 1464.[40] In Lancashire the rentals of Rossendale and Pendle Hill vaccaries faltered in mid-century, and in the peaks of Derbyshire 'the years 1448–56 witnessed a slump in pastoral activity of unprecedented proportions'.[41] The national series of cheese prices is not very robust but it too offers supporting testimony of glut in the later fifteenth century; for the price of a wey of cheese, having fluctuated narrowly between 9s. and 10s. from the 1370s to the 1440s, fell to 8.44s. in the 1450s and remained below 7s. over the next three decades.[42]

It is only to be expected that there were some exceptional regions and individuals who rode out the depression more successfully than most, and the flourishing of cattle grazing by the gentry and yeomanry of Warwickshire has been repeatedly proclaimed.[43] As we have seen, however, it cannot serve as an index of the performance of pastoral husbandry in England as a whole. Indeed, such was the repute of Warwickshire cattle that they were were sold not only to butchers in local towns but to Londoners, and in 1457–8 when the victualler of Calais bought 417 oxen for shipment, 186 came from Coventry and a mere 21 from nearby Romney marsh. Located centrally on the main droving routes from Cheshire and North Wales to London and with convenient access to the towns of the midlands, some Warwickshire graziers were endowed with enough advantages to enable them to survive relatively well even in these troubled decades.[44] But despite some exuberant support from its historians, the success of Warwickshire cattle grazing in mid-century was a qualified one: the size of most of the herds in the county was relatively small before the closing decades of the century, and none of the county aristocracy and few of the gentry kept cattle commercially, using them instead primarily to supply meat and dairy produce to their households.

[40] Pollard, *North-Eastern England*, pp. 51, 61–2; R.B. Dobson, *Durham Priory, 1400–1450* (Cambridge, 1973), p. 277.

[41] I.S.W. Blanchard (ed.), *The Duchy of Lancaster's Estates in Derbyshire, 1485–1540* (Derbyshire Archaeological Society Record Series, 3, 1967), p. 11.

[42] Farmer, 'Prices and Wages, 1350–1500', in *AHEW*, III, p. 467. In the troubled years of the 1430s the calculated price rose exceptionally to 12.33s per wey. The quality of cheese is, of course, far from homogeneous (Mate, 'Pastoral Farming', pp. 528–9).

[43] See, for example, C. Dyer, 'A Small Landowner in the Fifteenth Century', *Midland History*, 1 (1972); *Dyer, Warwickshire Farming*, pp. 17–21; Carpenter, *Locality and Polity*, pp. 176–93; Watkins, 'Cattle Grazing in the Forest of Arden'.

[44] Dyer, *Warwickshire Farming*, p. 20; Mate, 'Pastoral Farming', p. 527.

The aptly named Deys of Drakenage did thrive, apparently via cattle grazing, but records of their activities in the 1450s and 1460s are frustratingly indirect, and much of the renowned John Brome's profits would appear to have come from using his privileged position as an influential member of Henry VI's household to supply it with meat at inflated prices during its residence at Coventry or Kenilworth; when Brome was forced to dispose of his livestock on the open market he usually had to accept lower prices or even a loss.[45]

The rabbit was a rare and expensive beast in the early fourteenth century, and the rise of commercial rabbiting after the Black Death testifies both to the rapidity with which consumer demand – in this case for both meat and cheap fur – could grow and the enterprise with which landlords could respond to the opportunities of investing in new profitable ventures.[46] As a result the supply of rabbits soared as more and more warrens were constructed and expanded, and in a few ideal locations revenues rose to significant levels: in Suffolk sales from the manors of Brandon and Lakenheath reached £40 in the mid-1380s, and an extraordinary £75 at Methwold in 1391. However, as the supply of rabbits spiralled ever higher so their price plunged ever lower: the producer price of East Anglian rabbits in the century before 1350 had averaged 3½d. each, in the half-century after 1350 it averaged 2½d., in the first half of the fifteenth century less than 2d., and in the 1460s only 1¾d.[47] Inevitably the profit margins of commercial rabbiting were severely eroded, and landlords progressively abandoned direct management of their warrens. By the middle decades of the fifteenth century some warrens were difficult to lease even at much reduced rents, and arrears accumulated. Although rabbits continued to provide a welcome source of additional protein and income for some lords – the Catesby's, for example, kept rabbits at Radbourne (Warws.), killing for home consumption and sale 100–300 couples annually from 1448–58[48] – they were a significant source of wealth for very few.

Woodlands have been identified by some historians as assets with immense potential for many owners, but in reality their value was often hard to unlock and even more difficult to sustain. In the remoter parts of England the general standard of woodland management tended to be poor, and in order to be of significant and consistent longer-term commercial value woodlands

[45] Carpenter, *Locality and Polity*, pp. 189–90.
[46] M. Bailey, 'The Rabbit and the Medieval East Anglian Economy', *Agric. Hist. Rev.*, 36 (1988), pp. 1–20.
[47] *Ibid.*, p. 11. The eclectic price series collected by Thorold Rogers shows the price of a couple, which had been 6d. in the 1400s, remaining at 4d.–4½d. from the 1430s to the end of the century (J.E.T. Rogers, *A History of Agriculture and Prices in England*, 7 vols. (Oxford, 1866–1902), IV, pp. 345, 355.
[48] Dyer, *Warwickshire Farming*, pp. 19–20.

needed careful husbandry as well as convenient access to sizable markets, which in practice meant that they had to be located very close to towns, to industries like iron making which used substantial amounts of fuel, or to water communications. Certainly, if the timber could be conveniently transported, handsome profits might be gained by the wholesale felling of mature trees, but the extreme length of the growth cycles in forestry meant that excessive felling inevitably resulted in the erosion of future income. What is more, the market for timber and firewood was competitive and conditions deteriorated in the late fourteenth and fifteenth centuries.[49] Falling population led both to reduced demand and increased supply: as the pressure on the land eased and cultivation contracted, the numbers of non-woodland trees rose, and the depredations of woodlands by owners desperate to boost their flagging incomes swelled the glut. Not surprisingly prices tumbled.[50] In consequence it was only for a fortunate few that woodland constituted a source of income which was both substantial and regular.[51] Margaret Paston, in straitened circumstances in 1471 when unable to collect rents or sell her farm produce, appreciated the dilemma far better than many of the historians who have followed her: she was forced to contemplate felling her woods but it was against her inclination towards good husbandry, and all the more so 'since other landlords were resorting to the same expedient and prices were low'.[52]

IV

It was inevitable that the sharp deterioration which took place in the markets for almost all agricultural commodities in mid-fifteenth-century England should have further undermined the land market and led to an intensification of the downward pressure on rents. With relatively few exceptions, wherever surviving documentation is good enough to record it, the demand for land slumped decisively below the already depleted levels of the preceding decades. From region after region, estate after estate, and manor after manor comes testimony of falling rents and of difficulties in collecting rents, of a scarcity of tenants and of an abundance of vacant holdings and dilapidated

[49] J. Hatcher, *The History of the British Coal Industry*, I: *Before 1700* (Oxford, 1993), p. 28.
[50] Rogers, *History of Agriculture and Prices*, III, pp. 255–72; O. Rackham, *Ancient Woodland: Its History, Vegetation and Uses in England* (London 1980), p. 167; P. Bowden, 'Statistical Appendix', in J. Thirsk (ed.), *AHEW*, IV: *1500–1640* (Cambridge, 1967), pp. 845–50; E.H.P. Brown and S.V. Hopkins, *A Perspective of Wages and Prices* (London 1981), pp. 45–9.
[51] See, for example, the small sums normally yielded by the bishop of Worcester's woodlands (Dyer, *Lords and Peasants*, pp. 175–6).
[52] Britnell, 'Occupation of the Land: Eastern England', in *AHEW*, III, pp. 59, 61.

buildings – and all on a heightened scale.[53] That such developments had an adverse effect upon the incomes which landlords were able to extract from their estates is beyond question, but quantification is no easy matter, especially since it involves the separation of these revenues from other non-landed sources of income.

The accurate measurement of the incomes which landlords drew from their farms and tenants requires plentiful and precise records of the cash which they actually received. In the majority of cases, however, documents in adequate numbers and of sufficient quality have not survived, and instead historians have sometimes been tempted to place undue reliance upon intuition and upon sources which detail the aspirations of landlords rather than their concrete achievements. Reconstructing rudimentary profit and loss accounts and balance sheets from medieval financial records is a formidable task, even for the best-documented of estates, and one which has scarcely been started. The difficulties are further compounded by accounting conventions which often obscure as much as they reveal, and by the conventions of an age which was loath to admit losses and obdurate in its insistence on treating arrears as the personal debts of the officials under whom they had accumulated. It is frequently left to the historian to break arrears down into more meaningful categories, and to reveal that they often included, in addition to recent defaults, such divers elements as long-standing and irrecoverable debts, instalments due to be paid in the future, and shortfalls arising from legitimate reductions in the rents of particular holdings which had been agreed by estate officials. The absence of arrears in a series of intermittent accounts is no less inconclusive, for it may well reflect a recent writing-off of debts rather than the collection in full of all dues; and valors drawn up on the basis of a theoretical maximum potential income have many times been shown to be grossly misleading because a substantial proportion of that income was unable to be collected.[54] The auditors of the bishop of Durham in 1463–4 placed an annual value of £2,940 on the bishopric estates, but the contemporaneous series of receiver-general's accounts reveal that the bishop actually received a very substantially lower income: less than £1,900 on average in the decade from 1459 to 1469, and only £1,761 in 1459–60, the worst year for which record survives in the fifteenth century.

---

[53] The evidence was summarised some years ago in J. Hatcher, *Plague, Population and the English Economy, 1348–1530* (London, 1977) pp. 36–43; an up-to-date and far more detailed review of national experience is contained in E. Miller (ed.), *AHEW*, III.

[54] See, for example, the careful discussion of sources and their limitations in A.J. Pollard, 'Estate Management in the Later Middle Ages: The Talbots and Whitchurch, 1383–1525, *Econ. Hist. Rev.*, 2nd ser., 25 (1972); J.T. Rosenthal, 'The Estates and Finances of Richard, Duke of York (1411–1460)', *Studies in Medieval and Renaissance History*, 2 (1965), pp. 122–46; R.R. Davies, 'Baronial Accounts, Incomes and Arrears in the Later Middle Ages', *Econ. Hist. Rev.*, 2nd ser., 21 (1968).

The artificiality of the 1463–4 valor is highlighted by the fact that the receiver-general's account of that very year shows that receipts from current dues amounted to only £1,100.[55] In similar vein, the archbishop of Canterbury's bailiwick of Otford, which according to a valor of 1446 should have been worth £413 annually, produced on average no more than £303 in the 1450s and £262 in the 1460s.[56]

This is not to say, of course, that landlords as a class were hopelessly inefficient, or that more than a small minority of them failed to make determined efforts to maintain their incomes. The bishop of Worcester, for instance, resolutely attempted to swim against the mid-century tide of economic adversity by instituting 'an orgy of administrative activity', which included a general inquiry into the condition of his estates and a thoroughgoing tightening of procedures. As a result lands which had been 'lost' were rediscovered, defaulters were threatened with distraint of goods and eviction, and the rents of some holdings were even raised. But, almost inevitably, conditions in the real world soon swamped the bishop's paper aspirations, and arrears escalated alarmingly as tenants failed to pay in full the rents demanded of them.[57] At the same time, it has sometimes been maintained that the gentry, lacking the reserves of fat bestowed by the immense wealth of most members of the lay and ecclesiastical aristocracies, kept more closely in touch with conditions on their manors and with the markets for the produce which they yielded, were able to satisfy much of their needs from the produce of their own farms, and were more enterprising and efficient in the management of their tenants. But even if this were true, and it may well have been, it would fall far short of demonstrating the general applicability of the recently expressed opinion that 'a combination of careful attention to the administration of rents and assiduous exploitation of the limited opportunities for profit could carry a lesser landowner triumphantly through the worst conditions of the fifteenth century'.[58]

Any indiscriminately optimistic conclusions must derive whatever plausibility they possess from the inadequacy of surviving gentry records which, when they exist at all, normally consist of little more than a thin scattering of manorial accounts and an occasional valor or survey, and often centre on the running of home farms rather than commercial operations. Almost all those who have studied the fortunes of this important landholding stratum would concur that fifteenth-century records are 'not adequate for a general

---

[55] Pollard, *North-Eastern England*, pp. 53–4.
[56] Hatcher, *Plague, Population and the English Economy*, p. 41.
[57] Dyer, *Lords and Peasants*, cf. pp. 165–7 with 183–9.
[58] Carpenter, *Locality and Polity*, p. 193. See also E. Acheson, *A Gentry Community: Leicestershire in the Fifteenth Century, c. 1422–c. 1485* (Cambridge, 1992), pp. 59–68.

assessment of the economic fortunes of the class as a whole', and the deficiency is often especially pronounced in the the mid-century. Thus at present it is impossible to construct from them 'a general assessment of the economic fortunes of the class as a whole' in any county.[59] In the absence of satisfactory estate records the balance of probabilities has to be drawn with the assistance of a wider range of less specific but still powerful inferences from the behaviour of the economy at large; the tenor of which, as we have seen, is to restrain firmly any excess of confidence. The fortunes of gentry families in the mid-fifteenth century were far more likely to have been boosted by the beneficence of their superiors, by inheritances, by marriages to heiresses and by the receipt of fat professional fees and annuities than by the profits of estate management.

A favourable interpretation of the experiences of the general run of lesser landlords at the height of the mid-century slump is rendered less plausible still by the uniquely informative correspondence of the Pastons, a Norfolk gentry family for whom only a very thin scattering of estate records survives. Because the correspondence provides the comments, reflections and advice received and given by the family and its officers, it is capable of illuminating crucial areas where the records of more conventionally documented estates cannot reach.[60] The Pastons were rentiers and, in common with a number of Norfolk landlords who held manors in the fertile and conveniently located eastern coastal regions of the county, they received rents in both cash and kind, most notably in barley which they usually malted before it was sold. The letters passing between members of the family and their employees in the 1460s and 1470s reveal starkly the chronic problems which they faced not only in finding tenants and in collecting the rents that had been agreed with them, but in disposing of the commodities which they received by way of rent. The local market seems frequently to have been glutted with malt and wool, and both the Pastons and their neighbours at Ormesby Hall were repeatedly forced to search for merchants in more distant places, including Yarmouth, London, Newcastle upon Tyne and Flanders, who were capable of purchasing significant quantities without depressing prices further. This involved them in delays and substantial extra costs in travel and transport,

---

[59] Carpenter, *Locality and Polity*, pp. 163–4. For similar comments relating to Leicestershire see Acheson, *A Gentry Community*, p. 56. For C. Richmond the lack of estate records 'may be a blessing. It makes impossible a discussion of what financial value to the Pastons their estates may have been, which would have been, as such discussions invariably are, drawn-out, tedious and necessarily inconclusive' (*The Paston Family: The First Phase* (Cambridge, 1990), p. 30).

[60] See in particular the perceptive article written by R.H. Britnell, 'The Pastons and their Norfolk', *Agric. Hist. Rev.*, 36 (1988), pp. 132–44; together with Richmond, *The Paston Family*, pp. 23–31; C.E. Moreton, *The Townshends and their World: Gentry, Law and Land in Norfolk, c. 1450–1551* (Oxford, 1992), pp. 141–2.

but even so sales were far from being assured. In April 1465 Margaret Paston lamented that the price of malt had fallen to 2s. 2d. a comb of four bushels; the next month a servant wrote to John I saying that he was unable to find a merchant who would pay more than 1s. 10d. a comb, and in August Margaret informed John that the price in Yarmouth was only 1s. 4d. In such circumstances 'even their most strenuous endeavours could achieve no more than making the best of a bad job'.[61]

V

Those who have searched for silver linings among the black clouds of the mid-century depression have sometimes found them in the contention that falling rents constituted a redistribution of income from landlords to their tenants, from the richer strata of society to the poorer. But this is a proposition that needs to be applied to this period with caution. For the fundamental cause of the downward spiral of rents and the accumulation of arrears at this time lay not in the deteriorating efficiency of seigneurial management, nor yet in the ability of tenants to win concessions in excess of those warranted by market conditions: it lay in an acutely depressed land market, within which prices, profits and rents all moved downwards in accordance with the classical laws of economics. It was also a time of sharply reduced levels of economic activity. The manner in which the slump impacted on the various strata in rural society depended on the mix of sources from which they derived their incomes: the extent to which they farmed for the market or for subsistence, and the degree to which they relied on wages and therefore on opportunities for paid employment. It is an eccentric inversion of the normal consequences of any slump to judge that tenant farmers whose livelihoods primarily depended upon the sale of produce were typically net beneficiaries from the combined effects of falling prices and lowered rents. In the mid-fifteenth century when incomes generated by land were falling there was less to be distributed between owners and occupiers, and even substantial reductions in rent might well prove insufficient to compensate farmers for the reduced prices which they obtained when they sold their produce.

The Paston's servants understood the situation well, and advised against insisting on payments which would undermine the solvency of farmers, and against the rigorous enforcement of clauses in their leases which might lead to their eviction. For, as James Gresham pointed out in the early 1460s, tenants faced problems in disposing of the produce of their farms comparable

---

[61] Britnell, 'The Pastons', p. 139.

to those faced by the Pastons themselves, and he reported to his master that 'Halman can not yet gete monay, for his cornes arn at so litell price that he can not utter them, and yet ther noman wole bye it for al the gret chep'. In 1467 the Pastons were counselled that the rents for the demesne lands of Snailwell and Spore should be lowered, and Sir James Gloys, the family chaplain, advised that 'if ye vndo your tenauntes with ouer-charging of your fermes it shall distroy your tenauntes and lordshepes'.[62] Richard Calle even advised his master to withdraw a legal action against a man whom he believed would prove 'a gret fermour of your the next yere'. Such 'pampering' of tenants might well reveal 'how unusually, how uniquely disadvantaged mid-fifteenth-century landowners were', but it also reveals how reluctant tenants were to take up land and how difficult many of them found it to continue in occupancy despite the concessions which were granted to them.[63] The advice given to the Pastons was good advice, and it is virtually identical to that which many commercial and agricultural landlords have received from their agents in the recession of recent years. When general trading conditions are adverse and bankruptcies and vacancies proliferating it is often more prudent to assist defaulting tenants in their struggles to continue in business than to enforce strictly the terms of leases and face the daunting prospect of having to find new tenants who would prove more remunerative.

The terms upon which demesnes were leased were largely determined by market forces. Land was usually demised for a cash rent, uncluttered by custom; the lessee was commonly under an obligation to keep the manorial buildings in a good state of repair at his own expense; and the landlord was expressly permitted to repossess the land and distrain the property of the farmer if the rent was not paid promptly. In practice, however, during the worst decades of the mid- and later fifteenth century many farmers were permitted to remain in occupation despite falling seriously into arrears. The bishops of Worcester suffered chronically but not exceptionally in this regard. When the demesne at Stoke Bishop, just two miles from the centre of Bristol, was leased in 1447 along with the park and some other lands to Richard Baylly, a Bristol merchant, for a term of sixty years at a rent of £8 annually, it must have seemed a satisfactory deal in the circumstances. But by 1456 Baylly owed £54 and had failed to pay any rent at all since 1451. However, despite the scale of his debts, eviction and distraint were not resorted to: instead in 1458 a deal was struck whereby Baylly was pardoned £34 of his arrears in return for paying £10 in cash. He was still in possession of the demesne and park in the 1470s, when his arrears amounted to more than £17. Nicholas Poyntz, the farmer of the bishop's demesne at Bibury,

[62] Quoted in *ibid.*, pp. 137, 141.
[63] Richmond, *The Paston Family*, p. 29.

did eventually suffer eviction in 1449–50, but only after he had repeatedly failed to meet his obligations in full over a period of fifteen years, despite securing a reduction of 30 per cent in the agreed rent. However, the bishop fared little if any better with the new tenant, for in 1459 he too was in arrears, to the tune of £22.[64]

There are many other signs of the extreme slackness of the land market in the mid-fifteenth century in addition to the readiness with which landlords granted remissions of entry fines and rents, and the reluctance with which they resorted to eviction as a means of dealing with debt-ridden tenants; these included a marked increase in investment by landlords in the repair of the cottages and farm buildings of unoccupied holdings in order to entice potential tenants.[65] But commercial farming required investment by the farmer and, since money was short, land abundant and the prospects for making a good profit were slim, it was sometimes impossible to find anyone who was prepared to pay anything at all. John Paston was told in 1460–1 that there were no takers at any price for forty acres of arable at Bolton (Norf.) because it was out of tilth and the buildings needed repair, but also that it was not possible to find a farmer for Mautby demesne, which was good land and situated only three miles from the coast, and that some of the land at 'Spitlynges' had to be let 'in smale parcelles because I cowde gete no fermour for it'.[66] In order to find tenants in the 1450s and 1460s many of the demesnes of the archbishop of Canterbury had also to be split into small parcels and let piecemeal for short terms, and even then some were left vacant. The archbishop's demesne at Wrotham, for instance, lay untenanted from 1463 to 1486.[67]

While more substantial men were limiting their commitment to commercial farming and suffering from poor and uncertain returns, lower down the scale among the peasantry the occupiers of large landholdings could sometimes be 'afflicted by extreme poverty'.[68] Large peasant tenancies of thirty acres or more were often difficult to let and not infrequently surrendered. Most significantly, evidence from virtually all parts of the country shows

[64] Dyer, *Lords and Peasants*, pp. 181–2, 184; C. Dyer, 'A Redistribution of Incomes in Fifteenth Century England', *Post and Present*, 39 (1968), p. 29.

[65] R.H. Hilton, *The English Peasantry in the Later Middle Ages* (Oxford, 1975), pp. 191–3; C. Dyer, 'Occupation of the Land: The West Midlands', and H.S.A. Fox, 'Occupation of the Land: Devon and Cornwall', in *AHEW*, III, pp. 88, 171.

[66] Britnell, 'The Pastons', pp. 137, 141; Moreton, *Townshends*, p. 141; Richmond, *The Paston Family*, p. 26n.

[67] F.R.H. Du Boulay, 'Who Were Farming the English Demesnes at the End of the Middle Ages', *Econ. Hist. Rev.*, 2nd ser., 17 (1965), pp. 444–61.

[68] C. Dyer, 'Tenant Farming and Farmers: The West Midlands', in *AHEW*, III, p. 642; M. Mate, 'The Economic and Social Roots of Medieval Popular Rebellion: Sussex in 1450–1451', *Econ. Hist. Rev.*, 2nd ser., 46 (1992), 672.

that, despite the cheapness and abundance of land, relatively few clusters of holdings were built up by aspirant 'proto-yeomen' before the closing decades of the century, and those that were seldom survived intact beyond the death of the men who had acquired them. Only twelve of the forty holdings of forty-five acres and more which were assembled on the great manor of Halesowen from 1431 to 1500 survived for more than one generation.[69] Of course, the failure to produce heirs may have played a part in the transience of multiple landholdings, but so too did the forces relentlessly undermining the profitability of commercial farming. Nor must it be assumed that all the larger peasant landholdings were farmed intact: subletting in small parcels could often prove more lucrative.

Wage labourers and smallholders who farmed primarily to feed themselves were the undoubted beneficiaries of the long-term economic trends of the later Middle Ages, for their standards of living and quality of life soared as real wages rose, rents fell and the bonds of villeinage dissolved. They undoubtedly continued to enjoy prosperity in the mid-century decades, but it is questionable whether the slump brought them yet further gains. Cheaper food had obvious advantages for those who were net purchasers, as had falling rents for those who occupied land and buildings, but eventually the conditions which forced down both the profits which could be derived from farming and the intensity with which the land was cultivated must also have curtailed the opportunities which the landless and smallholders had to secure casual work in agriculture, and the widespread contraction of industrial and craft activity must have further restricted employment. Moreover, the obstacles in the way of making much money out of production for the market, even using family labour, must have severely curtailed the scope for further economic and social advancement. The period has more the flavour of comfortable bucolic sufficiency than of rampant rising prosperity.

Our knowledge of the earnings of labour in the Middle Ages is relatively thin and unsophisticated. There is an excessive reliance upon the records of institutional employers, which have a strong bias towards stable money wages punctuated by short, sharp movements which are almost invariably upwards, and we know very little about fringe benefits, the extent of the duties of employees, or the number of days which they worked. The notoriously 'sticky' nature of wage rates, that is the extraordinary absence of falls, is a striking feature of all periods of history and it is especially pronounced

[69] Z. Razi, 'The Myth of the Immutable English Family', *Past and Present*, 140 (1993), pp. 30–1; M. Mate, 'Tenant Farming and Farmers: Kent and Sussex', in *AHEW*, III, p. 702; H.S.A. Fox, 'Tenant Farming and Farmers: Devon and Cornwall', in *AHEW*, III, p. 731; Dyer, *Lords and Peasants*, pp. 311–12.

in the data which we rely most heavily upon. In the seven centuries of building workers' wages spanned by the Phelps Brown and Hopkins series the only recorded reduction before the late nineteenth century occurred in craftsmen's rates in the deflation of the 1330s.[70] But the absence of reiterations of the Statute of Labourers between 1444 and 1495 may reflect an easing of the demand for labour, and some evidence has been gathered from manorial records which suggests that there was discernible downward pressure on the wages of a range of labourers, servants and artisans between the 1440s and the 1480s.

The series constructed by J.H. Munro from a variety of sources display a fall of 21 per cent in agricultural wages and almost 8 per cent in the wages of craftsmen during this period, although much of this admittedly took the form of a retreat from the short-term peaks to which wages had risen in the later 1430s when harvest failures had forced up the price of foodstuffs.[71] Although it would obviously be unwise to place too much weight upon the precise movements of such aggregations of data drawn from different places and the performance of different tasks, a number of supporting instances have been gathered by M. Mate from Kent and Sussex: at Barton (Kent) the pay for mowing an acre which had been 8d. in the early fifteenth century, and had risen to 10d. in the troubled years of the 1430s, subsequently dropped to 7d. where it remained for three decades; and at Lullington and Alciston (Suss.) the wages of some carpenters were reduced from 5d. to 4d. a day in the late 1440s. Falling food prices, of course, helped to offset reductions in money wages, but as food became cheaper in mid-century it became increasingly common in Sussex for the money wages of craftsmen to be cut in return for allowing them to eat at the lord's table.[72] The net impact upon the incomes of the poorer strata of the countervailing influences of occasional wage cuts, probable reductions in the availability of work and lower food prices, must at present be a matter of conjecture, but no such doubt exists about the impact of trade depressions upon those families who derived substantial parts of their incomes from working part time in slump-afflicted industries. As J.N. Hare has demonstrated, depression in Wiltshire cloth-making brought misery to the families of husbandmen and cottagers as well as to artisans and clothiers.[73]

---

[70] Brown and Hopkins, *A Perspective of Wages and Prices*, pp. 1–12.

[71] J.H. Munro, 'The Behaviour of Wages and Prices during Deflation in Late Medieval England and the Low Countries', paper presented to the Ninth International Economic History Congress (Berne, 1982).

[72] M. Mate, 'Tenant Farming and Farmers: Kent and Sussex', *AHEW*, III, p. 695.

[73] J.N. Hare, 'The Wiltshire Risings of 1450: Political and Economic Discontent in Mid-Fifteenth Century England', *Southern History*, 4 (1982), pp. 15–19.

VI

The ebbs and flows in the incomes of each noble and gentry family and each ecclesiastical household depended upon changes in the number of assets which they held as well as upon fluctuations in the revenues which each of those assets produced, but since rents and the profits of farming fell overall so too must the aggregate incomes of those who lived off them. The appetites of those in the upper and middle strata of society spanned the whole range of commodities available in fifteenth-century England, from wooden trenchers to gold dishes, from blanket cloth to embroidered silks, and from major building works in stone and brick to the repair of humble cottages and fences, and any reductions in their levels of consumption impacted upon the urban, commercial and industrial sectors of the economy as well as upon the agricultural. The pressure to economise must have been especially sharp in the worst decades of the mid-century, and it must have severely affected the businesses of those merchants and manufacturers who supplied them and the levels of employment in the neighbourhoods where they resided.

Although experience varied in accordance with fortunes and inclinations, a number of general features have been discerned in the management of the households of the rich.[74] Steps were often taken to achieve a tighter control over household expenditure, which paralleled the steps which were taken to improve the collection of revenues: accounts were audited more thoroughly and new administrative systems introduced to eliminate waste and fraud.[75] Reductions were also made in the size of many households, and in the comfort with which their lesser members were sustained. Contemporaries complained of a decline in traditional standards of hospitality and largesse among the magnates, engendered by a creeping parsimony which expressed itself in the evolution of more private life-styles in which the consumption of the most expensive luxuries was increasingly restricted to a diminishing circle of family, friends and high officials. Fewer guests and visitors were entertained, and some were even expected to pay for their keep. Although the quality and furnishings of prime residences were often improved, magnates were becoming more sedentary and it was common for the number of houses which they maintained to be reduced, with the result that total

[74] The expenditure patterns and management of the households of the nobility and religious institutions are examined in ch. 4 of C. Dyer, *Standards of Living in the Later Middle Ages: Social Change in England, c. 1200–1520* (Cambridge, 1989).
[75] The series of exceptionally detailed accounts kept by Thetford Priory are an extreme example of the painstaking accounting procedures introduced by many households in the mid- and later fifteenth century; they are being edited by Dr D. Dymond for publication by the British Academy.

expenditure on buildings was diminished. The number of residences used by the bishops of Worcester, for example, was cut from fifteen to six.[76]

It has been estimated that the numbers of monks, canons, friars and nuns in England fell from around 17,000–18,000 in *c.* 1300 to some 11,000–12,000 two hundred years later. Reducing the size of religious houses was an effective means of balancing income and expenditure, but sometimes thrift went much further. Although there were only around fifty monks at Bury St Edmunds abbey under abbot William Curteys in the later 1430s, compared with some eighty in the late thirteenth century, he introduced a stringent financial code which laid down that the whole monastery was to be fed for no more than £480 11s. 4d. a year, with 2s. 6d. allowed weekly for each monk and 10d. for each groom.[77] Expenditure on English monastic and cathedral buildings plummeted; religious, social and cultural factors all had a part to play, of course, but perhaps it is no mere coincidence that the numbers of major cathedral and monastic projects begun and in progress tracked the path of economic fortunes and slumped to their lowest point in mid-century.[78]

Once again the sparsity of surviving documents makes comparable analysis of gentry household expenditure far more tenuous, and it is usually possible to speak only in the most general terms and without much reference to changes over time.[79] That few gentry families faced ruin is manifest, and although their more limited financial resources meant that they were to this extent more vulnerable to economic fluctuations than their superiors, they commonly ran home farms from which they were able to provision their households relatively cheaply, and they were often able to draw fees and annuities from the crown, the magnates and the church for the performance of administrative and legal duties and for past or future service in war. Nonetheless, many, probably most, gentry families must have felt the pinch in the worst decades of the fifteenth century, and have been forced to economise. When John Paston I sought a financial favour from Sir John Heveringham he was refused, for Heveringham claimed that, because he could not collect what was due to him, he was experiencing difficulties in maintaining his own 'livelihood'; and Margaret Paston in the early 1470s learnt that her cousin Sir William Calthorpe was in such straitened circumstances because 'he can not be payd of his tenauntes as he has before this tyme',

---

[76] Dyer, *Standards of Living*, p. 100.

[77] *Ibid.*, p. 98.

[78] R. Morris, *The Cathedrals and Abbeys of England and Wales* (London, 1979), p. 180.

[79] For recent discussions emphasising the paucity of records, see Carpenter, *Locality and Polity*, pp. 196–211; Acheson, *A Gentry Community*, pp. 135–42; S.M. Wright, *The Derbyshire Gentry in the Fifteenth Century* (Derbyshire Record Society, 8, Chesterfield, 1983), pp. 22–5.

that he was planning to reduce the size of his household. It was a fate which Margaret had herself faced in 1469 when she confessed to her son to be 'so symppely payed thereof that I fere me I xale be fayn to borrowe fore my-selfe ore ell to breke vp howsold, ore bothe'.[80] Even less is known about the expenditure levels of those lower down the social scale – the demesne lessees, yeomen farmers and peasants with large holdings – but it is inconceivable that many, perhaps most, did not also have to reduce their consumption as a consequence of the agricultural depression.

Rarely is it possible to quantify the scale of home demand, but some suggestive data exist for wine, tin, lead and furs, of which the upper social strata were the major consumers. The massive fall in the consumption of wine in England, which some of the lesser members of the gentry apparently entirely ceased to drink in the fifteenth century,[81] is directly reflected in the collapse of imports by 40 per cent or more noted above. Tin was primarily used for the manufacture of pewter tableware at home and abroad, and its output, for which there are very good data, halved between c. 1400 and the early 1460s.[82] The most important use of lead was in major building works, for roofing, guttering and piping, and its output too seems to have fallen sharply, although records of production are patchy.[83] The importation and consumption of furs also shrank, though conflicts with Hanseatic merchants and changes in fashion which dictated a preference for smaller quantities of the more expensive types accentuated the decline.[84]

VII

Urban economies were based in very large measure upon the production and trade of commodities consumed by those who derived their incomes from the land, and imports and exports passed through towns and were largely handled by townsmen. As volumes declined, less was spent in towns and on the products produced within their walls and traded through their markets. It would seem inevitable, therefore, that the general run of towns must have suffered appreciably as trading conditions worsened in the mid-fifteenth century, and this is precisely the conclusion to which urban sources seem unerringly to point. Whatever fortunes the economies of particular towns had experienced before c. 1450, with a remarkable degree of syn-

[80] Britnell, 'The Pastons', p. 142; Moreton, *Townshends*, p. 142.

[81] Dyer, *Standards of Living*, pp. 107–8.

[82] J. Hatcher, *English Tin Production and Trade before 1550* (Oxford, 1973), pp. 152–63.

[83] I.S.W. Blanchard, 'Derbyshire Lead Production, 1195–1505', *Derbyshire Archaeological Journal*, 91 (1971), pp. 128–9.

[84] E.M. Veale, *The English Fur Trade in the Later Middle Ages* (Oxford, 1966), pp. 138–42, 156–61.

chronisation they tended to weaken appreciably thereafter. There is little difficulty in finding examples from the later fourteenth century and the first half of the fifteenth century of larger towns which fared tolerably well and of smaller towns and industrial villages which throve, but afterwards plausible instances of improved or sustained prosperity become exceedingly rare. Moreover, a suspiciously close correlation exists between those towns which are still held up as possible exceptions to the general decline and those towns which lack adequate modern studies. Time and again, as our knowledge of the experiences of individual towns has advanced, it has proved necessary to remove them from the lists of those which might have sailed virtually unscathed through the worst storms of the fifteenth century.

High ratios of tax levied in 1515/24 compared with 1334 have been used to suggest that towns such as Coventry, Colchester, Exeter, Bury St Edmunds, Norwich, Salisbury and Worcester were faring better than most.[85] But even a sharply increased tax assessment does not of itself prove that a town was richer in the early sixteenth century than it had been 200 years earlier, not least because the basis upon which the two taxes were assessed was radically different; still less does it prove that such a town had enjoyed uninterrupted prosperity in the interim. Coventry had one of the very highest rates of increase in the amount of tax it was called upon to pay in 1524, which was once thought to imply 'notable achievements', and in 1977 the city was considered to be 'prosperous and intermittently growing' in the fifteenth century.[86] Two years later, however, Coventry was the subject of a book entitled *Desolation of a City*.[87] Proof of Colchester's late medieval resilience, a city whose tax obligations were increased even more strikingly than Coventry's, was once believed to lie in a thriving cloth industry and the extensive rebuilding of its parish churches,[88] but R.H. Britnell's detailed study has revealed instead that 'after 1449 it is impossible to speak of economic growth on the available evidence, which favours more the proposition that the economy of the town decayed'; and he has concluded that 'if Colchester did not grow through most of the period 1300–1525, it is very unlikely that any English town did so'.[89] Newcastle upon Tyne and Canterbury were on every optimist's list until A.F. Butcher's researches among rent rolls revealed that in the later fifteenth century vacancies, rent rebates and arrears

---

[85] This device was first used by Bridbury in 1962 (*Economic Growth*, pp. 77–82, 111–13), and has been close to the centre of the debate over late medieval urban fortunes ever since.

[86] *Ibid.*, p. 81; S. Reynolds, *An Introduction to the History of English Medieval Towns* (Oxford, 1977), p. 144.

[87] C. Phythian-Adams, *Desolation of a City: Coventry and the Urban Crisis of the Late Middle Ages* (Cambridge, 1979).

[88] Reynolds, *English Medieval Towns*, p. 155.

[89] Britnell, *Growth and Decline in Colchester*, pp. 266–8.

abounded.[90] Bristol, which was once thought to have benefited from the shift of wealth to the south-west of England, from an exceptionally entrepreneurial merchant elite, from buoyant cloth exports and from the growth of textile production in its vicinity, is now believed to have suffered one of the greatest population losses of any provincial city.[91] Even London's celebrated ability to grow regardless of the fate of the wider economy has been called into question by D. Keene's painstaking reconstruction of the history of Cheapside; while in nearby Westminster, whose taxable capacity increased by a staggering forty-three-fold between 1334 and 1524, population losses in the middle decades of the fifteenth century 'inevitably entailed, overall, a marked economic recession'.[92] The list of significant towns whose fortunes might not have deteriorated after *c*. 1450 is therefore now extremely short, but even so it would be prudent to wait until detailed studies have been completed of the economies of Norwich, Salisbury, Bury St Edmunds, Worcester and Exeter before confirming that they warrant a place upon it.

Nor has recent scholarship lessened the scale of the difficulties undergone by the indisputable urban casualties of this period, and as new studies are written, for example of Winchester, Durham and Chester, the place of their subjects among the victims of the depression is duly confirmed.[93] Whereas the evidence for the decline of the east coast ports could once be described as patchy, recent studies of Hull, Beverley and Yarmouth have painted an irrefutably dismal picture;[94] and whereas it was claimed of Grimsby that 'the townspeople's complaints of poverty from depopulation look disingenuous', S.H. Rigby's recently published study concludes that in the later fifteenth century this Lincolnshire port 'suffered from a decline in its population, a shrinkage of its economic functions, a fall in the volume of its trade, a shortage of richer townspeople, an inability to attract migrants, and problems in its municipal revenues'.[95] York, the leading east coast town was, in

[90] A.F. Butcher, 'Rent, Population and Economic Change in Late-Medieval Newcastle', *Northern History*, 14 (1978); A.F. Butcher 'Rent and the Urban Economy: Oxford and Canterbury in the Later Middle Ages', *Southern History*, 1 (1979).

[91] Reynolds, *English Medieval Towns*, p. 152; Dyer, *Decline and Growth*, p. 30.

[92] D. Keene, 'A New Study of London before the Great Fire', *Urban History Yearbook*, 1984; D. Keene, 'Medieval London and its Region', *London Journal*, 14 (1989); G. Rosser, *Medieval Westminster, 1200–1540* (Oxford, 1989), pp. 74–81, 171–3.

[93] D. Keene, *Survey of Medieval Winchester*, 2 vols. (Winchester Studies, 2, Oxford, 1985), I, pp. 237–48; M. Bonney, *Lordship and the Urban Community: Durham and its Overlords, 1250–1540* (Cambridge, 1990), pp. 130–1; J.W. Laughton, 'Aspects of the Social and Economic History of Later Medieval Chester, 1350–*c*. 1500' (Univ. of Cambridge University PhD thesis, 1994), pp. 385–405.

[94] J.I. Kermode, 'Merchants, Overseas Trade, and Urban Decline: York, Beverley and Hull c. 1380–1500', *Northern History*, 23 (1987); A.R. Saul, 'English Towns in the Later Middle Ages: The Case of Great Yarmouth', *Journal of Medieval History*, 8 (1982).

[95] Reynolds, *Medieval English Towns*, p. 151; S.H. Rigby, *Medieval Grimsby: Growth and Decline* (Hull, 1993), p. 146.

the words of A.J. Pollard, reduced in the course of the fifteenth century, and especially after 1440, 'from a great international trading city to little more than a large provincial market town'.[96]

When assessing the urban sector as a whole it is, of course, necessary to balance thriving smaller towns and industrialising villages against the deteriorating fortunes of larger older towns. The profound changes which occurred in the structure and location of industry in the later Middle Ages produced many spectacular examples of development in rural England, including most notably an abundance of flourishing clothworking villages and small towns in East Anglia, the West Riding, north-west Yorkshire, the Cotswolds and the west country. But this is not to say that their growth was uninterrupted, nor that they were unaffected by the slump in the cloth export trade in the third quarter of the fifteenth century. Moreover, the expansion of some rural districts took place at the expense of others: the supremacy enjoyed by north-west Yorkshire at the close of the fourteenth century, for example, was not only subsequently eclipsed by the West Riding, but the closing down of many of its fulling mills by the 1470s suggests that it experienced absolute as well as relative decline; and in Essex, Suffolk and Norfolk, the lesser centres of production often lost ground to a few larger ones.[97] Similarly contrasting sequences of rise and decline could also be based upon trade rather than manufacturing. We now know that Buntingford in north-east Hertfordshire succeeded in the century and a half after the Black Death largely by capturing the trade of of nearby Standon, which experienced a severe contraction, but even so Buntingford was not exempted from suffering 'some economic decline between 1440 and 1490'.[98]

Though urban historians may continue to debate the precise meanings of 'growth' and 'decline', 'prosperity' and 'decay', the actual evidence from the overwhelming majority of English towns, great and small, from the mid-fifteenth century onwards displays a plethora of incontrovertibly inauspicious signs. Whereas falling commercial and residential rents, vacant premises and abandoned town churches might by themselves denote merely declining population rather than diminishing *per capita* prosperity, we can also discern, where records permit, not merely a contraction in the numbers of merchants and craftsmen but a reduction in their average wealth. This did not mean, of course, that the most favourably sited and structured towns suffered as badly as those whose trades were in near-terminal decline, nor that the leading inhabitants of ailing towns were reduced to poverty, nor yet

---

[96] Pollard, *North-Eastern England*, p. 74.
[97] *Ibid.*, pp. 72–3; Britnell, *Growth and Decline in Colchester*, pp. 187–9.
[98] M. Bailey, 'A Tale of Two Towns: Buntingford and Standon in the Later Middle Ages', *Journal of Medieval History*, 19 (1993), p. 365.

that weakened urban communities were incapable of raising sizable sums to loan to the crown when pressed hard to do so; but it did mean that for most townsfolk life became appreciably harder. This worsening economic environment derives further confirmation from the protectionist legislation by which urban craftsmen and merchants sought to secure their interests, as well as from the marked slowing of the rate of migration to towns.[99]

VII

The end of what must constitute one of the deepest, most pervasive and enduring of all depressions is no more a matter of precise determination than its onset, yet we must be wary of setting too early a date. Although in the last quarter of the fifteenth century the experience of the urban sector became somewhat less uniformly dismal, the position of many leading towns failed to improve substantially while others continued to decline or stagnate.[100] On the other hand, the rally in overseas trade from the 1470s, which drew support from a general revival of European transcontinental trade, was both strong and widely based, and some branches positively boomed: by 1479–82 annual imports and exports of merchandise paying *ad valorem* duties were valued at almost three times the levels they had fallen to between 1456 and 1471. Even so it was not until the first decade of the sixteenth century that cloth exports consistently exceeded the levels they had attained in the 1440s, and wool exports continued on an irregular but distinctly downward path.[101] The production and export of tin and lead recovered strongly, but once again it was not until the early sixteenth century that the output of the stannaries of Cornwall and Devon surpassed previous records.[102]

[99] E. Lipson, *The Economic History of England*, 3 vols. (1949–56 edns), I, pp. 308–439, surveys the ordinances promulgated by craft guilds in the fifteenth century; see also Bolton, *Medieval English Economy*, p. 265. H. Swanson has suggested that much of this legislative activity was ineffective ('The Illusion of Economic Structure: Craft Gilds in Late Medieval English Towns', *Past and Present*, 121 (1988).

[100] D.M. Palliser, 'Urban Decay Revisited', in J.A.F. Thomson (ed.), *Towns and Townspeople in the Fifteenth Century* (Gloucester, 1988), pp. 1–21.

[101] P. Ramsey, 'Overseas Trade in the Reign of Henry VII: The Evidence of the Customs Accounts', *Econ. Hist. Rev.*, 2nd ser., 6 (1953); E.M. Carus-Wilson and O. Coleman, *England's Export Trade, 1275–1547* (Oxford, 1963).

[102] Hatcher, *English Tin Production*, pp. 152–63; Blanchard, 'Derbyshire Lead Production', pp. 128–9. Blanchard has claimed that tin exports were substantially higher and domestic consumption substantially lower at the close of the fifteenth century than they had been in the early fourteenth century (*Econ. Hist. Rev.*, 2nd ser., 27 (1974), pp. 473–4). In fact all the evidence unerringly points to the opposite conclusions. For the early fourteenth century, a period for which no remotely comprehensive records of tin exports exist, Blanchard has taken a few incidental notices of particular shipments by a single Italian

The trough of the slump in the rural economy had also been passed by the 1480s, and the prospects for rentiers and agricultural producers improved thereafter: in general rents firmed somewhat, demesnes became easier to let and larger peasant farms increased in both number and durability. But for some decades the recovery in most regions remained patchy and partial, constituting more of a bounce back from extreme depression than the commencement of a strong upward trend.[103] Although it may well have become less difficult to dispose of crops, to judge from price movements there was no substantial improvement in the market for grain before the 1520s. Whereas decennial averages register a sharp increase in the prices of many grains and legumes in the 1480s, annual data reveal it to have been primarily the result of an abnormal cluster of bad harvests. In the 1490s the average price of wheat sank to its lowest level since the 1440s, while oats and peas sold for less than at any time since the first half of the thirteenth century. Not surprisingly the demand for arable remained subdued. Similarly, the average price of wool was lower in the 1490s than it had been at any time since the opening decades of the thirteenth century, and the prices of meat, cheese, sheep, horses and cattle were either below or only marginally higher than they had been in the 1440s. Sustained substantial increases in the prices of animal products and dairy produce took place only in the 1530s, and accordingly the recovery in the demand for pasture land before then was fitful in most regions.[104]

Clearly it would be unwise to place too early a date on the commencement of the sustained long-term upswing in agricultural activity and profitability that was to characterise so much of the early modern era. There is much to commend William Harrison's view that it was well into the reign of Henry VIII before the decisive turning point occurred. Writing in the 1570s Harrison drew attention to a number of things that had been 'marvellously altered in England [within] . . . the sound remembrance . . . of old men yet dwelling

merchant house as indicative of the total level of exports to all parts of Europe. As for domestic consumption, he fails to take account of the crucial fact that tin is both durable and recyclable, and that consequently any new output retained in England was an addition to existing stocks, largely held in the form of pewterware which was periodically melted down and re-worked to make new items.

[103] For continuing problems and the lack of sustained recovery in many agricultural regions at the close of the fifteenth century see, for example, Mate, 'Tenant Farming and Farmers: Kent and Sussex', in *AHEW*, III, p. 688; P.F. Brandon, 'The Common Lands and Wastes of Sussex' (Univ. of London PhD, thesis, 1963), p. 319; Britnell, *Growth and Decline in Colchester*, p. 264; B.J. Harris, 'Landlords and Tenants in England in the Later Middle Ages: The Buckingham Estates', *Past and Present*, 43 (1969), pp. 146–8 (for lands in Staffordshire, Shropshire, Cheshire, Yorkshire and Wales); Pollard, *North-Eastern England*, pp. 56–9.

[104] Farmer, 'Prices and Wages', in *AHEW*, II; *Farmer*, 'Prices and Wages, 1350–1500', in *AHEW*, III; Lloyd, *Wool Prices*, pp. 45–7; Bowden, 'Statistical Appendix', in *AHEW*, IV, pp. 814–79.

in the village where I remain'. One such matter was a dramatic improvement in the circumstances of farmers who in times past, perhaps in the 1520s or 1530s, for all their 'frugality . . . were scarce able to live and pay their rents at their days without selling of a cow or an horse or more'. In those times, he goes on, 'such was their poverty that if some odd farmer or husbandman . . . did cast down his purse [containing] . . . a noble or 6s. in silver' before his fellows

it was very likely that all the rest could not lay down so much against it; whereas in my time, although peradventure £4 of old rent be improved to £40, £50 or £100, yet will the farmer . . . think his gains very small towards the end of his term if he have not six or seven years' rent lying by him, therewith to purchase a new lease, beside a fair garnish of pewter on his cupboard, with so much more in odd vessel going about the house, three or four feather beds, so many coverlets and carpets of tapestry, a silver salt, a bowl for wine (if not an whole nest), and a dozen spoons to furnish up the suit.[105]

[105] William Harrison, *The Description of England*, ed. G. Edelen (New York, 1968), pp. 201–2.

13

Lorenzo de' Medici's London branch

GEORGE HOLMES

WHY DID the Medici bank go downhill under the management of Lorenzo de' Medici, 1469 to 1492? The present article is about one section only, the London branch, but it may have some usefulness for illuminating the general problem. Since Lorenzo's servants were deeply involved in the trade and politics of London it may also shed some light on English history. The Medici bank was very fully and helpfully investigated by Raymond de Roover.[1] De Roover quoted the general judgements of Machiavelli and Guicciardini that Lorenzo had no commercial luck and stood aside from the business of the bank, leaving it to his representatives.[2] In the case of the English branch he attributed much importance to independent loans to King Edward IV[3] parallel to the Bruges branch's loans to Charles the Bold duke of Burgundy.[4] De Roover made a good deal of progress but his account is not final. There is a vast amount of documentary material relevant to the London branch in the Mediceo avanti il Principato collection in the Archivio di Stato, Florence, and in the exchequer records at the Public Record Office in London. De Roover did not use any of the unpublished London material, and did not refer to many of the relevant records in Florence. This article will not be final either – the Medici bank is an endlessly complicated subject with ramifications in so many areas of European history – but I hope to push a little further into the complex web of evidence and make the conclusions a little stronger.

I am greatly indebted for help in the production of this essay to Dr Giovanni Ciappelli and Professor Nicolai Rubinstein.

[1] Raymond de Roover, *The Rise and Decline of the Medici Bank 1397–1494* (Cambridge, Mass., 1963), Italian translation with extra documents, *Il banco Medici dalle origini al declino (1397–1494)*, trans. G. Corti (Florence, 1970).

[2] De Roover, *Medici Bank*, p. 364.

[3] *Ibid.*, pp. 333–4.

[4] Discounted as an explanation of the Bruges branch's troubles by R. Vaughan, *Charles the Bold* (London, 1973), pp. 258–60.

The precise legal status of the London branch at this time is not clear. In 1465 it was planned to set up an *accomanda* with most of the money supplied by Piero di Cosimo de' Medici and Tommaso Portinari, the Medici manager at Bruges, but most of the work in London was done by Gherardo Canigiani, already active in London for many years,[5] and Giovanni de' Bardi. Whether this scheme actually came into effect and, if so, how long it lasted are unknown. It is clear from the records, however, that the lead was taken in London by Canigiani in the late 1460s and early 1470s. His is the name that nearly always appears in the records, either alone or with the description 'merchant of Florence'. It is impossible to distinguish between actions on behalf of the Medici bank and actions on his own account but most of the time he was probably using Medici money. In 1472, or, more probably, in 1473, Lorenzo broke with Canigiani, who continued to work in London on his own and indeed to do business with the Medici branch, now apparently placed under the control of Tommaso Guidetti.[6]

Piero di Cosimo de' Medici died on 2 December 1469, to be succeeded by his son Lorenzo, aged only twenty. It was probably unfortunate for Lorenzo, as far as his London branch was concerned, that his succession happened to coincide with the upheaval in English politics caused by the differences between King Edward IV and the earl of Warwick. Edward's sister, Margaret, was married to Charles the Bold duke of Burgundy in July 1468. Risings against the king in the north started in the spring of 1469; the king's forces were defeated at Edgecote in July and the king himself captured. Edward fled to the Low Countries in October 1470 and did not recover his position until the battles of Barnet and Tewkesbury in April and May 1471. So Lorenzo's early days as the guardian of his family's interests were also the period when the English court was most disturbed, and no doubt repayment of loans was held up for this reason as well as others. Lorenzo also found the political career forced on him in Florence an enormous distraction from his business interests. 'If I have been rather later than you would have wished and as I also would have wished,' he wrote to Tommaso Portinari, his manager at Bruges and the most important Florentine merchant in northern Europe, on 31 July 1470, 'you will excuse me because the assiduous and continuous business of the Palace [i.e. the Palazzo della Signoria] does not allow me to be attentive to my own affairs, as by chance may be necessary.

---

[5] Biography of Canigiani by M. Mallett, *Dizionario Biografico degli Italiani*, XVIII (Rome, 1975), pp. 91–3.

[6] De Roover, *Medici Bank*, pp. 330–6. De Roover says (p. 332) that the change occurred in 1472. It seems to me more likely that it was after the events following the capture of the Burgundian galley in 1473. Canigiani can be seen doing business with the separate Medici branch in the fragment of accounts for 1477: Archivio di Stato, Florence, Mediceo avanti il Principato (henceforward MAP) 99/3.

I find myself at this time with a great burden, public and private, on my shoulders.'[7] Lorenzo, the owner of a vast international business, remained always somewhat detached from his widespread branches and this may have been a main reason for his relative lack of financial success.

Gherardo Canigiani, the Medici manager in London, appears to have lent Edward IV £5,254 19s. 10d. in November 1466.[8] This loan was apparently still partly outstanding several years later. When Canigiani's payment of customs dues was questioned in the exchequer, he produced a privy seal letter dated 5 July 1472, pardoning him for having recovered £3,893 2s. 1¼d. from customs on wool and cloth at London and Southampton.[9] It is impossible to know whether the whole of the loan had been repaid but it is clear that the major part had. On 20 December 1467 Canigiani was granted repayment of another loan of £8,468 18s. 8d., apparently made on 28 November, to come from a variety of wardships, marriages, reliefs, escheats, forfeitures, custodies of heirs and temporalities and customs and subsidies at south coast ports, and from permission to export wool, cloths and tin via the Straits of Morocco quit of customs and subsidies at the rate of four marks.[10] On 20 July 1468 he was granted assignments to repay this loan of £2,999 15s. 3d. and £2,625 3s. 10d.[11] and on 9 August an assignment of £2,477 2s. 5d.[12]. On 30 September he was granted a further assignment of £3000.[13] On 13 May 1469 Canigiani was granted £500 cash as compensation for surrendering the letter of 20 December 1467 which had allowed him to recover his loan by not paying customs.[14]

A letter produced in the exchequer in Michaelmas Term 1471 stated that between 31 May and 25 December 1468 Canigiani had quite properly

---

[7] Lorenzo de' Medici, *Lettere*, ed. N. Rubinstein (Florence, 1977–), I, ed. R. Fubini, pp. 186–8.

[8] C.L. Scofield, *The Life and Reign of Edward the Fourth* (London, 1923), II, p. 423 and note.

[9] Public Record Office (hereafter PRO) (documents quoted in future are here unless otherwise stated), E159/248, Recorda Trinity, rot. xix.

[10] Scofield, *Edward the Fourth*, II, p. 423 and note, *Cal. Pat. Rolls, 1467–77*, p. 11. A privy seal letter of 11 December 1467 instructed the exchequer to record as *mutuum* payments of £8,468 18s. 8d. by Canigiani and another £8,468 18s. 8d. by Earl Rivers, the treasurer and others (E404/73/3/72).

[11] E403/840: 'Gerard Canyzian mercatori de fflorencia in denariis sibi liberatis per assignamentum isto die factum per manus proprias in persolutionem viijMl iiijC lxviij l. xviij s.viij d. quos domino Regi ad Receptam scaccarii sui xxviij die Novembris ultimo preterito vt patet in Rotulo Recepte de eodem die – ijMl ixC iiij xix li. xv s. iij d. de ista summa – ij Ml DCxxv li. iij s. x d. ob.' In the right hand margin: 'Memorandum quod ccclxxiiij li. xi d qd.ob parcella ij Ml ixC iiij xix li. xv d. infrascriptorum non debent computari infra summam huius diei.' The reference to this entry by Scofield, *Edward the Fourth*, II, p. 423, n. 4, appears to be erroneous.

[12] E403/840.

[13] Scofield, *Edward the Fourth*, II, p. 423 n. 4.

[14] E403/842.

retained half of the £1,478 10s. 9¼d. which he should have paid for 392½ sacks and 17 nails of wool which he shipped from London, in accordance with a 'wrytte showed by the said Gerard vnto the same late customers in that behalf'.[15] A letter of 5 July 1472 pardoned him for recovering £1,047 10s. 9d. from the collectors of customs in the port of London. He was also pardoned for exporting pewter to Zealand: 'the said statute not ponderyng at London in the parysshe of Saint Mary of Berkyng in the warde of the Tower of London', he had shipped 'ij litell barellis with Dl.lb of vessels of tynne of the value of vij li. vj s. viij d in a Galey of Laurence Zane [Lorenzo Zane?] patron'.[16]

The next loan, of £1,000, was made on 9 August 1468.[17] On 12 September Canigiani apparently had an assignment worth £633 6s. 8d. towards repayment of it which he admitted receiving.[18] On 26 November 1468 there was a further loan of £2,610 9s. 0d. for which an assignment was issued on 1 December.[19] Canigiani's assignment was also entered on the issue roll but there it was stated that £2,283 15s. 8d. of the repayment were cancelled because Canigiani, it was reported, later said he had been satisfied by letters patent of 30 August 1471.[20] This was the date of the letters patent granting repayment of another loan, of £6,600; the connection is not made clear. On 18 January 1469 Canigiani loaned £3,225 6s. 8d.[21] On 1 February he was allowed to recover the money lent by shipping from London, Southampton and Sandwich provided wool went by way of the Straits of Gibraltar.[22] On 13 July 1471 Canigiani loaned £6,600.[23] On 30 August he was allowed to ship without paying customs to get the money back.[24] On 12 February 1473 this permission was extended to exporting by factors and attorneys of Canigiani, in addition to export in his own name.[25] There was then a gap until 2 March 1474 when Canigiani loaned £4,566 1s. 8d. which was apparently to be repaid by assignments.[26]

[15] E159/248, Recorda Trinity, rot. xix.
[16] E368/245, Recorda Trinity, rot. xxii.
[17] E401/892.
[18] E403/840. The payment is entered as £1,000 but with the addition: 'de ista summa ccclxvi li.xiij s.iiij d non computantur infra summam huius diei sed summa de claro DCxxxiij li. vj s. viij d.'. In the right-hand margin: 'Memorandum quod Gerardus Canizian fatetur se de ista summa infrascripta.'
[19] E401/893: 'persolutum per assignamentum primo die Decembris proximo sequente'.
[20] E403/841.
[21] E401/893.
[22] Cal. Pat. Rolls. 1467–77, p. 132.
[23] A. Steel, The Receipt of the Exchequer 1377–1485 (Cambridge, 1954), pp, 297–8; E405/53.
[24] Cal. Pat. Rolls, 1467–77, p. 273.
[25] E159/249, Brevia directa baronibus, Hilary, rot. vii.
[26] The loan is entered on E401/913, 914 and 915. E401/915 includes the addition 'persoluti per assignamentum [or assignamenta] per breve de priuato sigillo hoc termino'.

The size of the London loans to Edward IV caused considerable anxiety. Angelo Tani, sent to London by Piero de' Medici in January 1468 was disturbed by their size and by the slowness of repayment.[27] Lorenzo's first recorded statements about London were in July 1470, as the political crisis between Edward IV and Warwick blew up. The Medici agent in Bruges, Tommaso Portinari, had written to him on 9 June rather reassuringly, hoping the political and financial situation in London would improve. Lorenzo wrote back to Portinari on 31 July, 'I have at present no business or weight on my shoulders which gives me more concern or greater trouble than the question of London, for I think we have neither on this side nor on the other a matter of greater importance.' He besought Portinari to keep the matter under control. He saw Warwick preparing war against the debtor to the Medici branch, Edward IV, with the help of France. His opinion was that 'when the time and the season will bear it, it would be wise to bind his [Canigiani's] hands so that they cannot soil us any more.' Lorenzo was also anxious to use English exports of wool and cloth to balance the movement of alum from Tolfa to northern Europe.[28] In May 1472 he sent Cristofano Spini to Bruges and London with instructions to encourage Portinari to keep his hands on London and to point out to Canigiani 'the dangers in which he has put us and that he has served the king with our money and not his own and that if it is so bad it will be a matter of harming us not him'.[29]

It is difficult to know whether Lorenzo was right in thinking that London was in a dangerous condition. It is true that there is no loan of which it can be shown that all the money was repaid. On the other hand repayment was certainly going on and there is no reason why it should not have been largely completed. Canigiani was being used by the crown for other business, for example the payment of the £10,000 dowry for the marriage of Margaret of York to Charles the Bold in 1468, which was no doubt profitable.[30] Canigiani's support must have been important to Edward. In February 1473 the Milanese ambassador in France reported to his lord the anger of King Louis XI, complaining about the effects of Lorenzo's money in London, 'saying that his money makes him [King Louis] more wars than the enemy, because for this fleet which they are preparing in London, numbers of his [King Edward's] troops are paid at his bank in London':[31] a garbled account, no

[27] De Roover, *Medici Bank*, p. 474.
[28] Lorenzo de' Medici, *Lettere*, I, pp. 191–6.
[29] *Ibid.*, I, p. 371.
[30] Scofield, *Edward the Fourth*, I, pp. 453–4; cf. G. Daumont, *Calais sous la Domination anglaise* (Arras 1902), pp. 185–8.
[31] *Calendar of State Papers and Manuscripts Existing in the Archives and Collections of Milan*, ed. A.B. Hinds (HMSO, London), p. 173.

doubt, but related to the truth. Apart from the loans Canigiani was also doing a great deal of normal trading. A customs account for London in 1471 shows substantial imports by him on the galleys of Jeronimo Morosini and Lorenzo Contarini which were entered on the rolls on 13 and 15 November. On the first galley his total imports were valued at £2,358 5s. 1d. They included pepper, silk, carpets and cloth of gold. A similar cargo on the other galley was valued at £872 6s. 8d. In January 1472 came a northern ship carrying alum for him worth £100.[32] A merchant carrying on business on that scale could not fail to benefit from the close association with the court which Canigiani enjoyed.

In April 1473 the Medici business was hit by an unexpected disaster, of a kind which, on a smaller scale, was common enough. The two, so called, Burgundian galleys, built earlier for a crusading project of the duke of Burgundy which came to nothing, were bound from Zealand to England, on their way to Pisa, carrying a considerable quantity of merchandise meant for the English market, with the intention that after being emptied here they should carry English wool and cloth to the Mediterranean. On 27 April they were attacked by a Baltic pirate. One galley was captured, the other escaped. The event is famous because the captured galley was carrying Memling's *Last Judgement*, the property of Angelo Tani, whom Lorenzo had earlier sent to look into his branches at Bruges and London. The picture was on its way to Florence but it was now carried off to Danzig.[33]

There were some imports in the galleys belonging to English merchants and it is interesting that the Mercers' Company, on receiving news of the event, reacted immediately by securing Canigiani's help on 1 May. 'Wherefore we appoynted in the same Courte diuers persones with the Wardens to goo to speak with Garard Canysyan for to understonde what comford or Councell that he knew or cowde gyf us in this mater.' The galley which had escaped capture went on to Southampton but would not enter the port until Canigiani, who had instructions to have the cargo unloaded at London, gave permission.[34] This galley, the San Giorgio, had aboard as a passenger Girolamo Strozzi of Florence who left a record of his voyage. He made use

[32] E122/194/19.
[33] A. von Reumont, 'Di alcune relazioni dei Fiorentini colla città di Danzica: memoria', *Archivio Storico Italiano*, n.s., 13, part 1 (1861), pp. 37–47; G. van der Ropp, Zur Geschichte des Alaunhandels im 15. Jahrhundert', *Hansische Geschichtsblätter* (1900); O. Meltzing, 'Tommaso Portinari und sein Konflikt mit der Hanse', *Hansische Geschichtsblätter* (1906); *Hanserecesse, 1431–76*, ed. G. von der Ropp, 7 vols. (Leipzig, 1876–92), VII, pp. 115–17; *Hanserecesse, 1477–1530*, ed. D. Schäfer, 9 vols. (Leipzig, 1881–1913), I, p. 70; A. Warburg, 'Flandrische Kunst und Florentinische Frührenaissance', *Gesammelte Schriften*, I, (Berlin, 1932).
[34] *Acts of Court of the Mercers' Company 1453–1527*, ed. L. Lyell and F.D. Watney (Cambridge, 1936), pp. 68–74.

of the three-month stay at Southampton to go to London and bring back cloth, tin and brass candlesticks to take to Pisa.[35] Canigiani too appears to have done his best to fill up the Burgundian galley with profitable exports because he is recorded as sending more than a thousand cloths in carts to Southampton in May to July 1473.[36]

There are one or two documents which shed light on the relations between the representatives of the Medici in London after the affair of the Burgundian galley. They do not make its business dealings or its profits clear, though they do shed light on that aspect of the matter, but they make absolutely clear that there was intense rivalry and bitterness between Canigiani and Cristofano Spini, who had been sent by Lorenzo to look into the London scene. There is a petition by Canigiani to the English chancellor claiming money from Spini, presumably written in 1473. Spini, he said, had asked him for help in exporting goods on a galley of Genoa at Southampton, of which Paolo Nigero (*de Negri*) was patron, and two galleys of Naples about to arrive from Flanders. Canigiani had a licence to ship exports without paying custom in order to secure repayment of a loan of £6,600, a licence, which, as we have seen, had been granted to him in 1471. Spini proposed that 500 or 600 sacks of wool should be exported using that licence, the profit later to be divided between them. They were both acting as 'factors and attorneys' of the 'feloushipp of the Medicis of fflorence'. They bought 711 sacks and 20 nails of wool for £6,795 16s. 5d. Canigiani paid for the packing of the wool and transport to the galleys at a cost of £952. The licence saved custom to the sum of £1,738 12s. 3d. Spini had still not paid the £311 16s. 4d. due to John Tame, from whom wool had been bought, or another £952.[37]

Attached to the petition is a schedule of the woolmen from whom the 711 sacks had been bought and the exact sums due to them, which, as it happens, provides quite an interesting insight into the English wool trade, illustrating the large quantities of wool available in the Cotswolds and the system of paying for it by instalments spread over several years.[38] This instalment system, which saved the buyer from immediate payment and in most cases must have allowed final payments to be made after the wool had been sold abroad is also, incidentally, relevant to the loans made to the king. The

[35] F.E. De Roover, 'Le voyage de Girolamo Strozzi de Pisa à Bruges et retour à bord de la galère bourguignonne "San Giorgio"', *Annales de la Société d'Emulation de Bruges*, 91 (1954).

[36] E.g. 'In biga petri hopkyn versus Southampton eodem die De Gerardo Canyzean pro ij balis cum xliiij pannis et dimidio sine grano', E122/194/20, with many similar entries following.

[37] Cl/50/414.

[38] Cl/50/415.

loans were payments out by merchants, with a slow return. Wool was an immediate receipt with slow payment. To some extent loans by Italians like Canigiani or by the Staplers would have been balanced by the system of wool purchase. The first entry on the schedule of wool purchases is as follows, the others being in the same form.

> Fyrst bought of William Flodgate of Borford xlv sakks xxviij naylys of Cotiswold woll at xiiij marc a sakke – summa iiij C xxv. li.
> Whereof payed in hond in redy money ij C xv li.
> Item payable the xv day of may nexte cominyng cv. li.
> Item payable the xv day of march anno Ml iiij C lxxv cv li.

The people from whom wool had been bought, apart from the last entry, which is illegible, were

William Flodgate of Burford	45 sacks	28 nails
Thomas Alan of Stow	62 sacks	4 nails
John Croke and Richard Chestre	55 sacks	11 nails
Jane Kent widow of London	78 sacks	7 nails
Thomas Jerveyse of Norton	45½sacks	23 nails
William Saunders of Banbury	79 sacks	24 nails
John Tame[39] of Fairford	96 sacks	40 nails
John Forte of Cirencester	43½sacks	18 nails
Richard Golfers mercer of London	28½sacks	13 nails
Jane Lenarde and Richard Lombard of Campden	28 sacks	23 nails
Harry Bysshopp of Burford	35 sacks	6 nails
John Pynnok of Burford	58½sacks	17 nails

The petition has an entry on the back recording that on 5 February 1474 it was decided in court that Spini must pay £2,000 to Richard Lumbard, William Saunders, John Pymcok, Richard Chestre, Richard Golofre and Joan Kent.

There are also in the Medici archives at Florence two conflicting statements by Canigiani and Spini about other deals in which they had been involved. Canigiani, writing on 1 July 1475, claimed that he had bought 107 sacks of wool, costing £837 17s. and fleeces costing £121, on which the custom had been £64 7s. 2d., to be put on the 'galea di Borghogna padron Francesco Tedaldi', that is the galley which came into Southampton in the spring of 1473. In repayment for this he had received only a tapestry worth £36 5s. 0d., bought from Piero

---

[39] John Tame, or Thame, John Forte, or Fortey, and John Lennard were among those prosecuted for offences against wool statutes in 1455–60 (E. Power and M.M. Postan, *Studies in English Trade in the Fifteenth Century* (London, 1933), p. 53).

Bandini, and cloth of gold and silk and other things worth £136 13s. 8d. Other goods had been sold to the king: cloths of gold and silk worth £455 15s. 6d., a damask worth £185 10s. 0d., a white damask worth £130; the total £809 5s. 6d. The king would not make an assignment for the payment of this money because he was waiting for Spini's return. Spini, he claimed, had made £300 or £400 out of goods sent to Francesco Villani in Spain. He had sent cloths to Pisa and made £150 out of exchanging them with Carlo Martelli for silk cloth. He had bought wool in London on which he had made £200 which should be repaid to Canigiani. He had used a patent obtained by Canigiani for making money at Calais. And there were other misdeeds. The tenor of Canigiani's statement was that Spini had refused to pay money owed to him and had exploited Canigiani's ability to obtain favours from the crown for his own advantage. 'The whole world marvels at his methods and especially at what he has done at Calais at the time when he frequented that voyage . . . If I could be face to face with you', said Canigiani, presumably addressing Lorenzo, 'I would stupefy you with what he had had the heart to do.'[40] Later in the document Canigiani appears to be claiming that Spini had shipped ten pokes of fine wool to his own profit on the Genoese ship on which the large consignment which figured in the English chancery case had been exported, taking for himself profit which should have gone to the Medici firm at Bruges.[41] At the end of his statement Canigiani accused Spini of being responsible for the loss of the goods on the Burgundian galley captured by the Danzigers.[42]

Spini replied to this at length refuting the 'articles forged and compiled and false information given about me by Gherardo Canigiani to Messer Lorenzo di Medici'.[43] 'When I went last to London sent by Tommaso [Portinari]', he wrote to Lorenzo, 'I understood that they had decided to betray

[40] MAP, 82/114. 'El detto à fatto di qua altri ghuadagni, chome intenderete per altra, e tutto il mondo sta marauigliato de'modi sua e maxime di quello à fatto a Chalixe nel tempo frequetaua quello viagio; et lo so è anchora per le ratione d'inghilesi medesimi che s'io potessi essere a bocha con uoi, ui farei stupefare di quello che gl'à hauuto quore di fare questo chauestro.'

[41] 'El detto charicho sulla naue Negrona in suo nome p°x di lane della più fine auessimo et secondo intendiamo le mando a Gienoua a Negroni et per tanto uedete che ue ne fatti la diliberansa che sono a vostro conto, c[i]oè de'uostri di Bruggia, chè lo'ntenderamo al contar con loro.'

[42] 'Angnolo Tani ci domanda certi denari[?] di drappi che si presono sulla ghalea di Borghogna presa da li Ostarlini i quali non siamo tenuti di paghare, perchè detta perdita fu a chagione di detto Christofano, chome si chiarira a luogho e tempo; e sechondo intendamo, e Medici di Bruggia aueano ordine di seghuire la uolontà di detto Cristofano e chosì feciono, e di sua [MS "suo"] testa li charicho in su detta ghalea.'

[43] MAP 82/113. 'Risposta si fa per me Christofano Spini a li articholi forgiati e chonpilati e falsa informazione data di me Gherardo Chanigiani à lo Mre L. de'Medici, e tutto per indegnazione e mala volonta per avere io chon grande sollecitudine e arte senza avere auto righuardo ho rispetto alchuno trouato in grande parte lo modo e rimedio a la sua grande e isfrenata malizia.'

and cheat you and not give you the wools they had promised and to send back the protests [i.e. refusals to cash letters of exchange] to your greatest harm and shame.'[44]

A long letter from Canigiani to Lorenzo defending himself in very general terms, without much specification of precise events, is dated 1 July 1475, clearly some time after he had ceased to act for the Medici.[45] Presumably the break between them had come in late 1473 when Canigiani received letters of denization.[46] Canigiani appears to have remained on very good terms with the crown. On 13 January 1474 he was granted protection for five years against Spini 'and other merchants of the society of the Medici' who were said to be hostile to him 'on account of his services to the king and his marriage solemnised in this realm'.[47] On 23 June 1475 a privy seal letter to the exchequer stated, rather mysteriously,

> Where processe is made oute of oure seid Eschequier directed to the Shirief of London and Middlesex to distraign Gerard Canizian to make vnto vs homage lawfull as in oure seid Exchequier more plainly it appiereth of record we for certaine causes vs specially moevyng woll and straitly charge you that ye surcease of al maner of processe made or to be made for vs agenste the seid Gerard for the seid homage unto suche tyme as ye have othrewise in comandement frome vs.[48]

In March 1476 he accepted in settlement of all past debts from the crown £3,000, of which £1,000 was to be assignments and the rest in two instalments of cash to be paid at Easter and Michaelmas.[49]

The Medici representatives, however, continued their activities independently of Canigiani. A loan of £5,000 made to the king on 6 April 1475 was in the names of Giuliano de' Medici, Lorenzo's brother, and Tommaso Portinari, manager of the Bruges branch, and other Florentine merchants.[50] A letter close of 6 June 1475 allowed Lorenzo, Giuliano, Portinari and Alessandro Portinari to export wool without customs to repay the loan.[51] The

[44] 'Quando ío andai a Londra v[l]timamente mandato da Tomimaso inteso, aueano deliberato di tradirvi e inchanarui e di non darui le lane aveano promesse e di lasciar tornar li protesti chon grandissimo vostro danno e verghogna.'

[45] 'Io credo che debiate avere inteso come nel tempo ch'io [ho] auto a ffare le facende vostre delle vostre chompagnie, mi sono senpre portato lealmente e giustamente', MAP 26/160.

[46] Scofield, *Edward the Fourth*, II, p. 425.

[47] *Cal. Pat. Rolls, 1467–77*, pp. 481–2.

[48] E159/252. Brevia Directa Baronibus, Trinity, rot vii.

[49] Scofield *Edward the Fourth*, II, p. 215.

[50] E401/920: 'Mutuum De Juliano de Medicis Thomam de Portynariis et alios mercatores de fflorencia v Ml li.de mutuo. Persolutum per litteras Regis patentes de data vi to die Junii anno xv Regis nunc. Sol.'

[51] *Cal. Close Rolls, 1468–76*, p. 388; in full in T. Rymer, *Foedera* (The Hague 1739–45), V, part III, pp. 62–3. A privy seal letter of 12 June 1475 stated that the £5,000 was 'money delivered to our persone in oure Chambre' (E404/76/1/27).

continuation of the Medici business at London is shown most clearly by two pages of an account for the branch dated 12 November 1477.[52] In this account substantial sums are stated to be owing to the London branch from Bruges and Florence: £554 17s. 1d. due from the Medici and Portinari of Bruges for the payment of instalments for wool sent;[53] £579 10s. 8d. in two halves due from Tommaso and Giovanni Portinari also for instalments on wool (wool was, of course, commonly bought in England on payment of a deposit, the rest of the purchase price to be paid in later instalments); a further £303 2s. 0d. and £171 15s. 0d. from the Medici and Portinari of Bruges, unspecified; £519 15s. 0d. from the Medici of Florence for goods sent to them on a ship of Naples insured for 2,827 florins.[54] On the other side of the account the biggest item is £666 13s. 4d. due to the Medici branch at Bruges as part repayment of the £5,000 loaned in April 1475.[55] The sum of £506 12s. 2d. was owed to four men defined as 'lanieri di paese', woolmen in the country, for wool: William 'Sandres', Thomas 'Aleno', John 'Heueninghe' and John 'Pinochio'. Three of these were identical with the William 'Sandres' of Banbury, Thomas 'Alan' of Stow and John 'Pynnok' of Burford from whom Canigiani had bought wool in 1473.[56] In January 1479 the king acknowledged a debt of £433 6s. 8d. to Canigiani for wools bought for him from Pynnok, Alan and Fortey.[57] Other substantial debts were to Italian firms: to Marco da Pesaro e Paolo Tiepolo, Venetians, to the Medici of Venice for Corinth raisins, to Federigo da Prioli, probably also of Venice, and to Francesco Micheli, Venetian. The essence of the business is fairly clear. The London branch exported substantial quantities of wool either to Bruges, or in association with the Medici and Portinari of Bruges, and perhaps cloth or tin to Florence. It also imported goods, largely unspecified, from Venice.

A partly illegible sheet in the Medici archive,[58] apparently relating to the year 1478, runs as follows:

Gherardo Canigiani e compagnia di Londra restorono a dare alla ragione di Bruggia £18093.s.15 d. 7 di grossi di Londra che erano debitori a'detti di Bruggia come appare a'libri loro et anche appare in su'bilancio di detta ragione de l'anno 1478 che loro mettono per debitori perduti, e

---

[52] MAP 99/3. This is analysed in a different way by De Roover, *Medici Bank*, pp. 336–8.

[53] 'Medici e portinari de Bruggia per loro conto aparte di tempi per lane fornite'.

[54] 'Medici di Firenze per noi remiss loro dal padrone della na [?nave] di napoli e . . . andare il costo alla sichurta ff 2827 s i d i a Londra stanno £519.15'.

[55] 'Medici di bruggia conto apparte di denari ritratti dal re di la patente di £ vM'.

[56] Above, p. 280.

[57] Privy seal letter, 31 January 1479, E404/76/4/110.

[58] MAP 99 no. 6.

noi gli habbiamo paghati a detti di Brugia in somma di
£31500 come appare pel frastaglio e per lo accordo che fece
con Tomaso Portinari Rinieri da Ricasoli nostro procura-
tore li quali £18093 e s. valsono   f. 63328
Et più mandano debitore Tomaso Guidetti di Londra di
£1267 di grossi dipendenti da detta ragione per uno resto
di £5000, quali alsi sono perduti   f. 5068
Et per più debitori da Londra perduti £140   f.560
                                                                    ———————
                                                                     68956

This corresponds fairly well with Lorenzo's statement in his 'Promemoria' of December 1478[59] that the London losses were £18,982 5s. 10d. equivalent to 70,000 ducats. The unprinted document indicates that it was made up of £1,267 sterling still not recovered from the 1475 loan of £5,000 and £18,093 owed by Canigiani, that is to say, presumably, a debt still owing from him dating from the period before 1473, when he had been running the Medici branch.

These documents enable us to say with a little more confidence what the situation in London was. First, there was money to be made by exporting wool, cloth and tin and importing Mediterranean goods. Second, Canigiani had perhaps been foolish in lending money to Edward, not all of which, probably, was going to be repaid. He may, of course, have profited personally by this and so may the branch. It is interesting that the Medici made a loan of £5,000 in 1475 after they had taken the company from Canigiani, some of which had not been repaid three years later. They presumably judged that it was worth running that risk to secure the king's favour and perhaps felt particularly bound to make the loan, if they wanted to carry on doing business in London, because they had ditched the king's favourite, Canigiani, and might therefore be unpopular. Canigiani had followed the same path excessively. But the £5,000 loan makes fairly clear that generous lending might be regarded as a proper way of securing conditions needed for profit-able business. Thirdly, one reason why the Medici were relatively unsuccess-ful at this time was that they were no longer operating, as Lorenzo's grand-father Cosimo had done, as monopolistic controllers of ecclesiastical finance. That kind of business clearly played a relatively small part of the London business in the 1470s, limited to a few letters sent to Italy for priests. The Medici branch was now an ordinary commercial concern, dependent on making a profit out of exporting and importing ordinary commodities. That kind of business was not a goldmine; it had to be handled carefully and

---

[59] *Lettere*, III, pp. 350–4, also printed by De Roover, *Banco Medici*, pp. 565–7.

conscientiously. This was difficult when the head of the firm was totally involved in politics a thousand miles away.

The failure of the London branch had been due to the absence of that kind of management. The big figures in northern Europe in the late 1460s and early 1470s, Tommaso Portinari, Angelo Tani, Cristofano Spini and Gherardo Canigiani, had not been working efficiently together. Portinari and Tani had been suspicious of Canigiani, Spini had become his bitter enemy. Far away in Florence was the head of the international corporation, Lorenzo, who had never visited northern Europe or been trained as a banker. His exquisite aesthetic and political judgement, for he was unquestionably a man of very great ability, was useless. And as he said at the beginning, pressing business in the Palace of the Signoria, to which he had to devote himself continually as head of the regime, claimed his attention first. There is no indication in these documents that commercial business at London was essentially unprofitable. Other firms, Florentine, Venetian and, in particular, Genoese, carried on a similar business of exporting English wool, cloth and tin and importing Mediterranean goods. Lorenzo retained his interest in London and we find him as late as 1490 employing the same Tommaso Portinari and Cristofano Spini to investigate the rather fanciful plan of attracting English wool exports to Pisa and cutting out the Venetians from that trade.[60]

That is another story, which need not concern us here. The Medici branch in London was regarded as a failure by the late 1470s. The loans were probably a factor but the imperfect record of repayments of, for example, the loan of £8,468 in 1467 and the loan of £6,600 in 1471, indicate that most of the money lent was probably repaid and that the losses might well have been worthwhile in order to secure royal favour for a substantial commercial business. Lending to kings was never regarded as a profitable activity: it was always done in order to secure royal favour for other business which really was profitable. The failure at London seems to have been largely the result of a conflict of personalities which made rational management of the business impossible and also, perhaps, of the dishonesty of which the principal participants accused each other.

---

[60] M.E. Mallett, 'Anglo-Florentine Commercial Relations, 1465–1491', *Economic History Review*, 2nd Ser., 15 (1962), pp. 260–3.

14

The trade of late medieval Chester, 1500–1550

JENNY KERMODE

CHESTER IS an interesting exception to the generality of medieval English port towns at the end of the Middle Ages.[1] It was on the commercial periphery of England, and the capital of an undeveloped region, yet while most of the larger centres in more prosperous areas were struggling through the aftermath of recession,[2] Chester's trade was increasing and its population expanding.[3] In part this was because the scale of Chester's commerce required a relatively small increase to trigger growth as new markets became accessible in Spain and Portugal, and in part because of the emerging Lancashire textile industry.

By 1500 Chester was a primary centre which had drawn a multiplicity of functions to itself over the centuries. It had prospered during the late Saxon period, and then under William the Conqueror and Edward I, as a strategic supply base for military operations in Wales and Ireland. The Palatinate generated a unique flow of administrative business[4] to augment the town's markets, and in spite of its virtual exclusion from the wool trade and a

---

[1] I am grateful to Wendy Childs and Jane Laughton for their comments on this essay.

[2] For the debate on late medieval urban decline, see A.R. Bridbury, 'English Provincial Towns in the Later Middle Ages', *Econ. Hist. Rev.*, 2nd ser., 34 (1981), pp. 1–24; R.B. Dobson, 'Urban Decline in Late Medieval England', *Trans. Royal Hist. Soc.*, 27 (1977), pp. 1–22; and for the most recent wide-ranging assessment, see A.D. Dyer, *Decline and Growth in English Towns, 1400–1640* (London, 1991), esp. pp. 25–36.

[3] For Chester's economic fortunes before 1500, see Jane Laughton, 'Aspects of the Social and Economic History of Late Medieval Chester 1350–*c*. 1500' (Univ. of Cambridge PhD thesis, 1994). I am grateful to Dr Laughton for her comments and for references in nn. 5, 8 and 9.

[4] As a Palatinate, Cheshire had its own chancellor and exchequer court. The county courts enjoyed an extraordinary level of jurisdiction which, coupled with the tradition of maintaining law and order through recognisances, required the presence of large numbers of local gentry in the city during the frequent county court sessions. D.J. Clayton, *The Administration of the County Palatine of Chester, 1442–85* (Chetham Soc., 3rd ser., no. 35, Manchester, 1990), pp. 132–7, 230–1, 226, 241–60; R.C. Palmer, *The County Courts of Medieval England, 1150–1350* (Princeton, 1982), pp. 56–8; T. Thornton, 'Political

marginal investment in the wine trade, Chester became the only town of significant size north of Shrewsbury and west of the Pennines.

Chester's hinterland was famously undeveloped. The Lancashire textile industry was scarcely visible before 1500[5] and Cheshire itself was a poorly drained county, routinely milked of its surplus by a succession of royal servants with short-term leases on Cheshire estates.[6] Welsh wool and even minerals were not super-abundant, and Welsh wool and cloth were traded by Shropshire men through Shrewsbury and Ludlow, and later Bristol, with Welsh merchants claiming an increasing share from *c.* 1500.[7] Cattle trading was another regional speciality. The major drove roads out of North Wales bypassed Chester, turning south at Abergele, through Dyffryn Clwyd to Wrexham. Wales, though, was Chester's major source of cattle, which were sometimes fattened up at Christleton and Eccleston before being sold in the city's markets and fairs. Cheshire cattle and sheep were traded through Chester, some for stock breeding, some for consumption and hides.[8] As the point of exchange within a region concentrated on north and west Cheshire, North Wales, south-east Lancashire and the Irish Sea ports, Chester had sustained a role as regional entrepot.

Between 1463 and 1563, the city's population increased by some 30–40 per cent from about 3,000–3,500 to about 4,500–5,000. Evidence of epidemics in the city together with the patchy evidence of freemen entries suggests that the period of most rapid growth was between 1520 and 1550. Chester was small, in the same rank as Leicester, Oxford and Shrewsbury. Its nearest urban rivals in *c.* 1550 were Nantwich at 2,000, Wrexham at about 1,000 and Denbigh and Liverpool at about 600–800 each (Map

Society in Early Tudor Cheshire, 1480–1560' (Univ. of Oxford DPhil thesis, 1994), pp. 30–3, 118–22, 126–8. *VCH Ches.*, II, pp. 35–8.

[5] N. Lowe, *The Lancashire Textile Industry in the Sixteenth Century* (Chetham Soc., 3rd ser., no. 20, Manchester, 1972), pp. 1–5; F. Walker, *Historical Geography of Southwest Lancashire before the Industrial Revolution* (Chetham Soc., n.s., no. 103, Manchester, 1939), pp. 36, 60–1.

[6] A.E. Currie, 'The Demesne of the County Palatine of Chester in the Early Fifteenth Century' (Univ. of Manchester MA thesis, 1977), pp. 284ff. See also H.J. Hewitt, *Medieval Cheshire* (Chetham Soc., n.s., no. 88, Manchester, 1929), p. 4; *The Letters and Accounts of Sir William Brereton of Malpas*, ed. E.W. Ives (Lancs. and Ches. Rec. Soc., no. 116, Liverpool, 1976), pp. 15, 48.

[7] T.C. Mendenhall, *The Shrewsbury Drapers and the Welsh Wool Trade in the XVI and XVII Centuries* (London, 1953), pp. 2–3; E.A. Lewis, 'The Development of Industry and Commerce in Wales During the Middle Ages', *Trans. Royal Hist. Soc.*, n.s., 17 (1903), pp. 121–73: 142–8, 159–161; E.A. Lewis,' A Contribution to the Commercial History of Medieval Wales with Tabulated Accounts from 1301–1547 A.D.', *Y Cymmrodorion*, 24 (1913), pp. 86–188: 97.

[8] *Letters and Accounts of Sir William Brereton*, pp. 43, 45–6; Laughton, 'Aspects of Social and Economic History', pp. 168–9, 223, 234–5; C. Skeel, 'The Cattle Trade between Wales and England from the Fifteenth to the Nineteenth Centuries', *Trans. Royal Hist. Soc.*, 4th ser., 9 (1926), pp. 135–58: 149.

Map 14.1 Late Medieval Chester and its region.

14.1).The rural population was sparse and may have been roughly fifty to sixty per square mile in Cheshire and adjacent North Wales and forty-four in Lancashire.[9] There were at least thirteen markets: five were the eastern Cheshire boroughs, Altrincham, Congleton, Knutsford, Macclesfield and Stockport: three were the salt wiches of central Cheshire, while Chester and Tarvin dominated western Cheshire and the border.[10]

---

[9] N.J. Alldridge, 'The Mechanics of Decline: Immigration and Economy in Early Modern Chester', in M. Reed (ed.), *English Towns in Decline 1350–1800* (Centre for Urban History, University of Leicester, 1986); N. Alldridge, 'Population', in *VCH Chester* (forthcoming); Laughton, 'Aspects of Social and Economic History', pp. 44–9; C.B. Phillips and J.H. Smith, *Lancashire and Cheshire from* A.D. 1540 (London, 1994), pp. 5–9.
[10] A. Everitt, 'The Marketing of Agricultural Produce', in *AHEW*, IV, pp. 470–1.

In 1484 the city had claimed that it was 'wholly destroyed' because no merchant ship had been able to approach within twelve miles for sixty years. Two years later, the claim was that the city was 'thoroughly ruined . . . nearly one quarter destroyed' because access for shipping had been impossible for 200 years, and Welsh traders avoided the city because of high tolls. Allowing for due exaggeration, these petitions reflected Chester's physical disadvantages as a port. To avoid the shifting sands and silting of the river, trade was maintained by using anchorages in the Dee estuary as outports: West Kirby, Redbank, Heswall, Gayton, Neston, Newquay, Denhall, Burton, Shotwick and Portpool.[11] 'Chester has no merchant ship of its own', claimed the petition of 1484, and when Cestrians were licensed to trade with Gascony in 1496, they were allowed to use foreign vessels 'since they had none suitable of their own'.[12] Shipowning was not a characteristic of Chester's merchants, although it was increasing in the early sixteenth century, and instead Chester merchants ventured their cargoes in ships from other ports.[13] Facing increasing competition from Liverpool, the council attempted to improve port facilities with the construction of a quay at Neston some ten miles downriver from Chester. This was underway by 1541 and although the New Haven was used, it was never completed.[14]

Our view of Chester's trade can only be partial. The evidence for exports is slight until the systematic recording of the duties which were imposed on hides in 1536. We know even less about Chester's inland trade with its hinterland and so this discussion unavoidably focusses on the visible import trade.

During the first half of the sixteenth century there were changes in the pattern of trade around the Irish Sea which initially boosted Chester's port activity but eventually led to its decline. From the 1490s, the south-east Lancashire textile industry began to develop, trade with the Iberian peninsula and Brittany expanded, ships from Chester's creek ports in Lancashire began to appear south of the Ribble and Welsh merchants increasingly took over the sea trade of west Wales. Although the port of Chester increased its business during this period, there was no automatic increased investment by Cestrians in trade and their level of participation fluctuated.[15]

[11] Chester RO (hereafter CRO), CH/30, charter of Richard III reprinted in R.H. Morris, *Chester in the Plantagenet and Tudor Reigns* (Chester, [1893]), pp. 516–21. For Henry VII's remission of the fee farm, see CH/31 and Morris, *ibid.*, pp. 21–4.

[12] *Deputy Keeper's Reports*, XXXVII (1876), p. 143.

[13] K.P. Wilson, 'The Port of Chester in the Later Middle Ages' (Univ. of Liverpool PhD thesis, 1965), pp. 148–9.

[14] E. Rideout, 'The Chester Companies and the Old Quay', *Trans. Historic Soc. of Lancs. and Ches.*, 79 (1928), pp. 141–74.

[15] Southampton, a town with few local merchants and trade, was dominated by Italians and Londoners. O. Coleman, 'Trade and Prosperity in the Fifteenth Century: Some Aspects of the Trade of Southampton', *Econ. Hist. Rev.*, 2nd ser., 16 (1963–4), pp. 7–22; A.A.

IRISH AND COASTAL TRADE

The major flow of Chester's sea-borne trade was with Ireland, Brittany, Spain and Portugal.[16] The sources do not allow a precise valuation of trade, but Irish and coastal trade generally accounted for over 75 per cent of all inward sailings to Chester, rising to 95 per cent in 1548–9 (Map 14.2).[17] Outward sailings cannot be ennumerated, and it is not possible to guess how many ships left Chester in ballast. There was an active re-export trade between Chester and Ireland in both directions, suggesting that Irish merchants picked up what they could as return cargoes, perhaps more concerned with selling than with buying.[18] However, some traditional commodities had apparently disappeared. There is no record of Cheshire salt being exported *via* Chester after 1450, and it may have been replaced in Irish markets by salt from the bay of Bourgneuf carried in Breton and Gascon ships.[19] Irish corn imports faded following a ban in 1472.[20] The majority of cargoes were a mixture of cloth, fish, hides and skins, linen (cloth and yarn), wool (fells, flocks and yarn), a miscellany of honey, tallow, wax and occasional re-exports such as silk.[21] This trade was concentrated in the Pale, on the west coast of Ireland, and not with wealthier Waterford, Cork and Kinsale.[22]

Fish exceeded any other single commodity in quantity.[23] Eels, milwell (cod), herrings from the Irish Sea fisheries and salmon were regularly imported in ships from Ireland, Chester, Cumbria, the Isle of Man and Wales. Salmon was the most valuable, customed at more than double the

---

Ruddock, 'London Capitalists and the Decline of Southampton in the Early Tudor Period', *Econ. Hist. Rev.*, 2nd ser., 2 (1949), pp. 137–51. For Chester see below pp. 302–3.

[16] This analysis is derived from the Palatinate Customs Accounts and Local Customs Accounts recorded in Chester Sheriffs' Books. For an explanation of the two systems see Wilson, 'Port of Chester', chs. 1–2; *Chester Customs Accounts 1301–1566*, ed. K.P. Wilson (Lancs. and Ches. Rec. Soc, no. 111, Liverpool, 1969), pp. 1–18.

[17] The number of ships rose from 83 in 1494–8, 101 in 1520–9, 125 in 1530–9 to 179 in 1540–9: Wilson, 'Port of Chester', pp. 105–7. In so far as the provenance and destinations of ships in the port of Chester are known, Irish trade accounted for 80 per cent of arrivals and departures in 1404–5, and over 67 per cent in 1422: W. Childs and T. O'Neill, 'Overseas Trade', in A. Cosgrove (ed.), *A New History of Ireland, II: Medieval Ireland* (1987), p. 512.

[18] A Wexford man sueing for detinue of goods worth £40 in Chester: CRO, Pentice Court Roll, SR 535, m. 34d.

[19] Childs and O'Neill, 'Overseas Trade', p. 507; CRO, Sheriffs Book (hereafter SB), v, fol. 176.

[20] T. O'Neill, *Merchants and Mariners in Medieval Ireland* (Dublin, 1987), p. 27.

[21] For example CRO, SB, v, fols. 174–5.

[22] Wilson, 'Port of Chester', p. 96; Childs and O'Neill, 'Overseas Trade', p. 495.

[23] This was the same pattern in late fifteenth-century Bristol. W. Childs, 'Ireland's Trade with England in the Later Middle Ages', *Irish Econ. and Soc. Hist.*, 9 (1982), pp. 5–33: 6. See also O'Neill, *Merchants and Mariners*, pp. 31–40.

Map 14.2   Ports of origin of ships arriving at Chester, *c.* 1450–1550.
Source: CRO, Sheriffs Books. Map redrawn from Wilson, 'The Port of Chester in the Later Middle Ages'.

rate for herring,[24] but accounting for smaller quantities. In 1525–6 over 103 tons of herrings were shipped in but only half a ton of salmon. A Chester merchant, Otwell Corbet, leased the Bann salmon fishery in northern Ireland in 1519 for an annual rent of £60. In July 1526 he shipped eighty butts of salmon into Chester, and in August the *Anne Corbet* carried a further sixty

[24] CRO, Assembly Book, fol. 41.

butts.[25] Salmon continued to find a market and a regular place in Chester's imports.[26] Country fishmongers regularly paid fines[27] to retail fish in Chester and probably beyond. In 1501, for instance, Thomas Corbet of Chester sold herrings to a Nantwich butcher,[28] and fish from Drogheda was carted *via* Chester to Shrewsbury in 1476–7.[29]

Skins and hides continued as a regular Irish export, the bulk of the hides being shipped directly to continental ports.[30] Chester imported both tanned and raw hides, together with tallow used to waterproof hides. Skins were imported in greater quantities. In 1525–6, whereas some 2,200 Irish hides entered Chester, so did over 13,000 lambskins (at least 6,300 of them black), 10,200 sheepskins, 2,300 badger pelts, 1,100 calfskins, 320 each of marten and otter skins, 300 fox skins, including cases (skins stitched into squares), 90 goat skins and 50 hart skins.[31] Alum and the oil used by glovers and tawyers to prepare light leathers also came from Ireland.[32] Prices for skins in the London luxury market rose fast between 1500 and 1550, marten tripling in price and otter quadrupling, and it is likely that some Irish skins were sold in London after preparation in Chester.[33]

The pattern of Chester's textile trade with Ireland underwent a transformation in the early sixteenth century. The falling demand for clipped wool in the textile industry of Coventry and its region was increasingly met by midland growers,[34] and only small quantities were imported *via* Chester after 1500. About nine or ten sacks were imported in 1525–6, and unspecified quantities of flock, wool or cloth shearings.[35] Wool from imported sheepskins would have been sold as a by-product by Chester's leatherworkers.

[25] O'Neill, *Merchants and Mariners*, pp. 31–40; CRO, SB, v, fol. 177v.
[26] CRO, SB, viii, fos. 39–99, and see, for example, William Goodman, SB, v, fol. 187; vii, fols. 23, 61v–63; viii, fols. 20, 89v.
[27] For example CRO, SB, iv, fols. 5–7, 11–2; v, fol. 47v.
[28] CRO, SR 445, m. 1d.
[29] CRO, Mayors Book, vi, fol. 36.
[30] O'Neill, *Merchants and Mariners*, pp. 78–9.
[31] CRO, SB, v, fols. 174–97d; viii, fols. 59–93 (1543–4); *Chester Customs Accounts*, pp. 132–42.
[32] CRO, SB, v, fol. 176.
[33] A.D. Longfield, *Anglo Irish Trade in the Sixteenth Century* (London, 1929), pp. 62–3; E.M. Veale, *The English Fur Trade in the Later Middle Ages* (Oxford, 1966), p. 169; D.M. Woodward, 'The Chester Leather Industry, 1558–1625', *Trans. Historic Soc. of Lancs. and Ches.*, 119 (1967), p. 71.
[34] Wilson, 'Port of Chester', p. 91; C. Gill, *Studies in Midland History* (Oxford, 1930), pp. 81–3; W.G. Hoskins, 'English Provincial Towns in the Early Sixteenth Century', *Trans. Royal Hist. Soc.*, 5th ser., 6 (1956), pp. 1–19; C. Phythian-Adams, *Desolation of a City. Coventry and the Urban Crisis of the Late Middle Ages* (Cambridge, 1979), pp. 33–67.
[35] CRO, SB, v, fols. 174–187v.

Coarse friezes, checkers, mantles, blankets, rugs (perhaps some higher-quality Waterford rugs) accounted for most imports.[36] Quantification is difficult, but checkers predominated and at least 2,000 yards plus 1,500 yards or pieces were imported in 1525–6, together with at least 300 yards plus 550 yards or pieces of linen cloth. In the same year one cargo contained 12 lb of 'Irish silk', but this was probably a re-export from the continent. Yarn accounted for a large part of Irish exports, some 8,000 lb into Chester in 1525–6, but the record did not differentiate between woollen and linen yarn. Smaller quantities of fine and middling yarn were shipped from time to time.[37]

By 1550, the balance of this import trade had shifted away from finished Irish cloth to sheepskins and to yarn supplied to the expanding Lancashire textile industry. In 1522 and 1537 Irish legislation vainly tried to defend domestic textile producers against English competition,[38] but from the 1540s, a coarse woollen cloth disarmingly called Manchester Cotton, quickly dominated the north-western textile industry. Linen cloth manufactured in Lancashire competed successfully with Irish linen products. As imports of Irish yarn through Chester and Liverpool rose, so did the export of northern cloth to Ireland while Irish cloth exports to England inevitably fell.

Butchered beef, honey and small quantities of Irish barley, rye and occasionally wheat were shipped in to Chester, a trade which increased in 1536 during the grain shortage.[39] Battry, old and new brass and pewter, together with glass and turpentine were irregular imports.[40] From time to time Chester's role as the port of embarkation for English campaigns is in evidence as a further aspect of the town's involvement with Ireland. Soldiers passed through the city in 1539–40 and munitions in 1558. Church dignatories lodged in the city *en route*: Archbishop Rokeby in 1514, and the dean of St

[36] Waterford rugs were often russet, and a few russet mantles were included in Chester's imports, e.g. CRO, SB, v, fol. 178, and fledges were a staple commodity during the first half of the sixteenth century: Longfield, *Anglo-Irish Trade*, pp. 80–1; CRO, SB, viii, fols. 39–99. Bristol's Irish textile imports in 1492–3 were dominated by mantles worth £202, followed by frieze, worth £60. Childs, 'Ireland's Trade with England', pp. 6, 19.

[37] For example CRO, SB, v, fols. 175, 177.

[38] Longfield, *Anglo-Irish Trade*, p. 77.

[39] For example CRO, SB, v, fol. 179v; vii, fol. 97v; viii, fols. 23, 81v, 82v, 84, 89. For grain imports in 1536 see SB, vii, fols. 58–62, 100. There is no evidence of imported Irish grain into Chester from about the 1420s, and a possible prohibition of exports from Ireland in the 1430s prolonged its absence. E.M. Carus-Wilson, 'The Overseas Trade of Bristol', in E. Power and M.M. Postan (eds.), *Studies in English Trade in the Fifteenth Century* (London, 1933), p. 199; K. Down, 'Colonial Society and Economy in the High Middle Ages', in A. Cosgrove (ed.), *Late Medieval Ireland, 1370–1541* (Dublin, 1981), p. 485.

[40] For example CRO, SB, v, fol. 178v; x, fol. 175; Longfield, *Anglo-Irish Trade*, pp. 126–7.

Paul's in 1558. Some expeditions, like those of Sir William Brereton and Sir William Skeffington of 1534, used Beaumaris in preference to Chester.[41]

Ships from the Cumbrian and Lancashire coasts were shipping herrings, salmon, cod and hides into Chester during the early sixteenth century. This was probably local produce intended for retail in the city's markets.[42]

There is little direct evidence of what was exported to Ireland from Chester at this time, but it is likely that it matched the coal, cloth (straights and rays), exported from Bristol in 1504.[43] Assertive Welsh merchants were developing their own trade in such traditional items as slate and millstones, as well as in small quantities of local cloth.[44] Salt, wine and Breton canvas were re-exported from Chester to Ireland, and vice versa from Ireland to Chester.[45]

The beginning of the sixteenth century was a turning point in terms of investment in the Irish trade. After almost a century Coventry merchants virtually disappeared as traders in Irish wool and Coventry cloth: only eight were active in 1500–1, two in 1508–9 and one or two from time to time thereafter. Occasionally a Coventry draper appeared in Chester's pentice court to recover debts from Chester men.[46] From 1500 Drogheda merchants abandoned Chester in favour of Liverpool and became the largest single group there. Dubliners remained to dominate the Irish trade through Chester, comprising the largest single group there between 1520 and 1540: their number included a dozen or so Dublin mayors and bailiffs.

It is difficult to identify all the denizen merchants but it seems as though the direct involvement of Chester men in this trade varied. After 1539 there were more non-freemen than freemen shipping into the port. Relatively few Chester merchants were involved in the Irish trade and generally were outnumbered by nine to one.[47] They preferred to focus their investment in continental ventures.

[41] R. Bagwell, *Ireland under the Tudors*, 3 vols. (London, 1885–90), I, p. 169; CRO, SB, vii, fol. 121.

[42] CRO, SB, v, fols 11v, 79v, 103, 125, 146–7, 174; vi, fols. 3v, 15; vii, fols. 5, 23, 62, 74v, 98v, 126v; viii, fols. 66v, 71v; Wilson, 'Port of Chester', pp. 97–8. For the 1460s, see SB, ii, fols. 72, 73v, 78; iii, fols. 12, 29, 32.

[43] Longfield, *Anglo-Irish Trade*, p. 170. For Chester as a market for coal, see J. Hatcher, *The History of the British Coal Industry, I: Before 1700* (Oxford, 1993), pp. 131–2. Coal was definitely exported from Chester in 1565–6. Wilson, 'Port of Chester', p. 87.

[44] Lewis, 'Industry and Commerce in Wales', pp. 146, 160; Lewis, 'Contribution to the Commercial History of Medieval Wales', p. 90; Wilson, 'Port of Chester', p. 97.

[45] For example, CRO, SB, v, fols. 174, 179.

[46] For example: in 1522 a debt of £21 16s. against three Cestrians, and in 1531, 33s. 4d. against two. CRO, SFB 2/13; SBC 1, fol. 13v.

[47] Wilson, 'Port of Chester', pp. 94, 163, 166.

CONTINENTAL TRADE

From the 1490s[48] up to the early 1540s, Chester enjoyed a boom in its trade with Europe. The port was well placed to take advantage of the expansion in trade with the Iberian peninsula in the more politically stable climate which followed the 1466 Anglo-Spanish treaty.[49] Imported Spanish iron, wine from Portugal, Spain and Gascony became the basis for a dramatic expansion in overseas trade, which allowed other Mediterranean commodities to reach Chester, and carried back hides and northern cloth. This was a short-lived boom since deteriorating political relations between England and Spain in the 1540s adversely affected trade with the region thereafter.

Trade with Spain focussed on the Basque region and its local iron mines. Iron imports rose from 939 tons in 1490–1500 to 2,506 tons in 1510–20, and 4,273 tons in 1530–40, and although dropping below 1,000 tons thereafter, survived international tension as a regular item in Chester's trade.[50] Iron was carried in local and Iberian ships, and up to 1540 alien merchants shipped the largest quantities: 77 per cent in 1490–1500, 36 per cent in 1510–20, 61 per cent in 1523–30, 52 per cent in 1530–40, and 28 per cent in 1540–50.[51] Although iron was the major consignment in most cargoes, small quantities of angora, silk and velvet, liquorice, train oil, woad and Cordovan skins might be added.[52] Trade with Portugal and Andalusia (*via* the northern Spanish ports), brought cork, dyestuffs, figs and raisins, litmus, pepper and herbs, oil, sugar, wax and sweet wines to Chester from *c.* 1509.[53] It was never extensive and dwindled to only two shipments between 1542 and 1560.[54] From at least 1494–5, small loads of Spanish wine reached Chester, and from time to time southern ships also carried cargoes of Gascon wine.[55]

Northern cloth, hides and skins comprised the main return cargoes. In 1539 Manchester cottons, frieze, kersey, broad dozens and goatskins were carted from Chester to four Spanish ships at anchor in the Dee estuary.[56] In 1536 Chester was brought into the national customs system for leather and in 1537–8, 10,681 tanned hides were customed in five Spanish and five

---

[48] Some Spanish ships with wine reached Chester in 1484–5: CRO, SB, iii, fol. 105–105v.
[49] Wendy Childs confirms that Iberian trade with southern English ports was increasing in the 1470s and 1480s.
[50] Wilson, 'Port of Chester', pp. 124, 137: *Chester Customs Accounts*, p. 71; Woodward, *Elizabethan Chester*, p. 130.
[51] Wilson, 'Port of Chester' p. 124: *Chester Customs Accounts*, pp. 69–71.
[52] Wilson, 'Port of Chester', p. 130: e.g. CRO, SB, v, fol. 167; vii, fols. 21v, 23v, 59, 61, 141.
[53] For example CRO, SB, v, fols. 164v, 176v, 179; vii, fols. 4, 58, 73v; viii, fol. 44v; Wilson, *Chester Customs Accounts*, pp. 138–9, 142.
[54] Wilson, 'Port of Chester', p. 13.
[55] CRO, SB, iv, fols. 52–62v; *Chester Customs Accounts*, p. 35.
[56] CRO, SB, vii, fols. 122v, 125–6v. See also vii, fol. 74.

Chester ships. Figures for subsequent years ranged from 700 to 1,600 hides, with Spanish merchants exporting the larger share. Thus in 1537–8, six Spaniards shipped 5,739 hides in five cargoes, while fifteen Cestrians shipped 4,830 hides also in five ships.[57]

Chester was the most north-westerly port regularly handling wine. Even though it may have been the terminus for voyages which had already called at Bristol or Dublin and intermediate ports,[58] Chester's wine imports doubled from 1,131 tuns in 1490–1500 to 2,451 tuns in 1510–20, the highest ever. Imports remained high through the 1520s peaking at 2,335 tuns in the 1530s before falling away to 698 tuns the following decade.[59] Chester regularly accounted for 3–4 per cent of national imports except for 1509–10 when a staggering 9 per cent of imported wine came through Chester.[60] Gascony was the main source of Chester's wine imports, augmented by tiny quantities of Portuguese and Spanish wine. This was one branch of trade which Chester freemen dominated, denizens accounting for about 90 per cent between 1510 and 1540.[61]

Ships from Gascony also carried alum, dyestuffs, honey, linen cloth, pitch, tar, train oil, salt, vinegar and woad. Some of these commodities may have been taken on as ships called into Breton ports *en route* for England, and Breton ships certainly carried Gascon products to Chester, in addition to Breton canvas.[62] It is unlikely that French ships ventured so far to return in ballast and it is probable that their return cargoes were mainly hides and northern cloths.[63]

Trade with distant markets brought foreign merchants to Chester. They sued and were sued in the city courts.[64] Spaniards anchored their ships in the Dee, waiting for return cargoes and in 1532, a Spaniard was killed during a fracas with his fellows.[65] Trade was conducted directly by Cestrians at the port of dispatch or through agents. Peter Grey of Lupe Quinto (perhaps Lequeitio), was contracted in 1511 to conduct business on behalf of Roger Barrowe in Biscay, Spain, Bordeaux and Aquitaine, but he failed to give satisfaction and was pursued by Barrowe and others through the Chester city courts for over a decade.[66] Anglo-Spanish and Portuguese co-operation

[57] *Chester Customs Accounts*, pp. 57–62.
[58] As in the fifteenth century, Wilson, 'Port of Chester', p. 119.
[59] *Ibid.*, p. 121: *Chester Customs Accounts*, pp. 70–1.
[60] *Chester Customs Accounts*, p. 72.
[61] *Ibid.*, p. 71; Wilson, 'Port of Chester', p. 124.
[62] Wilson, 'Port of Chester', p. 135; CRO, SB, v, fols. 103, 164–5v, 176v; vii, fols. 5, 7, 22, 38–54, 58, 73v.
[63] Wilson, 'Port of Chester', p. 136; CRO, SB, viii, fol. 16.
[64] For example CRO, Portmote Court Rolls, MR 111, mm. 6,11; SR 535, mm. 28, 37; SR 543, m. 1; SFB 2/30.
[65] University of Liverpool, Sidney Jones Library, MS23.5, 52 (Archdeacon Roger's manuscript).
[66] CRO, MR 111, mm. 8–11; MR 112, m. 8v.

was achieved, to the extent that Chester merchant Henry Gee could leave £5 to 'Salse the Spaynard for the good love that I ber unto hyme and in recompense of all suche rekenyngs be twixte hym and me'.[67]

CHESTER'S TRADE AND THE REGION

The impact of external trade upon a local economy can be difficult to gauge. Although Chester's outports were busy, the volume of goods carried the twelve miles or so into the city and the distant destination of the goods imported through the Chester customs system are unknown. A county whose cash was regularly skimmed by its earl to maintain English garrisons in Wales, and routinely exploited by the numerous lessees of the earl's land seeking short–term profit,[68] may have been a limited market for imported goods. Sir William Brereton bought eighty-two yards of Irish rugg from two Chester merchants in 1531 but he also bought 300 lb of cloth for his house-hold's livery from London *via* Nantwich.[69] Other gentry households pre-ferred to shop in London for items such as Sir William Booth of Dunham's gold chain, Sir Thomas Butler of Bewsey's blackbird and cage, Anthony Calveley of Lea's silver spoons and Richard Cholmondeley of Cholmonde-ley's saddles.[70]

Imported iron, oil, resin, salt, wine and woad were sold in Chester's markets[71] alongside regional products. Sales of wool and of cloth, whatever its provenance, were regular causes of disputes in the city courts and included Manchester cottons, coverlets, kerseys, London russet, Welsh mantles and straights.[72] Rye and wheat, Irish salmon and herrings, local cheese, Welsh lead, tanned hides and livestock were traded in the city.[73] Although barley, oats and wheat were grown, livestock was the basis of the county's agriculture and Chester was its main market place. The city horse fairs attracted large

[67] Cheshire RO, EDA 2/1 fols. 188–9. See CRO, SB, v, fol. 121, for another example of international partnerships.

[68] See nn. 3 and 6 above.

[69] *Letters and Accounts of Sir William Brereton*, pp. 238, 241.

[70] *Lancashire and Cheshire Wills and Inventories*, ed. G.J. Piccope, 3 vols. (Chetham Soc., nos. 33, 51, 54, Manchester, 1851–61), I, pp. 139–42, II, pp. 65, 126, III, p. 43.

[71] CRO, SR 444, m.1; SR 445, m.1; SR 504, mm. 9 (a dyer buying 218 lb of woad), 23; SR 522, mm. 6d., 28, 34; SR 535, m. 26; SFB 3/2.

[72] For example CRO, SR 444, m. 1; SR 445 m. 1d; SR 504 m. 35d; SR 506 mm. 47d–48d, 49d, 60, 64; SR 522 m. 33d; SR 543 m. 12; SB, v, fol. 156 (garment made of London russet); SB, vii, fol. 89; *Letters and Accounts of Sir William Brereton*, p. 45; *Lancs. and Ches. Wills and Inventories*, III, p. 47, a Denbigh mantle in the will of the rector of St Peter's.

[73] For example CRO, SR 444, m. 1d; SR 445, m. 1d; SR 504, mm. 9, 14, 17d, 26d; SR 506, mm. 53, 54, 57; SR 522, m. 32; SR 554, m. 1d; SB, vi, fol. 18v., vii, fol. 31; SBC 1, fol. 8.

numbers especially from Shropshire and North Wales. Horses were bred for sale in London as well as Chester, and cattle and sheep for stock breeding and for local and possibly London consumption.[74] Warrington butchers bought cattle from Welsh farmers and haggled over payment in Chester's pentice court. The demands of the Chester leather industry drew on Cheshire, Lancashire and the farmers of North Wales,[75] drovers bringing in large herds of 200 or more animals for sale.[76]

COURTS AND FINANCE

Even before Chester's trade became a significant element in the north-western economy, the taxation and judicial processes developed by the palatine administration created a pool of financial expertise and formal services,[77] crucial to economic and commercial expansion. The city courts afforded easy access for the enrolment and recovery of debts,[78] and for the enforcement of contracts and awards of compensation. As the taxation and customs centre for the Palatinate, Chester had a key role to play in the circulation of coins and in facilitating credit.

There was a significant presence of goldsmiths working in the city: 1 per cent of the 930 new freemen between 1500 and 1560. They were very active in the city courts, frequently appearing as pledges and as creditors and debtors. John Belyn, William Bexwith and Richard Woodward in particular engaged in business sometimes involving exceptionally large sums of money.[79] In 1531, two Manchester merchants, Thomas Bakke and Thomas Bewe, separately impleaded Richard Woodward and William Bexwith, Chester goldsmiths, for three debts of £18, suspiciously uniform sums suggestive

---

[74] *Letters and Accounts of Sir William Brereton*, pp. 43, 45–6. A.M. Johnson, 'Some Aspects of the Political, Constitutional, Social, and Economic History of the City of Chester, 1550–1662' (Univ. of Oxford DPhil thesis, 1970), p. 234.

[75] For example CRO, SR 504, mm. 23, 37.

[76] Butchers were notorious forestallers, and in Chester industrial as well as food supply was affected when cattle were kept back. Butchers and drovers were blamed for manipulating market prices. CRO, SB, vi, fol. 19v. For an instance of drovers and carriers brawling see SB, v, fol. 61.

[77] For the early history of the development of the earldom of Chester's administration and mint, see D. Crouch, 'The Administration of the Norman Earldom', in A.T. Thacker (ed.), *The Earldom of Chester and its Charters: A Tribute to Geoffrey Barraclough*, *Journal of the Chester and North Wales Archaeological Society*, 71 (1991), pp. 69–96; B.M.C. Husain, *Cheshire under the Norman Earls 1066–1237* (Chester, 1973), pp. 38–40, 47; *VCH Ches.*, I, pp. 260–3, 325–7.

[78] Chester mayors could enrol debts under Statute Merchant, *Cal. Pat. Rolls, 1281–92*, p. 449, and although no separate roll has survived, statutory debts were recorded in the mayor's pentice court rolls occasionally. E.g. CRO, MR 112, m. 1.

[79] Thomas Belyn (perhaps John's son), appeared in the Chester courts in 1551, as goldsmith of London. For goldsmiths, see CRO, SR 535, m. 26; SR 543, m. 12; SR 554, m. 1; SBC 1, fols. 38v., 39, 69v.

of loans.[80] Credit and maybe cash loans flowed into Chester from further afield. A Dubliner impleaded a Chester goldsmith in 1540 for a debt of 30s. and in 1551, a London goldsmith Thomas Belyn was pursuing Chester merchant John Haward for a debt of £10.[81] There is evidence of a bullion shortage in Cheshire in the early sixteenth century: orders were sent to the mayor of Chester in 1499 that all coins were to be accepted in the city, however small, with the exception of Irish spurret pennies,[82] and in 1535 counterfeit coins were said to be circulating from Valle Crucis and Norton Priory.[83]

A shortage of good coins encouraged alternatives. Pawning was quite common in the city, notably in the 1530s,[84] and in pastoral Cheshire, livestock were often bequeathed. Chester testators Katherine Brown, widow, Ralph Aldersey, merchant, and Richard Massy, merchant, left cattle as legacies[85] and Richard Grosvenor of Eaton made several bequests of cattle as cash equivalents – such as £40 in kyne, 100 marks in oxen – in his will of 1549.[86] There is also some evidence of coin hoards. In 1551 the *post mortem* estate of Mancunian draper, James Williamson, contained a hoard of mixed coins and a Liverpool merchant called Raynford, whose first name is unknown, impleaded a Manchester merchant, James Wrest in the Chester pentice court for withholding a large amount of coins.[87]

Outsiders brought to the city courts all sorts of actions, that often ended up as actions for debt as a legal convenience, and their appearance is perhaps indicative of the extent and level of regional trade chanelled through Chester. The numbers of such outsiders were small, accounting for between 4 per cent and 7 per cent of cases between 1500 and 1551.[88] The largest groups represented Chester's immediate trading contacts with Cheshire and Wales.[89] The former group was drawn mainly from north and west Cheshire, a few from the salt wiches and Frodsham.[90] Most Welsh litigants came from Denbigh, Wrexham, Mold and Flintshire, with one or two from Beaumaris,

[80] CRO, SBC 1, fols. 38v., 69v. See also SFB 2/17.

[81] CRO, SR 543, m. 6; SR 554, m. 1.

[82] *Deputy Keeper's Reports*, XXXVII, p. 144.

[83] *Letters and Accounts of Sir William Brereton*, pp. 40–1.

[84] CRO, SB, v, fols. 130–1, 157; vii, fols. 9, 31, 67, 85.

[85] *A Collection of Lancashire and Cheshire Wills*, ed. W. Fergusson (Lancs. and Ches. Rec. Soc., no. 30, 1895), pp. 169–70, and also pp. 168, 174–5: Cheshire RO, WS 5/1, 6/7.

[86] *Cheshire Sheaf*, 17 (1920), pp. 106–7.

[87] CRO, SR 554, m. 1.

[88] Cf. Colchester where actions involving outsiders comprised some 20 per cent. R.H. Britnell, *Growth and Decline in Colchester, 1300–1525* (Cambridge, 1986), pp. 106–7.

[89] This discussion is based on an analysis of the records of the courts of the pentice and portmote, sampled by decade from 1500 to 1551. I am grateful to the Nuffield Foundation for the grant, SOC/181 (2660), which made the research possible. See also Wilson, 'Port of Chester', p. 97.

[90] For example CRO, SR 443, m. 4: SR 445, m. 1d: SR 506, m. 64d: SB, vii, fol. 70v.

Caernarfon, Conway and Colwyn.[91] The ratio of Welsh plaintiffs to Welsh defendants was about 60:40, and although the restructuring of local government in North Wales might have led to a decrease in the Welsh use of the city courts after 1541, there is no visible evidence of such a change.

Lancashire, and in particular Manchester and its region, accounted for the next significant group of outsiders, appearing more often as plaintiffs than as defendants.[92] They played an increasingly active role in the textile trade.[93] Leland in 1535 noted Manchester merchants buying flax in Liverpool but they were shipping through Chester from the late fifteenth century. There is some evidence of Cestrians joining with Mancunians to trade further up country. In 1540 Hugh Aldersey of Chester alone, and Henry Gee of Chester in partnership with Edward Jannys of Manchester, bought iron in Manchester.[94] Richard Crompton, merchant of Bury, claimed in 1547 that he regularly sold cottons to John Offeley of Chester.[95] Kendal cloth continued to be sold and exported through Chester in the sixteenth century,[96] and in 1547 specific imposts were demanded of Kendal and Manchester merchants selling in the city.[97]

Merchants sought trade wherever there was a profit, and from time to time men from as far afield as Canterbury, Kendal, London, Solihull, Shropshire, Staffordshire and Yorkshire pleaded cases of debt in Chester.[98] Londoners almost always appeared pursuing local debtors and for sums larger than usual, ranging from 27s. to £100. They included a brewer indebted to Chester ironmonger Roger Barrowe for £100, a grocer, haberdashers, a mercer, merchants, salters and aldermen John Champanel and James Spen-

---

[91] For example CRO, SR 504, mm. 10–11, 29, 35–6; SR 506 m. 73d; MR 111, m. 1: SBC 1, fol. 6; SBC 7, fols. 66, 107.

[92] For example CRO, SR 522, m. 13; SR 535, mm. 12, 25d, 40; SR 543, m. 12; SR 554, mm. 1, 6–6d; SBC 1, fols. 50, 64, 69v; SBC 7, fol. 34.

[93] Wilson, 'Port of Chester', p. 100.

[94] *Pleadings and Depositions in the Duchy Court of Lancaster*, ed. H. Fishwick, 3 vols. (Lancs. and Ches. Rec. Soc., nos. 32, 35, 40, 1896–9), I, p. 136.

[95] *Ibid.*, I, pp. 3, 8–11. Business relations merged into closer ties with marriages between Chester and Manchester families. Either Henry Gee of Chester or his sister married into Edward Jannys of Manchester's family, and his son Edmund Gee married the sister of a Manchester merchant Richard Shawcross, who subsequently acted as his executor. Cheshire RO EDA 2/1, fols. 188–9; CRO, SR 554 m. 6: *Lancs. and Ches. Wills and Inventories*, I, p. 159. The daughter of another Chester merchant, Thomas Aldersey, married the Manchester merchant Thomas Bakke: CRO, EDA 2/1, fols. 163–4.

[96] For example, CRO, MR 111, m. 6; SFB 2/11, 12; SBC 1, fols. 20, 30; Wilson, 'Port of Chester', p. 103.

[97] CRO, AB 1, fol. 77–77v.

[98] For example CRO, SR 522, m. 11; SR 535 m. 23d; SR 554, m. 22; SBC 1, fols. 20, 30, 35, 53v: SBC 7, fols. 28, 72, 82, 83, 96, 98, 103.

cer.[99] Londoners might ship goods from Spain to Chester[100] but their claim to trade toll free in the city was disputed, and there was concerted opposition in 1537 by 'influential men' to prevent a London grocer from retailing wine in the city.[101]

The convenience of the city and palatine courts encouraged merchants and others to negotiate agreements and to enrol debts from transactions possibly concluded away from the city. Walter Jobson of Hull brought an action against Edward Clayton of Rotherham for a debt of £54 in 1551 and in the same year John Both, a mercer of Prescot (Lancs.), impleaded George Orme, yeoman of Lee (Lancs.), for a debt of £16.[102] In 1516 a Denbigh merchant, William Dakers, took fellow-townsmen to court in Chester for a debt of 26s. 8d.,[103] and Howell ap David ap Tudor and David ap Robert ap Ithell took Edmund ap Parry to court over a breach of contract. Business spanned the region: in 1512 Thomas Pygot of Halifax impleaded Morgan Hewik, draper of Denbigh, for 36s.,[104] and a Warrington butcher and Nicholas Blundell of Crosby were jointly liable for a debt of £10. In 1531 two Cestrians, Richard Hoket, merchant, and Richard Mason, weaver, were jointly indebted with Hugh Prycke, gentleman of Conway, to Thomas Middleton of Chester.[105]

CITY ECONOMY

An unquantifiable volume of Chester's trade was in raw materials and it is possible to identify craftsmen whose employment was in complementary industries. The most numerous were associated with textile production and leather working, accounting for around 28 per cent and 20 per cent respectively of the new freemen entering Chester between 1500 and 1510. About 20 per cent of the textile workers were weavers and about 50 per cent were in

---

[99] Barrowe v. John Churston, brewer: CRO, SR 504, mm. 36, 36 (a) d. See also SR 522, mm. 5, 30d; SR 535, m. 27d; SR 554, mm. 1, 3, 7; SBC 1, fols. 3, 25v, 35, 45, 53v: SBC 7, fols. 5, 49, 52, 78, 98, 103, 122–3: MR 111, m. 2.

[100] CRO, AB 1, fol. 78v. For Londoners shipping through Chester, see *Chester Customs Accounts*, pp. 76–9, 83, 85–6, 88, 90, 94, 96, 99.

[101] The Londoner complained that previously two Bristol men had been allowed to sell sugar in the city and that foreigners sold wine at the Portpool from time to time. *Letters and Papers, Foreign and Domestic, of the Reign of Henry VIII*, ed. J.S. Brewer, J. Gairdner and R.H. Brodie, 2nd edn, 21 vols, in 33 parts (HMSO, London, 1862–1932), VI, no. 202, p. 92.

[102] CRO, SR 554, mm. 2 (Both), 7 (Jobson).

[103] One was a weaver. CRO, SFB 2/1–6. See also SR 506, mm. 68, 73v.

[104] CRO, SR 506, mm. 37 (Tudor), 41 (Pygot), 69d (abbot of Basingwerk v. Wrexham men for a debt of fourteen marks).

[105] CRO, SFB 2/9 (Blundell), 2/15 (Hoket).

the finishing and commercial branches of the textile trade in 1500–10.[106] Chester fullers attracted distant customers and in 1560 the *Bee* of Whitehaven landed sixty yards of cloth to be fulled in the city.[107]

The basic occupations – building, provisioning (including butchers), clothing (cappers, drapers, girdlers, hatmakers, tailors, shoemakers) – accounted for 34 per cent of admissions between 1500–1550, a pattern matching that of many early sixteenth-century towns.[108] Although there were some thirty craft guilds or companies in 1499/1500,[109] members of fifty-three different crafts and trades were involved in cases before the pentice court, excluding clergy, gentlemen, husbandmen and yeomen – the number of different occupations recorded in the court records fluctuating between thirty and thirty-seven in any single year. The court rolls confirm the importance of leather and textile workers in the city. Wholesalers – that is mercers, merchants, drapers and ironmongers – were a slightly smaller group and acted as middlemen between different craftsmen, selling buckles and stirrups to saddlers for instance, or acting as agents in the sale of Cheshire wool in the city as well as selling imports.[110]

From around the 1530s the basis of the city's economy shifted slightly so that by the 1560s, freemen entering textile trades had fallen to about 21 per cent while those entering leather trades had risen to 27 per cent: notably they were glovers, shoemakers and cordwainers. Butchers often acted as middlemen trading in hides, and if the forty-seven butchers were included amongst leatherworkers, that group comprised 30 per cent of all new freemen between 1500 and 1560. Chester butchers and glovers traded in hides, mainly light skins from Ireland and heavier hides from neighbouring counties. Hides were finished in Chester and forwarded to London, although some were kept back for local shoemakers.[111]

Of the new freemen entering Chester between 1500 and 1510, the most rapidly growing group were those associated with trade. Admissions almost trebled between 1500 and 1560, doubling between the mid-1530s and 1540s and matching the peak in overseas trade. Occupational ascriptions do not

---

[106] Analysis based on *The Rolls of the Freemen of the City of Chester*, ed. J.H.E. Bennett, 2 vols. (Lancs. and Ches. Rec. Soc., nos. 51, 55, Liverpool, 1906–8), I; D.M. Palliser, 'A Revised List of Chester Freemen' (typescript, CRO); CRO, Mayors Books.

[107] CRO, MUB/2.

[108] Cf. the 23–30 per cent estimated by N. Goose, 'English pre-industrial urban economies', *Urban Hist. Yearbook* (1982), pp. 24–30: 24–5, and the 35–40 per cent estimated by W. G. Hoskins, *Provincial England* (London, 1965), p. 88.

[109] British Library (hereafter BL), Harleian MS 2104, fol. 4.

[110] CRO, SR 444, m. 1d (Mannyng v. Barker and [blank] v. Hamnet); SR 543, m. 12 (Johnson v. Brerewood).

[111] D.M. Woodward, 'The Chester Leather Industry, 1558–1625', *Trans. Historic Soc. of Lancs. and Ches.*, 119 (1967), pp. 68–73.

tell the whole story though. Ironmongers were active in overseas trade and by the early sixteenth century were combined in one powerful company with the mercers.[112] Wholesale traders turned to all manner of enterprises.[113] For instance several merchant oligarchs, including William Davison, William Goodman, Hugh and Robert Aldersey and David Middleton, were said to own taverns in 1533. In 1557 the council identified victualling as an occupation 'for the common weale', and agreed on a reduced entry fine in an apparent attempt to attract more victuallers to the city.[114]

During the sixteenth century, the assembly tightened its control over the city's craftsmen and trade in general, in order to advantage the freemen of the city,[115] and its management of local port customs also favoured freemen.[116] Nonetheless, although Cestrians were continuously engaged in trade, their share fluctuated. Dubliners dominated the Irish Sea trade, and other English and Welsh merchants, together with continental merchants, competed for the trade with France, Portugal and Spain. In 1538–42, during Chester's trading zenith, 40–5 per cent of traders identified in the local customs were Chester freemen.[117] Most were probably occasional traders, and between 1500 and 1550 there were about forty or so significant Chester merchants, sometimes several members of one family, who shipped through the port.[118]

Their investment was predominantly in iron and wine imports and cloth and hide exports, but not exclusively so, and the top half-dozen traders continued to trade in Irish commodities. Richard Grymesdiche for example, whose career lasted over forty years of regularly importing wine and iron, bought dyed kersey and other cloth from Irish merchants in Chester.[119] William Goodman, another long-lived trader, had three to five wine ship-

[112] Johnson, 'Aspects of Political, Constitutional, Social, and Economic History', p. 277.

[113] The Cappers accused mercers, amongst others, of unfairly competing by retailing caps: Morris, *Chester*, pp. 316–17.

[114] *Letters and Papers*, VI, no. 202, p. 92. Davidson and two Aldersays owned taverns between 1546 and 1554, BL, Harleian MS 2054, fols. 14v–15v; CRO, AB 1, fol. 91. In a decadal sample of court records between 1500 and 1550, one innkeeper, one taverner and one vintner were found.

[115] For example, CRO, AB 1, fol. 79v.

[116] *Chester Customs Accounts*, pp. 8–17.

[117] Wilson, 'Port of Chester', p. 163.

[118] These included Hugh, Ralph and William Aldersey, Roger and Thomas Barrowe, Thomas Bavand, Randolph Brereton, Hugh Clerke, Philip Costerdyne, Edward and Ralph Davenport, William Davidson, John Dymmock, Charles Eaton, Edmund and Henry Gee, Ralph, Robert and William Goodman, two Richard Grymsdiches, Henry Hamnet, Thomas Martin, David Middleton, John and William Offeley, John Pike, Ralph, Thomas and William Rogerson, Richard Talbot, Thomas Smyth, John Thorneton, Robert Walley, Richard Wright. CRO, SB, *passim*: *Chester Customs Accounts*, *passim*.

[119] Grymesdiche senior was active between 1508 and 1550. CRO, SB, *passim*. He occurs buying kerseys in SB, ix, fol. 68v.

ments each year alongside regular imports of fish, particularly salmon.[120] The records of landward trade are sparse, but it would be surprising if some of the overseas merchants were not drawn deeper into trade up country. In the 1540s John Offeley was said to buy cottons regularly from Richard Crompton of Bury, and Hugh Aldersey and Henry Gee of Chester were buying iron in Manchester.[121] We can see from the 1547 inventory of Hugh Aldersey, that although an active wine importer, he also invested in domestic provisioning: 328 bushels of barley, 65 of wheat, 54 of peas, 30 of rye, 21 of barley malt, 20 of oats and 12 of oat malt were listed.[122] Such large quantities were unlikely to be from his own farming.

Although some individuals sustained a high level of trade over their life-time, few seem to have accumulated great disposable wealth and for the handful whose wills survive, the evidence suggests that real estate absorbed some of their surplus.[123] The overseas traders were a mixed group of incomers and others from established county families, sometimes investing in trade while retaining agricultural property. Despite its port tradition and strong manufacturing base in textiles and leather, Chester retained a hybrid character. There were gardens, orchards and tofts within the city walls, barns scattered throughout the city and common fields close by. Several merchants displayed a strongly persistent agricultural interests owning farms and leasing agricultural land.

Ralph and William Aldersey both owned farms, as did Ralph Bostock and Henry Gee who owned an estate at Little Mouldsworth and had recently purchased the manor of Manley.[124] It is difficult to tell which way investment flowed: some property was inherited and other newly acquired. Henry Hardware and Richard Massy's wills sharply reflected this joint interest in farming and trade. Hardware left land and water mills in Great Mouldsworth, closes in Flookersbrook, houses in the city and twenty-two tons of Spanish iron in his cellar. Massy left a newly purchased estate, land mortgaged to him, cattle, corn and farming implements, as well as current ventures in three different ships.[125]

---

[120] He was active between 1509 and 1547. For examples of his salmon shipments, see CRO, SB, v, fol. 187; viii, fols. 23, 61v–63; viii, fols. 6, 20, 63, 89v.

[121] *Pleadings and Depositions*, II, p. 136, and III, pp. 6–10.

[122] BL, Harleian MS 2119, fol. 33: *Lancs. and Ches. Wills and Inventories*, III, p. 71.

[123] There are few extant wills for Chester at this date. Of those for whom we have evidence William Rogerson (1519) left over £102, Ralph Rogerson (1540) £200, Thomas Aldersey (1557) £420, and Fulk Dutton (1558) £120. *Cheshire Sheaf*, 13 (1914), p. 40; *ibid.*, 18 (1921), p. 99; Cheshire RO, EDA 2/1, fols. 163–4; WS 8/1, 3.

[124] Cheshire RO, WS 5/1; EDA 2/1, fols. 188–9; *Cheshire Sheaf*, 11 (1914), pp. 1–2; *ibid.*, 17 (1920), p. 30. See also Cheshire RO, WS6/3, 4, 7; 8/1, 3; *Collection of Lancs. and Ches. Wills*, pp. 189–90.

[125] *Lancs. and Ches. Wills and Inventories*, III, pp. 26–30; Cheshire RO, WS6/7.

COMPETITION AND DECLINE

Overall, 1500–40 was a time of increasing imports, ended by hostilities with Spain, and growing competition from other north-western ports.[126] Chester's administrative dominance over its creek ports guaranteed the Palatinate's income from customs but not the presence of merchants or the carriage of goods into Chester. The ports of North Wales, especially Beaumaris, Caernarfon and Conway, were regularly visited by Spanish, French and Irish ships from the 1490s.[127] Beaumaris was convenient for the middle marches and wine taken in prisage there was conveyed to the prince's household at Ludlow in 1493. Demand was growing in Wales for a variety of manufactured goods, as well as iron and wine. A Dieppe merchant imported ninety-six reams of paper, eight gross of combs, six gross of looking glasses, bonnets, earthen bottles, shovels and trenchers in 1531.[128] Welsh ports were busier and although Welsh merchants were taking over Welsh coastal trade,[129] a number of Chester merchants such as John and Richard Goodman, David Middleton, Richard Shawe, Edward Smyth and Ralph Rogerson imported Breton canvas, iron and wine through Beaumaris between 1517 and 1520.[130] In 1534 Thomas Osley or Ofeley of London was importing wine through Beaumaris.[131] English cloth was exported to Spain through Beaumaris: York and Kendal cloth in 1519–20, northern cloth and Manchester cottons in 1530–40.[132] Beaumaris was also used as a port of military embarkation for Ireland in the 1530s, a role at other times claimed by Chester.[133]

The river Mersey was a more direct waterway to northern Cheshire and into south-eastern Lancashire. Although the river currents shifted sand banks, as in the Dee, there was always a navigable passage up the Mersey. Runcorn, close to the mouth of the river Weaver, attracted merchants avoiding the high customs duties charged at Chester,[134] triggering a defensive response from the earl's officals. In 1481, any ship trying to discharge at Runcorn was to be arrested but in the same month, James Walsh of Ireland was licensed to unload at Runcorn and return home with any non-staple goods.[135]

[126] Wilson, 'Port of Chester', p. 128.
[127] Lewis, 'Contribution to the Commercial History of Medieval Wales', pp. 170ff.
[128] Ibid., p. 181.
[129] Ibid., p. 99.
[130] Ibid., pp. 172–4.
[131] Ibid., p. 183.
[132] Ibid., pp. 129–33, 170–88.
[133] Bagwell, Ireland under the Tudors, I, p. 169.
[134] Imposts at Chester included the customs levied by the Palatinate in lieu of national customs, and local customs, levied by the city council. See Wilson, 'Port of Chester', chs. 1–2; Chester Customs Accounts, pp. 1–18. For the differential rates, see below p. 306.
[135] Deputy Keeper's Reports, XXXVII (1876), pp. 222, 760.

Chester's greatest and ultimately triumphant rival was Liverpool, located at the mouth of the Mersey with a natural anchorage and clear access to the sea. Fiercest competition was over the import of Irish yarn and export of English cloth, and successive Chester councils tried to legislate against its own and Dublin citizens shipping through Liverpool. In 1532, bargaining with Irish merchants at Liverpool or elsewhere was forbidden.[136] Reacting to Dublin's attempts to divert its trade away from Chester and into Beaumaris, Conway and Liverpool in 1549–50, Cestrians were forbidden to buy Irish goods which had not been through the city customs' registration system, nor to ship their own goods through Liverpool, even in chartered vessels.[137] By 1535 Leland had been able to describe Liverpool as the natural entrepot for Irish yarn.[138] In the mid-sixteenth century, the export of cloth to the continent from Chester was considerably greater than from Liverpool: 25,600 goads of cottons compared with 6,900 goads in 1565–6[139] Liverpool had overtaken Chester, however, in exporting cloth to Ireland, and in importing yarn and wool.[140]

Liverpool's success was due in part to its location close to the rapidly expanding textile centres of south-east Lancashire and in part to Chester's reluctance to accommodate to market forces at a critical time. No exemptions from Chester's local customs were allowed, except in a reciprocal agreement with men of Wexford.[141] While Chester freemen made a single payment of 4d., foreigners paid on every major item imported and exported. The schedule of dues was restated in 1533.[142] Specific customs duties were committed to individual city officials by civic ordinance, and non-freemen had to pay at least 2½d. in the pound sterling on bulk commodities, while freemen paid nothing except 4d. per vessel to the sheriffs. All duties payable to the sheriffs were doubled for a fortnight before and after Midsummer and for one week before and after Michaelmas. Common bargains, the sale of forfeit goods, was also managed to the citizens' advantage.[143]

All trading ventures had to carry the extra costs incurred by using the Dee estuary ports, and the council stipulated precise rates for off-loading into lighters and for the carriage of goods overland to the city. Portering rates were regulated so that in addition to 8d. per ton for transport from

---

[136] CRO, Assembly Files 1, fol. 18.
[137] CRO, AB 1, fols. 81v–82v; Wilson, 'Port of Chester', p. 169.
[138] Wilson, 'Port of Chester', p. 102; J. Leland, *The Itinerary*, ed. L. Toulmin Smith, 5 vols. (London, 1906–10), V, pp. 40–1.
[139] Wilson, 'Port of Chester', p. 102; Lowe, *The Lancashire Textile Industry in the Sixteenth Century*, p. 79.
[140] Woodward, *Elizabethan Trade*, pp. 7, 8, 13, 15.
[141] BL, Harleian MS 2057, fol. 129.
[142] CRO, AB 1, fols. 41–2.
[143] *Ibid.*, fols. 41–6v.

Shotwick a merchant had to pay a further 2d. per ton for goods moved within the city, and 4d. for moving and setting up a barrel in a cellar.[144] Only merchants with a sizeable turnover could carry such costs.

Dubliners claimed the lower dues payable at Liverpool as a major attraction in 1533,[145] and in 1550 the mayor of Dublin complained to his counterpart in Chester that increases in the level of dues encouraged merchants to seek 'their advantage in els wher as they do se good'.[146] Chester merchants were not averse to seeking the best advantage either and could be found importing wine into Liverpool in the 1540s.[147] The balance was already tipping away from Chester, and by 1581–2, the Stanleys of Hornby Castle were buying their wine from Liverpool.[148] Chester, outpaced in trade, clung on to shreds of its former dominance by virtue of its administrative functions and its role as the marketing centre for west Cheshire and North Wales: a capital, still, but of a commercially diminished region.

---

[144] *Ibid.*, fols. 42–3.
[145] *Letters and Papers*, VI, no. 319, p. 148.
[146] CRO, Mayors' Letters 5/1.
[147] *Pleadings and Depositions*, III, pp. 135–7.
[148] *A Sixteenth-Century Survey and Year's Account of the Estates of Hornby Castle, Lancashire*, ed. W.H. Chippindall (Chetham Soc., n.s., no. 102, Manchester, 1939), pp. 113–9.

Bibliography of Edward Miller's
published works

1938

Review article: A.E. Levett, *Studies in Manorial History*, in *St Albans and Herts. Archit. and Arch. Soc. Trans.*, pp. 285–300.

1944

Reviews of: R.A.L. Smith, *Canterbury Cathedral Priory*, and P.H. Reaney, *Place Names of Cambridgeshire and the Isle of Ely*, in *Econ. Hist. Rev.*, 1st ser., 14, p. 104.

1947

'The Ely Land Pleas in the Reign of William I', *Econ. Hist. Rev.*, 62, pp. 438–56.

1948

With H.C. Darby, 'Political History of Cambridgeshire to the End of the Middle Ages', in *VCH Cambs.*, II, pp. 377–402.
'Baldwin Blancgernun and his Family: Early Benefactors of the Hospital of St John the Evangelist in Cambridge', *The Eagle*, 53, pp. 73–9.

1950

Reviews of: M. Bassett, *Knights of the Shire for Bedfordshire during the Middle Ages*, in *Econ. Hist. Rev.*, 2nd ser., 2, pp. 332–3; T.F.T. Plucknett, *The Legislation of Edward I*, in *ibid.*, 3, pp. 240–2; G.L. Haskins, *The Growth of English Representative Government*, in *History*, 35, pp. 263–4.

1951

The Abbey and Bishopric of Ely: The Social History of an Ecclesiastical Estate from the Tenth Century to the Early Fourteenth Century (Cambridge).

Review of: H.C. Peyer, *Zur Getreidepolitik oberitalienishe Städte im 13 Jahrhundert*, in *Eng. Hist. Rev.*, 66, pp. 288–9.

1952

'The State and Landed Interests in Thirteenth-Century France and England', *Trans. Royal Hist. Soc.*, 5th ser., 2, pp. 109–29; rep. S.L. Thrupp (ed.), *Change in Medieval Society* (New York, 1964), pp. 116–32.

'The Norman Conquest', in Martin Charlesworth (ed.), *The Heritage of Early Britain* (London), pp. 153–73.

Reviews of: R.S. Hoyt, *The Royal Demesne in English Constitutional History, 1066–1272*, in *Econ. Hist. Rev.*, 2nd ser., 4, pp. 385–6; and A.R. Lewis, *Naval Power and Trade in the Mediterranean, 500–1100*, in *Eng. Hist. Rev.*, 67, pp. 286–7.

1953

'The liberty of Ely', *VCH Cambs.*, IV, pp. 1–27.

1954

Reviews of: V. Chomel and J. Ebersolt, *Cinq siècles de circulation internationale vue de Jougne*, *Econ. Hist. Rev.*, 2nd ser., 7, p. 109; *VCH Wilts.*, VII, in *ibid.*, p. 264; R.W. Southern, *The Making of the Middle Ages*, *Eng. Hist. Rev.*, 69, pp. 431–2; R.H.C. Davis (ed.), *The Kalendar of Abbot Samson of Bury St Edmunds and Related Documents*, in *ibid.*, pp. 652–3; H.C. Darby and I.B. Terrett, *The Domesday Geography of Midland England*, in *Cambridge Review*, 30 Oct. p. 129.

1956

Reviews of: G.H. Martin, *Court Rolls of the Borough of Ipswich*, *Econ. Hist. Rev.*, 2nd ser., 9, p. 137; E.G. Kimball (ed.), *Some Sessions of the Peace in Lincolnshire, 1381–1396*, in *ibid.*, pp. 138–9; M. Bloch, *Esquisse d'une histoire monétaire de l'Europe*, in *ibid.*, p. 158; I.J. Sanders, *Feudal Military Service in England*, in *ibid.*, p. 369; J.H. Mundy, *Liberty and Political Power in Toulouse, 1050–1230*, in *Eng. Hist. Rev.*, 71, pp. 87–8; F. Barlow, *The Feudal Kingdom of England, 1042–1216*, in *ibid.*, pp. 138–9.

1957

Reviews of: E.A. Kosminsky, *Studies in the Agrarian History of England in the Thirteenth Century*, in *Econ. Hist. Rev.*, 2nd ser., 9, pp. 499–501; G.V. Scammell, *Hugh de Puiset, Bishop of Durham*, in *ibid.*, p. 505; J. Stiennon, *Etude sur le chartrier et le domaine de l'abbaye de Saint-Jacques de Liège (1015–1209)*, in *ibid.*, 2nd ser., 10, pp. 300–1; C. Verlinden, *L'esclavage dans l'Europe médiévale: péninsule ibérique – France*, in *Eng. Hist. Rev.*, 72, pp. 91–3; R. Latouche, *Les origines de l'économie occidentale (IVᵉ–XIᵉ siècle)*, in *ibid.*, pp. 486–8; R. Coulborn (ed.), *Feudalism in History*, in *ibid.*, pp. 489–91.

1958

Reviews of: *VCH Wilts.*, III, in *Econ. Hist. Rev.*, 2nd ser., 10, pp. 485–6; J. Conway Davies (ed.), *Studies Presented to Sir Hilary Jenkinson*, in *ibid.*, 2nd ser., 11, pp. 171–2; C. Hart, *The Early Charters of Essex (Saxon and Norman Periods)*, in *ibid.*, p. 174; F. Lot and R. Fawtier (eds.), *Histoire des institutions francaises au moyen âge: institutions seigneuriales*, in *Eng. Hist. Rev.*, 73, pp. 470–2.

1959

'St John's College', *VCH Cambs.*, III, pp. 437–50.

Reviews of: K. Major (ed.), *Registrum Antiquissimum of the Cathedral Church of Lincoln*, VIII, in *Econ. Hist. Rev.*, 2nd ser., 11, pp. 530–1; T.F.F. Plucknett, *Early English Legal Literature*, in *ibid.*, pp. 529–30; B.D. Lyon, *From Fief to Indenture: The Transition from Feudal to Non-Feudal Contract in Western Europe*, in *Eng. Hist. Rev.*, 74, pp. 286–7; J.A. Raftis, *The Estates of Ramsey Abbey*, in *ibid.*, p. 338; M. Bloch, *La France sous les derniers Capétiens, 1223–1328*, in *ibid.*, p. 521; D. van Derveeghde (ed.), *La polyptique de 1280 du chapitre de la cathédrale Saint-Lambert à Liège*, in *ibid.*, pp. 720–1.

1960

'The last will and testament of the Lady Margaret Beaufort', *The Eagle*, 57, pp. 1–7.

The Origins of Parliament (Historical Association Pamplet, General Ser., no. 44, London).

War in the North: The Anglo-Scottish Wars of the Middle Ages (St John's College Lecture, University of Hull).

Introduction to F.W. Maitland, *Domesday Book and Beyond* (Glasgow and London), pp. 15–22.

Reviews of: R. Brentano, *York Metropolitan Jurisdiction and Papal Judges Delegate, 1279–1296*, in *Econ. Hist. Rev.*, 2nd ser., 12, pp. 477–8; C.D. Ross (ed.), *Cartulary of St Mark's Hospital, Bristol*, in *ibid.*, 2nd ser., 13, pp. 282–3; A.E. Verhulst, *De Sint-Baafsabdij te Gent en haar Grondbezit, VIIe–XIVe Eeuw*, in *Eng. Hist. Rev.*, 75, pp. 486–7.

1961

Portrait of a College: a History of the College of St John the Evangelist, Cambridge (Cambridge).

'Medieval York', *VCH Yorks.: The City of York*, pp. 25–116.

Reviews of: H.G. Richardson, *The English Jewry under the Angevin Kings*, in *Econ. Hist. Rev.*, 2nd ser., 14, pp. 342–3; F.B. Stitt (ed.), *Lenton Priory Estate Accounts, 1296 to 1298*, in *Eng. Hist. Rev.*, 76, p. 131; M.W. Farr (ed.), *Accounts and Surveys of the Wiltshire Lands of Adam of Stratton*, in *ibid.*, pp. 350–1; A. Joris, *La ville de Huy au moyen âge*, in *ibid.*, p. 699; A. Sabin (ed.), *Some Manorial Accounts of St Augustine's Abbey, Bristol*, A.H. Denney (ed.), *Sibton Abbey Estate: Select Documents 1325–1509*, and R.H. Hilton (ed.), *The Stoneleigh Leger Book*, in *History*, 46, pp. 128–31.

1962

'Fishpond Close and its Pondyards', *The Eagle*, 59.

Review article: 'The Background of Magna Carta', on J.C. Holt, *The Northerners: A Study in the Reign of King John*, in *Past and Present*, 23, pp. 72–83.

Reviews of: R.F. Hunnisett (ed.), *Bedfordshire Cononers' Rolls*, in *Econ. Hist. Rev.*, 2nd ser., 14, p. 554; J.A. Cazel jnr (ed.), *Feudalism and Liberty: Essays and Addresses of Sidney Painter*, in *ibid.*, 2nd ser., 15, p. 370; R.B. Smith, *Blackburnshire: A Study in Early Lancashire History*, in *ibid*. p. 372; M. Castaing-Sicard, *Les contrats dans le très ancien droit toulousain, X^e–XIIIe siècle*, in *Eng. Hist. Rev.*, 77, pp. 134–5; R. Welldon Finn, *The Domesday Inquest and the Making of Domesday Book*, in *ibid.*, pp. 147–8.

1963

Joint ed., with M.M. Postan and E.E. Rich, *Cambridge Economic History of Europe*, III: *Economic Policies and Organization in the Middle Ages* (Cambridge).

'The Economic Policies of Governments: I. Introductions; II. France and England', in *Cambridge Economic History of Europe*, III, pp. 281–340.

Reviews of: E.B. Fryde (ed.), *Book of Prests of the King's Wardrobe for 1294–5*, in *Econ. Hist. Rev.*, 2nd ser., 16, p. 163; G.A. Williams, *Medieval London: From Commune to Capital*, in *ibid.*, pp. 364–6; M. Keen, *Outlaws of Medieval Legend*, in *Eng. Hist. Rev.*, 78, p. 155.

1964

'The English Economy in the Thirteenth Century: Implications of Recent Research', *Past and Present*, 28, pp. 21–40.

'Expanding Christendom: The Colonization of Europe', *The Listener*, 16 January.

'Expanding Christendom: Banking and International Trade', *ibid.*, 30 January.

Reviews of: T.J. Hunt (ed.), *Medieval Customs of the Manors of Taunton and Bradford on Tone*, in *Eng. Hist Rev.*, 79, pp. 398–9; A.E. Wilson (ed.), *Customs of the Manors of Laughton, Willingdon and Goring*, in *ibid.*, pp. 399–400.

1965

'The Fortunes of the English Textile Industry during the Thirteenth Century', *Econ. Hist. Rev.*, 2nd ser., 18, pp. 64–82.

Review of: C.W. Hollister, *The Military Organization of Norman England*, in *Econ. Hist. Rev.*, 2nd ser., 18, pp. 416–17.

1966

The Relevance of Medieval History (inaugural lecture, Sheffield University).

'Some Twelfth-Century Documents concerning St Peter's church at Barbraham', *Proc. Cambridge Antiquarian Soc.*, 59, pp. 113–23.

'La société rurale en Angleterre, X^e–XIIe siècles', *Agricoltura e mondo rurale in occidente nell' alto medioevo* (Settimane di Studio, Spoleto, XIII), pp. 111–34.

Review articles: 'The Elizabethan and Early Stuart Peerage', on L. Stone, *The Crisis of the Aristocracy, 1558–1641*, in *Historical Jnl*, 9, pp. 133–6; 'Pre-industrial Society', on P. Laslett, *The World We Have Lost*, in *ibid.*, pp. 374–9.

Reviews of: G.T. Beech, *A Rural Society in Medieval France: The Gâtine of Poitou in the Eleventh and Twelfth Centuries*, in *Eng. Hist. Rev.*, 81, pp. 142–3; E.M. Veale, *The English Fur Trade in the Later Middle Ages*, in *Cambridge Review*, 29 October, p. 71; E.B. Fryde, *The Wool Accounts of William de la Pole* and *Some Business Transactions of York Merchants . . . 1336–49*, *Northern Hist.*, 1, pp. 152–3; C.T. Clay (ed.), *Early Yorkshire Charters*, XII, in *ibid.*, pp. 147–8; W.E. Wightman, *The Lacy Family in Normandy and England, 1066–1194*, in *ibid.*, pp. 148–9.

1967

Reviews of: M. Bloch, *French Rural History: An Essay on its Basic Characteristics*, trans. J. Sondheimer, in *Econ. Hist. Rev.*, 2nd ser., 20, pp. 411–12; R.H. Hilton, *A Medieval Society: The West Midlands at the End of the Thirteenth Century*, in *ibid.*, p. 555; M. Altschul, *A Baronial Family of Medieval England: The Clares, 1217–1314*, in *Eng. Hist. Rev.*, 82, pp. 594–5; F.W. Brooks, *Domesday Book and the East Riding*, in *Northern Hist.*, 2, pp. 166–7; M. Roper (ed.), *Feet of Fines for the County of York, 1300–1314*, in *ibid.*, pp. 172–3.

1968

Review article: 'Medieval New Towns', on M. Beresford, *New Towns of the Middle Ages*, in *Northern Hist.*, 3, pp. 192–7.

Reviews of: P. Gérard, E. Magnou and P. Wolff (eds.), *Cartulaires des Templiers de Douzens*, in *Eng. Hist. Rev.*, 83, p. 154; L. Knabe (ed.), *Die zweite Wismarische Stadtbuch, 1272–1297*, in *ibid.*, pp. 585–6; U. Dirlmeier, *Mittelalterliche Hoheitsträger im Wirtschaftlichen Wettbewerb*, in *ibid.*, pp. 825–6.

1969

Reviews of: R.W. Southern (ed.), *Essays in Medieval History Selected from the Transactions of the Royal Historical Society*, *Econ. Hist. Rev.*, 2nd ser., 22, pp. 157–8; J.Z. Titow, *English Rural Society, 1200–1350*, in *ibid.*, p. 556; E. Searle and B. Ross (eds.), *Cellarers' Rolls of Battle Abbey, 1275–1513*, in *Eng. Hist. Rev.*, 84, p. 384; A. Marongiu, *Medieval Parliaments: A Comparative Study*, in *ibid.*, p. 834.

1970

Joint ed., with E.B. Fryde, *Historical Studies of the English Parliament*, 2 vols. (Cambridge). Reviews of: D. Styles (ed.), *Ministers' Accounts of the Collegiate Church of St. Mary, Warwick, 1432–1485*, in *Econ. Hist. Rev.*, 2nd ser., 23, pp. 564–5; N. Denholm-Young, *The Country Gentry in the Fourteenth Century with Special Reference to the Heraldic Rolls of Arms*, in *Welsh History Review*, 5, pp. 182–3.

1971

'England in the Twelfth and Thirteenth Centuries: An Economic Contrast?', *Econ. Hist. Rev.*, 2nd ser., 24, pp. 1–14.

Reviews of: H. Gilles (ed.), *Les coutumes de Toulouse (1286) et leur premier commentaire*, *Eng. Hist Rev.*, 86, pp. 830–1; *VCH Yorks East Riding*, I: *The City of Kingston upon Hull*, in *Northern Hist.*, 6, pp. 156–9; R.B. Smith, *Land and Politics in the England of Henry VIII: The West Riding of Yorkshire, 1530–1546*, in *ibid.*, pp. 161–3.

1972

'Government Economic Policies and Public Finance 1000–1500', in C.M. Cipolla (ed.), *The Fontana Economic History of Europe*, I: *The Middle Ages* (London and Glasgow), pp. 339–73.

Reviews of: R. Welldon Finn, *Domesday Studies: The Norman Conquest and its Effect on the Economy, 1066–1086*, in *Econ. Hist. Rev.*, 2nd ser., 25, p. 155; D. Herlihy (ed.), *The History of Feudalism*, in *ibid.*, pp. 371–2; B.P. Wolffe, *The Royal Demesne in English History*, in *ibid.*, pp. 509–10; R.B. Pugh (ed.), *Court Rolls of the Wiltshire Manors of Adam de Stratton*, in *Eng. Hist. Rev.*, 77, pp. 395–6; W.P. Hedley, *Northumberland Families*, II, in *Northern Hist.*, 7, pp. 139–40.

1973

'Farming of Manors and Direct Management', *Econ. Hist. Rev.*, 2nd ser., 26, pp. 138–40.

Review article: 'The Economy Expands', on G. Duby, *Hommes et structures du moyen âge* and *Guerriers et paysans, VIIe–XIIe siècle*; M. Lombard, *Espaces et réseaux du haut moyen âge*; M.M. Postan, *Essays on Medieval Agriculture and General Problems of the Medieval Economy* and *Medieval Trade and Finance*, in *The Times Literary Supplement*, 17 August, repr. in *TLS: Essays and Reviews from the Times Literary Supplement*, 12, pp. 94–102.

Review of: M. Prestwich, *War, Politics and Finance under Edward I*, in *Econ. Hist. Rev.*, 2nd ser., 26, pp. 524–5.

1974

Reviews of: M.M. Postan, *Essays on Medieval Agriculture and General Problems of the Medieval Economy* and *Medieval Trade and Finance*, in *Econ. Hist. Rev.*, 2nd ser., 27, pp. 681–2; R. Welldon Finn, *The Making and Limitations of the Yorkshire Domesday*, in *Northern Hist.*, 9, pp. 171–2; D.E. Greenway (ed.), *Charters of the Honour of Mowbray, 1107–1191*, in *ibid.*, pp. 172–3.

1975

'Farming in Northern England during the Twelfth and Thirteenth Centuries', *Northern Hist.*, 11, pp. 1–16.

'War Taxation and the English Economy in the Late Thirteenth and Early Fourteenth Centuries', in J.M. Winter (ed.), *War and Economic Development: Essays in Memory of David Joslin* (Cambridge) pp. 11–31.

Reviews of: R.M. Timson (ed.), *The Cartulary of Blyth Priory*, in *Econ. Hist. Rev.*, 2nd ser., 28, pp. 116–17; *Calendar of Inquisitions Post Mortem*, XVI, in *ibid.*, pp. 708–9; R.W. Kaeuper, *Bankers to the Crown: The Riccardi of Lucca and Edward I*, in *Eng. Hist. Rev.*, 90, p. 174; G. Devailly, *Le Berry du Xe siècle au milieu du XIIIe*, in *ibid.*, pp. 877–8; A. Chédeville, *Chartres et ses campagnes, XIe–XIIIe siècles*, in *ibid.*, pp. 880–1; C.T. Clay (ed.), *Early Yorkshire Families*, in *Northern Hist.*, 11, p. 239; I. Kershaw, *Bolton Priory: The Economy of a Northern Monastery, 1286–1325*, in *ibid.*, pp. 240–1; R.B. Dobson, *Durham Priory, 1400–1450*, in *ibid.*, pp. 243–5.

1976

Reviews of: G.L. Harriss, *King, Parliament and Public Finance in England to 1369*, in *Eng. Hist. Rev.*, 91, pp. 841–3; J.R. Maddicott, *The English Peasantry and the Demands of the Crown, 1294–1341*, in *ibid.*, pp. 897–8; T.F. Reddaway and L.E.M. Walker, *The Early History of the Goldsmith's Company, 1327–1509*, in *The Times Literary Supplement*, 20 February; D.J.H. Michelmore (ed.), *The Fountains Abbey Rental, 1495–6*, in *Northern Hist.*, 12, p. 261.

1977

Reviews of: B. Dodwell (ed.), *The Charters of Norwich Cathedral Priory*, I, in *Eng. Hist. Rev.*, 92, pp. 186–7; M. Prestwich, *York Civic Ordinances, 1301*, in *Northern Hist.*, 13, pp. 294–5.

1978

Jointly, with John Hatcher, *Medieval England: Rural Society and Economic Change, 1086–1348* (London).

Review of: P.H. Sawyer (ed.), *Medieval Settlement: Continuity and Change*, in *Northern Hist.*, 14, pp. 268–9.

1979

Reviews of: *VCH Cambs.*, VI, in *Econ. Hist. Rev.*, 2nd ser., 32, pp. 118–119; P. Morgan (ed.), *Domesday Book: Cheshire*, *Northern Hist.*, 15, pp. 242–3; A. Young, *William Cumin: Border Politics and the Bishopric of Durham*, in *ibid.*, pp. 246–7.

1980

'Grossbrittanien im Hoch- und Spätmittelalter', in J.A. van Houtte (ed.), *Handbuch der europäische Wirtschafts- und Sozialgeschichte* (Stuttgart), II, pp. 227–58.

1981

'Glyn Daniel and Cambridge', in J.E. Evans, B. Cunliffe and C. Renfrew (eds.), *Antiquity and Man: Essays in Honour of Glyn Daniel* (London), pp. 243–6.

Review article: 'The Making of Northern England', on P.H. Sawyer, *From Roman Britain to Norman England*, W.E. Kapelle, *The Norman Conquest of the North*, and B. English, *The Lords of Holderness, 1086–1250*, in *Northern Hist.*, 17, pp. 274–8.

Review of: J.L. Bolton, *The Medieval English Economy, 1150–1500*, in *Econ. Hist. Rev.*, 2nd ser., 34, pp. 150–1.

1982

Reviews of: H.G. Richardson and G.O. Sayles, *The English Parliament in the Middle Ages*, and R.G. Davies and J.H. Denton (eds.), *The English Parliament in the Middle Ages*, in *Parliamentary History: A Yearbook*, 1, pp. 217–20; T.H. Lloyd, *Alien Merchants in England in the High Middle Ages*, in *The Times Literary Supplement*, 22 October; G.W.S. Barrow, *The Anglo-Norman Era in Scottish History*, in *Northern Hist.*, 18, pp. 290–1.

1983

'Michael Moissey Postan, 1899–1981', *Proc. British Academy*, 69, pp. 543–57.

'Introduction', T.H. Aston *et al.* (eds.), *Social Relations and Ideas: Essays in Honour of R.H. Hilton* (Cambridge), pp. ix–xiii.

Reviews of: J. McDonnell, *Inland Fisheries in Medieval Yorkshire*, in *Northern Hist.*, 19, p. 259; H.M. Jewell (ed.), *Court Rolls of the Manor of Wakefield, 1348–1350*, in *ibid.*, pp. 260–2; D.J.H. Michelmore (ed.), *The Fountains Abbey Lease Book*, in *ibid.*, pp. 263–4.

Reviews of: D. Austin (ed.), *Boldon Book*, *Northern Hist.*, 20, pp. 241–2; R. Horrox (ed.), *Selected Rentals and Accounts of Medieval Hull, 1293–1528*, in *ibid.*, pp. 243–4; C.M. Fraser (ed.), *Northern Petitions Illustrative of Life in Cumbria, Berwick and Durham in the Fourteenth Century*, in *ibid.*, pp. 244–5; S.S. Walker (ed.), *Court Rolls of the Manor of Wakefield, 1331–1333*, in *ibid.*, pp. 246–7; H. Swanson, *Building Craftsmen in Late Medieval York*, in *ibid.*, pp. 248–9.

1986

'Rulers of Thirteenth-Century Towns: The Cases of York and Newcastle upon Tyne', P.R. Coss and S.D. Lloyd (eds.), *Thirteenth-Century England* (Woodbridge), I, pp. 128–41.

Reviews of: K. Emsley and C.M. Fraser, *The Courts of the County Palatine of Durham from the Earliest Times to 1971*, in *Northern Hist.*, 22, p. 316; P.D.A. Harvey (ed.), *The Peasant Land Market in Medieval England*, in *ibid.*, pp. 318–20; G.R. Price (ed.), *A Transcript of the Court Rolls of Yeadon, 1361–1476*, in *ibid.*, p. 322.

1987

Joint ed., with M.M. Postan, *Cambridge Economic History of Europe*, II: *Trade and Industry in the Middle Ages*, 2nd edn.

Reviews of: M.L. Faull and M. Stinson (eds.), *Domesday Book: Yorkshire*, in *Northern Hist.*, 23, pp. 248–9; W.R. Childs (ed.), *The Customs Accounts of Hull, 1453–90*, in *ibid.*, pp. 252–3.

1988

'New Settlement: Northern England', 'Farming Techniques: Northern England' and 'Social Structure: Northern England', in *AHEW*, II, pp. 245–59, 399–411, 685–98.

Reviews of: B. Dodwell (ed.), *The Charters of Norwich Cathedral Priory*, II, in *Eng. Hist. Rev.*, 103, p. 1028; J. Taylor, *English Historical Literature in the Fourteenth Century*, *Northern Hist.*, 24, pp. 239–40; E. White, *The St Christopher and St George Guild of York*, in *ibid.*, pp. 240–1.

1989

Reviews of: M.K. McIntosh, *Autonomy and Continuity: The Royal Manor of Havering, 1200–1500*, in *Eng. Hist. Rev.*, 104, pp. 722–3; G. Barraclough (ed.), *The Charters of the Anglo-Norman Earls of Chester, c. 1071–1237*, in *Northern Hist.*, 25, pp. 312–14; P. Morgan, *War and Society in Medieval Cheshire, 1277–1403*, in *ibid.*, pp. 318–19.

1990

'English Town Patricians, c. 1200–1350', in A. Guarducci (ed.), *Gerarchie Economiche e Gerarchie Sociali, secolo XII–XVIII* (Instituto F. Datini, Florence), pp. 217–40.

Reviews of: J. Wardrop, *Fountains Abbey and its Benefactors, 1132–1300*, in *Eng. Hist. Rev.*, 105, pp. 1005–6; C. Fink, *Marc Bloch: A Life in History*, and Marc Bloch, *Feudal Society*, trans. L. Manyon, in *French History*, 4, pp. 389–91; R. Robson, *The Rise and Fall of the English Highland Clans: Tudor Responses to a Medieval Problem*, in *Northern Hist.*, 26, pp. 240–1; H. Swanson, *Medieval Artisans: An Urban Class in Late Medieval England*, in *ibid.*, pp. 242–3; R. Lomas and A.J. Piper (eds.), *Durham Cathedral Priory Rentals: Bursar's Rentals*, in *ibid.*, pp. 243–4.

1991

Ed., *Agrarian History of England and Wales*, III: *1348–1500* (Cambridge).

'Introduction: Land and People', 'The Occupation of the Land: Yorkshire and Lancashire', 'The Occupation of the Land: The Southern Counties', 'Farming Practices and Techniques: Yorkshire and Lancashire', 'Farming Practices and Techniques: The Southern Counties', 'Tenant Farming and Tenant Farmers: Yorkshire and Lancashire', 'Tenant Farming and Tenant Farmers: The Southern Counties', in *AHEW*, III, pp. 1–33, 42–52, 136–51, 182–94, 285–303, 596–611, 703–22.

Reviews of: T.H. Aston (ed.), *Landlords and Peasants in Medieval England*, in *Eng. Hist. Rev.*, 106, p. 164; J.A.F. Thompson (ed.), *Towns and Townspeople in the Fifteenth Century*, in *ibid.*, pp. 987–8; M. Beresford and J. Hurst, *Wharram Percy:*

Deserted Medieval Village, in *Northern Hist.*, 27, pp. 286–7; M. Bonney, *Lordship and Urban Community: Durham and its Overlords*, in *ibid.*, pp. 289–90; W.R. Childs, *The Trade and Shipping of Hull, 1300–1500*, in *ibid.*, pp. 290–1.

1992

Reviews of: F. Musgrove, *The North of England: A History from Roman Times to the Present Day*, in *Northern Hist.*, 28, pp. 267–9; P.H.W. Booth and A.D. Carr, *The Account of Master John de Burnham, Chamberlain of Chester, . . . 1361–1362*, in *ibid.*, p. 274; D.S. Reid, *The Durham Crown Lordships in the Sixteenth and Seventeenth Centuries*, in *ibid.*, pp. 277–8.

1993

Reviews of: K. Biddick, *The Other Economy: Pastoral Husbandry on a Medieval Estate*, in *Eng. Hist. Rev.*, 108, pp. 142–3; R. Lomas, *North-East England in the Middle Ages*, in *Northern Hist.*, 29, pp. 218–19; A.T. Thacker (ed.), *The Earldom of Chester and its Charters: A Tribute to Geoffrey Barraclough*, in *ibid.*, pp. 219–20; P.H. Cullum, *Cremetts and Corrodies: Care of the Poor and Sick at St Leonard's Hospital, York, in the Middle Ages*, in *ibid.*, p. 221; W.R. Childs and J. Taylor (eds.), *The Anonimalle Chronicle, 1307 to 1334, from Brotherton Collection Ms. 29*, in *ibid.*, pp. 221–2.

1994

Reviews of: D.A. Crowley (ed.), *The Wiltshire Tax List of 1332*, in *Eng. Hist. Rev.*, 109, pp. 415–16; A. Goodman and Anthony Tuck (eds.), *War and Border Society in the Middle Ages*, in *Northern Hist.*, 30, pp. 232–3.

1995

Jointly, with John Hatcher, *Medieval England: Towns, Commerce and Crafts, 1086–1348* (London).

'A Judge of the Early Fourteenth Century and his Cambridgeshire Manor', in C. Richmond and I. Harvey (eds.), *Recognitions: Essays Presented to Edmund Fryde* (National Library of Wales, Aberystwyth), pp. 133–46.